THE SINGING SIXTIES

The Spirit of Civil War Days
Drawn from the Music of the Times

THE SINGING SIXTIES

****

*The Spirit of Civil War Days
Drawn from the Music of the Times*

****

by Willard A. and Porter W. Heaps

NORMAN : UNIVERSITY OF OKLAHOMA PRESS

The publication of this volume has been aided by a grant from
THE FORD FOUNDATION

Library of Congress Catalog Card Number: 60-7739

****

TO MOTHER

who, as a young girl, sang many of these songs

****

Preface

THE TRAGIC AMERICAN CIVIL WAR of 1861–65 gave birth to hundreds of songs which reflect the principles and ideals of the opposing sides, mirror the differences in temperament between the North and the South, and narrate events and movements. In this volume we have attempted to arrange a representative number of these war songs in a way which will illustrate the human as well as the historical and contemporary elements involved in the conflict. The few collections of Civil War melodies still available contain little or no explanation of their origins or purposes. Most anthologies of poems of the 1860's, while sometimes including accounts of their backgrounds, do not follow any logical sequence. A few out-of-print books tell how some of the more popular ballads came to be written. Nowhere have the words of many songs of every type, both Northern and Southern, been collected to stress historical quality and purpose.

It is not our intention to provide a history of the war, and our emphasis on events, personages, and contestants has been determined solely on the basis of their contribution to our primary purpose of showing the spirit of the Civil War period reflected in its music. We have aimed to avoid regional bias. More compositions of Union origin are included only because the musical output of the Confederate States was considerably less. In addition, many songs overcame the barriers of sectionalism and loyalty and were popular in both North and South.

As originally planned, the volume was to have included musical scores of the most important songs. However, the majority of tunes, with the exception of at most fifty-odd compositions, have outlived their popularity and follow stilted patterns which make them unmusical and interesting only as "period pieces."

Opinions, sentiments, and ideas expressed in the lyrics have proved more important than the musical settings. However, no poem has been included which was not set to music and published in that form. All have been examined in their original sheet music formats. With few exceptions they were published between 1860 and 1865 and are therefore truly representative of the tunes sung while the struggle was taking place.

The book had its beginning in a thesis undertaken in the Department of History of Northwestern University by Porter Heaps. We received valuable assistance in our research from Mr. J. K. Lilly, of Indianapolis, when his collection of Fosteriana was housed on his estate in that city, and from Mr. Fletcher Hodges, Jr., curator of Foster Hall before and after it became a part of the University of Pittsburgh. Miss Mary Porter Pratt lent us contemporary song books. Interested Southerners—among them Miss Louisiana R. Blackmar, Mr. E. D. Pope, then editor of *The Confederate Veteran,* Miss Sally B. Staton, and Mrs. John H. Anderson, historian-general of the United Daughters of the Confederacy—were exceedingly helpful.

Highest praise and thanks are due to librarians in various parts of the country, working in all types of collections, who were both patient and co-operative. Without their aid in making materials available and in following up clues, this volume could not have been written. Particular gratitude is due to Mr. Richard Hill, Mr. W. J. Lichtenwanger, Mr. Frank C. Campbell, and Mr. Oliver Dudley of the Music Division of the Library of Congress, and to Miss Margaret Hackett and Mr. Walter Whitehill of the Boston Athenaeum for aid in special research. The recording laboratory of the Library of Congress Music Division permitted use of its facilities in recording the words of more than 400 songs in its collection, not elsewhere available. Miss India Thomas of the Confederate Museum in Richmond, Virginia, was also particularly helpful. Collections of sheet music in the Boston, Chicago, and New York public libraries, the Library of Congress, the Boston Athenaeum, and Brown University were the main sources of lyrics included in this volume.

Librarians of the Cooper Union (New York City), Newberry Library (Chicago), the Chicago Historical Society, the Confederate Museum and Valentine Museum (Richmond), Tennessee State Library, the University of Chicago, Northwestern University, Ohio State University, and the public libraries of Cincinnati, Evanston, Louisville, Nashville, and New Orleans lent materials and gave aid in their use.

Much of the background material for chapters 4 and 5 was obtained from *The Life of Johnny Reb* and *The Life of Billy Yank,* two excellent volumes by Bell Irvin Wiley, to whom acknowledgment is gratefully tendered, as well as to Harcourt, Brace and Company for permission to use quotations from Carl Sandburg's *Storm Over the Land* in chapters 3 and 9.

WILLARD A. HEAPS
PORTER W. HEAPS

Evanston, Illinois
March 1, 1960

Contents

army: drummers and fifers; off-duty recreation; the serious side; picket duty; rations; the struggle against lice; the life of the sailor.

Illustrations

The illustrations reproduced in this volume are used through the courtesy of the Library of Congress.

Musical Examples

THE SINGING SIXTIES

The Spirit of Civil War Days
Drawn from the Music of the Times

****

CHAPTER I

****

The Nation Sings in Wartime

ON SUNDAY AFTERNOON, December 7, 1941, a large portion of the thirty million radio sets in homes throughout the length and breadth of the United States was in operation. Suddenly all network programs were simultaneously interrupted. Millions of Americans of diverse racial backgrounds in all classes and conditions of life listened in unbelieving dismay to the news that their forces had been attacked by the Japanese at Pearl Harbor. Throughout that day and evening, regular programs were interrupted as bulletin crowded bulletin with added bits of news. Metropolitan newspapers issued extra editions.

From an initial feeling of numbed shock, the mood changed to anger, chagrin, rage, and, finally, to a demand for revenge. Swept along in a tide of surging patriotism, young men rushed to recruiting stations. Formal declaration of war with Japan came the next day, with Germany four days later. The die was cast. No longer merely the observer of a gigantic struggle, the United States became an active participant in a life and death contest for world survival.

How were these emotions expressed in music? The radios continually echoed *God Bless America,* which had been suggested as a national anthem two years previously without success. The airways resounded with the strains of *The Star-Spangled Banner,* which, as usual, few could sing properly because of its vocal range. The times called for stirring and rousing musical compositions, and composers met the challenge with tunes such as *Remember Pearl Harbor, Good-bye, Mama, I'm Off to Yokohama,* and *You're a Sap, Mr. Jap.*

3

Before the United States became a part of that world-wide conflict, American composers had written a number of popular songs sympathetic to the country's undeclared allies during the months of the Nazi holocaust in Europe. Britain's struggle received tributes sentimentally in *The White Cliffs of Dover* and martially in *There'll Always Be an England*. *My Sister and I,* a popular ballad in the spring of 1941, commemorated the rape of Holland. *The Last Time I Saw Paris* recalled the fall of that great European capital.

The reality of actual war, however, found the nation with few songs appropriate to the stirring times. After Pearl Harbor the United States drafted its manpower to the banal strains of *He's My Uncle* and *I Am an American*. And, strangely enough, the music makers were almost completely impotent throughout the four years of World War II. What songs of enduring quality have survived?

Songs of patriotism? *God Bless America* was not composed as a result of the war, though its revival made it the most sincere song of the period. *Praise the Lord and Pass the Ammunition* had only a brief day, plugged to death over the radio. The contributions of Tin Pan Alley, such as *Let's Put the Axe to the Axis, Put Another Nail in Hitler's Coffin,* and *Taps for the Japs,* were hardly designed to stir up patriotic emotions. The songs of the various military and naval services were widely sung, but these were not true expressions of the national feeling.

Songs of sentiment? Civilians continued singing the ordinary undistinguished ballads. Rollicking nonsense songs, such as *The Hut-Sut Song, You Are My Sunshine, Deep in the Heart of Texas, Pistol Packin' Mama,* and *Mairzy-Doats,* were typical of the most popular tunes. The loneliness of enforced separation and the glamour of the uniform were chief topics of sentimental melodies; ballads like *No Love, No Nuthin', Till My Baby Comes Home, I Lost My Heart at the Stage Door Canteen,* and *Goodnight, Wherever You Are* had fleeting popularity. The picturesque activities of the Army Air Corps worked song writers into a frenzy of composition; *Comin' In on a Wing and a Prayer* and similar ballads had their brief day. Of all the songs of sentiment, *White Christmas* possessed the greatest appeal to the heart, though it made no reference to the war. But deep and true sentiment was strangely lacking in the songs of the people.

Songs of the soldier and sailor? Those in uniform sang only the popular service tunes and songs of the moment. They borrowed *Waltzing Matilda* from the Australians, *I've Got Sixpence* from the British, and

Lili Marlene from their German enemies. Our servicemen glorified *Gertie from Bizerte* and a score of other females in all parts of the world. The final European victory was pictured in *There'll Be a Hot Time in the Town of Berlin When the Yanks Go Marching In* and *Der Fuehrer's Face,* both of which offered an excellent opportunity for a loud "Bronx cheer" in the chorus.

A survey of the songs during this great war shows that the events which touched every life failed to inspire lyrics of enduring merit. With few exceptions, the output of composers was singularly mediocre. World War II was *not* a singing war, nor was its successor, the struggle in Korea.

Going back in memory to World War I, one finds it similarly unproductive, although a few tuneful melodies of that period have come to be loved by Americans. Ballads there were in plenty, ballads which are still singable—*Smiles, There's a Long, Long Trail, Roses of Picardy, Dear Old Pal of Mine,* and *My Buddy.* The French contributed *Madelon,* the British *Tipperary* and *Keep the Home Fires Burning.* Soldiers sang the rousing choruses of *Pack Up Your Troubles, You're in the Army Now, Where Do We Go from Here?, K-K-K-Katy, Oh, How I Hate to Get Up in the Morning,* and *Good-bye Broadway, Hello France. The Rose of No Man's Land* was the best seller of the war years, some five million copies having been printed. *Over There* is still remembered because it embodied the martial spirit then needed. But few truly stirring songs of patriotism have endured from World War I.

The Spanish-American War of 1898 was responsible for the adoption of *The Star-Spangled Banner* as a national anthem. The "gay nineties" atmosphere with its ragtime and minstrelsy, caused *On the Banks of the Wabash* to bring tears to the eyes of every homesick soldier boy. *Just Break the News to Mother,* by Charles Harris, the composer of *After the Ball,* entered the lists as the number one song of sentiment, and *A Hot Time in the Old Town Tonight* was fantastically popular. But the musical legacy of this war was negligible.

The War of 1812 produced *The Star-Spangled Banner,* which memorialized a single incident—the bombing of Fort McHenry in Baltimore Harbor.

In 1798, the words of *Hail, Columbia!* were set to a tune known as *The President's March,* which had been composed for George Washington's inauguration in 1789. *Yankee Doodle,* though borrowed from the British, was the only product of the Revolutionary War.

A deep sincerity distinguishes the music of the conflict which tore the United States asunder in the 1860's. Whether termed the Civil War, the War Between the States, the War of the Rebellion, or the War of Secession, this struggle was the most tragic in the entire span of American history. And because this was the conflict of a house divided, of brother against brother, of state against state, and region against region, it touched the lives of every one of the over thirty-one million citizens comprising the country's population at that time. This was no war to drive out an invader from overseas or to aid an ally; it was a bloody contest between ruptured elements of "one nation, indivisible."

The people, individually and collectively, whatever their loyalties, were receptive to the appeal of song, and so sincere and gripping were some of the musical creations born of the conflict that a treasured few have outlived their immediate aims and are equally appealing today. The gay notes of *Dixie* and *When Johnny Comes Marching Home,* the patriotic stateliness of *John Brown's Body (The Battle Hymn of the Republic)* and *The Battle Cry of Freedom,* the martial rhythm of *Marching Through Georgia,* and the moving melody of *Tenting on the Old Camp Ground* make them as singable today as when they were written.

Enjoyment of those songs which have endured does not require an understanding of their significance in the 1860's. Most present-day Americans, for example, will sing the words

> Tramp, tramp, tramp, the boys are marching,
> Cheer up, comrades, they will come;
> And beneath the starry flag we will breathe the air again
> Of the freeland in our own beloved home

with small notion of their meaning in 1864. When George F. Root wrote *Tramp, Tramp, Tramp; or, The Prisoner's Hope,* however, possibly 200,000 Union prisoners were being held by the Confederates. The song, therefore, had a personal meaning for almost every Northerner, since the capitulation of forts and cities as troops advanced deep into the South resulted in the release of thousands of captives. They must have listened eagerly for the "tramp, tramp, tramp" of their liberating comrades.

The original significance of Julia Ward Howe's *The Battle Hymn of the Republic,* with its "He is trampling out the vintage where the grapes of wrath are stored" and "I have read the fiery gospel writ on burnished rows of steel," is lost to the millions who sing it in Sunday schools and churches today. Nevertheless, it remains a deeply moving song.

Such songs have retained their popularity because the music has universal and stirring appeal. Whether sung by civilians at home or by soldiers in the field, war songs are always the expression of emotion related to the times. In periods of conflict, the basic sentiments of people are the same as in times of peace—the love of home, family, and friends and the security of the family group and the nation. During a war, however, these emotions are intensified, and this magnification is evidenced in the subject content of songs which the people sing—individually and collectively.

A song does not become "national" or "patriotic" merely because it expresses love of country or lofty sentiments of patriotism, but rather because author and composer intensify or strengthen in musical form what the populace is already thinking and feeling. The rallying song, for example, is one of the propaganda weapons turned upon civilians in wartime to unify them in support of a common cause; a ringing composition will stir their hearts. Songs about lonely, wounded, and dying soldier boys strike basic human emotions.

The populace takes to its heart those compositions which echo currently widespread ideas or universal emotions, thus making them national songs. When a composer or an author strikes this common chord during a war period, he can wield tremendous power.

The similarity of human emotions accounts for the acceptance by both North and South of certain nonpolitical ballads of the American Civil War. Neither geographical nor ideological differences were able to overcome the basic thrill of those songs which appealed to the hearts of Unionists and Confederates alike, even when it was necessary to make changes or substitutions in the words to fit the region.

A chain of music houses covered the North in 1860, and through their issuances, music came to play almost as important a part as journalism in influencing the emotions of Union sympathizers. Several dominant publishers formed chains. Individual titles were often simultaneously issued by five firms—Oliver Ditson and Company in Boston; Firth, Pond and Company (and successors) in New York City; Lee and Walker in Philadelphia; Lyon and Healy in Chicago; and John C. Church in Cincinnati— in one alliance, and four firms—Root and Cady in Chicago; Henry Tolman and Company in Boston; S. Brainard and Company in Cleveland; and H. N. Hempsted in Milwaukee—in another.

In the Southern states the most prominent and productive publishing firm was A. E. Blackmar and Brothers of New Orleans. Its entire stock was destroyed on General Benjamin Butler's orders after the capture of the city in 1862, all of its Confederate States copyrights being confiscated by him. Blackmar removed the remnants of his company from Union-occupied territory to Augusta, Georgia, where he continued to publish for the duration of the war. He had a chain of dealers and agents in the South—in Richmond, Goldsboro, Macon, Savannah, Mobile, Montgomery, Raleigh, Columbia, and Atlanta. Most of his titles were simultaneously published in these cities. Next to Blackmar in importance was the firm of John C. Schreiner and Son of Macon and Savannah. Mr. Schreiner began publishing after the beginning of the war with a font of music type which had successfully gone through the Union lines from Philadelphia via Nashville, Louisville, and Cincinnati to Macon. His outlets extended to Atlanta, Athens, Columbia, Wilmington, Augusta, Mobile, Huntsville, Raleigh, and Selma. After Blackmar's removal from New Orleans, Schreiner's firm became the leader in the South until the capture of Savannah in December, 1864. George Dunn and Company of Richmond published jointly with Julian A. Selby of Columbia, South Carolina. P. P. Werlein of New Orleans, later Werlein and Halsey, had representatives in Mobile, Natchez, and Memphis.

Sheet music was the most frequent form of publication. Covers pictured bloody and stirring battle scenes when the subject was martial, and garlands of flowers and flourishing ornamental borders when it was sentimental. The portrait of many a soulful-eyed maiden graced the covers of the love ballads. Titles included the reprinting of old favorites as well as new compositions, and varied arrangements of standard tunes. Many poems of the 1860's were set to the minstrel show airs, gospel hymn tunes, and English sentimental ballads then so admired.

Early in the war sheet music was printed on heavy paper from high-quality plates. But as the conflict progressed, the paper became increasingly poor in quality, the ink dim. Yet the prices were higher. Northern publishers used the five-pointed star, with a number inside, to indicate the price of the copy. This star, engraved on the plate, was generally centered at the bottom of the cover directly above the firm's name. If the figure was 2½, the price was 25¢; if 3, 30¢; if 5, 50¢; and so forth.

8

Southern publishers began copying this device early in 1863, but it was abandoned in the next year when inflationary prices of $1.50, $2.00, and even $2.50 for a single copy were not uncommon. However, these prices were plainly stated on the covers. Concurrently the size changed from the standard 10½ x 13 inches to a more handy and economical 8½ x 11 inches, or even smaller. Toward the end of the war, paper of Confederate imprints was so thin that printing on the reverse side made reading difficult, and copies could no longer be stood upright on the piano music rack without support. The ink was nothing more than blackened water, and the plates were inferior in quality. On the other hand, the quality of Northern printing was comparatively high throughout the war.

In supplying new words to well-known airs, both Northern and Southern publishers issued a mass of pocket-sized "songsters," with words only. Many of the poems included were of only passing interest, and words were set to all types of currently popular tunes which the average purchaser would be expected to know. These songsters are now extremely rare. Often the editor of a songster was the author of most of the words set to the popular tunes. Among those printed in the North were the Beadle Dime Series (*Knapsack Songster, Military Song Book,* and *Union Song Book,* the latter published in New York annually throughout the war years), *Flag of Our Union Songster* (Philadelphia, 1861), *Songs for the Union* (Philadelphia, 1861), *Little Mac Songster* (New York, 1862), *Red, White, and Blue Songster* (New York, 1862), *The Soldier's Companion* (New York, annually after 1862), *Tony Pastor's Union Song Book* (New York, 1862), *Touch the Elbow Songster* (New York, 1862), *John Brown Songster* (San Francisco, 1863), *The Union, Right or Wrong Songster* (San Francisco, 1863), *Camp Fire Songster* (New York, 1864), *Tony Pastor's New Union Song Book* (New York, 1864), and *The Drum Beat* (New York, 1865).

The South was no less prolific, with *Hopkins' New Orleans 5 Cent Song Book* (New Orleans, 1861), *Bonnie Blue Flag Song Book* (1861), *Dixie Land Songster* (Augusta, 1863), *Songs of the South* (Richmond, 1863), *Stonewall Song Book* (Richmond, 1863), *Beauregard Songster* (Macon and Savannah, 1864), *General Lee Songster* (Macon and Savannah, 1864), *Jack Morgan Songster* (Raleigh, 1864), *New Confederate Flag Song Book* (Mobile, 1864), *Rebel Songster* (Richmond, 1864), *Songs of Love and Liberty* (Raleigh, 1864), *Southern Flag Songbook* (Mobile, 1864), *The Southern Soldier's Prize Songster* (Mobile, 1864), and *The Cavalier Songster* (Staunton, 1865).

9

To supplement sheet music and the pocket songsters, broadsides poured from the presses, designed as "penny ballads," for the singer who was already familiar with the tune. One of Stephen Foster's[1] most interesting compositions, copyrighted in December, 1863, mentioned titles of the sheet music and broadsides which could be seen "sticking up in a row" in a walk through the town. "Old songs! new songs! every kind of song, I noted them down as I read them along," he says, and the rhymed titles make up *The Song of All Songs,* of which the following two verses are typical:

> There was "Abraham's Daughter" "Going Out upon a Spree,"
> With "Old Uncle Snow" "In the Cottage by the Sea."
> "If your Foot is Pretty, Show It" "At Lanigan's Ball;"
> And "Why Did She Leave Him" "On the Raging Canawl?"
> There was "Bonnie Annie" with "A Jockey Hat and Feather."
> "I Don't Think Much of You" "We Were Boys and Girls Together!"
> "Do They Think of Me at Home?" "I'll Be Free and Easy Still;"
> "Give Us Now a Good Commander" with "The Sword of
>   Bunker Hill."
>
> "When This Cruel War Is Over," "No Irish Need Apply,"
> "For Everything Is Lovely" and "The Goose Hangs High."
> "The Young Gal from New Jersey," "Oh! Wilt Thou Be My Bride?"
> And "Oft in the Stilly Night," "We'll All Take a Ride."
> "Let Me Kiss Him for His Mother," "He's a Gay Young Gambolier;"
> "I'm Going to Fight mit Sigel" and "De Bully Lager-bier."
> "Hunkey Boy Is Yankee Doodle," "When the Cannons Loudly Roar,"
> "We Are Coming, Father Abraham, Six Hundred Thousand More!"

These titles indicate the strange mixture of sentiment, melancholy, and humor—often forced—which made up the musical fare during the four years of the war.

[1] Stephen Collins Foster (1826–64) is typical of the professional composers of the period, for writing music was his sole means of support. As a free lance, he had no connection with a large publishing house, as did George F. Root, Henry Clay Work, and A. E. Blackmar. His most famous and enduring compositions were published during the late forties and fifties, generally made popular through performances in minstrel shows. His wartime melodies never obtained widespread acceptance because his sensitive nature totally unfitted him, as the composer of *Old Folks at Home, My Old Kentucky Home,* and *Old Black Joe,* to write anything martial. Foster's nineteen songs produced during the war years (eighteen of which are mentioned herein) were examples of four types—patriotic, martial, sentimental, and humorous.

Musical expressions of the 1860's fell into a logical sequence. When the first shots were fired at Fort Sumter, this climax of the bitter feelings which had marked early threats of secession produced martial rallying songs and inspired expressions of patriotism and love of flag and country. As the increasing needs of war called for more and more soldiers, the loneliness caused by enforced separations and the breaking of family ties was reflected in the plaintive ballads. Finally, an inexpressible weariness settled over all; individual battles and campaigns, with their accompanying fear, sadness, and tragedy, were merely steps toward the glorious and long-anticipated day when the war might end.

The soldiers in blue and gray constantly wanted to know "Do they miss me at home, do they miss me?" They dreamed of home, of sweethearts, of Dixie Land where Mother was waiting for news of the battle. Did her Willie think of her as he lay dying? Little Sonny asked if the battle was over and if his father was safe. Mother thought her boy was coming from the war, but fate had determined otherwise, and instead, "Somebody's darling" was sleeping on the battlefield where he died for the flag he loved, gasping his last words, "Who will care for mother now?" Maidens prayed, soldiers prayed, mothers prayed; they prayed just before the battle, and they prayed after the battle, while the boys were dying far from those they loved. But none seemed afraid to die, for their souls would go marching on like that of John Brown, or their deaths would confer glory to the Confederate cause.

The soldiers on both sides had an identical objective—"preservation of freedom" as each saw it. To the boy in gray this signified upholding the newly formed Confederacy against "Northern oppression" and the "invasion" of Southern soil. To the boy in blue it meant saving the Union at all costs. On the one side he remained loyal to the Bonnie Blue Flag and the Stars and Bars and fought for his Dixie Land; on the other, he rallied round the flag and shouted the Battle Cry of Freedom.

Songs, many of them inferior both musically and poetically, appeared in ever increasing numbers from the outbreak of hostilities until the end at Appomattox Court House, and even thereafter. An audience could always be found for any sentiment which afforded even momentary release from care, sorrow, and anxiety. The words did not need to possess any exceptional poetic quality, and were often uninspired, even banal.

In many aspects the most interesting songs from a modern point of view are those of sentiment. So changed are musical tastes that the glowing, flowery prose of sentiment—in which sweethearts bid good-bye, mother hears the news of a son's death or wounds, soldiers dream of loved ones, and a thousand and one incidents and thoughts of love are expressed—seems often strange, outmoded, and quaint today. Yet in the sixties, when such ballads were popular, these songs were highly effective and moving. Examined as museum pieces representative of a dated style, they have unique interest.

The religious songs and prayers, with their stilted verses and appeals to the Deity, are set in the contemporary mode of expression. Yet the sincerity of feeling behind the words is evident. Each side believing its cause to be just and deserving of success, both Northern and Southern prayers for victory and peace were honest and genuine. Supplications for God's protection of the boys under fire were deeply rooted in current religious faith; Confederates and Unionists alike prayed that their loved ones might be spared if it were "God's will." Mothers, wives, and sweethearts prayed for courage to endure the forced separations, and for strength to bear their grief.

The most transitory Civil War songs were those celebrating specific events and incidents. The volunteering or "loyalty" songs used a vocabulary and high-sounding phrases which appear stilted and almost insincere a century later. Their emotional appeal is gone, and the songs no longer thrill as of yesteryear.

The music of historical periods always follows a definite and set pattern which is a reflection of contemporary style and taste. The cultural trend of the Civil War period was toward reverence of anything foreign. The best European vocal and instrumental artists had visited the United States, bringing with them the Continental type of music. Reflecting this influence, American solo pianists reveled in florid keyboard embroiderings, with abundant use of arpeggios, crashing chords, and difficult pyrotechnic passages.

Yet, strangely, the developing native American music was simple and unaffected. The music of the people lacked Continental showiness, appealing instead to the inner feelings. Popularity of the sentimental ballad and the simple songs of Stephen Foster was in strong contrast to the musical fare of concert halls. Emphasis upon the romantic was reflected in the vocal music.

Since the great foreign piano makers had only recently invaded the American market, persons who could play acceptably were in a minority.

The accompanist was usually a musical amateur, hence the score was of necessity not difficult. Common patterns were followed as slavishly as modern popular song writers now follow the eight-bar repetitive pattern. Without exception melodies were based on a routine pattern of "ump-ah" or accented beats. Simple arrangements were necessary not only because of the average "parlor" pianist's limited ability but also because the accompaniment was only incidental. The modern popular tune, on the contrary, is performed by dance bands, pianists, organists, accordionists, and a variety of solo instrumentalists, with or without a vocalist. The song of the sixties was not a dance tune; it was not a piano solo; it was a vocal ballad. Consequently, the accompaniment was made as simple as possible, merely a succession of chords to give harmonic and rhythmic background to the lyrics of the ballad.

The piano parts fell into several basic variations of the "ump-ah" pattern designed to express the spirit of a piece through chords and accents. Simplest and most obvious were those involving the repetition of the single chord. The repeated chord, accented chord, and the broken (or arpeggio) chord, formed the basic types. Most songs were in four-four tempo.

Choral singing was at the height of its popularity in the 1860's. A feature of many printed songs of the period was the quartet arrangement of choruses, adapted from the minstrel quartets then popular. These choruses possessed the essential elements of "barbershop" harmony, which was to become popular later in the 1890's. Since many contemporary versions buried chorus melodies in male quartet arrangements, it was clear that the choruses were not to be sung by a soloist, but that the melody was assigned to the tenor or baritone of the quartet. This type of arrangement was sung at encampments of the Grand Army of the Republic and the United Confederate Veterans after the war.

The most noticeable difference between modern popular songs and those of the Civil War, however, is the importance given the verse in contrast to the short choral refrain or chorus. Verses of today's songs are rarely sung and are unimportant to the development of the mood of a ballad. Those of Civil War melodies are long and sometimes complicated. The story is told in verses, the chorus forming a short refrain or division between stanzas. Sometimes the latter was a mere repetition of lines in the verses. Parlor entertainment in the sixties, during which the young lady of the house sang current airs after dinner to her own accompaniment, lent itself to long and detailed verses which could be readily absorbed by polite and attentive listeners.

13

In an 1864 issue of a magazine no longer in existence is an article entitled "War Songs and Their Influence in History," by Charles G. Leland, which traces the function of music in wars since the time of the Vikings and Norsemen. In a concluding paragraph, Mr. Leland wrote:

> I have heard from a collector that during the first year of the present war two thousand songs were published upon it, and the subsequent rate of increase has been somewhat greater! . . . I would not conclude these remarks without expressing the hope that those who may chance to think that we are without good war-songs will take pains to ascertain what really exists. I trust that no pains will be spared in collecting, for our historical and other libraries, all the current literature of the war, since there is a time coming when its every fragment will be of inestimable value.

Mr. Leland's warnings were not heeded, for copies of many of the songs have completely disappeared, and others have been preserved only in collections generally unavailable to the public. But those which remain reveal the spirit of the 1860's; they tell the story of the soldier as a man, as a living and breathing human being; and they portray the anxiety, sorrow, and disappointment of the people at home. They commemorate victories and defeats, and they glorify heroes. Above all, they fully and accurately reflect American public opinion and life from late 1860 to 1865.

CHAPTER 2

Rallying Round the Flags

WHEN PRESIDENT-ELECT Abraham Lincoln was inaugurated on March 4, 1861, the national situation was tense with suspense. South Carolina had seceded from the Union in December; Mississippi, Florida, Alabama, Georgia, Louisiana, and Texas had followed within a month. In February the Confederate States of America had been established as a provisional government, with Jefferson Davis as president, and had organized its own army. Lincoln said in his inaugural address:

> In your hands, my dissatisfied fellow-countrymen, and not in mine, is the momentous issue of civil war. You have no oath registered in heaven to destroy the Government, while I shall have the most solemn one to "preserve, protect and defend" it. . . . We are not enemies but friends. We must not be enemies. Though passion may have strained, it must not break our bonds of affection. The mystic cords of memory, stretching from every battlefield and patriot grave to every living heart and hearthstone all over this broad land, will yet swell the chorus of the Union when again touched, as surely they will be, by the better angels of our nature.

The Federal forts which had been seized by the Confederate government were the immediate causes of contention. Fort Sumter, in Charleston Harbor, was particularly important, and *The Flag of Fort Sumter* (words by J. Harry Hayward, music by Thomas D. Sullivan) became a symbol:

Unfurl the banner upon the ramparts high
    Where Columbia's fold may descrie it;
The stars and stripes we now swear to defend
    Though they in perfidy defy it.
The shouts of the rebels may fall on our ears
    The cannon their thunder may rattle,
But while God is with us its folds still shall wave
    In triumph throughout every battle.

CHORUS:
Its bright stars shall be o'er land and o'er sea
    By us e'er sustained and defended.
The balls of the rebels must pierce our true hearts
    Ere the flag of Fort Sumter be rendered.

When, after two days of bombardment, the fort was surrendered on April 14, 1861, the die was cast for war. The song continued:

Unfurl the banner upon the ramparts high,
    The base traitors' guns thunder 'round us;
The balls crush our walls, the shells burst in air
    And the fierce destruction surrounds us.
See! See in our midst 'mid the terrors of strife
    New horrors of war rise before us;
The Fort is on fire, the magazine explodes,
    Still our flag in triumph waves o'er us!

The house of the United States was now divided. Major Robert Anderson, Fort Sumter's commanding officer, at once became a Union hero and was praised in *The Hero of Fort Sumter* (words by Anna Baché, music by C. Munzinger):

When factioned hand debased the flag
    Our fathers raised so high
A darkening orb fell sadly down
    From Union's starry sky.

CHORUS:
Hurrah, the Union flag unrolls
    Its glories on the air;

Three cheers for Robert Anderson
  The man that keeps it there.

Fort Moultrie bears a brand of shame
  But Sumter hence will be
A shrine where honor's steadfast sons
  May kneel in loyalty.

Another Union song dedicated to Major Anderson was *The Stars and Stripes Are Still Unfurled* (words by W. H. Conkle, music by J. E. Kochersperger), which was somewhat extreme in its estimates of Union naval strength:

Shall star by star fade out of sight
  Which spangled once our banner free?
Shall hostile arms tear down that flag
  Which crowns our million ships at sea?
Arouse, ye patriots of the land;
Arrest the wild uplifted hand;
  The stars and stripes are still unfurled.

Abundant musical evidence exists of the fact that the Southern states were seriously considering such overt warlike acts as far back as the middle months of 1860. For example, P. P. Werlein, the New Orleans publisher, had at that time issued a song entitled *Minute Men, Form; the Anthem of the South,* the cover of which reproduced a large shield with the labeled escutcheons of fifteen states—Maryland, Arkansas, Missouri, Kentucky, Tennessee, Virginia, Georgia, South Carolina, Louisiana, Alabama, North Carolina, Mississippi, Florida, Texas, and Delaware—which the designer arbitrarily joined in the secession movement. The words of the song refer to the "sound of thunder afar, a storm in the sky that darkens the day—the storm of battle and thunder of war." It urges the minute men to forget their civilian life for a while—"better a loss of a crop or so, Than wait to see our homes in flames." The chorus cried:

Form, form, be ready to do or die;
  Form, respond to your country's call,
Be not deaf to the sound that warns,
  Be not gulled by an enemy's pleas.

The North was outraged by such defiance of the authority of the national government. Fear, apprehension, and distrust were everywhere, for no one could foretell the future. Nevertheless, all realized the gravity of the situation, and while waiting to see what would be done, George F. Root wrote the first popular Union song of the war.[2] It called upon free-

The First Gun Is Fired! "May God Protect the Right"

[2] George Frederick Root (1820–95) was the most prolific, if not the greatest, Northern composer. He had been a pioneer, with Lowell Mason and William Bradbury, in the compilation of church hymnals and the organization of religious singing schools. His loyalty to the Union cause was due in part to the fact that he was an ardent Abolitionist, and his forty-odd war songs furnished incentives to enlistment, aroused patriotism and loyalty, brought cheer to soldiers in camp, and helped in

born sons of the North "to heed the signal and rise in the strength of freedom to prevent the ruthless sundering of the glorious Union by trait'rous foes." Now that *The First Gun Is Fired! "May God Protect the Right"*:

> The first gun is fired!
>   May God protect the right!
> Let the free-born sons of the North arise
>   In pow'r's avenging night;
> Shall the glorious Union our fathers made
>   By ruthless hands be sunder'd?
> And we of freedom's sacred rights
>   By trait'rous foes be plunder'd?
>
> CHORUS:
> Arise, arise, arise!
>   And gird ye for the fight . . .
> And let our watch-word ever be
>   "May God protect the right."
>
> The first gun is fired!
>   Its echoes thrill the land,
> And the bounding hearts of the patriot throng
>   Now firmly take their stand.
> We will bow no more to the tyrant foe
>   Who scorn our long forbearing,
> But with Columbia's stars and stripes
>   We'll quench their trait'rous daring.

The song reached citizens of Northern states at a time when patriotism was at fever heat. The colors red, white, and blue were used everywhere—in shops, as neckties and rosettes, and on hats. Loyal Unionists purchased packs of playing cards in which a colonel was substituted for the king, the Goddess of Liberty for the queen and a major for the jack; eagles, shields, stars, and flags were the suits. American flags floated from housetops, windows, and doors, were used as decorations in parlors, offices, shops, and stores, ornamented the heads of horses in the streets, and fluttered from every mast-peak. Everyone declared himself for *The Union, Right or Wrong* (words by George P. Morris, music by William Plain):

relieving the shock of battle. His publishing firm in Chicago, Root and Cady, was outstanding during the war. His most famous non-war songs were *Hazel Dell* and *There's Music in the Air*. He often wrote under the pseudonym "Wurzel."

It is the duty of us all
    To check rebellion's sway;
To rally at the nation's call,
    And we that voice obey.
Then like a band of brothers go,
    A hostile league to break,
To rout a spoil-encumbered foe
    And what is ours retake.

Then come, ye hardy volunteers,
    Around our standard throng
And pledge man's hope of coming years,
    The Union—right or wrong!
The Union right or wrong inspires
    The burden of our song;
It was the glory of our sires—
    The Union—right or wrong!

The success of *The First Gun Is Fired* led George Root to write the words and music of one of the first of his many martial and patriotic songs, titled *Stand Up for Uncle Sam, My Boys:*

Stand up for Uncle Sam, my boys,
    With hearts brave and true;
Stand up for Uncle Sam, my boys,
    For he has stood by you.

He's made your home the brightest
    The sun e'er shone upon;
For honor, right and freedom
    He's many a battle won.

CHORUS:
Stand up for Uncle Sam, my boys,
    With hearts brave and true;
Stand up for Uncle Sam, my boys,
    For he has stood by you.

Oh, strike for Uncle Sam, my boys,
    For danger is near;
Yes, strike for Uncle Sam, my boys,
    And all to you most dear.

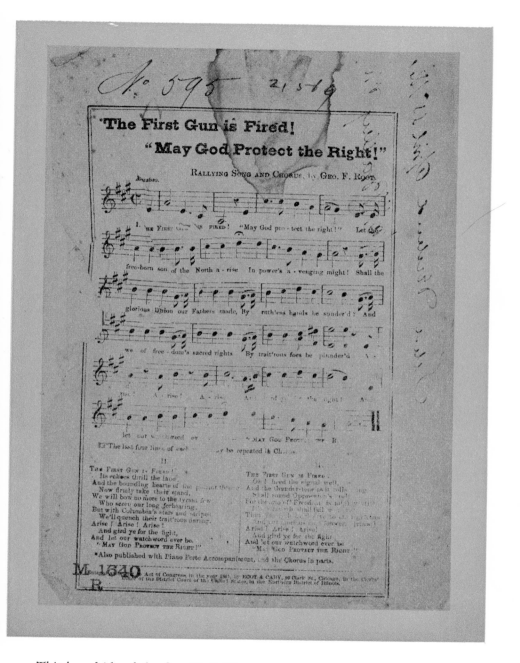

This broadside of the first Civil War song was copyrighted on April 18, 1861, and published simultaneously in full sheet music form.

Rebellious sons are plotting
    To lay the homestead low,
Their hands are madly lifted
    To give the fatal blow.

However, a Northern poet, "A. E.," thoroughly shocked at the sight of a large army (7,000 Confederate troops) arrayed against the Sumter garrison of only 84 men, composed an energetic song of denunciation, *A Southern Paean,* to the tune of *Kitty Tyrrell* (composed by Charles W. Glover):

I'll sing you a song worth the singing,
    Of Sumter chivalrously won,
By the brave chiefs who brought to the contest
    Just seventy hundred to one!
Fair odds was the good Saxon usage,
    When men boasted of worsting a foe;
But such musty old saws are exploded,
    And we are all heroes, you know.

But a truce to all questions of reason,
    Fort Sumter is gloriously won.
And who cares a jot for the treason,
    If the black-hearted North is undone?
'Tis true this may rouse indignation,
    And parties may possibly jar,
But we can defy the whole nation,
    Since we've taken Fort Sumter—hurrah!

The understandable joy of the Southerners was expressed in *Sumter, a Ballad of 1861* (words by O. E. M., music by Elizabeth Sloman):

Now ring the bells a joyous peal,
    And rend with shouts the air,
We've torn the hated banner down
    And placed the "Crescent" there.
All honor to our gallant boys,
    Bring forth the roll of fame
And there in glowing words inscribe
    Each patriot hero's name.

And in New Orleans, where *Dixie* had just been introduced, Margaret Weir composed a verse of *Dixie Doodle:*

Dixie whipped old Yankee Doodle early in the morning,
So Yankeedom had best look out and take a timely warning.

Yankee Doodle, grease your heels, make ready to be running,
For Dixie boys are near at hand, surpassing you in cunning.

Union publishing houses immediately hired hack poets to write words fitted to popular tunes of the day, particularly English ballads, and printed them in pamphlet form or as broadsides. Hundreds of spirited lyrics, expressing the feelings of anxiety and alarm which the bombardment at Charleston and the subsequent military activities had aroused, were hastily printed. The excitement of the times was expressed in an anonymous ballad entitled *Rather Too Much for a Shilling,* to the tune of *Over the Water to Charlie:*

Come, rouse up, ye freemen, give ear to my song,
 And muster your forces for action.
Our foemen are marching—their armies are strong—
 But we'll conquer this treacherous faction.
We read in the papers strange stories of late,
 Our noodles they're constantly filling
With threats of secession, disunion and hate,
 Which is rather too much for a shilling.

In the midst of the clamor, a lone Northern voice defended free speech, but warned against fanatical oratory. *Our Thirty-four Bright Stars,* to the tune of *A Wet Sheet and a Flowing Sea,* offered the suggestion:

Let's spurn the traitors North and South
 Who'd aid in Treason's plot,
Or from our Union's glorious flag
 One star would dare to blot.
Let's spurn fanatics now whose tongues
 Do naught but threat and teach,
Oh, bid them cease their fiery slang,
 But still respect Free Speech.

Send men to Congress now to work
    As public servants should,
Whose actions louder speak than words,
    And for our country's good.
Keep ranting orators at home,
    They only agitate,
We've souls as pure, as days of yore,
    To guard our ship of state.

But the North was now aroused, and began to call Southerners assassins and traitors, as in *The Defenders* (words by Thomas Buchanan Read, music by Werner Steinbrecher):

'Spite of the sword or assassin's stiletto
    Whilst throbs a heart in the breast of the brave
The oak of the north or the southern palmetto
    Shall shelter no foe except in his grave.
While the Gulf billow breaks, echoing the northern lakes
    And ocean replies unto ocean afar
Yielding no inch of land while there's a patriot's hand
    Grasping the bolts of the thunders of war.

The mustering for war was long overdue, said *Liberty's Reveille* (words by W. S. Hurlocke, music by James W. Porter):

The stern braves of the north, in order arrayed
    The east with her yeomen of steel
South's patriot sons in proud strength undismayed
    Stalwart giants of the west in line wheel.

And the flag must be defended at any cost (*Traitor, Spare That Flag,* words by William J. Wetmore, music by Henry Russell):

Traitor, spare that flag,
    Touch not a single star
'Twill rouse each loyal heart
    And light the flames of war.
Still let that standard wave,
    The symbol of our land
Raised by our patriot sires,
    A brave and noble band.

The discovery was soon made that lyrics of none of the existing patriotic songs did justice to the stirring events. As a national hymn *The Star-Spangled Banner* was then, as now, almost useless. The range of the air, one and one-half octaves, placed it out of the compass of average voices; the words were almost entirely descriptive of a particular event in the War of 1812; they painted a picture but expressed no sentiments. The lines were involved and difficult to remember, and the rhythm was complicated. *Yankee Doodle* was too undignified; the tune was as light as the words. *Hail, Columbia,* originally composed as a military march, was stilted. Efforts were made in both North and South to add verses to *The Star-Spangled Banner* to suit the emergency. The South at first wished to appropriate both the flag and the song celebrating it, since the verses had been written by a native of Maryland, a Northern slaveholding state. Even Oliver Wendell Holmes attempted an added verse of contemporary significance, his contribution appearing in the *Boston Evening Transcript* during the year 1861:

When our land is illumined with Liberty's smile,
If a foe from within strike a blow at her glory,
Down, down with the traitor who dares to defile
The flag of her stars and the page of her story!
   By the millions unchained
   Who their birthright have gained
   We will keep her bright blazon forever unstained.
And the Star-Spangled Banner in triumph shall wave
While the land of the free is the home of the brave.

In the hope that an entirely new national song might be composed, a group of New York City patriots privately organized a competition and offered a prize of $500. This contest, given widespread publicity in newspapers throughout the Northern states, was announced on May 17, 1861, with a deadline set for June 20. The rules of the contest as outlined in Richard Grant White's *National Hymns: How They Are Written and How They Are Not Written,* 1861, stated:

(1) The Hymn is to be purely patriotic, adapted to the whole country—not a war-song or only appropriate to the present moment, (2) It must consist of not less than sixteen lines, and is not to exceed forty, exclusive of a chorus, or burden, which is essential, and (3) It

25

should be of the simplest form and most marked rhythm; the words easy to be retained by the popular memory, and the melody and harmony such as may be readily sung by ordinary voices.

Twelve hundred contributions, three hundred accompanied by music, were received—from every Northern and Western state, and even from England, Germany, and Italy. A committee of thirteen inspected the compositions submitted. Following weeks of hard labor in examination, the disheartening decision, issued on August 9, was that not one of the works was found powerful enough to be classed as a genuinely worthy national anthem. However, even as the judges were pondering their decisions, events were creating the first popular songs of the war.

As a result of the assault on Fort Sumter, Lincoln found several states already prepared to supply their allotted quotas when, on April 15, he issued his call for 75,000 three-month volunteers "to curb the rebellion." The Massachusetts Militia had always been well organized, and when a struggle seemed imminent, Governor John Andrew took immediate steps to mobilize his men, with the result that within three days after the proclamation, the Sixth Massachusetts Regiment was armed and ready to leave for Washington, where it was to be a garrison outfit.

The direct route to the capital lay through Baltimore, where secessionist feeling naturally ran high. Maryland's territory ran north of Washington, cutting off the national capital from that portion of the Union which supported the Federal government.

On the eighteenth of April, a band of 460 Pennsylvania volunteers was mobbed while passing through Baltimore. The first blood shed in the war was drawn by this crowd; it was that of a Negro, Nicholas Biddle, who was accompanying the recruits. Upon arrival in Washington, his bloody bandages created a sensation.

The following day, the nineteenth, witnessed a much greater demonstration on the streets of Baltimore when the Sixth Massachusetts, passing through, was attacked by a band of Southern sympathizers. Paving stones, available in large quantities because streets repairs were in progress, were freely used by members of the mob as they screamed accusations such as "black Republicans," "nigger thieves," and "Yankee hirelings." Contemporary reports differ on the number of casualties, but it is probable that four soldiers and twelve civilians were killed and thirty-one soldiers wounded.

Governor Andrew had requested that the mayor of Baltimore "Care for them tenderly," and this outrage prompted a song titled *All Hail to the Stars and Stripes: Care for Them Tenderly*" (words by Whitney L. Needham, music by Rev. J. N. Collier, another setting by C. L. Stevens):

> Care for them tenderly, send back our dead,
> Who in their country's cause nobly have bled.
> Send us our cherished ones who in Spring's bloom
> First on the battlefield, first found their tomb.
>
> Care for them tenderly and as they come
> Lower their much-loved flag, muffle the drum.
> Send up your prayers to Heav'n, let teardrops fall,
> Scatter fresh laurel leaves, meet for their pall.

Another Boston composer, J. W. Turner, wrote the words and music to *The Martyrs of Baltimore:*

> Defenders of the Union, immortal you will be,
> You scorned at base disunion and died for Liberty.
> The ruffians that so basely left you weltering in gore
> Shall rue the day, brave soldiers, you fell at Baltimore!
>
> CHORUS:
> > We'll not forget the soldiers
> > Who fell at Baltimore!
>
> 'Twas Massachusetts soldiers who fell upon that day;
> They died like noble heroes as life's blood flowed away;
> Let each one then remember, though much we may deplore,
> They died for us most nobly, who fell at Baltimore.

An individual casualty was lauded in *The Dying Volunteer of the 6th Massachusetts Regiment* (words and music by G. Gumpert):

> He was the first whose blood was spilled;
> > By traitor's hand he died.
> His country's love his bosom filled
> > And dying still he cried
> "All hail to the stars and stripes."
> Oh, Massachusetts' noble son
> > May laurels crown thy grave;

27

Thy country's freedom must be won,
    The Union still we'll save.

Indignation ran high in the North as the story was relayed throughout the Union. Jubilation simultaneously fired the Confederates to greater and greater activity.

James Ryder Randall, a native of Maryland who was teaching at a small college near New Orleans, was particularly affected by the news since the first man to fall in this riot was a good friend. In a burst of sincere emotion, he wrote *My Maryland* and submitted it for publication in the New Orleans *Delta*. The stirring stanzas appeared at a psychological moment when they were able to exert a great influence. Oliver Wendell Holmes later praised it as the best poem produced by the war.

The opening lines indicate that the poem was inspired in a white heat of patriotism:

The despot's heel is on thy shore, Maryland, my Maryland!
His torch is at thy temple door, Maryland, my Maryland!
Avenge the patriotic gore That flecked the streets of Baltimore
And be the battle queen of yore, Maryland, my Maryland!

Randall's absence from Maryland explains lines in the second stanza:

Hark to an exiled son's appeal, Maryland, my Maryland!
My mother state, to thee I kneel, Maryland, my Maryland!
For life or death, for woe or weal Thy peerless chivalry reveal,
And gird thy beauteous limbs with steel, Maryland, my Maryland!

Some history of the glorious state was cited in the third and fourth verses:

Thou wilt not cower in the dust, Maryland, my Maryland!
Thy beaming sword shall never rust, Maryland, my Maryland!
Remember Carroll's sacred trust, Remember Howard's warlike thrust,
And all thy slumberers with the just, Maryland, my Maryland!

Come! 'Tis the red dawn of the day, Maryland, my Maryland!
Come with thy panoplied array, Maryland, my Maryland!
With Ringgold's spirit for the fray, With Watson's blood at Monterey,
With fearless Lowe and dashing May, Maryland, my Maryland!

Randall then appealed to the state's Southern sympathies:

> Dear mother, burst the tyrant's chain, Maryland, my Maryland!
> Virginia should not call in vain, Maryland, my Maryland!
> She meets her sisters on the plain, "Sic semper," 'tis the proud refrain
> That baffles minion's back amain, Maryland, my Maryland!
>
> Come! for thy shield is bright and strong, Maryland, my Maryland!
> Come! for thy dalliance does thee wrong, Maryland, my Maryland!
> Come to thine own heroic throng, Stalking with liberty along,
> And chant thy dauntless slogan-song, Maryland, my Maryland!

The state's loyalties lay with the South, he continued:

> I see the blush upon thy cheek, Maryland, my Maryland!
> But thou wast ever bravely meek, Maryland, my Maryland!
> But lo! there surges forth a shriek, From hill to hill, from creek to creek,
> Potomac calls to Chesapeake, Maryland, my Maryland!
>
> Thou wilt not yield the vandal toll, Maryland, my Maryland!
> Thou wilt not crook to his control, Maryland, my Maryland!
> Better the fire upon the roll, Better the shot, the blade, the bowl,
> Than crucifixion of the soul, Maryland, my Maryland!

His final verse burst forth with a zealous hope that the state would join the Confederacy. This hope, however, never materialized:

> I hear the distant thunder-hum, Maryland, my Maryland!
> The "Old Line's" bugle, fife and drum, Maryland, my Maryland!
> She is not dead, nor deaf nor dumb; Huzza! she spurns
>   the Northern scum—
> She breathes! She burns! She'll come! She'll come!
>   Maryland, my Maryland!

Historically these verses are important, for they record feelings of that hour throughout the South, even if not entirely accurate for Baltimore.

When the poem reached Baltimore, the Cary sisters, Jennie and Hetty, famous beauties who were well acquainted with rousing college songs of the day, discovered that the music of *Lauriger Horatius*—the German folk air *Tannenbaum, Oh, Tannenbaum*—long a favorite in colleges, fitted the words of *My Maryland* perfectly, with the addition of two extra "My

Marylands." The music's martial beat served to enhance the value of the lyrics. From that day to the present, *My Maryland* has retained its popularity. Its contemporary influence was said to have been greater than a hundred victorious battles.

An indication of the song's rousing nature was the fact that a Union parallel version was composed and sung to the same tune, with six instead of nine verses. The contrast between the two versions is rather striking. In the first verse, "despot" became "traitor:"

> The traitor's foot is on thy soil, Maryland, my Maryland!
> Let not his touch thy honor spoil, Maryland, my Maryland!
> Wipe out the unpatriotic gore That flecked the streets of Baltimore,
> And be the loyal state of yore, Maryland, my Maryland!

and in the fifth verse the situations of Virginia and Carolina were substituted, respectively, for those of Maryland and Virginia in Randall's version:

> Virginia feels the tyrant's chain, Maryland, my Maryland!
> Her children lie around her slain, Maryland, my Maryland!
> Let Carolina call in vain: Our rights we know and will maintain:
> Our rise shall be her fall again, Maryland, my Maryland!

Then followed an appeal that Maryland ally herself with the Union:

> I hear the distant battle's hum, Maryland, my Maryland!
> I hear the bugle, fife and drum, Maryland, my Maryland!
> Thou art not deaf, thou art not dumb: Thou wilt not falter or succumb:
> I hear thee cry, We come, we come! Maryland, my Maryland!

> Ten hundred thousand, brave and free, Maryland, my Maryland!
> Are ready now to strike with thee, Maryland, my Maryland!
> A million more still yet agree To help thee hold thy liberty,
> For thou shalt ever, ever be, Maryland, my Maryland!

The North could scarcely allow these impassioned pleas to pass unnoticed, and Marylanders who were loyal to the Union urged their state in poems and songs to join the Federal cause; *Answer to My Maryland* (words by William H. C. Hosmer), reviewing the history of the state and appealing to the patriotism of her inhabitants, was typical of such songs. It called upon citizens not to forget how Howard had beaten back Tarleton at Cowpens; not to forget their citizen-patriots Charles Carroll of Carrollton, the last signer of the Declaration of Independence, and Francis Scott Key, writer of *The Star-Spangled Banner*. The state should ally herself on the side of the right, it concluded:

> One sword-strike for the good old flag, Maryland, my Maryland!
> Down with secession's shameless rag, Maryland, our Maryland!
> The glorious Stars and Stripes uphold, That over Yorktown
>   were unrolled—
> Oh! March beneath that banner fold, Maryland, our Maryland!
>
> Let the drums beat "To arms, to arms!," Maryland, our Maryland!
> Leave cottage homes, and shops, and farms, Maryland, our Maryland!
> Rush, as your sires to conflict rushed, Rebellion's war cry
>   must be hushed,
> The serpent of Secession crushed, Maryland, our Maryland!

Southern promises of aid in driving the "hireling host" from her soil reached Maryland in the form of many songs and poems. As late as January 13, 1862, one Southern writer, Robert E. Holst, using the tune of *Gideon's Band* (composer, Charles R. Dodworth), promised that *We'll Be Free in Maryland*:

> The boys down South in Dixie's land
> Will come and rescue Maryland.
>
> The Northern foes have trod us down
> But we will rise with true renown.
>
> The tyrants they must leave our door,
> Then we'll be free in Baltimore.
>
> CHORUS:
>   If you will join the Dixie band,
>   Here's my heart and here's my hand,
>   If you will join the Dixie band,
>   We're fighting for a home.

And when the Confederates inaugurated their Maryland campaign, a Boston poet, Finley Johnson, using the tune of *My Maryland,* paraphrased the original:

31

The "liberating army" came, Maryland, my Maryland!
Polluting thy soil in freedom's name, Maryland, my Maryland!
They came with proclamations loud, They came with ragged,
    squalid crowd,
To wrap thee in Secession's shroud. Maryland, my Maryland!

They marched along in bold array, Maryland, my Maryland!
Expecting on thy soil to stay, Maryland, my Maryland!
They came with bugle and with drum, They came from Hades,
    the very scum,
To strike the sons of freedom dumb. Maryland, my Maryland!

We hear the marching Union song, Maryland, my Maryland!
We see thee coming thousands strong, Maryland, my Maryland!
We hear the bugle and the drum, We're chasing off the rebel scum,
Thank God, the Union forces come. Maryland, my Maryland!

This song is a good example of typical Northern references to the Southerners as "rebel scum" and "a traitor crew." Indeed, in the early war years invective was hurled with high emotional intensity by both sides.

If any force could have drawn Maryland to the side of the Confederacy, it would have been that exerted by *My Maryland* and its fiery patriotic appeal. However, in the fall elections Maryland voted overwhelmingly in favor of remaining with the Union, though sentiment in the city of Baltimore itself was always pro-Confederate, in spite of its occupation by Union forces.

Words of the Confederate rallying songs tended to be stilted and artificial, referring, for example to the "foeman" instead of the "enemy," to "gore" rather than "blood," to Northern "hosts and vandals," to the "spoilers and minions" of Lincoln, to the "clank of the tyrant's chains," and included exalted poetic passages which failed to express the deep and genuine emotion affecting the people. A song entitled *The South* (words by Charlie Wildwood, music by John H. Hewitt), issued in 1861, was typical; the land of chivalry, the home of liberty, it said, was being overrun by "swarms of foul demons" and "these base tyrants would crush to the earth and mangle and bruise on the soil of their birth." Another Southern melody of this type was *Stars of Our Banner* (words by M. F. Bigney, music by Alice Lane), the chorus of which ran:

With "God and the Right!"
Our cry in the fight,
We'll drive the invader afar.

The readiness of Southerners to defend their land had already been expressed in two 1860 songs published in Baltimore, one of which was *Dear Land of the South* (words and music by Eugene Raymond):

The stalwart and brave are all ready to band
For the cause that is just and their own native land;
"The union of states, and the union of hands"
Is blazed on their standard wherever it stands.

And another, *The South* (words by J. H. H., music by Arnaud Préot):

Men of the South! your homes
    Where peace and plenty smiled
Have been assailed by thieving bands
    And by their tread defiled.
The canting traitors of the North
    With lying tongues declaim
And spit at you their slime and froth,
    Their venom and their flame.

Rather than wait for composers to produce stirring tunes for arousing war enthusiasm, Southerners adapted words to the strains of well-known airs. The tune of *Bruce's Address,* a traditional Scottish air which accompanied the "Scots wha' hae wi' Wallace bled" of Robert Burns, was stirring enough to express prevailing sentiments in many settings. Mrs. F. T. H. Cross, using this tune in her *Address of the Women to the Southern Troops,* expressed the loyalty of women to the cause:

We—may God so give us grace!—
Sons will rear, to take your place;
Strong the foeman's steel to face—
Strong in heart and hand!

Though our land be left forlorn,
Spirit of the Southern-born,
Northern rage shall laugh to scorn—
Northern hosts defy.

33

Death your serried ranks may sweep,
Proud shall be the tears we weep,
Sacredly our hearts shall keep
Memory of your deeds!

He that last is doomed to die,
Shall, with his expiring sigh,
Send aloft the battle-cry
"God defend the right!"

The tune was also used in *The Rallying Song of the Virginians* (words by Susan A. Talley) and *A Southern War Cry,* which was published in the New Orleans *Times-Picayune.*

A stream of Confederate songs followed in which Southerners vowed to conquer or die and dedicated themselves to battle to the end. *God and Our Rights* (words by William M. Johnston, music by A. E. Blackmar), "dedicated to the friends of Southern independence," urged:

Hearts of the South, though peace no more
May visit again your sunny shore,
Yield no inch of your dear-bought right,
Yield, if you yield, a life in the fight,
And, as with your feet to the foe you lie,
 Let the red field echo your last deep cry:
  "God and our rights!"

No Surrender (words and music by Henry Douglas) was the word:

Constant and courageous still,
 Mind the word is "No Surrender";
Battle though it be uphill,
 Stagger not at seeming ill.
Hope, and thus your hope fulfil,
 There's a way where there's a will
And the way all fears to kill
 It's to give them No Surrender.

It was to be a battle to the death, said *We Conquer or Die* (words and music by James Pierpont):

The trumpet is sounding from mountain and shore
Your swords and your lances must slumber no more.

Fling forth to the sunlight your banner on high
Inscribed with the watchword "We conquer or die."

The South, Our Country (words by E. M. Thompson, music by J. A. Butterfield) must be defended:

But *Union* still gladdens our own sunny home,
Whose bright blades and brave hearts will ever defend her,
And though wreck and disaster and ruin may come
While the bright sun shines o'er them they ne'er will surrender.
Let the foeman come on in his daring effrontery,
Let him trample the loved soil we call our dear country,
And for every fair flower which fades in his path
A proud heart shall bleed 'neath the sword of our wrath.

The Land of the South (words by A. F. Leonard, music by Julius E. Müller) *will* be defended:

Men of the South! A freeborn race,
    They vouch a patriot line;
Ready the foeman's van to face
    And guard their country's shrine.

The Southern Boys (adapted by Hermann L. Schreiner) will rise up:

Cheer, boys, cheer, for our sweethearts and our wives.
Cheer, boys, cheer, we'll nobly do our duty
And give to the South our hearts, our arms, our lives.

Finally, a Louisiana *Confederate Song* called on the "sons of chivalry" to rally against Northern vandals, who

... tread our soil,
Forth they come for blood and spoil
To the homes we've gained with toil,
Shouting "Slavery."

Traitorous Lincoln's bloody band
Now invades the freeman's land,
Arm'd with sword and firebrand,
'Gainst the brave and free.

Arm ye, then, for fray and fight,
March ye forth both day and night,
Stop not 'till the foe's in sight,
Sons of chivalry.

North Carolina, which withdrew from the Union on the twentieth day of May, called her troops in words set to the rousing tune of the state anthem, *The Old North State*. *A North Carolina Call to Arms* (words by Mrs. Willis L. Miller, "Luola") urged the brave sons of Carolina to awake from their dreaming and, waiting neither for argument, call, nor persuasion, to fly to the rescue of sweethearts, wives, and mothers in a heroic effort to prevent the ghastly fate outlined in the third and fourth stanzas, an invasion by bands of fanatics:

The national eagle, above us floating,
Will soon on the vitals of loved ones be gloating;
His talons will tear and his beak will devour;
Oh! spurn ye his sway, and delay not the hour.

The Star-Spangled Banner, dishonored, is streaming
O'er bands of fanatics; their swords now are gleaming;
They thirst for the life-blood of those you most cherish;
With brave hearts and true, then, arouse, or we perish!

Carolina's Sons (words by H. W., music by T. S. Whitaker) were called into battle:

Hurry on to meet the wretches, Heaven's vengeance waits for them.
Take your knapsacks on your shoulder, meet the foe, the
        Northern men.

Up! and leave your wives and daughters, who would gladly follow on,
But their duty promptly tells them they must stay, you must be gone.

May the God of Battles guide you and kind angels hover o'er
'Till you drive the black fanatics from our dear loved Southern shore.

On a more elevated level, *Chicora, the Indian Name of Carolina* (words by Dr. E. Marks, music by Prof. A. Hatschek) declaimed:

Lone Star of nations! Chicora! Chicora!
Hail midst the darkness of tyranny's might,

36

Shine in thy heavens, alone in thy glory,
Justice our buckler and freedom our might!

This state was entitled to issue stirring appeals, for she was to bear a full portion of suffering. The first man reported killed on the Confederate side was a North Carolinian, and it was claimed that the last volleys at Appomattox were fired by a North Carolina regiment. Reliable records indicate that almost one-half of the state's troops were either killed or wounded.

Alabama, true to the meaning of her name "Here we rest," was at first unwilling to follow the other Southern states; this was perhaps due to her remoteness from actual combat. But the issue of slavery eventually won her to the cause, and *Ye Men of Alabama* (words by John D. Phelan), set to the tune of *Ye Mariners of England,* were called upon to rend asunder the coils of the "abolition snake":

Ye men of Alabama,
    Awake, arise, awake!
And rend the coils asunder
    Of this abolition snake.
If another fold he fastens—
    If this final coil he plies—
In the cold clasp of hate and power,
    Fair Alabama dies.

Though 'round your lower limbs and waist
    His deadly coils I see,
Yet, yet! thank Heaven! your head and arms
    And good right arm are free;
And in that hand there glistens—
    Oh God! what joy to feel—
A polished blade full sharp and keen
    Of tempered State Right's steel!

The men of the South were pictured as standing "shoulder to shoulder in solid phalanx with poised spears and locked shields," guarding their native land.

The response of Texas to the call was signified in *The Song of the Texas Rangers* (words by Mrs. M. J. [Fuller] Young), to the tune of *Yellow Rose of Texas* (composed in 1858), which has been termed the rallying song of the West:

The morning star is paling, the camp-fires flicker low,
Our steeds are madly neighing, for the bugle bids us go:
So put the foot in the stirrup and shake the bridle free,
For today the Texas Rangers must cross the Tennessee.
With Wharton for our leader, we'll chase the dastard foe
'Till our horses bathe their fetlocks in the deep blue Ohio.

As a border and slave state, Missouri was wooed by both the Union
and the Confederacy. Throughout 1861 she remained in the Union, with
the people about equally divided in loyalty. Harry Macarthy,[3] the Arkansas comedian, urged that the state ally herself with the South in *Missouri;
or, A Voice from the South:*

Missouri! Missouri! Bright land of the West,
    Where the wayworn emigrant always found rest,
Who gave to the farmer reward for the toil
    Expended in breaking and turning the soil;
Awake to the notes of the bugle and drum!
    Awake from your peace, for the tyrant hath come.

CHORUS:
And swear by your honor that your chains shall be riven,
    And add your bright star to our Flag of Eleven.

Missouri! Missouri! Where is thy proud fame?
    Free land of the West, thy once cherished name?
Trod in the dust by a tyrant's command
    Proclaiming there's martial law in the land.
Men of Missouri! Strike without fear!
    McCulloch, Jackson and brave men are near.

The struggle over Missouri was met by a Union song, *Belle Missouri,* in
reply to *Maryland, My Maryland* and set to that tune (words by Howard
Glyndon):

Arise and join the patriot train, Belle Missouri, Belle Missouri!
They should not plead and plead in vain, Belle Missouri, My Missouri!

[3] Macarthy traveled widely throughout the Confederacy giving "impersonation"
concerts and was thus able to popularize his own and other Southern songs. He visited
his good friend A. E. Blackmar whenever he appeared in New Orleans and regularly
acquired the manuscripts of newly published songs, which he later featured in his
concerts. He joined the Confederate army from Arkansas.

The precious blood of all thy slain arises from each reeking plain.
Wipe out this foul disloyal stain, Belle Missouri, Belle Missouri!

Up with the loyal stripes and stars, Belle Missouri, My Missouri!
Down with the traitor stars and bars, Belle Missouri, My Missouri!
Now by the crimson crest of Mars and Liberty's appealing scars
We'll lay the demon of these wars, Belle Missouri, My Missouri!

Although the state remained with the Union, Confederate sympathies were always strong.

The other border states, Kentucky and Tennessee, were urged to join the Southern coalition in *The Song of the South* (words by Lena Lyle of Tennessee, music by James H. Huber of Kentucky):

Oh! Southern boys for their fireside joys,
With their hearts so brave and tender,
Will relentlessly fight and to death's dark night
Alone will they surrender.

Promises to conquer or to die were common among Southerners in 1861. References to the "bloody torrents" were made with scarcely a thought that encounters would soon make them a reality. Typical of such songs was *The Cavaliers of Dixie* (words by Benjamin F. Porter), set to the tune of *Ye Mariners of England:*

Ye Cavaliers of Dixie!
    Though dark the tempest lower,
What arms will wear the tyrant's chains
    What dastard heart will cower?
Bright o'er the night a sign shall rise
    To lead to victory!
And your swords reap their hordes,
    Where the battle tempests blow;

CHORUS:
Where the iron hail in floods descends
And the bloody torrents flow.

The Union sought to temper the resolution for war by urging a rational and unemotional consideration of what this break might signify.

39

North and South (words by Beulah Wynne, music by George F. Root) presented a dialog of 1861:

North:

Ah, wherefore woulds't thou leave our band,
    Why turn ye from our Union?
Why wander from the happy land,
    Long joined in close communion?
My sister, pause, oh cans't thou go?
    Cans't leave the cause we've loved together?
The bond our fathers did bestow
    Oh, cans't thou break it and forever?

South:

Why should I pause or wherefore stay?
    The tie is broken now.
We will not brook thy northern sway,
    Will not to tyrants bow.
Nay, urge me not, for well you know
    Our progress you've retarded.
We start anew, we from you go
    Our rights you've disregarded.

North:

My dark-eyed sister, say not so
This erring step will lead to woe.

South:

'Twill lead to peace, 'twill give new life
Though bought by sorrow, war and strife.

And in *Jonathan's Appeal to Caroline; or, Mr. North to Madame South* (words and music by Miss M. Stoddard), Jonathan (the Union) reminds Caroline (the Confederacy) of the long record of past co-operation and the happiness which had been theirs in the Union, continuing:

Now because for once my votes
    Outdo your swindling plan

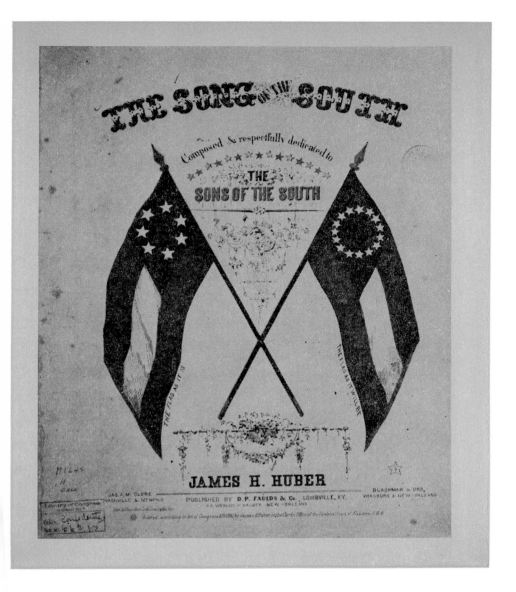

According to this 1861 sheet music cover, the seven states of the Confederacy would eventually be increased to fifteen. Note the figure 5 in the star, indicating the price of fifty cents.

You mean to break the unit up
   And do what harm you can.
Think to please you how I worked,
   Down upon my knees I've toiled,
While for my sake you've never once
   Your dainty fingers soiled.
Then you've called me wicked names
   "Yankee," "Mudsills," "Farmer," "Small,"
Yet have I a Christian been
   And borne in meekness all.
Yes, you know I've borne all this
   And a thousand other ills,
Just to live in peace with you
   And run my cotton mills.

Then you know I've active been
   Mobbin' preachers if they dared
Say aught against your darling sin,
   Hard was the fate they shared.
Then to think I caught your slaves
   When they tried to run away,
And never let them stop to rest
   This side of Canaday.
Now it really makes me mad
   To think how foolish I have been
How for your sake I lost my peace
   And steeped my soul in sin.
And yet you have a traitor proved
   And stole my guns away
But as I have a few more left
   I guess I'll stop your play.

Madame, you will trouble see
   'Less your temper soon is mended,
And much you'll wish you'd stayed with me
   Before the war is ended.
Yet since you the war have brought,
   Blame yourself for all the sorrow
That now enshrouds all hearts and homes
   And fills our land with horror.
Though I fight but for the laws
   And stand on Constitution,

Yet blame yourself if 'midst the crash
    Down comes your Institution.
And devoutly good men pray
    For such a consummation,
And wise ones tell us, peace can come
    But in Emancipation.

The North, after the Baltimore riots, could not but enter the fray, declared *Once More the Rebels' Bugle* (words and music by George H. Thurston):

Once more the rebels' bugle insults our northern air
    Once more their steps pollute our Maryland so fair.
So gather from your workshops and gather from your farms
    From the sweet pursuits of peace to the war-blast's rude alarms.

Hence, the Union boys must be ready, says *Come, Rouse Up! Brave Boys* (words by Avanelle L. Holmes):

Rouse up, brave boys, there's a foe on the farm
    And Uncle Sam calls on his children to arm.
Oh, come from the workshop, the plow and the loom,
    From highway and byway and every way, come!

Come, rouse up, brave boys, 'tis no trifling campaign
    Each heart must be bold and each nerve on the strain.
The greater the danger, the greater the need
    Of arms that can strike and of feet that can speed.

The stirring strains of the French national anthem found favor on both sides of the Potomac, and poets responded with words of equal vigor. *The Marseillaise* was a stimulating and rousing war song, unique among national anthems. As an enthusiastic call for liberty, it was perfect as a marching song. This outburst against eighteenth-century tyranny was easily translated into modern American terms; the chorus "To arms, citizens, form your battalions" became a mutual call "To arms, to arms, ye brave! Th' avenging sword unsheathe." Through a pointed coincidence, the choruses of both Union and Confederate versions were identical.

The Southern Marseillaise (words by A. E. Blackmar[4]) called on all

[4] Armand Edward Blackmar was a native of Vermont who went to the South when nineteen years of age. After operating music stores in Huntsville, Alabama,

citizens to meet and subdue the "hireling Northern band that comes to desolate the land":

Sons of the South, awake to glory,
    A thousand voices bid you rise.
Your children, wives and grandsires hoary
    Gaze on you now with trusting eyes,
Gaze on you now with trusting eyes.
Your country ev'ry strong arm calling,
    To meet the hireling Northern band
That comes to desolate the land
    With fire and blood and scenes appalling.

CHORUS:
To arms, to arms, ye brave;
    Th' avenging sword unsheath!
March on! March on! All hearts resolve
    On victory or death.

The French population of New Orleans, where Blackmar had his publishing house, took the song particularly to their hearts, often coupling it with *Dixie* when arousing patriotic enthusiasm at rallies.

Another Southern version was titled *The Hour's Arrived, Awake from Slumber!*:

The hour's arrived, awake from slumber!
    Hark, the trumpet's war-like call!
See the host's advancing number,
    Rise to meet them one and all,
    Rise to meet them one and all,
Can you not hear their exultation
    As now they trespass on our soil?
Thus bent upon our subjugation
    Let their acts on them recoil!

CHORUS:
To arms! then, one and all!
Come lay th' usurper low!

---

and Vicksburg, Mississippi, he established his New Orleans store in 1860. He often purchased poems and patriotic verses and set them to music of his own composition, as well as sponsoring several of the most noted Confederate composers. His own songs made him known as the "voice of the South."

March on! March on! our country's call
Now bids us strike the blow!

Both these versions were also sung in the original French. New Orleans publishers were liberal in issuing an avalanche of highly emotional French songs, the French-speaking Zouaves of Louisiana being favored subjects of many compositions. A popular song topic was a mother of French ancestry sending her son off to the struggle in tears, recalling the glories of the old country's fight for similar freedom sixty-five years previously. Some ballads of the period were translated into non-metrical French and distributed as broadsides.

Virginia had her *Virginian Marseillaise* (arranged by F. W. Rosier), which expressed the following ideas:

Virginia hears the dreadful summons
Sounding hoarsely from afar,
On her sons she calls, and calmly
Bids them now prepare for war.

The Union took up the strain, and *The Northmen's Marseillaise*, patterned closely on the Southern version, urged all citizens to prevent the desolation of the land by "hateful minions, terror-breeding . . . a ruffian band":

Ye sons of Freedom, wake to glory!
    Hark! hark! what thousands bid you rise!
Hark! children, wives and grandsires hoary,
    Prevent their tears and save their cries!
    Prevent their tears and save their cries!
Shall hateful minions, terror-breeding,
    With Southern hosts, a ruffian band,
Affright and desolate our land
    While peace and liberty lie bleeding?

While the stirring strains of *My Maryland* were being sung far and wide, a light minstrel air was sweeping the Confederate States and being adopted by popular acclaim as its "national" song—*I Wish I Was in Dixie's Land*. Hurriedly written overnight in the spring of 1859 by Daniel Decatur ("Dan") Emmett, an Ohioan, as a walk-around (a musical feature sung and danced by a few soloists in the foreground of the stage with the rest of the company in the background) for the Bryant Minstrels in New York City, it became known throughout the whole country from its performance as a repertoire number in other minstrel companies.

On the eve of the war, the music of *Dixie,* the popular title of Emmett's melody, was being used in a minstrel show at New Orleans, and its rendition was spontaneously received as almost an inspiration. As war sentiment grew, the South began to apply the words of this song to its cause, recognizing themselves as a separate people occupying their own territory, Dixie Land. They were, therefore, resolved to live and die in this newly born, as yet unrecognized, Dixie. P. P. Werlein was said to have pirated *Dixie* from a copy sent by Emmett to Billy Newcomb, the minstrel, in New Orleans.

Many a Confederate regiment was given a send-off to the lilting tune. At the inauguration of Jefferson Davis as president of the Confederate States of America on February 22, 1862 (he had been elected a year before), the program was so arranged that the band led off with *Dixie* (in an arrangement by Herman Arnold) just as Davis set out from the Old Exchange Hotel toward the Capitol in Richmond. This was equivalent to its official adoption as the national "anthem" of the Confederacy. It is a strange contradiction that a Northern composer should have given to the South its outstanding song and that a Southerner wrote the tune *Glory Hallelujah!* to which *John Brown's Body,* the North's most popular and stirring song, was set.

The first stanza as composed by Emmett was never used, because Mrs. Bryant, the wife of the minstrel company manager, feared that the lines might offend the religious-minded:

> Dis worl' was made in jiss six days,
> An' finished up in various ways;
> > Look away! Look away! Look away! Dixie Land!
> Dey den made Dixie trim and nice,
> But Adam called it "paradise,"
> > Look away! Look away! Look away! Dixie Land!

As a result, the modern version of the song generally begins with the second stanza.

I Wish I Was in Dixie's Land

I wish I was in de land ob cotton,
Old times dar am not forgotten,
    Look away! Look away! Look away! Dixie land.
In Dixie land whar I was born in
Early on one frosty mornin'
    Look away! Look away! Look away! Dixie land.

CHORUS:
Den I wish I was in Dixie, Hooray! Hooray!
In Dixie Land I'll take my stand,
To lib and die in Dixie,
Away, away, away down south in Dixie.
Away, away, away down south in Dixie.

Old Missus marry "Will-de-weaber,"
Willyum was a gay deceber,
    Look away! Look away! Look away! Dixie land.
But when he put his arms around her,
He smiled as fierce as a forty-pounder.
    Look away! Look away! Look away! Dixie land.

His face was sharp as a butcher's cleaber,
But dat did not seem to grieb 'er,
    Look away! Look away! Look away! Dixie land.
Old Missus acted de foolish part,
And died for a man dat broke her heart.
    Look away! Look away! Look away! Dixie land.

Now here's a health to de next old Missus,
An' all de gals dat want to kiss us;
    Look away! Look away! Look away! Dixie land.
But if you want to drive 'way sorrow,
Come and hear dis song tomorrow.
    Look away! Look away! Look away! Dixie land.

Dar's buckwheat cakes and Injun batter,
Makes you fat, or a little fatter,
    Look away! Look away! Look away! Dixie land.
Den hoe it down and scratch your grabble,
To Dixie's land I'm bound to trabble.
    Look away! Look away! Look away! Dixie land.

During the war other words were written to the air of *Dixie* in both North and South. The Daughters of the Confederacy have discovered twenty-two Southern versions. Elliott Shapiro has listed thirty-nine versions issued between 1860 and 1866, arranged for piano, violin, minstrel band, plantation dance, polka, reel, rondo, caprice, cornet band, olio, and all vocal combinations—solo, duet, quartet, quintet, chorus (mixed, male, and female), and minstrel walk-around. Although titles of Northern and Southern versions vary, the spirit is generally the same, for it is difficult to resist matching the rollicking and gay notes with equally light verses.

It was inevitable that authors would attempt to couple the tune with lofty sentiments. Such versions, however, were doomed to failure since the music negated the seriousness of the words. The most famous of such verses, composed by General Albert Pike, Indian commissioner to the Confederate government, first appeared in the Natchez *Courier* on April 30, 1861. Published under the title *The War Song of Dixie; or, Southrons, Hear Your Country Call You!,* it was "inscribed to our Gallant Volunteers." In spite of the somewhat stilted poetic form, *Pike's Dixie,* as it came to be popularly known, enjoyed immense success. Two of its eight verses will serve to show its theme:

> Southrons, hear your country call you!
> Up! lest worse than death befall you!
> To arms! to arms! to arms! in Dixie!
> Lo, all the beacon-fires are lighted,
> Let all hearts be now united!
> To arms! to arms! to arms! in Dixie!
>
> CHORUS:
> Advance the flag of Dixie! Hurrah! Hurrah!
> For Dixie's land we'll take our stand,
> To live or die for Dixie.
> To arms! to arms! and conquer peace for Dixie!
> To arms! to arms! and conquer peace for Dixie!
>
> Strong as lions, swift as eagles,
> Back to their kennels hunt these beagles!
> To arms! to arms! to arms! in Dixie!
> Cut the unequal swords asunder,
> Let them then each other plunder!
> To arms! to arms! to arms! in Dixie!

H. T. Stanton titled his version *The Dixie War Song; or, Fly to Arms in Dixie*. Following are two of the six verses:

Hear ye not the sounds of battle,
Sabre's clash and muskets' rattle?
  To arms! to arms! to arms! in Dixie!
Hostile footsteps on our border,
Hostile columns tread in order!
  To arms! to arms! to arms! in Dixie!

CHORUS:
Oh, fly to arms in Dixie! to arms! to arms!
From Dixie's land we'll rout the band
That comes to conquer Dixie.
To arms! to arms! and rout the foe from Dixie!
To arms! to arms! and rout the foe from Dixie!

Shall this boasting, mad invader
Trample Dixie and degrade her?
  To arms! to arms! to arms! in Dixie!
By our father's proud example
Southern soil they shall not trample!
To arms! to arms! to arms! in Dixie!

A local version titled *Awake to Arms in Texas* parodied Stanton's verses by substituting "Texas" wherever "Dixie" was used.

Southern versions were most successful when they retained the sprightly spirit of the original. The exuberance which inflamed the South after its first victories is shown in *The Bayou City Guards' Dixie*:

From Houston city to Brazos bottom,
From selling goods and making cotton,
  Look away! Look away! Look away! Dixie land!
We go to meet our country's foes,
To win or die in freedom's cause;
  Look away! Look away! Look away! Dixie land!

CHORUS:
We're going to old Virginia, hooray! hooray!
To join the fight for Southern rights.
We'll live or die for Davis!
Hooray! hooray! We'll live or die for Davis!
Hooray! hooray! We'll live or die for Davis!

You've heard of Abe, the gay deceiver,
Who sent to Sumter to relieve her;
   Look away! Look away! Look away! Dixie land!
But Beauregard said, "Save your bacon!
Sumter's ours and must be taken!"
   Look away! Look away! Look away! Dixie land!

The Northerners were not long in realizing the effect of the catchy
tune, in spite of the fact that the South had adopted the song as its own.
The Wolverines were apparently quite concerned with the fate of the Stars
and Stripes, but more particularly the Stars, as indicated in the *Michigan
Dixie* song:

Away down South where grows the cotton,
Seventy-six seems quite forgotten;
   Far away, far away, far away, Dixie land.
And men with rebel shout and thunder
Tear our good old flag asunder;
   Far away, far away, far away, Dixie land.

CHORUS:
Then we're bound for the land of Dixie. Hooray! Hooray!
In Dixie land we'll take our stand,
And plant our flag in Dixie.
Away, away, away down South in Dixie.
Away, away, away down South in Dixie.

Almost every Northern state used the tune of *Dixie* for a similar call to arms.

In 1915, *The Confederate Veteran* instituted a campaign for new words
of greater dignity, "more in the spirit of the Confederacy," patriotic words
to be sung to the glorious, soul-stirring air, but it was found that not even
the Sons and Daughters of the Confederacy could lightly discard the words
which are even today beloved wherever rousing tunes are sung.

The fanaticism of a Kansas Abolitionist gave to the North its most
rousing lyric. The story of John Brown's unsuccessful invasion of Virginia,
his capture at Harpers Ferry, and his hanging late in 1859 is familiar.

The tune was composed some time before 1855 by William Steffe, a
South Carolinian, and had become a popular camp-meeting air, with the
refrain, "Say, brothers, will you meet us on Canaan's happy shore?" When

the "Tiger" battalion of the Twelfth Massachusetts Regiment was stationed at Fort Warren in Boston Harbor early in the war, its members used the air to taunt a fellow-soldier named John Brown. The transition to the Abolitionist of the same name was quite natural.

Published in Boston late in 1861, under the title *Glory Hallelujah!*, it became the marching song of the regiment and quickly spread when the unit departed for the front. The catchy rhythm made it easy to sing. Soldiers shouted the refrain with gusto on marches, and many units added verses to fit their own experiences. When the abolition of slavery became an accepted reason for the war, the song was a part of every civilian political rally and fund-raising meeting. It was variously known as *The John Brown Song, John Brown's Body,* and *Glory Hallelujah!*:

John Brown's body lies a-mouldering in the grave [repeat three times]
His soul is marching on.

CHORUS:
Glory, glory, hallelujah! [repeat three times]
His soul is marching on!

The stars of heaven are looking kindly down
On the grave of old John Brown.

He's gone to be a soldier in the army of the Lord
His soul is marching on.

John Brown's knapsack is strapped upon his back
His soul is marching on.

His pet lambs will meet him on the way
And they'll go marching on.

They will hang Jeff Davis to a sour apple tree
As they go marching on.

A reminder of the wish expressed in the sixth verse was included in in *Good-bye, Jeff,* issued at the end of the war:

But the soul of famous old John Brown
    Has not stopped marching, Jeff,
And the last of Southern chivalry we'll see
    When the echo of the
        Hallelujah Chorus, Jeff,
Finds you hanging on a "sour apple tree."

51

The rousing music of *Glory Hallelujah* had literally scores of poems set to it, many containing no reference whatever to John Brown. For example, *Raise Up the Banner,* by an anonymous poet, said:

Raise up the banner, let it float wide and free
Over every valley, every hill and every sea;
Victory shall crown it wherever it may be
As they go marching on!

CHORUS:
Glory, glory, hallelujah!
Glory, glory, hallelujah!
Glory, glory, hallelujah!
    Hurrah, hip, hip, hurrah!

Friends of the Union, let us sing, one and all,
Cheering those who volunteer at our country's call;
Fighting for the banner that never shall fall
As they go marching on!

Because it immediately became a popular Union marching song, other versions were composed for individual Northern regiments, always, however, using the original tune of the Southern composer. The Thirteenth Massachusetts Volunteer Regiment marched away to these words:

Cheer for the banner as we rally 'neath its stars,
As we join the Northern legion and are off for the wars,
Ready for the onset, for bullet, blood and scars!
Cheer for the dear old flag!

CHORUS:
Glory! Glory! Glory for the North!
Glory to the soldiers she is sending forth!
Glory! Glory! Glory for the North!
They'll conquer as they go.

As in the case of *Dixie,* attempts to provide intelligent words in good grammatical form to replace the nonsense verses resulted in failure. Edna Dean Proctor's *The Presidential Proclamation,* dealing with the Emancipation Proclamation (see Chapter VII), was strangely matched to such a doggerel tune. However, the melody was so widely sung that it was inevitable that fitting words would eventually be composed to fit it. Julia Ward Howe achieved this.

In November, 1861, a party which included Rev. James F. Clarke and Mrs. Samuel (Julia Ward) Howe, whose husband was editor of an antislavery paper in Boston, visited an outpost of the Army of the Potomac in Virginia to witness a review of the troops. However, an unexpected Confederate assault cancelled the review, and instead they witnessed the skirmish and heard the returning soldiers singing *John Brown's Body.* On the return trip to Washington, Mr. Clarke suggested that she write grander and more dignified words to fit the sturdy martial rhythm of the music. Inspired during the early morning hours, she wrote the words down by candlelight in her room at the Willard Hotel. James T. Fields, editor of the *Atlantic Monthly,* accepted them for publication, paying her five dollars. *The Battle Hymn of the Republic,* the title he gave the poem, appeared in the February, 1862, issue, without identification of the author. Later, after her name was revealed, the fame of Julia Ward Howe increased, and the poem came to be ranked with *My Maryland* as one of the finest produced by the war. The picturesque words formed a truly majestic and militant religious marching song still included in every present-day hymnal:

Mine eyes have seen the glory of the coming of the Lord;
He is trampling out the vintage where the grapes of wrath are stored;
He hath loosed the fateful lightning of His terrible swift sword;
His truth is marching on.

CHORUS:
Glory! Glory! Hallelujah!
Glory! Glory! Hallelujah!
Glory! Glory! Hallelujah!
His truth is marching on.

I have seen Him in the watch-fires of a hundred circling camps;
They have builded Him an altar in the evening dews and damps;
I can read His righteous sentence by the dim and flaring lamps;
His day is marching on.

I have read a fiery gospel writ in burnish'd rows of steel;
"As ye deal with my condemners, so with you my grace shall deal!
Let the Hero, born of woman, crush the serpent with his heel,"
Since God is marching on.

He has sounded forth the trumpet that shall never call retreat;
He is sifting out the hearts of men before His judgment-seat;
Oh, be swift, my soul, to answer Him! be jubilant, my feet!
    Our God is marching on.

In the beauty of the lilies Christ was born across the sea,
With a glory in His bosom that transfigures you and me;
As he died to make men holy, let us die to make men free,
    While God is marching on.

After South Carolina withdrew from the Union on December 20, 1860, a blue flag, with a single centered white star representing the state was used until her official flag as a member of the Confederacy (blue with a palmetto tree and crescent in the left upper corner) was adopted on January 28, 1861. So, while the pros and cons of secession were being heatedly discussed throughout the South, the words and music of *The Bonnie Blue Flag* attained a popularity which lasted throughout the war. Harry Macarthy, the comedian who was a native of Arkansas, set the words to the old and well-known Irish air, *The Irish Jaunting Car,* and by means of his impersonation concerts, the piece reached every important city in the Confederacy. The tune was sung at the Mississippi Convention which passed the act of secession in Jackson on January 9, 1861, at which time this first flag was displayed. For over four turbulent months, this simple flag was the only one around which the seceding states could rally.

We are a band of brothers, and native to the soil,
Fighting for the property we gained by honest toil;
And when our rights were threatened, the cry rose near and far,
"Hurrah for the Bonnie Blue Flag that bears a single star!"

CHORUS:
Hurrah! Hurrah! for Southern rights, hurrah!
Hurrah for the Bonnie Blue Flag that bears a single star.

As long as the Union was faithful to her trust,
Like friends and like brethren, kind were we and just;
But now, when Northern treachery attempts our rights to mar,
We hoist on high the Bonnie Blue Flag that bears a single star.

Then here's to our Confederacy, strong we are and brave,
Like patriots of old, we'll fight, our heritage to save;

And rather than submit to shame, to die we would prefer,
So cheer for the Bonnie Blue Flag that bears a single star.

Verses not reproduced here listed the various states of the Confederacy and outlined their contribution to the cause. As the war progressed, it was necessary to add other verses to include the new states. When, at last, Arkansas, North Carolina, and Tennessee joined the Confederacy, a seventh stanza was added:

Then cheer, boys, cheer, raise a joyous shout,
For Arkansas and North Carolina now have both gone out,
And let another rousing cheer for Tennessee be given,
The single star of the Bonnie Blue Flag has grown to be eleven.

Numerous were the alternative versions which were introduced by patriotic lyricists to emphasize the part some particular state was playing in rallying round the Bonnie Blue Flag.

The Northerners, however, could not be expected to overlook the fact that the flag was a traitorous emblem and that it possessed only one star, whereas the Union flag, the old Stars and Stripes of their forefathers, glittered with many stars. Verses from several Northern songs expressed this feeling. *A Reply to the Bonnie Blue Flag* (words by Mrs. C. Sterett, music by H. M. Frank) ended with the verse:

We're in the right and will prevail, the Stars and Stripes must fly!
The "Bonnie Blue Flag" be haul'd down and every traitor die.
Freedom and Peace enjoyed by all, as ne'er was known before,
Our spangled Banner wave on high with stars just Thirty-Four.

The Stars and Stripes of Old (words by C. Jays, to the tune of the *Bonnie Blue Flag*) was the only true flag:

The rebel host may gather, with savage fury fight,
But they can never conquer our strength as in our right
We follow on triumphant, where on the breeze unrolled
Waves high our glorious banner, The Stars and Stripes of Old.

And *Our Beautiful Flag; or, The Bonnie Red, White, and Blue* (words and music by J. C. J.) would ever fly over the brave:

55

Oh, no, the "bonnie blue flag"
    With one white ghastly star,
Never shall float before our ranks
    To lead the brave afar,
But blend the hue of sunset,
    The bonnie red, white, and blue,
Shall fire our souls with patriot zeal,
    With hope and courage true.

The Flag with Thirty-four Stars (words by Gen. W. H. Hayward, music by C. S. Root) had the subtitle *Hurrah! for the Dear Old Flag with Every Stripe and Star,* while *The War Song for '61* (words by Thomas Mitchell, music by John R. Mitchell) termed the Southern flag one of serpents:

Coming like vandals for plunder and prey,
With barbaric spirits and hands for the fray,
Madly, blindly, rushing to ruin they fly.
Rattlesnake's emblem these minions,
Torn from the Eagle his pinions.
Not o'er the land of rebellion the flag of our Union doth wave!

Resentment towards the single star was expressed in *Shoulder Arms* (words and music by John Fickeison):

Woe to the cunning false advisers, The deceivers and surmisers
Who caused this most unholy war.
South Carolina's ill-taught manner Brought dishonor to our banner
By raising first the lonely star.

Down with the Traitors' Serpent Flag (words by C. C. Flint, music by A. J. Higgins) was even more pointed:

But the vipers whom our fire hath warmed
    And wretches whom our hand hath fed
Hath dared tear down our nation's flag
    And raised their ensign in its stead.

CHORUS:
Down with the traitors' serpent flag
Death to the wretch o'er whom it waves.

And let our heaven-borne banner float
O'er freemen's homes and traitors' graves.

In elegance and proud disdain
      The tyrants lord it o'er the South
But never, never can they reign
      O'er the freemen of northern birth.

Although *The Bonnie Blue Flag* fired the imagination of Southerners
during the war, it possessed no musical quality to insure its permanence,
even had the Confederate cause been triumphant. There is nothing particularly Southern in feeling or temperament about the word "bonnie,"
and the words are a mere recital of the order in which the states seceded,
and not even historically correct order, at that. Because of its popularity,
Major General Benjamin Butler, commander of the Union troops occupying New Orleans after its capture on April 28, 1862, threatened to levy a
fine of twenty-five dollars on any man, woman, or child who sang, played,
or even whistled the song. He then arrested Blackmar, its publisher, fined
him five hundred dollars, and destroyed all copies of the tune.

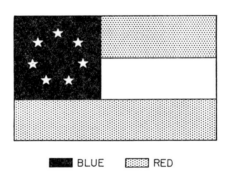

BLUE   RED

Obviously the seceded states
could not retain the flag of the government from which they had
withdrawn. The Montgomery Convention in February, 1861, therefore appointed a Committee on
Flag, Seal, Coat of Arms, and
Motto*; and over two hundred de-
signs were submitted, accompanied by letters explaining their sym-
bolic meanings. The majority of
the plans formed some combination of stars or stripes, or of both—symbols
intentionally retained because of old associations. At the first session of the
provisional Congress, the committee chairman, William P. Miles, sub-

---

* The history of the Confederate flags is best treated in E. Merton Coulter, "The
Flags of the Confederacy," *Georgia Historical Quarterly,* Vol. XXXVII (September,
1953), 188–99, in which dimensions are quoted from the official legislation and from
the *Journal of the Congress of the Confederate States.* See also George H. Preble,
History of the Flag of the United States of America, 2nd Revised Edition (Boston,
1880), II, 525–31.

mitted the committee's report, recommending the adoption of the "Stars and Bars," thus described: "To consist of a red field, with a white space extending horizontally through the center, and equal in width to one-third the width of the flag; the red space, above and below, to be of the same width as the white; the union blue extending down through the white space and stopping at the lower red space; in the center of the union a circle of white stars corresponding in number with the states of the Confederacy." Seven white stars, representing the seceded states of Alabama, Florida, Georgia, Louisiana, Mississippi, South Carolina and Texas, were included, the intention being to add stars as new states withdrew from the Union.

Ever alert to use of topics of the moment as song subjects, Harry Macarthy took the lead in publicizing the new emblem, maintaining that the flag of his youth—of the North—no longer deserved his loyalty, and outlined *The Origin of the Stars and Bars; or, Our Flag*:

> Young stranger, what land claims thy birth?
> For thy flag is but new to the sea,
> And where is the nation on earth
> That the right of this flag gives to thee;
> Thy banner reminds us of one
> By the Champions of Freedom unfurled,
> And the proudest of nations have owned,
> 'Twas a glory and pride to the world;
> That flag was the Stripes and the Stars
> And the colors of thine are the same,
> But thou hast the Stars and the Bars,
> Oh, stranger, pray tell us thy name.
>
> That flag, with its garland of fame
> Proudly waved o'er my fathers and me,
> And my grandsires died to proclaim
> It the flag of the brave and the free;
> But alas, for the flag of my youth;
> I have sighed and dropped my last tear,
> For the North has forgotten her truth
> And would tread on the rights we hold dear;
> They envied the South her bright stars,
> Her glory, her honor, her fame,
> So we unfurled the Stars and the Bars
> And the Confederate Flag is its name.

With the new emblem as an object of devotion, songs began to glorify its significance and to predict the addition of more and more stars. The banner was to signify the glory of the Southern crusade, asserted *The Confederate Flag* (words by Mrs. Charles D. Elder, music by Sig. C. George):

Bright banner of freedom! with pride I unfold thee,
Fair flag of my country, with love I behold thee,
Gleaming above us in freshness and youth,
Emblem of Liberty, symbol of Truth.

CHORUS:
For this flag of my country in triumph shall wave
O'er the Southerners' home and the Southerners' grave.

All bright are the stars that are beaming upon us,
And bold are the bars that are gleaming above us,
The one shall increase in their number and light,
The other grow bolder in power and might.

Those bars of bright red show our firm resolution
To die, if need be, shielding thee from pollution;
For man in this hour must give all he holds dear,
And woman her prayers and her words of high cheer.

A native of South Carolina, the palmetto state, celebrated the possibility of thirteen stars on the Southern flag and predicted an eventual total of fifteen in *Farewell Forever to the Star-Spangled Banner* (words and music by Mrs. E. D. Hundley):

CHORUS:
Farewell, forever, the Star-Spangled Banner
No longer shall wave o'er the land of the free;
But we'll unfurl to the broad breeze of Heaven
Thirteen bright stars 'round the palmetto tree.

When the fair fifteen sisters a bright constellation
Shall dazzlingly shine in a nation's pure skies
With no hands to oppose, no foes to oppress them,
They'll gleam there forever, a light to all eyes.

The duplication of the red, white, and blue was noted in *Hurrah for our Flag!* (words and music by Rev. T. B. Russell), and the new flag was

59

Let ty-rants and slaves sub-miss-ive-ly trem-ble, And

bow down their necks 'neath the jug-ger-naut car; But

brave men will rise in the strength of a na-tion, And

cry "Give me free-dom, or else give me war."

Chorus

Fare-well, for-ev-er, the Star-Spang-led Ban-ner No

long-er shall wave o'er the land of the free;

But we'll un-furl to the broad breeze of Heav-en

Thir-teen bright stars 'round the pal-met-to tree.

Farewell Forever to the Star-Spangled Banner

60

welcomed in *Adieu to the Star-Spangled Banner Forever* (words by Ella D. Clark, music by J. R. Boulcott):

> Adieu to the star-spangled banner forever,
> Its once joyful folds are now trailing in dust.
> The ties that endeared it in sorrow we sever
> And give to the flag that redeemed us our trust.

The flag called for loyalty, affirmed *Flag of the Sunny South* (words by E. V. Sharp, music by John H. Hewitt):

> Flag of the sunny South still wave
> Where first from gloom thy stars arose,
> Thy dazzling lustre ne'er shall pale
> Where freedom's martyr'd sons repose.

And the new flag was to be the one flag, said *Our Southern Flag* (words by J. P. Caulfield, music by Samuel L. Hammond):

> Yes, we've lifted our flag, we've raised it at last!
> We've nailed it on high at the top of the mast!
> And grandly it flashes, and proudly it blows,
> And sternly it dashes defiance to foes!

Other less popular Confederate songs welcoming the new flag and bowing out the old were *The Banner of the South* (words by P. E. Collins, music by Newton Fitz), *The Flag of the Free Eleven* (words by M. F. Bigney, music by J. C. Viereck), *The Flag of the South* (words by Mrs. Anna K. Hearn, music by Dr. O. Becker) and *The New Red, White and Blue* (words by General M. Jeff Thompson, music by Theodore von La Hache), which was a song urging Missouri to join the Confederacy and "make the stripes of the Union flag trail in the dust."

To the tune of *The Bowld Soger Boy*, a witty Northerner summed up the story of the origin of the Stars and Bars in a few sarcastic verses, predicting its eventual doom:

> Oh, there's a dark secession wag,
> Made a flag from a rag
> Torn from a cotton bag
> > By a privateering crew.

But the people couldn't see it,
  And the timid had to flee it,
While all honest men agree it
  Is rebellion's dying cue.

One Union song, *Down with the Stars and Bars* (words by Frank Macneill, music by William M. Weckerly), berated this flag and urged, "up with the starry banner."

So similar was the Stars and Bars to the Stars and Stripes that the difference was not easily detected in combat. At a crucial stage in the First Battle of Bull Run (referred to by Confederates as Manassas) in July, 1861, when General P. G. T. Beauregard, commander of the Confederate Army of the Potomac, was expecting momentary aid during a lull in the fighting, he saw a column of troops approaching but was unable to determine whether they were Union or Confederate soldiers. The uniforms of both sides were similar and colors carried by the opposing armies were so much alike that the flag could not be identified amid the clouds of dust. The day was hot, without a sign of a breeze; the flag of this column hung drooping from the staff and could not be identified through binoculars. However, a sudden puff of wind spread the emblem—the Stars and Bars— and knowing that help had arrived, the General ordered combat renewed, with a Confederate victory resulting. After the battle, General Beauregard announced that the Confederate soldiers must have a flag so distinct from that of the enemy that there would never again be any difficulty in distinguishing it in combat.

BLUE   RED

A special battle flag was therefore designed, using the St. Andrew's cross with the ground red, the bars blue, and thirteen white stars, the number of seceding states having increased. The first flags were made from dresses belonging to the Cary sisters, Jennie and Hetty, of Baltimore, the same belles who suggested the music of *Tannenbaum* to fit the poem *My Maryland*.

The term "Stars and Bars" was dropped for the more fitting one of "the Southern Cross." To the tune of *The Star-Spangled Banner,* St. George Tucker of Virginia, then professor of law at the College of William and

Mary, memorialized this emblem in his verses entitled *The Southern Cross* (set to music by C. L. Peticolas and published as *The Cross of the South,* and by Charles Ellerbrock as *The Southern Cross*):

> Oh, say, can you see through the gloom and the storm,
>> More bright for the darkness, that pure constellation?
> Like the symbol of love and redemption its form,
>> As it points to the haven of hope for the nation.
> How radiant each star! as they beacon afar,
>> Giving promise of peace, or assurance in war;
>
> CHORUS:
> 'Tis the cross of the South, which shall ever remain
> To light us to Freedom and Glory again.

Though never officially adopted by the Confederate Congress, the Southern Cross supplanted the Stars and Bars on the battlefield, and most soldiers knew no other flag during the war.

After the Confederate government replaced the provisional government, the flag question was reopened, and the appointed committee recommended a new standard, completely eliminating stars and substituting a white cross on a red field, centered with a Norman shield bearing the sun, the rays of which were intended to represent the member states. This device, however, was not adopted.

BLUE   RED

The battle flag proved so satisfactory that it was used for the next one and one-half years. In April, 1863, General Beauregard wrote: "Why change our battle flag, consecrated by the best blood of our country in so many battlefields? A good design for the national flag would be the present battle flag as union jack, and the rest all white or all blue." The design chosen by the Confederate Congress on May 1, 1863, was a white ground with the battle flag as the union in the upper left corner. The thirteen five-pointed stars corresponded to the number of Confederate states at that time. The emblem was first used on May 10 as the pall of General "Stonewall" Jackson. The flag was celebrated anonymously in *The Star-Spangled Cross and the Pure Field of White* (words and music by "Subaltern") :

The star-spangled cross and the pure field of white
    Is the banner we give to the breeze;
'Tis the emblem of freedom, unfurled in the right,
    O'er our homes and our lands and our seas.

CHORUS:

We'll stand by the cross and the pure field of white
    While a shred's left to float on the air,
Our trust is in God, who can help us in fight,
    And defend those who ask Him in prayer.

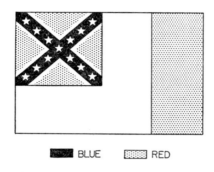

BLUE   RED

Then it was discovered that when this flag fell limp around the staff, it resembled a flag of truce or surrender; hence, on March 4, 1865, a vertical red bar was added to the right border of the white field.

The Unionists clung to the national emblem even as they jeered at the audacity of those who would supplant it. There was *No Flag but the Old Flag* (words by Jennie M. Parker, music by Charles G. Degenhard):

Up, up with the stars and stripes and go forth
    To save our great Union, brave men of the North.
No rest 'till the Star-Spangled Banner you see
    Triumphantly float from the palmetto tree.

The Bonnie Flag with the Stripes and Stars (words by Colonel J. L. Geddes, music by Henry Werner) is the one flag:

We treated you as brothers until you drew the sword
With impious hands at Sumter you cut the silver cord,
So now you hear our bugles, we come, the sons of Mars,
We rally 'round that brave old flag which bears the stripes and stars.

We do not want your cotton, we care not for your slaves,
But rather than divide this land, we'll fill your Southern graves.
With Lincoln as our chieftain, we'll wear our country's scars.
We rally 'round that brave old flag which bears the stripes and stars.

Every Star—Thirty Four (words by G. Simcoe Lee, music by Charles G. Degenhard) was needed:

Let it gallantly wave, that proud flag of the free,
A protector in peace, but a terror in war!
Let it flaunt to the breeze, let it skim every sea,
And bear on its folds every star—thirty four.

The Stars and Stripes was a favorite subject for rallying allegiance to the Union, and scores of songs appeared extolling it and the virtues it represented. *The American Standard* (words by George P. Morris, music by A. Bagioli) termed its stars "the forget-me-nots of Heaven"; *The Flag of the Constellation* (words by T. Buchanan Read, music by Charles R. Crosby) said, "It sails as it sailed, by our forefathers hailed, O'er battles that made us a nation."[5]

The Union standard elicited feelings of pride, according to *The Patriot Flag* (words by H. Markinfield Addey, music by J. R. Thomas):

Fling to the breeze the patriot flag,
    Its starry fold unfurl

[5] Many of these songs referred specifically to the idea of union which the emblem represented and to the dangers which threatened, while others followed a pattern of rallying the patriots under it. Among such Union songs, none of which were outstanding in any way, were: *Madman, Spare That Flag* (words by Mrs. Lena Drake, music by Augustus Cull), *One Flag or No Flag* (words and music by Clara M. Brinkerhoff), *No Slave Beneath That Starry Flag* (words and music by G. A. Burdett), *No Flag but the Old Flag* (words and music by Charles G. Degenhard), *Not a Star from Our Flag* (words and music by George W. H. Griffin), *Stand By the Flag of the Nation* (words by C. C. Butler, music by R. Hastings), *The Spirit of '61; Our Banner Shall Wave Forever* (words by W. W. Story, music by T. H. Howe), *The Triple Hued Banner* (words by Mrs. C. A. Mason, music by Asa B. Hutchinson), *Up with the Flag of the Stars and Stripes* (words by W. W. Story, music by T. H. Howe), *Our Flag and the Union Forever* (words by Rev. J. Matlock, music by Isaiah Ickes), *Our Banner; or, The Star-Spangled Banner of '61* (words by J. N., music by Edward Mack), *Stand by the Banner of Columbia* (words by W. Dexter Smith, Jr., music by R. J. Martin), *God Save the Flag of Our Native Land* (words by Mary McAboy, music by George Martyn), *The Stars and Stripes of Old* (words by C. Jays, music by Ferdinand Mayer), *Flag of the Free* (words and music by Harrison Millard), *Stand By the Banner* (words by Lieutenant James F. Fitts, music by H. R. Palmer), *God Save Our Country's Flag* (words and music by J. S. Porter), *The Bonnie Old Flag* (words and music by Father Reed), *I Will Be True to the Stripes and Stars* (words by Mrs. Kidder, music by S. J. Vail), *Our Country's Flag Forever* (words by Harry Heine, music by George Webb), *The New Star-Spangled Banner* (words by Edna Dean Proctor, music by J. P. Webster), and *Hurrah for Our Flag* (words and music by J. H. Wheeler).

Though rebels flaunt their recreant rag
And fierce defiance hurl.

There is no need for a new flag, affirmed *The Banner of the Stars* (words
and music by R. W. Raymond):

We'll never have a new flag,
For ours is the true flag.
The true flag, the true flag,
The red, white and blue flag.
Hurrah for it, hurrah! We'll carry to the wars
The old flag, the free flag, the banner of the stars.

Will you come with me, my Phyl-lis dear, To yon blue mount -ain free? Where

blos – soms smell the sweet – est, Come rove a – long with me.   It's

ev – 'ry Sun – day morn – ing, When I am by your   side,   We 'll

jump in – to the   wag – on   And   all take a   ride.

Chorus
Wait   for   the   wag – on,   Wait   for   the   wag – on,

Wait   for   the   wag – on And   we'll   all   take   a   ride.

Wait for the Wagon

The song *Wait for the Wagon,* which had been composed by R. B. Buckley in the fifties, was at the height of its popularity at the outbreak of hostilities, and the air caught the fancy of versifiers not so much because of its tune as because the chorus, "Wait for the wagon, and we'll all take a ride," could be made to suit either side, with the wagon either the Union or the Confederacy. *The Old Union Wagon* (words by Robert M. Hart) was originally built by Uncle Sam and had enjoyed a great history:

The eagle of Columbia, in majesty and pride,
Still soars aloft in glory, though traitors have defied
The flag we dearly cherish, the emblem of our will,
Baptized in blood of heroes, 'way down on Bunker Hill.

CHORUS:
Sam built the wagon,
The old Union wagon,
The star-crested wagon,
To give the boys a ride.

It was a good, strong wagon, built on sturdy principles:

There's none can smash the wagon, 'tis patented and strong,
And built of pure devotion, by those who hate the wrong;
Its wheels are made of freedom, which patriots adore,
The spokes, when rightly counted, just number thirty-four.

CHORUS:
Keep in the wagon,
The old Union wagon,
The oft-tested wagon,
While millions take a ride.

It turned out that more than 350,000 boys were to be taken on their last "ride" in the old Union wagon.

Under the same title, with words by John H. Lozier, the background of the wagon was extolled:

The makers of our wagon were men of solid wit
They made it out of charter oak that would not rot or split.
Its wheels are of materials, the strongest and the best;

And two are named the North and South, and two the
    East and West.

This good old Union wagon the nations all admired
    Her wheels had run for four score years and never once been tired;
Her passengers were happy as along her way she whirled
    For the good old Union wagon was the glory of the world.

But when old Abram took command, the South wheel got displeased
    Because the public fat was gone that kept her axle greased.
And when he gathered up the reins and started on his route
    She plunged into secession and knocked some fellers out.

This song was a great favorite with the Hutchinson family, who sang it
under the title *The Union Wagon* throughout the North in their patriotic
concerts.

Another version, *The Good Old Union Wagon* (words by S. Mat-
thews), claimed that the wagon was just the thing for that moment:

Our wagon's in good order, the running gear is sound
    It's filled with bone and muscle and well guarded all around.
Then come, ye Union people, we'll stand up side by side
    With our starry flag and banner, we'll all take a ride.

Our cause is just and holy, our men are brave and true
    And if they catch the traitors, they'll pepper them a few.
God bless our noble army, in it we'll all confide
    So jump into the wagon and we'll all take a ride.

That Southern Wagon (words by Will S. Hays under the pseudonym
"Jerry Blossom") details the progress of secession:

Jeff Davis built a wagon and on it put his name
    And Beauregard was driver of secession's ugly frame.
The horse he would get hungry as most of horses do
    They had to keep the collar tight to keep from pulling through.

The axles wanted greasing, the body was not wide,
    North Carolina jumped into it, Mississippi by her side;
Virginia took a cushioned seat and Lou'siana next,
    South Carolina got to scrounging and Florida got vexed.

They asked Kentuck to take a ride, she said the horse was blind;
   She shook her head at seeing Tennessee jump on behind.
But Jeff assured her all was right, the wagon it was new.
   Missouri winked at Beauregard and said it would not do.

The Southern Wagon, the dedication of which stated that it was
"Respectfully hitched up for the President, officers, and men of the Confederate Army," was written when only seven states were "on the wagon,"
and called on the others to hurry and jump on or be left behind. It is a
good example of the type of topical song popular for short periods.

Secession is our watchword, our rights we all demand;
   To defend our homes and firesides we pledge our hearts and hand.
Jeff Davis is our President, with Stephens by his side;
   Brave Beauregard, our General, will join us in our ride.

CHORUS:
Oh, wait for the wagon,
The Dissolution wagon;
The South is our wagon,
And we'll all take a ride.

Our wagon is the very best, the running-gear is good;
   Stuffed 'round the sides with cotton, and made of Southern wood;
Carolina is the driver, with Georgia by her side;
   Virginia holds the flag up while we'll all take a ride.

There are Tennessee and Texas also in the ring;
   They wouldn't have a government where cotton wasn't king.
Alabama and Florida have long ago replied;
   Mississippi and Louisiana are anxious for the ride.

The divergent interests of the Northern states needed to be united
to present a solid front against the South. The North itself was divided
by sectionalism. New England was completely Abolitionist and economically independent, the Trans-Allegheny states felt they should fight to
keep the Middle West free from slavery, and the border slave states would
have been aliens in a cotton Confederacy, for they were economically tied
to the North.

George Root's *Battle Cry of Freedom,* more than any other composition, seemed to be the song most effective in sounding the call of Union

patriotism. The refrain had a natural swing which was easily learned by soldiers as well as civilians; the music afforded an excellent opportunity for the fifes and drums to display their showy techniques. The recurrent phrase "shouting the battle cry of freedom" was ideal for group vocalizing with a soloist singing the various verses. The tune represents perfectly those qualities essential in a patriotic song if it is to be accepted and widely sung. Root composed two sets of verses, one a civilian "rallying" song, the other a soldier or "battle" song. The first version was amazingly successful at patriotic gatherings and conscription rallies and was also sung in camp; the second version formed an ideal marching air for the soldiers. In addition to being a song of patriotism, it literally belonged to the soldiers. Fighting men shouted it to relieve the tedium of days in camps and on long marches; dying boys rallied their spirits to its rhythm; during battle, whole regiments renewed the attack to this air; in fact, no other single song was as much beloved by soldiers and civilians:

Rallying Song

Yes, we'll rally 'round the flag, boys, we'll rally once again,
    Shouting the battle-cry of freedom;
We will rally from the hillside, we'll gather from the plain,
    Shouting the battle-cry of freedom.

CHORUS:
The Union forever, Hurrah! boys, hurrah!
Down with the traitor and up with the star;
While we rally 'round the flag, boys, rally once again,
Shouting the battle-cry of freedom.

We are springing to the call of our Brothers gone before,
And we'll fill the vacant ranks with a million freemen more.

We will welcome to our numbers the loyal, true and brave,
And altho' they may be poor, not a man shall be a slave.

So we're springing to the call from the East and from the West,
And we'll hurl the rebel crew from the land we love the best.

Battle Song

We are marching to the field, boys, we're going to the fight,
    Shouting the battle-cry of freedom;
And we bear the glorious stars for the Union and the right,
    Shouting the battle-cry of freedom.

CHORUS:
The Union forever, Hurrah! boys, hurrah!
Down with the traitor, up with the star;
For we're marching to the field, boys, going to the fight
    Shouting the battle-cry of freedom.

We will meet the rebel host, boys, with fearless hearts and true,
And we'll show what Uncle Sam has for loyal boys to do.

If we fall amid the fray, boys, we'll face them to the last,
And our comrades brave shall hear us, as they go rushing past.

Yes, for Liberty and Union we're springing to the fight,
And the vict'ry shall be ours, for we're rising in our might.

The Battle Cry of Freedom is the type of rousing tune which appears seldom during a period of war and but once in a generation. Confederates naturally wished either to produce a Southern equivalent (or facsimile) or to write verses appropriate to their cause. Hermann L. Schreiner, one of the most prolific Southern composers, adapted Root's music to words composed by the manager of the Atlanta Amateurs, a volunteer group of entertainers who provided recreation for various soldier relief funds. With changes in the rhythm made by him, the almost identical music used words by William H. Barnes:

Our flag is proudly floating on the land and on the main,
    Shout, shout the battle cry of freedom;
Beneath it oft we've conquered and will conquer oft again,
    Shout, shout the battle cry of freedom.

CHORUS:
Our Dixie forever, she's never at a loss,
Down with the eagle and up with the cross;
We'll rally 'round the bonny flag, we'll rally once again,
Shouting the battle cry of freedom.

Our gallant boys have marched to the rolling of the drum,
And leaders in charge cry, "Come, boys, come."

They have laid down their lives on the bloody battle-field,
Their motto is resistance—"To tyrants we'll not yield!"

While our boys have responded and to the field have gone,
Our noble women also have aided them at home.

SPECIAL CHORUS FOR VERSE NO. 4:

Our women forever, God bless them, huzza!
With their smiles and favors, they aid us in the war;
In the tent and on the battle-field, the boys remember them,
And cheer for the daughters of freedom.

Let the joyous sound re-echo o'er the land and o'er the sea,
Our Southern sky is brightening and soon we will be free.

In the same spirit, and almost as popular, was the song *Rally 'Round the Flag,* resulting from the collaboration of James T. Fields and William B. Bradbury.[6] Although the lyrics are not particularly inspiring, the lilt of the music served to popularize it with men at the front:

Rally 'round the flag, boys, give it to the breeze,
That's the banner we love on the land and seas;
Brave hearts are under ours, hearts that need no brag,
    Gallant lads, fire away! and fight for the flag.
    Gallant lads, fire away! and fight for the flag.
Rally 'round the flag, boys, give it to the breeze,
That's the banner we love on the land and seas;
Let our colors fly, boys, guard them day and night,
For victory is liberty and God will bless the right.

CHORUS:
Then rally 'round the flag, boys, rally 'round, rally 'round.
Rally 'round the flag, boys, rally 'round the flag.

Floating high above us, glowing in the sun,
Speaking loud to all hearts of a freedom won.
Who dares to sully it, bought with precious blood?
    Gallant lads, we'll fight for it, tho' ours should swell the flood.
    Gallant lads, we'll fight for it, tho' ours should swell the flood.
Floating high above us, glowing in the sun,
Speaking loud to all hearts of a freedom won.
Let our colors fly, boys, guard them day and night,
For Victory is liberty and God will bless the right!

[6] Bradbury was a well-known gospel hymn writer, his most popular compositions being *Just As I Am, without One Plea, He Leadeth Me, O Blessed Thought,* and *I Think When I Read That Sweet Story of Old.*

Loyalty to, and love of, country is the basis of patriotism. Patriotism moves an able-bodied man to serve his homeland willingly in its defense, either in repelling an invasion or in protecting its rights and maintaining its laws and institutions. The people of the Southern states rallied to the defense of their sacred soil and to the preservation of their treasured doctrine of States' rights. Those of the North sought to bring the seceded states back into the Union.

The sweeping and instantaneous success of early songs such as *My Maryland, Dixie, John Brown's Body,* and *The Battle Cry of Freedom* was due to the first wave of patriotism in the face of peril. Patriotism had seized the minds of the people under the stress of quick-moving events.

But this first surge of emotionalism soon passed, leaving the populace to face the grimmer realities of the conflict. The task of the North, to preserve the Union, and of the South, to establish a Secessionist Confederacy, was soon found to require more effort than the shouting of a few hip—hip—hooray's. Manpower would be the key to eventual victory, and the donning of the blue or the gray must follow the vows of undying loyalty to flag and cause. Whether volunteers or draftees, men between the ages of eighteen and forty-five would be required to rally round the flag in camp, on the march, and in battle.

****

CHAPTER 3

****

Volunteering and Conscription

Part 1: THE BLUE RESPONDS TO THE CALL

THE DAY AFTER Fort Sumter fell to the Confederates (April 15, 1861), Lincoln called for seventy-five thousand state militiamen for ninety days' service "to curb the rebellion and repossess the Federal forts and other property." The Unionists generally believed that only a slight show of force would be needed to put an end to the secession movement. In an editorial, the New York *Times,* for example, called the "rebellion" an "unborn tadpole."

So convinced was Lincoln that a handful of militiamen, called up for this three-month period, could force the South into submission, that offers of additional troops from loyal states were actually refused by the Federal government. In the first flurry of patriotism, individual states were rushing their militia to the defense of the national capital; Massachusetts, New York, Pennsylvania, and Ohio, anticipating an open break, had theirs in readiness. On April 13, Wisconsin had passed a bill to raise troops, if needed; on the fifteenth, New York voted a grant of money to outfit 30,000 two-year troops; on the seventeenth, Rhode Island appropriated half a million dollars for military purposes. It is therefore little wonder that Governor Alexander Randall of Wisconsin was offended that his state was called upon for only one regiment. Indiana, New Jersey, Connecticut, Michigan, New Hampshire, and Ohio were likewise annoyed by the lack of initiative which, to their way of thinking, the Washington authorities were showing. Had they been given the opportunity, 500,000 men might have rushed to the Union colors during the first months of the war.

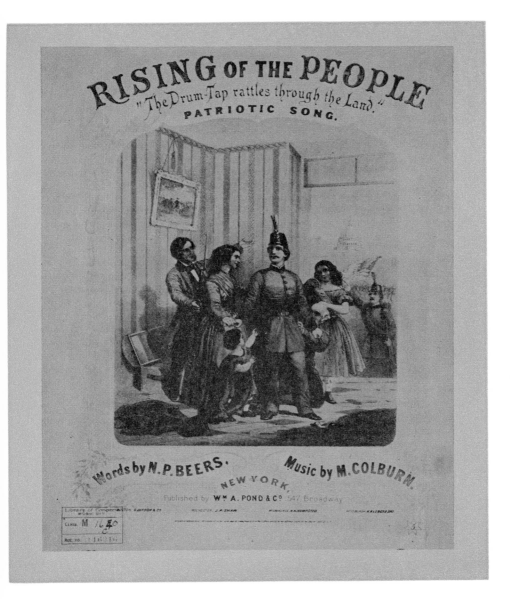

One father's farewell—evidently in Washington, since the Capitol is in the background—depicted each member of the assembled family handing him a piece of his gear.

The fever pitch to which the people were aroused was well expressed in *Going to the Wars* (words and music by A. B. Irving), which was inscribed "to all of Uncle Sam's boys":

Clergymen are mustering members of their flocks
   Satisfied they're able to inflict some knocks.
Sounding forth their doctrines, clearing up the mist
   From their eyes their discord ends " 'List, 'list, oh! 'list!"

CHORUS:
Hosts of freemen rushing 'round the stripes and stars!
Gracious, won't those South'rons get their full of war!

Editors are gathering and the walls of fame
   Soon will show their children how they carved a name.
Every inland steamer, every train of cars
   Bring their eager thousands going to the wars.

Tailors, clerks, mechanics, shoemakers to boot,
   Teachers tell their ideas, "Now's the time to shoot."
Bronzed and honest farmers say, "We're bound to jine"
   And the hardy fellows fall into the line.

Students, doctors, lawyers make a sight sublime,
   With the shoulder-hitters coming up to time.
Officers and seamen, salts and jolly tars
   All are now enlisting, going to the wars.

The infectious spirit of zeal and eagerness was expressed in *Hark! To Arms! Our Country Calls Us!* (words and music by E. W. Locke):

Tradesmen, close your doors and speed you
To the field, your brothers need you!
Herdsmen, leave your flocks and cattle,
Arm and hurry to the battle!

Young men, lithe and strong, we want you,
Quail, and age and cripples taunt you!
Seize the golden moments flying,
Meet your duty, living—dying!

Women true, no tears or sighing
Ease and luxuries denying!

Loving words and Spartan valor,
Not a lip or cheek of pallor!

East and West, they shout, "We're ready!"
On the columns firm and steady!
True as were our sires before us,
Marching steady to the chorus.

The willingness of the three-month volunteers in the North was later expressed by an Ohioan in *One Hundred Days Men* (words and music by
P. N. Wickersham):

You're wanted for a hundred days,
    Be ready in one minute
So General Cowan's order says,
    There must be something in it.
Now, lads, untackle from the plow,
    Unharness all the horses;
Quick, clap the saddle on them now
    To join the Union forces.

So farewell, hub; goodbye, sweet Sis,
    I have no time to tarry
Yet time enough to snatch one kiss
    From thee, my darling Mary.
Bear up, my love, the signal gun,
    How fast your heart is beating!
Weep not today, the rebels run
    And Grant pursues them fleeting.

We rendezvous and organize
    According to the order.
We march. Behold, our banner flies
    Beyond the Southern border.
Our officers are apt and kind,
    The men are raw but willing
And should it meet the colonel's mind,
    We'll go to rebel killing.

Fifty thousand militiamen went into training in and around Washington under General of the Armies Winfield Scott, a veteran of the Mexican War. So unskilled were these amateur soldiers in the use of firearms,

and so unaccustomed to military discipline, that he found himself unable to prepare them for success in the first encounter at Bull Run in Virginia on July 21, 1861. Some privates had been with their new units only a little over a week, since many of the April militiamen had already served their ninety-day terms and had returned to their homes. There had been practically no musket practice, and some of the green replacements went into battle without having ever previously fired a gun, an unbelievable but well-documented fact.

Yankee Robinson at Bull Run (words and music by George H. Briggs) describes the plight of a Vermonter who, during his term as a ninety-day volunteer, was sent to Washington and, after only a few drills, found himself at Bull Run:

> I fit sometime 'till I got a little tired,
>   And I began to feel sorta dry;
> As I raised my canteen up, I spied
>   The "Black Horse" Cavalry;
> So I cut dirt and run like a deer
>   (You couldn't see my coattail for the dust)
> At "two-forty" pace, ten thousand in the race,
>   Tew see who'd get to Washington fust.

These untrained volunteers were ordered into battle only because of the public clamor to take Richmond before the Confederate Congress could convene. The engagement was rightly termed "a battle of blunders," and from it originated the word "skedaddle," as recounted in *The New Skedaddle* (words by Eugene T. Johnston, music by John Durnal):

> By a man in Washington this movement was fomented
> But at the first Bull Run they say it was invented,
> Though our brave boys fought well, our officers in the saddle
> They made a move pell-mell, and people called skedaddle.

The humiliating defeat at Bull Run served to convince the Union that the war was truly serious business. To replace the ninety-day militiamen by long-term volunteers who could be carefully trained for continuous service, Lincoln issued a proclamation without Congressional clearance, calling for seventy thousand additional men to serve for periods of three years unless sooner discharged.

The fall of Fort Sumter and the gathering of troops from all the Northern states are pictured on this 1863 song cover.

Companies were usually formed from a city neighborhood or village, and volunteers were sworn in at noisy mass meetings. Battalions sometimes adopted colorful uniforms patterned after the French Army's Zouaves (Moorish soldiers). Their costumes were jackets, vests, and baggy breeches decorated with braid, turbans or fezzes of brilliant red with colored tassels, and white leggings, often accentuated by huge "handle-bar" mustaches which made them fearful and dazzling to behold. A New York maiden, deserted by her nineteen-year-old sweetheart, sang *My Love He Is A Zou-Zu:*

> My love he is a Zou-Zu, so gallant and bold,
> He's rough and he's handsome, scarce nineteen years old;
> To show off in Washington he has left his only dear,
> And my heart is abreaking because he's not here.
>
> CHORUS:
> For his spirit was brave, it was fierce to behold
> In a young man bred a Zou-Zu, only nineteen years old.

Many of these units were made up from the dregs of the city, plug-uglies and criminals. After the departure of the Wilson Fighting Zouaves from New York City, crimes were said to have decreased by 50 per cent. This battalion of rough-and-readies was praised in *Zouave Boys,* sung to the tune of Stephen Foster's *Nelly Bly:*

> Zouaves sly, shut one eye
>   When they go to sleep,
> But where spies and traitors lurk,
>   One eye they open keep.
>
> CHORUS:
> Hi, Zouaves! ho, Zouaves!
>   Don't be napping now,
> But day and night, just for the fight,
>   Be ready anyhow.
>
> When they sing, their roaring voice
>   So frightful is to hear
> That, at the sound, from all around,
>   The rebels cut and clear.

So fearful and dazzling were they that one verse of *Jeff Davis' Dream* (words and music by Bernard Covert) describes the Confederate president as awakening with a horrible scream:

He dreamed that a mudsill stood close by his bed
In the garb of a Zouave in flannel and red,
With a noose made of hemp slipping over his head,
Saying, "Come along, traitor, with me."

A member of one of these regiments, recruited from volunteer New York City fire departments, tells his story in one of the most popular songs of the war, *Abraham's Daughter; or, Raw Recruits* (words and music by Septimus Winner[7]):

Oh! kind folks listen to my song,
    It is no idle story;
It's all about a volunteer
    Who's goin' to fight for glory;
Now don't you think that I am right?
    For I am nothing shorter.

CHORUS:
And I belong to the Fire Zou-Zous,
    And don't you think I oughter?
We're goin' down to Washington
    To fight for Abraham's daughter.

Oh! should you ask me who she am,
    Columbia is her name, sir;
She is the child of Abraham,
    Or Uncle Sam, the same, sir.
Now if I fight, why ain't I right?
    And don't you think I oughter?

CHORUS:
The volunteers are pouring in
    From every loyal quarter,

[7] Septimus Winner, a music teacher and dealer in Philadelphia during the war, used the name "Alice Hawthorne" as composer of *Listen to the Mocking Bird* in 1855 and *Whispering Hope* in 1868. He wrote *Der Deitscher's Dog* ("Where, oh, where ish mine little dog gone?") in 1864; also *Ten Little Injuns* and *What Is Home without a Mother?*

Oh! kind folks lis-ten to my song, It is no i-dle sto-ry; It's

all a-bout a vol-un-teer Who's goin' to fight for glo-ry; Now

don't you think that I am right? For I am noth-in' short-er. And

I be-long to the Fire Zou-Zous, And don't you think I ought-er? We're

go-in' down to Wash-ing-ton To fight for A-bra-ham's daugh-ter.

Abraham's Daughter; or, Raw Recruits

    And I'm goin' 'long to Washington
      To fight for Abraham's daughter.

As the song says, Abraham's Daughter, or Columbia, certainly had her hands full, what with these raw recruits "pourin' in from every loyal quarter." The splendid accommodations the recruits had can be imagined from the fact that, on their arrival in Washington, the Capitol itself was turned over to the incoming regiments. The Massachusetts Sixth occupied the marble-trimmed Senate Chamber, while the New York Seventh took over the House of Representatives. Cooking and baking were done in the basement.

The third stanza stated:

    They say we have no officers,
      But ah! they are mistaken.

They certainly were mistaken. So liberal was the Secretary of War in the appointment of generals that there were at one time 2,357 of them.

These Fire Zouaves created something of a sensation on their arrival in the capital. When their leader, dashing Colonel Elmer E. Ellsworth, a friend of Lincoln's, was killed while tearing down a Confederate flag in Alexandria, Virginia, late in May, 1861, his memorial song, *The Zouaves* (words by J. Howard Wainwright), indicated the zest with which these roughneck soldiers approached their duties:

> Onward Zouaves,—Ellsworth's spirit leads us;
> For our country needs us;
> —For our banner floats o'er us;
> For the foe is before us.
>
> CHORUS:
> Onward, Zouaves!
> Do nothing by halves;
> Home to the hilt with the bay'net, Zouaves!
>
> Onward, Zouaves,—For the foe hath defied us:
> We have brave men to guide us;
> Let the sunlight and moonlight from bayonets glancing,
> Tell the foe the vanguard of the North is advancing.

During the month of July, Stephen C. Foster sent a song titled *I'll Be A Soldier* to the Copyright Office in Washington. Foster either sacrificed exactness for rhyme in the second verse, when he had the recruit "join in the *fray* with black shining belt and jacket of *gray*," or had not noted the color of the official Union uniform:

> I'll be a soldier and march to the drum,
> And lie in my tent when the night shadows come;
> I'll be a soldier with knapsack and gun,
> And stand to my post 'till the din of battle's done.
>
> CHORUS:
> Farewell! my own loved Jenny dear,
> Still will I dream of thee wherever I may stray;
> Farewell! before the coming year
> I'll be a soldier, far, far away.
>
> I'll be a soldier and join in the fray,

With black shining belt and jacket of gray;
I'll face up the battle as bold as a hawk,
As gay as a lark and as steady as a rock.

I'll be a soldier, "my country" is the cry,
I'll fly to defend her and conquer or die;
The land of my childhood, my love and my tears,
The land of my birth and my early sunny years.

I'll be a soldier, and when we have won,
I'll come back to thee with my knapsack and gun,
I'll come with a true heart and kiss off each tear,
And linger beside thee forever, Jenny dear.

Many looked upon the war as a lark at this time, and the young recruit
was feted widely.

With Congress finally in session, Lincoln, seeing the need for more
than the 150,000 men already called, asked for 400,000 more in mid-July
and received permission to raise half a million. Quotas of 600,000 were
assigned, and the states responded by furnishing 700,000. This rush to the
Union colors which followed the defeat at Bull Run is vividly portrayed
by an anonymous poet who composed *The Yankees are Coming* to the
minstrel tune *Jordan Am a Hard Road to Trabble:*

I harkened in the East, and I harkened in the West,
    And I heard a fifin' and a drummin'
And my heart bobbed up in the middle of my breast,
    For I knew that the Yankees were a-comin'!

CHORUS:
Then pull off your coat and roll up your sleeves,
    Yankee Doodle Dandy is a-comin'!
Oh, pull off your coat and roll up your sleeve,
    Yankee Doodle Dandy is a-comin', I believe!

There's a rattle in the East, and a rattle in the West,
    There's a Yankee Doodle fifin' and a-drummin'
When the rebels give us battle, you will find out the rest,
    And you'll know that the Yankees are a-comin'!

There was a great hurry to get into the fight, according to *The Volunteer's
Call to Arms* (words and music by Mrs. Lizzie A. Allan):

Come, brothers, come, let us hurry,
Now is the time for renown;
We'll give them a lesson to learn
That the Yankee boys can't be put down.
Better die than be conquered by rebels!
Our bugles in triumph shall sound
To cheer the hearts of the boys of New England
While our dead lie still on the ground.

The rush to defend the North was the subject of *Forward, Boys, Forward* (words by F. H. S., music by George F. Root):

From the mountain and the river, from the valley and the plain,
    We are sweeping to the rescue like the billows of the main.
For the traitor's hand is lifted o'er our fathers' sacred trust
    And our country's starry banner they would trample in the dust.

The Mudsills are Coming, mudsill being a Southern term for the common man and whites of low social standing (words by E. Bowers, music by G. L. J.), says:

The Union, the Union we're called on to save!
Fall in the ranks to join our brothers brave!
Chivalry, chivalry, old Abe's not a-funning
For six hundred thousand mudsills are coming.

One verse of *We Are Going to the Land of Dixie,* to the air of *Canaan,* relates the effect of all this "fifin' and a-drummin' " on President Davis:

Old Jeff, he hides behind the bales,
    We are going to the land of Dixie.
He thinks he sees the king of rails
    En route for the land of Dixie.

CHORUS:
Oh! Dixie, bright Dixie,
We're going to the land of Dixie.
    Oh! Jeff, beware,
    We'll soon be there,
We're going to the land of Dixie!

85

A lyric to the tune of the *Frankfort Apprentice's Song* explains the *Why and Wherefore* of all this excitement to get to the land of Dixie:

> Where, where, where and where,
> And where are you bound, young man?
> I'm off to the war with the good men and true,
> And hadn't you better come along too?
> I speak my mind quite freely, no ree'ly!

As this first stanza answers the question "where," so the second tells "why": to fight for the flag of freedom. The third stanza proclaims "which" is the flag of the free:

> Oh, Washington's flag with the stripes and the stars,
> Will you give such a name to the thing with the bars?

"Who goes with you?" asks the next stanza:

> Ten thousand brave lads, and if they should stay here
> The girls would cry shame, and they'd volunteer.

Finally the fifth and last stanza settles the question of "what" you would gain by that:

> Oh, I've gained enough, whatever the cost,
> If a free land, the hope of the world, isn't lost.

The first martial volunteering song which swept through the ranks was titled *Marching Along* (words and music by William B. Bradbury); it was said to have been known throughout the entire Army of the Potomac, and one could hear it wherever a group of soldiers gathered around a campfire. The tune was particularly catchy, easy to learn, and demanded only a very narrow vocal range. For the phrase "McClellan's our leader" the name of any other current military leader could be substituted. It was as good a rallying song as would appear for the Union forces:

> The army is gathering from near and from far;
> The trumpet is sounding the call for the war;
> McClellan's our leader, he's gallant and strong;
> We'll gird on our armor and be marching along.

The ar-my is gath-'ring from near and from far; The trump-et is sound-ing the

call for the war; Mc-Clel-lan's our lead-er, he's gal-lant and strong. We'll

gird on our ar-mor and be march-ing a-long. March-ing a-long, we are

march-ing a-long, Gird on the ar-mor and be

march-ing a-long; Mc-Clel-lan's our lead-er, he's

gal-lant and strong; For God and our coun-try we are march-ing a-long.

Marching Along

CHORUS:
Marching along, we are marching along,
Gird on the armor and be marching along;
McClellan's our leader, he's gallant and strong;
For God and our country we are marching along.

The foe is before us in battle array,
But let us not waver or turn from the way;
The Lord is our strength and the Union's our song;
With courage and faith, we are marching along.

87

The memory of demoralizing panic at Bull Run called for expressions of confidence in the innate bravery of Union soldiers. This battle had been looked upon as an opportunity for a Sunday afternoon outing, and the carriages of sightseers from Washington crowded roads near Warrenton. As Federal troops broke rank in their baptism of fire and ran toward the capital, they encountered civilians; and, when they were fired upon, complete panic resulted. This tendency to flee in fright was dealt with in *The Union Volunteers* (words and music by E. C. Saffery):

> Ye loyal Union Volunteers,
>   Your country claims your aid,
> Says Uncle Abe, a foe appears,
>   Are we to be afraid?
> Are we to be afraid, my boys?
>   No, at them we will go;
> On Potomac's banks we'll close our ranks,
>   And march to meet the foe.
>
> CHORUS:
> We'll just say who's afraid, my boys,
>   And at them we will go.
> On Potomac's banks we'll close our ranks,
>   And bravely charge the foe.
>
> Now where's the craven hearted slave
>   Who flies when he should stand?
> Why let him fill a coward's grave
>   Unwept as he's unmanned.
> But we will, at our country's call,
>   Inscribe our names on high.
> Hurrah, we'll muster one and all,
>   And bravely do or die.

A little training under experienced officers, the song contended, was all that was needed to produce men as brave as could be found anywhere.

The appointment of McClellan as commander of the Army of the Potomac instilled confidence in his troops, said a verse from *Whack-Row-De-Dow* (words by Fanny Herring, music by W. L. Hobbs), featured by Bryant's Minstrels.

There's a good time surely coming

And we think it soon will come
When our Northern boys are bound to make
    Their Southern rebels hum.
For we'll have no more Bull Run affairs
    Where the chivalry says we did knock under;
For we've got a brave McClellan now
    Who'll give them Northern thunder.

And, according to *Skedaddle* (words and music by George Danskin), this word would in the future be applied to the foe only when Union ranks were met:

Skedaddle, boys, skedaddle, that's Greek you all must know
Which means "Take to the saddle whene'er you see the foe."

Lincoln's 1862 call for the drafting of 300,000 additional troops was answered in a poem by an Abolitionist writer, James Sloan Gibbons, though it is often erroneously attributed to William Cullen Bryant. The swing of the words intrigued composers and several scores were written. The version by Luther O. Emerson, a writer of gospel hymns, was by all odds the most popular. Other settings were composed by S. J. Adams, L. S. Burditt, Stephen Foster, A. B. Irving, and George R. Poulton. The rhythm of the melody makes necessary the contraction "Abra'am" for "Abraham."

We are coming, Father Abra'am, three hundred thousand more,
    From Mississippi's winding stream and from New England's shore;
We leave our ploughs and workshops, our wives and children dear,
    With hearts too full for utterance, with but a silent tear;
We dare not look behind us, but steadfastly before—
    We are coming, Father Abra'am, three hundred thousand more!

CHORUS:

We are coming, we are coming, our Union to restore,
We are coming, Father Abra'am, with three hundred thousand more,
We are coming, Father Abra'am, with three hundred thousand more!

You have called us and we're coming, by Richmond's bloody tide,
    To lay us down, for freedom's sake, our brothers' bones beside;
Or from foul treason's grasp to wrench the murderous blade,
    And in the face of foreign foes its fragments to parade.

Six hundred thousand loyal men and true have gone before—
We are coming, Father Abra'am, three hundred thousand more!

When the actual quota was raised to 600,000, the same poem was set to music by Nathan Barker and Augustus Cull with the number changed to "full six hundred thousand more" and under the title *To Canaan: Song of the 600,000* by C. S. Brainard, Eben A. Kelly, and W. E. Thayer. J. W. Turner, in *Abraham's Draft,* said:

Six hundred thousand is the cry
  Come, rally to the call;
For Abra'am says he must have them
  Or else the Union'll fall!

So fond did the Union become of this tune that almost every Northern state furnished words for it. Excerpts from the *Song of the Hoosiers* (words by W. T. Dennis) show that Indiana was willing to do her part in filling the quota:

And here's thirty thousand more—list the thunder of their tread,
As they come to greet the living and avenge the honored dead.

Furthermore, these Hoosiers were true fighting men:

We are coming from the workshop, the office and plough
We've turned our faces from our homes, we are our country's now;
The foeman knows our banner and his face is blanched with fear,
As his scout repeats with quivering lips, "Indianians are near!"

Patriotism was at fever heat:

As the tempest sweeps the forest, as the lightning rends the oak,
So sweep our legions o'er the field, so falls our sabre-stroke.

From Rockford came *Illinois' Response* (by S. B. H.), from President Lincoln's own state:

We're coming, and we know your cheek will glow with honest pride,
When you see our spangled banner float our Sister States beside.

We're coming, for we trace the lines of care upon your brow,
And silver hairs are twining fast your "crown of glory" now.

We know that near your burdened heart our bleeding country lies,
We come with freedom's stalwart arm to meet her enemies.

William Bradbury, in *Hold on, Abraham, Uncle Sam's Boys Are Coming Right Along,* assured the president:

Hold on, Abraham, never say die to your Uncle Sam.
Uncle Sam's boys are coming right along
Six hundred thousand strong.

To these and similar responses, a word of thanks, in which each state is remembered individually, was given in *Father Abraham's Reply* (words and music by George F. Root):

I welcome you, my gallant boys, from Maine's resounding shore,
From far New England's granite hills I see your legions pour;
From Massachusetts' fertile vales, from old Vermont they come;
Connecticut wheels into line at the rolling of the drum,
And little Rhody springs to arms, like David in his might,
Upon rebellion's giant front to strike one blow for right.
One blow for right, my hero boys, for right and Uncle Sam,
Strike, and receive the blessings of the God of Abraham.

CHORUS:
'Tis glorious, 'tis glorious, to see your legions pour,
I welcome you, my gallant boys, SIX HUNDRED THOUSAND
    MORE!

I see from all her boundaries the glorious Empire State
A countless host is sending forth, with freemen's hopes elate;
From Delaware there comes a gleam of white and crimson bars
Where faithful hands are holding up the banner of the stars;
New Jersey answers to the call as if along her shore
Each grain of sand had said: "We come, three hundred thousand more;
We come to strike for liberty, for right and Uncle Sam,
Who gives us all the blessings of the God of Abraham."

And Pennsylvania, keystone of this glorious Union arch,
Is sounding through her thousand caves the thrilling order, "March!"

I see her dusky sons come forth from every darkened mine
And, like the clouds along her hills, swift forming into line;
Their eyes have such a fiery gleam, from glowing forges caught,
Their arms such strength, as if they were of iron sinews wrought;
I think when on Secession's head they strike for Uncle Sam
Each blow will fall like vengeance from the God of Abraham.

I see adown our Western vales your legions pour, my boys,
From the Buckeye, Indiana, and my own loved Illinois;
And Iowa, and Michigan, and Minnesota, too,
And far Wisconsin's prairies send their heroes tried and true.
Come on, O living avalanche! break into floods of light,
And roll your waves of truth along Secession's shores of night.
Drown out rebellion, as of old, and then with Uncle Sam,
Safe in the Ark of State we'll praise the God of Abraham.

In spite of the conscription rush, Stephen Foster's *We've a Million in the Field* was not true until much later in 1864:

The flags are flying and brave men are dying,
The din of battle is revealed;
The Union's quaking, the land is shaking
With the tramp of a million in the field.

CHORUS:
We've a million in the field,
A million in the field,
While our flag is slighted,
With hearts united,
We can bring a million more to the field.

We were peaceful hearted in days departed,
While foes kept their blighting plans concealed;
But they must now weather the storms they gather,
For they must meet a million in the field.

Down in old Kentucky, they're true and plucky;
They know that the Union is their shield!
And they'll do their duty in all its beauty,
When they find we've a million in the field.

During the feverish haste to enlist a large army, mothers, fathers, wives, and sweethearts were called upon to release their loved ones to the cause of freedom. A young lad eager to join the colors was not accepted without his parents' consent. *The Young Volunteer* (words and music by J. R. Osgood) asks his mother for permission:

Can you selfishly cling to your household joys,
    Refusing the smallest ties to yield,
While thousands of mothers are sending boys
    Beloved as yours to the battlefield?
Can you see my country call in vain
    And restrain my arm from the needful blow?
Not so, though your heart should break with pain,
    You'll kiss me, bless me, and let me go.

This song was also published under the title *Kiss Me, Mother, and Let Me Go* (music by L. B. Powell). An absent son begs his mother to let him enlist in *Mother, Can I Go?* (words by William B. Tremaine, music by J. P. Webster), also issued under the title *Tell Me, Mother, Can I Go?*:

I am young and slender, Mother; they would call me yet a boy,
    But I know the land I live in and the blessings I enjoy.
I am old enough, my Mother, to be loyal, proud and true
    To the faithful sense of duty I have ever learned from you.
We must conquer this rebellion; let the doubting heart be still
    We must conquer it or perish; we must conquer and we will!
But the faithful must not falter and shall I be wanting? No!
    Bid me go, my dearest Mother; tell me, Mother, can I go?

Another Northern boy, in *Your Blessing, Dearest Mother; or, The Soldier's Farewell* (words and music by T. H. Howe), spares his mother the sadness of parting:

Awaking at morning, should you call in vain
For me, who would spare you one moment of pain,
Remember, I could not part seeing you weep
And early departing, I kissed you, asleep.
My mother, my country, for thee will I fight.
I know that in time God will prosper the right.
Be cheerful, be hopeful, and calm, should you hear
I fell on the battlefield. Others as near
Will fall there, but then oh, remember this night.

Your blessing will linger in memory as bright.
Now once more, your blessing, so sweet to my ear
And then may God bless you, my mother dear.

Mothers of the North were quick to accept the inevitable and hero-
ically gave up their youngest, as in *The Soldier's Mother* (words by Mrs.
John C. Winans, music by Hermann T. Knake):

I may not kiss your brow again,
    I may not fold you here,
Nor ever more gaze fondly on
    The boy I love so dear;
But yet I bid you quickly don
    The soldier's bright array,
And foremost on the deadly fight
    Lead fearlessly the way.

See that your good sword worketh
    Where thickest lie the slain,
And wave our glorious banner
    O'er Southern soil again;
Away, boy! Fight and conquer,
    Turn not a thought to me;
Your country hath a nobler claim
    Help *her* to victory!

Mothers required bravery to part with their first-born,[8] according to *The
Conscript's Mother* (words and music by Henry Bedlow):

Away with all sighing! Away with all tears!
My boy shall behold not my grief but my pride.
Shall I taint his young manhood with womanish fears,
When the flag of his country is scorned and defied?

He's my all, he's my treasure! But take him, dear land,
And add him, a jewel to Liberty's crown.
One hero the more to your patriot band,
The widow's last mite to the nation's renown.

[8] Other mothers parted, bravely and tearfully, in *His Country Needs Him More
Than I* (words by M. P., music by T. Martin Towne), *The Volunteer's Mother* (two
songs by this title, one by Edwin Moore, the other by George A. Mietzke), and *She
Stood at the Door* (words and music by J. H. McNaughton).

Wives, too, expressed their willingness to bear the burden of separation. One voiced her spirit of sacrifice in *Take Your Gun and Go, John* (words and music by H. T. Merrill):

Don't stop a moment to think, John;
    Our country calls, then go.
Don't fear for me nor the children, John,
    I'll care for them, you know.
Leave the corn upon the stalk, John,
    The fruit upon the tree,
And all our little stores, John;
    Yes, leave them all to me.

CHORUS:
Then take your gun and go,
    Yes, take your gun and go,
For Ruth can drive the oxen, John,
    And I can use the hoe.

I've heard my grandsire tell, John,
    He fought at Bunker Hill,
He counted all his life and wealth
    His country's offering still.
Would I shame the brave old blood, John,
    That flowed on Monmouth plain?
No, take your gun and go, John,
    Tho' I ne'er see you again.

The army's short of blankets, John,
    Then take this heavy pair.
I spun and wove them when a girl
    And work'd them with great care,
A rose in every corner, John,
    And here's my name, you see!
On the cold ground they'll warmer feel
    Because they're made by me.

In the third stanza she gave him a pair of heavy blankets with roses in every corner and her name embroidered on them—pretty blankets that she had woven when she was a girl! Wives, sweethearts, and mothers often loaded down their loved ones with gifts which were soon discarded. When the first militia organizations arrived for the defense of Washington, they

95

"staggered under loads of parting gifts—pipes, tobacco, pills, needlebooks, Bibles, books, magazines, knives, towels, soap, slippers, water filters, and portable writing desks." The men found it impossible to keep knick-knacks on the long marches, for even some necessities had to be abandoned to lighten their burden. The boots, coats, and caps with which they started out were given up for lighter shoes, jackets, and soft felt hats. Heavy cartridge boxes, revolvers, and cooking utensils were thrown away as the shedding process continued. A private soldier was eventually defined as "one man, one hat, one jacket, one shirt, one pair of pants, one pair of drawers, one pair of shoes, and one pair of socks!" His baggage consisted of two blankets—one wool and one rubber—one haversack, one shelter tent, one canteen, and one rifle. The Confederate General Ewell was quoted as saying, "The road to glory cannot be followed with much baggage."

One mother, with her parting gift, said *Keep This Bible Near Your Heart* (words and music by H. S. Thompson):

"Go forth, my darling, to the conflict,"
Thus spoke a mother to her boy.
"Ne'er let me hear you turned away when traitors
Threatened our loved country to destroy.
Take a mother's blessing,
Keep this Bible near your heart;
Never forget a mother's prayers are ever with you
And her love for you will ne'er depart."

Later, the song recounts, the boy clutched the Bible as he lay dying. A brother, on parting, gave the soldier an old Revolutionary War musket in *The Corporal's Musket* (words by William S. Heath, music by C. Hatch Smith):

The rust has slowly settled
    In the years that since have flown,
Upon the good old barrel
    That once like silver shone.
It has a quaint and war-worn look.
    The fashion of the stock
Perhaps is only equalled
    By the fashion of the lock.
But slumbering stocks of '76

Within the flint remain;
Take down the corporal's musket,
    We need it once again.

To thee and me, my brother,
    Comes down the soldier's gun;
It tells a tale of mighty deeds
    By patriot valor done.
The hurried march, the daring charge,
    The onset and the strife;
Of clashing steel, of bursting shell,
    The stake, a nation's life.
Then seize once more that well-tried gun
    Which idle long has lain.
Quick, seize the corporal's musket,
    'Twill help us once again.

Sweethearts usually parted from their lovers with mixed feelings of sorrow and pride. Many were the sentimental farewells composed, but none more popular than the old Irish air of the seventeenth century, *The Girl I Left Behind Me* (music by Samuel Lover), which had many poetic settings. They would, indeed, be sorely missed, says *Glory Hallelujah* (a version for the Thirteenth Regiment of Massachusetts Volunteers):

Cheer for the sweethearts we are now forced to leave.
Think of us, lassies, but for us don't grieve.
Bright be the garlands that for us you'll weave
When we return to your smiles.

Almost invariably the sweethearts willingly let their lovers go, as in the case of *Dearest, Wilt Thou Bid Me Go?* (words by A. Alphonso Dayton, music by Matthias Keller):

Father, mother, brother, sister,
    All have bid their last adieu
And I come to thee, my darling,
    Come to ask consent of you.
Will thou give me thine own blessing,
    Bless me ere I go away?
Surely thou woulds't urge me forward;
    No, thou woulds't not bid me stay.

97

Early nineteenth-century immigrants had settled in the industrial areas of the North, and as a result, entire regiments were formed of those of foreign birth, some of whom spoke no English. Irishmen found an outlet for their inspired patriotism by the formation of several regiments, and Swedes from the Middle West made a substantial contribution to several campaigns. Naturalized Germans joined the rush to the colors, and the western general, picturesque Franz Sigel, hero of the Battle of Pea Ridge, Arkansas, himself a German *émigré,* attracted volunteers. A comic dialect song, *I Goes to Fight mit Sigel* (words by Fitch Poole, music by Samuel Lover), favored by minstrel soloists and impersonators, was based on their rallying cry:

> I've come shust now to tells you how
> > I goes mit regimentals,
> To schlauch dem voes of Liberty,
> > Like dem old Continentals
> Vot fights mit England long ago
> > To save der Yankee Eagle;
> Und now I gets my soldier clothes,
> > I'm going to fight mit Sigel.
>
> Dem Deutschen mens mit Sigel's band
> > At fighting have no rival;
> Und ven Cheff Davis mens we meet,
> > We schlauch 'em like de tuyvil;
> Dere's only von ting vot I fear
> > Ven pattling for der Eagle,
> I von't get not no lager beer
> > Ven I goes to fight mit Sigel.
>
> For rations dey gives salty pork,
> > I dinks dat vas a great sell;
> I petter likes de sauerkraut,
> > Der Schvitzer-kase und bretzel.
> If Fighting Joe will give us dem
> > Ve'll save der Yankee Eagle;
> Und I'll put mine vrou in breech-a-loons,
> > To go und fight mit Sigel.

The *Irish Volunteer* (words by S. Fillmore Bennett, music by J. P. Webster) is another song about an immigrant who is loyal to his adopted stars and stripes. *Corporal Schnapps* (words and music by Henry C. Work) later occupies a Southern town and receives short shrift from a local belle:

> I meets von laty repel in der schtreet
>> So handsome effer I see;
> I makes to her von ferry callant pow
>> Put oh! she schpits on me!

It was necessary to draft men from New York, Pennsylvania, New Jersey, New Hampshire, Vermont, Connecticut, Indiana, and Ohio to meet the established quotas. The procedure for this drafting consisted of assembling a mass meeting of all men in a certain community within the age limits of the draft, placing their names in a hat, and having a blindfolded person draw out enough slips to meet the quota. Another method employed was a wheel of chance. Prizes in the draft lottery were extolled in *Hurry Up, Conscripts* (words and music by W. J. Wetmore):

> The wheel is turning 'round, boys, hurrah now for the jam!
> How are you conscripts? Hurry up to fight for Uncle Sam!
> Come up, Bob, don't stand there shaking,
> Take your musket, shoulder arms!
> Stand in line with Larry Brady.
> Who now cares for war's alarms?

A draftee had the choice either of going to war himself or of providing a substitute in his place. The practice of substitution was quite common in Europe; hence, it was only natural that the custom should have been followed in the United States. The draft was, in reality, a method of placing upon a stated number of individuals the personal responsibility for procuring one soldier each, either himself or a substitute. Later, the practice of making a payment of $300 to the government as an alternative to procuring a substitute was established, but this did not render him immune to subsequent calls; whereas the procuring of another to take his place in the army absolved him from any further responsibility. The New York Draft Association would, for $10.00, guarantee a man against the draft and would supply a substitute for an additional $25.00. Such organizations advertised freely in the newspapers. Some crafty and unscrupulous individuals set themselves up in business to supply substitutes; the story of one is recounted in *The Substitute Broker* (words by John L. Zieber, music by Rudolph Wittig):

I am a broker, sir, and living in this city
    In substitutes I deal, and do it without pity.
I'm always on the hunt for some poor verdant fellow;
    I buy him with "soft soap" and liquor 'till he's mellow.

CHORUS:
That's the way we do, ain't we jolly jokers,
Making money being brokers?

I met a chap one day, a stranger, and a green one.
    Says I, "This is my man or I have never seen one."
I speedily hailed him and smiled most unresisting;
    Says I, "My dear young friend, do you think of enlisting?"

"Oh, yes," says he, "I am. 'Twas that which brought me hither;
I'll fight for Uncle Sam in March, I don't care whither."

Thus were the arrangements made, though later in the song the broker, under the influence of drink, was himself sold by the "greenie."

The substitute would inherit glory and honor says *Wanted, A Substitute* (words and music by Frank Wilder):

Wanted, a substitute, show me the man
That will buckle on his armor and fight for Uncle Sam.
He must have an arm of power and a heart of courage, too;
He must love his native country and the red, white, and blue.

CHORUS:
Wanted, a substitute, show me a man
That will buckle on his armor and fight for Uncle Sam.

Wanted, a substitute, three hundred I'll pay;
If you know of one who wants it, just send him along this way.
What glory he'll inherit when rebellion is put down!
No greater mark of merit could any mortal crown!

Wanted, a substitute, none need apply
Unless he's sound from head to foot, with perfect teeth and eye.
Now such a one is wanted, then who will go for me?
To fight his country's battles in the land of Dix-i-e?

The sad plight of a draftee who cannot raise the necessary $300 from his own resources or from friends, is celebrated in *Where Are You, $300* (words by W. Dexter Smith, Jr., music by R. J. Lessur):

Where are you, three hundred dollars? I'm hard up, I vow,
Never shall I need your greenbacks more than I do now.
Oh, the dollars I have wasted on all sorts of things!
If I had them now, I reckon grief would soon take wings.

CHORUS:
Where are you, three hundred dollars, where are you, I say?
They will sadly muss my collar if I do not pay!

Where are all the boys I've treated to ice cream and pie?
Will they see a little fellow like me go and die?
Though I'm well and able-bodied, yet I cannot fight.
Where are you, three hundred dollars, you would make it right!

This system naturally operated to the disadvantage of laboring men who could make no payments or financial arrangements and whose names, therefore, appeared in draft lists in much greater proportion than those of men of ample means. Such a situation precipitated the famous draft riot in New York City on July 13, 1863—a demonstration instigated to prevent official notification of the working men whose names had appeared in the Sunday papers the day before. Deaths from this four-day riot approached 500. Negroes were hanged in the streets, and police were unable to halt the burning of property.

The poor fellow who found himself drafted was remembered in a humorous song, the dialect of which reflects the education of the lower class to which Jimmy, who was unable to furnish the necessary $300 exemption fee, belonged. His mother, "a lone widder," says he was *Grafted into the Army* (words and music by Henry C. Work[9]):

Our Jimmy has gone for to live in a tent,
　They have grafted him into the army;
He finally puckered up courage and went,
　When they grafted him into the army.

[9] Henry Clay Work (1832–84), one of the three most prominent Union composers, was apprenticed at an early age to a printer and, throughout his successful career, composed by setting the notes directly in type without making any notes on paper. During the war years, he wrote exclusively for Root and Cady, the Chicago publishers. His non-war songs included *The Wreck of the Lady Elgin, Grandfather's Clock, The Ship That Never Returned,* and the famous temperance song *Come Home, Father* ("The song of little Mary, standing at the barroom door, While the shameful midnight revel rages wildly as before").

I told them the child was too young, alas!
At the captain's headquarters they said he would pass;
They'd train him up well in the infantry class,
    So they grafted him into the army.

CHORUS:
O Jimmy, farewell! your brothers fell
Way down in Alabamy;
I thought they would spare a lone widder's heir,
But they grafted him into the army.

Dressed up in his unicorn—dear little chap—
    They grafted him into the army.
It seems but a day since he sat in my lap,
    But they grafted him into the army.
And these are the trousies he used to wear—
The very same buttons, the patch and the tear—
But Uncle Sam gave him a bran' new pair
    When they grafted him into the army.

Now in my provisions I see him revealed,
    They have grafted him into the army;
A picket beside the contented field,
    They have grafted him into the army.
He looks kinder sickish—begins to cry—
A big volunteer standing right in his eye!
Oh, what if the ducky should up and die
    Now they've grafted him into the army!

A draftee was seldom eager to leave; but, if penniless, he became a
soldier "meek as any lamb," and his sweetheart could only exclaim hopelessly that *He's Gone to the Arms of Abraham* (words and music by Septimus Winner):

My true love is a soldier in the army now today.
It was the cruel war that made him have to go away;
The "draft" it was that took him, and it was a heavy blow.
It took him for a conscript but he didn't want to go.

CHORUS:
He's gone, he's gone, as meek as any lamb,
They took him, yes, they took him
To the arms of A-bra-ham.

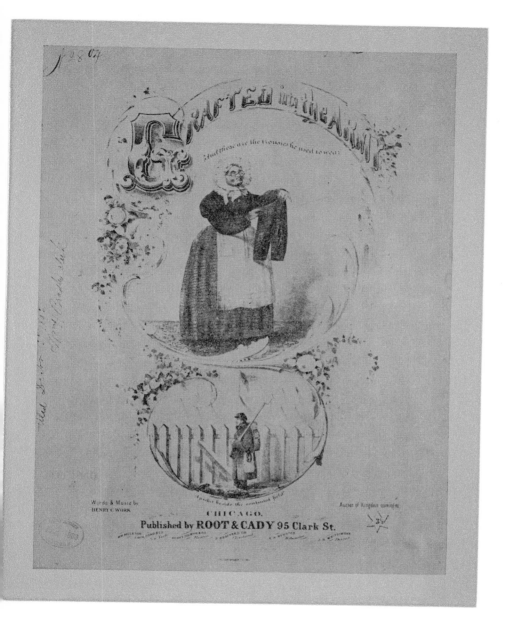

The large number of Northern citizens and soldiers of foreign ancestry and the current vogue of impersonation concerts led to the composition of many dialect songs, such as Henry C. Work's *Grafted into the Army*.

He's gone to be a soldier, with a knapsack on his back,
Afightin' for the Union and alivin' on hard tack;
O, how he looked like Christian in the Pilgrim Progress shown,
With a bundle on his shoulders, but with nuthin' of his own.

I haven't got a lover now, I haven't got a beau;
They took him as a raw recruit, but mustered him, I know.
He's nothing but a private and not for war inclined,
Although a hard old nut to crack, a colonelcy you might find.

Sweethearts lived in the fear that the draft would separate them from each other, as in *When This Cruel Draft Is Over,* sung to the tune of *When This Cruel War Is Over:*

Dearest love, I fear they'll draft you, they'll put you on the list;
And they'll turn the wheel to grind you into Lincoln grist.

But Old Abe I know will draft you and drag you far from me;
Oh, I cannot live without you, my heart so cold will be.

Methods of evading the draft were numerous. If a draftee could neither pay commutation nor furnish a substitute, he could simply remain at home and do nothing, hoping that his failure to report would not be discovered. The desperation of one draftee is expressed in a verse of *Come In Out of the Draft; or, The Disconsolate Conscript* (words by Ednor Rossiter, music by Frank Walters):

I've tried to get a wife, I've tried to get a "sub,"
But what I next shall do now, really is the rub;
My money's almost gone and I am nearly daft!
Will someone tell me what to do to get out of the draft?

The physical examination following the drawing of a draft number was the crucial test, and many frankly hoped for rejection and classification as exempts. One who failed to pass tells his story in *The Invalid Corps* (words and music by Frank Wilder):

I wanted much to be examined,
The surgeon looked me o'er and o'er;
My back and chest he hammered.
Said he, "You're not the man for me;

Your lungs are much affected and likewise
Both your eyes are cocked and defective otherwise.

CHORUS:
So now I'm with the invalids
    And cannot go and fight, sir.
The doctor told me so, you know;
    Of course, it must be right, sir.

Those who passed, while secretly jealous of the exempts, were not a
little sarcastic, as in *How Are You, Exempt?* (words and music by Frank
Wilder):

How are you, exempt?
    I s'pose you feel alright
As the surgeon said you'd never do
    To take your gun and fight.
What did he say the matter was,
    The trouble, man, with you?
Did he say you got the heart complaint
    And test you through and through?

CHORUS:
How are you, exempt?
    I s'pose you feel alright
As the surgeon said you'd never do
    To take your gun and fight.

How are you, exempt?
    Did he say that that was all?
Did he say you were too short,
    Or too slender, or too tall?
Was your case one of debility
    Once caused by a fall?
Did he say you could not see, sir,
    With but one eye at all?

To escape the draft, some few even mutilated their bodies; to cut off
the index finger on the right hand was the most common practice, since
it was the key to all weapons-firing. Others pretended physical ills. Twelve
out of every thirty men in Philadelphia wore trusses when they reported

for their medical examinations. Many preferred to strike out for the gold fields of the West, where anonymity was the order of the day.

Of the 292,441 names drawn in the first draft, only 9,881 were held to personal service; 26,002 furnished substitutes, while 52,288 paid commutation fees of $300 apiece. Nearly 40,000 did not report after being drafted, while over 164,000 were exempted because of physical defects. Knowledge of this blot on the Union record spread through the South, and as a result Confederate songs constantly referred to "Union hirelings," "hireling hosts," and the like. A phrase in *The Southron's Chaunt of Defiance* says:

> We may fall before the fire of your legions
> Paid with gold for murderous hire-bought allegiance.

A stanza of the Southern song *We Know That We Were Rebels,* written after the defeat, takes these draft dodgers to task:

> O, shame upon the coward band who, in the conflict dire,
> Went not to battle for their cause 'mid the ranks of steel and fire,
> Yet now, since all the fighting's done, are hourly heard to cry:
> "Down with the traitors! Hang them all! Each rebel dog shall die!"

The draft dodger was branded as a slacker, and the hunt for him was continuous. *How Are You, Conscript?* (words and music by Frank Wilder) deals with one such:

> How are you, Conscript, how are you today?
> The Provost Marshal's got you in a very tight place, they say,
> But oh, you should not mind it nor breathe another sigh,
> For you're only going to Dixie to fight and "mind your eye."
>
> CHORUS:
> How are you, Conscript, how are you today?
> The Provost Marshal's got you in a very tight place, they say.
>
> How are you, Conscript, how are you, my boy?
> I 'spose you take it rather hard since you're your mother's joy.
> But Uncle Sam says you're the one to go in hip and thigh,
> For you're only going to Dixie to fight and "mind your eye."
>
> How are you, Conscript, how are you, I say?
> Have you got three hundred greenbacks to pony up and pay?

If not you are a goner; and don't you fret and cry,
For you're only going to Dixie to fight and "mind your eye."

How are you, Conscript, how are you today?
You'll give us all a lock of hair before you go away.
And when you do come home again you'll see it same as I,
For you're only going to Dixie to fight and "mind your eye."

But of the 797,807 men comprising the Union Army at its peak strength on the first of May, 1865, nearly all were substitutes or volunteers influenced by bounty or fear of draft calls. A drafted man received no bounty, whereas an enlisted man was given payments from the national government, his state government, and local agencies, while some localities even guaranteed to take financial care of the family of the volunteer during his absence. One recruiting poster stated, "Men of Earnest Purpose, Good Habits and Resolute Hearts! Now is the Day and Hour to Defend your Free Government! The Well-being of Families will be the Special Care of Generous Friends!" Bounties often amounted to a great deal of money. A parody on *Abraham's Daughter* read as follows:

I'm a raw recruit with a bran' new suit, nine hundred dollars bounty;
And I've come down from Darbytown to fight for Oxford County.

One recruiting poster enumerated the benefits of enlistment:

County bounty (cash down)	$300
State bounty	75
U. S. bounty for new recruits	302
	$677

After a period of service, an additional $100 was added. Fifteen dollars "hand money" was paid to "any party who brings a recruit." In 1863, the veteran who re-enlisted for the duration was given $400.

A racket which caused many difficulties in filling quotas in actual rather than paper terms was that of "bounty jumping," wherein a recruit, having received the agreed sum of money, never reported for duty. If apprehended, he was imprisoned. Such an unfortunate forms the subject of *The Bounty-Jumper's Lament* (words by J. B. Murphy, music by W. Arlington):

In my prison cell I stand, thinking of you, Mary Ann,
And the gay old times we've had in days before
    When my sock was lined with "tin"
    And I thought it was no sin
For to jump a bounty every week or more.

CHORUS:
Tramp, tramp, tramp, the guard is coming,
Even now I hear them at my door.
    So goodbye, my Mary Ann,
    You must do the best you can,
For I'll never jump a bounty any more.

Oh, the gay old days and nights that we passed in fond delights
When my pockets they were brimming full of cash!
    And with oysters, cake and wine,
    We had such a bully time!
But I'm satisfied in dreaming now of hash.

Oh, goodbye, Mary Ann, I am now an altered man,
And I'm going away from you I love so well.
    Tell the boys to "all look out"
    And mind what they're about,
Or the provost guard will get them sure as you're born.

By 1864, as a result of the substitute and bounty systems with the continuance of the draft, Federal regiments were a curious mixture of all types of males between the ages of eighteen and forty-five. The rich and poor, the farmer and the city dweller, the mechanic and the clerk, the criminal and the upright citizen—all rubbed elbows in the same battalions and brigades. War, as always, became the great social leveler. The patriotic rallying songs had long since been forgotten, and the life of the soldier was the lot of over one million men—willingly or unwillingly.

Part 2: THE GRAY PREPARES FOR THE STRUGGLE

An army had been rapidly developed by the Confederacy early in 1861 as the cotton states were seceding one by one, and by April over 35,000 troops, fully equipped, were in active training. During the spring, 387 of the 1,100 officers in the United States [Regular] Army had resigned to join the Confederate cause, and President Jefferson Davis, himself a graduate of West Point, had by July selected five trained and experienced soldiers, all West Pointers, as his key military leaders—General Samuel Cooper (adjutant general), Albert Sidney Johnston, Robert E. Lee, Joseph E. Johnston, and P. G. T. Beauregard.

In April of 1862, the Confederate government passed a General Conscription Act calling out, with certain exceptions, all able-bodied white men between the ages of eighteen and thirty-five for the term of three years, and in September, a second one extending the upper limit to forty-five. A manuscript song in the State Historical Society of California, as reported in the *California Folklore Quarterly,* pictures the conscript's plight:

> Oh, weep not, conscript, weep not,
>   Old Jeff has called for thee.
> A soldier Congress makes you,
>   A soldier you must be!
> Make up your mind to stand in line,
>   And quake not at the Yanks,
> To shoot your gun and call it fun,
>   And for life return your thanks.

Later, in 1864, the law was extended to those between seventeen and fifty, the term was for the duration of the war, an act which was described by General Grant as "robbing the cradle and the grave." Since the total white male population between the ages of eighteen and forty-five in the census of 1860 was 984,475, the Confederacy possessed a numerical disadvantage from the start. From 200,000 to 300,000 youths reached the age of eighteen during the war years, and practically every able-bodied Southern male fought in the army at one time or another.

These calls exempted one white man on each plantation with twenty Negroes, thus favoring the moneyed, slaveholding aristocracy. Purchase of substitutes for those conscripted was permitted, and by 1863, Bragg and seventeen other generals, in a joint letter to Davis, declared that 150,000 possible soldiers had employed substitutes, not more than one in a hundred of whom were actually in the ranks for duty. By November, 1863, the price of substitutes had reached $6,000, leading to the use of the damning phrase "It's a rich man's war and a poor man's fight." In December, the Confederate Congress abolished the right to purchase substitutes. Estimates of the number in the Confederate forces varied from 25,000 to 150,000.

I leave my home and thee, dear, with sor-row at my heart, It is my coun-try's call, dear, to aid her I de-part; And on the blood-red bat-tle plain we'll con-quer or we'll die; 'Tis for our hon-or and our name, we raise the bat-tle-cry. Then weep not, dear-est, weep not, If in the cause I fall; O, weep not, dear-est, weep not, It is my coun-try's call.

The Volunteer; or, It Is My Country's Call
(Dedicated to the New Orleans Cadets)

Another advantage of wealth was in connection with the length of service pledged by volunteers. Shortages of equipment caused the Confederacy later to outfit only those volunteers who would enlist for three-year terms. Twelve-month volunteers were accepted, but only on condition that they provided their own equipment.

The Confederacy had no martial volunteering song which could be compared with the Union's *We Are Coming, Father Abraham*. The emotion felt by Secessionist patriots was therefore gratified through the many rousing songs of loyalty and devotion to the South. Fiery young men organized themselves into companies under such awe-inspiring names (located by Bell Irwin Wiley) as the King Cotton Guards, Spartan Band, Invincibles, Irrepressibles, Southern Avengers, Tallapoosa Thrashers, Baker Fire Eaters, Butler's Revengers, Bartow Yankee Killers, Chickasaw Desperados, Dixie Heroes, Hornet Nest Riflemen, Raccoon Roughs, Barbour Yankee Hunters, Bedford Yankee-Catchers, Southern Rejectors of Old Abe, and Yankee Terrors. Chivalry was reflected in names such as Ladies' Guards, Pocahontas Rescuers, and Ladies' Dragoons.

Some of these units were more resplendently dressed than were the Union Zouave organizations. The Emerald Guards of Mobile departed for Virginia clad in dark green, a color adopted in honor of Ireland, from which most of its members had come. Captain Patterson's company of East Tennesseans dressed themselves in suits of yellow to conform with their name of Yellow Jackets. The Granville Rifles of North Carolina sported uniforms featuring black trousers and flannel shirts of flame red. Some of the Maryland companies who allied themselves with the Confederate cause were clothed in uniforms of blue and orange. The Louisiana Zouaves, however, were the most resplendently attired—trousers of scarlet cloth, cut almost like bloomers, belted at the waist with large blue sashes and bound at the ankles with gaiters of white; jackets heavily adorned with varicolored lace; shirts of blue, cut low to reveal tanned throats and hairy chests; and headgear of jauntily perched fezzes.

The South's most popular recruiting song was *The Volunteer; or, It Is My Country's Call,* from the pen of Harry Macarthy, composer of *The Bonnie Blue Flag:*

I leave my home and thee, dear, with sorrow at my heart,
It is my country's call, dear, to aid her I depart;
And on the blood-red battle plain, we'll conquer or we'll die;
'Tis for our honor and our name, we raise the battle-cry.

CHORUS:
Then weep not, dearest, weep not,
If in the cause I fall;
Oh, weep not, dearest, weep not,
It is my country's call.

And yet my heart is sore, love, to see thee weeping thus;
But mark me, there's no fear, love, for in Heaven is our trust;
And if the heavy drooping tear swells in my mournful eye,
It is that Northmen of our land should cause the battle-cry.

Our rights have been usurp'd, dear, by Northmen of the land,
Fanatics raised the cry, dear, politicians fired the brand;
The Southrons spurn the galling yolk, the tyrants' threats defy;
They find we've sons like sturdy oaks to raise the battle-cry.

I knew you'd let me go, pet, I saw it in that tear,
To join the gallant men, pet, who never yet knew fear;
With Beauregard and Davis, we'll gain our cause or die,
Win battles like Manassas, and raise the battle-cry.

However, this was not at all a stirring song designed to influence volunteering through its emotional appeal, for it could not be sung by marching
soldiers. It had no swinging rhythm, and it recalled to the lad at the front
the sad farewells he had taken. *The Young Volunteer* (words and music
by John H. Hewitt[10]) was no better:

Our flag is unfurled and our arms flash bright
    As the sun wakes up in the sky;
But ere I join the doubtful fight,
    Lovely maid, I would say goodbye.
I'm a young volunteer, and my heart is true
    To our flag that woos the wind;
Then three cheers for that flag and our country, too,
    And the girls we leave behind.

CHORUS:
Then adieu, then adieu, 'tis the last bugle's strain
    That is falling on the ear;
Should it be so decreed that we ne'er meet again,
    Oh, remember the Young Volunteer.

When over the desert, through burning rays,
    With a heavy heart I tread;
Or when I breast the cannon's blaze
    And bemoan my comrades dead,
Then, then will I think of home and you
    And our flag shall kiss the wind;

[10] John Hill Hewitt was a student at West Point with Beauregard, Lee, Polk,
and Jackson, but military life had little appeal for him. His numerous musical compositions gained for him the title "father of the American ballad." In addition to his
many war songs, he was noted for *The Minstrel's Return from the War, Rock Me
to Sleep, Mother,* and *Carry Me Back to the Sweet Sunny South.*

With huzzah for our cause and country too,
    And the girls we leave behind.

Typical of a mass of Confederate "going-away" songs is the *Volunteer Song*, published in the New Orleans *Picayune* on April 28, 1861, and sung to the regiments departing for Virginia:

Go, soldiers, arm you for the fight,
God shield the cause of Justice, Might;
May all return with victory crowned,
May every heart with joy abound,
May each deserve the laurel crown,
Nor one to meet his lady's frown.

Your cause is good, 'tis honor bright,
'Tis virtue, country, home and right;
Then should you die for love of these,
We'll waft your names upon the breeze;
The waves will sing your lullaby,
Your country mourn your latest sigh.

The fact that the South had to call upon practically all of her available men is reflected in the song *My Warrior Boy* (words from *The Metropolitan Record,* music by A. E. A. Muse), in which a fifteen-year-old lad, a "babe in arms," goes to war along with "veterans grim and stalwart men":

Thou hast gone forth, my darling one,
To battle with the brave,
To strike in freedom's sacred cause
Or win an early grave;
With vet'rans grim, and stalwart men,
Thy pathway lieth now,
Though fifteen summers scarce have shed
Their blossoms on thy brow.

My babe in years, my warrior boy!
Oh, if a mother's tears
Could call thee back to be my joy
And still these anxious fears,
I'd dash the traitor drops away
That would unnerve thy hand,

113

Now raised to strike in Freedom's cause
For thy dear native land.

One mother even furnished the necessary battle sword and rifle for her
boy, in *The Mother's Farewell,* to the tune of *Jeannette and Jeannot:*

You are going to leave me, darling,
    Your country's foes to fight.
And though I grieve, I murmur not,
    I know we're in the right.
Here's your father's sword and rifle,
    Emulate him in the fight;
Let no coward stain be on your name
    That always has shone bright.

The soprano-tenor duet was currently popular at parlor recitals and
public entertainments. A song of this type was *Soldier, I Stay to Pray for
Thee* (words by J. S. Thovington, music by J. W. Groschel), supposedly
based on a "touching" incident which occurred in Montgomery, Alabama,
at the beginning of the war. A soldier met a lady in the street, touched
his hat, and said, "Lady, I'm going to fight for you." "Sir," she instantly
replied, "I am going to pray for you":

Soldier: Lady, I go to fight for thee, Where gory banners wave,
    To fight for thee, and oh, perchance To find a soldier's
    grave.

Lady: Soldier, I stay to pray for thee, A harder task is mine;
    To which, and long in lonely grief, That victory may be
    thine.

Soldier: Lady, I go and fight for thee.

Lady: Soldier, I stay to pray for thee.

Both: And strength and faith combined, Still form the magic
    sword,
    Wherewith the Southrons victory find, The Southrons
    victory find.

Soldier: Fare thee well!

Lady: Fare thee well!

In view of the traditional chivalry of Southern men, it was not unusual that many of the farewell songs were of sweethearts.[11] The most popular, in which the girl is afraid that, with such a beautiful uniform, her Willie will win the hearts of the pretty girls and forget all about her, was *You Are Going to the Wars, Willie Boy* (words and music by John H. Hewitt):

You are going to the wars, Willie boy, Willie boy,
    You are going to the wars far away,
To protect our rights and law, Willie boy, Willie boy,
    And the banner in the sun's golden ray;
    With your uniform all new,
    And your shining buttons, too,
    You'll win the hearts of pretty girls,
    But none like me so true.
Oh, won't you think of me, Willie boy, Willie boy?
    Oh, won't you think of me when far away?
I'll often think of ye, Willie boy, Willie boy,
    And ever for your life and glory pray.

You'll be fighting for the right, Willie boy, Willie boy,
    You'll be fighting for the right and your home;
And you'll strike the blow with might, Willie boy, Willie boy,
    'Mid the thundering of cannon and of drum.
    With an arm as true as steel,
    You'll make the foeman feel
    The vengeance of a Southerner,
    Too proud to cringe or kneel;
Oh, should you fall in strife, Willie boy, Willie boy,
    Oh, should you fall in strife on the plain,
I'll pine away my life, Willie boy, Willie boy,
    And never, never, never smile again.

The Southern belle's desire to have a victorious veteran for a husband

[11] Other sweetheart parting songs of Confederate authorship were *I'm Leaving Thee in Sorrow, Annie* (words by Edward J. Gill, music by George Barker), *The Good-bye at the Door* (words by J. E. Carpenter, music by Stephen Glover), *I Will Meet Thee* (words and music by John H. Hewitt), and *The Soldier's Farewell* (words and music by Albert Lindahl).

may have spurred enlistments, and at least one girl definitely entered the matrimonial market with the declaration *I Would Like to Change My Name* (words and music by Theodore von La Hache):

I would like to change my name
And share another's home,
With a heart that's kind and true,
And one that would not roam;
For my schooling days are over,
The books I've thrown aside,
I've often been a bridesmaid,
'Tis time I was a bride;
I've often been a bridesmaid,
'Tis time I was a bride.

I would like to change my name
And settle down in life,
Here's a chance for some young man
That's seeking for a wife;
But he must be a soldier,
A vet'ran from the wars,
One who has fought for Southern rights
Beneath the Bars and Stars;
One who has fought for Southern rights
Beneath the Bars and Stars.

Many a maiden looked forward to happiness at the close of the war and sent her beloved away reassured by his promise to return to her. Sung at Richmond in 1863 by Sallie Partington, "the prima donna of the Confederacy," *My Southern Soldier Boy* (words by Capt. G. W. Alexander, to the tune of *The Boy with the Auburn Hair*) attained a degree of popularity, particularly in music halls where "The Virginia Cavalier" played and the audience could join in the series of "Yo, ho, ho's" of the chorus:

Bob Roebuck is my sweetheart's name,
    He's off to the wars and gone,
He's fighting for his Nannie dear,
    His sword is buckled on;

He's fighting for his own true love,
    His foes he does defy;
He is the darling of my heart,
    My Southern soldier boy.

CHORUS:

Yo! ho! Yo! ho! Yo! ho! ho! ho! ho! ho! ho!
He is my only joy,
He is the darling of my heart,
My Southern soldier boy.

The soldier anticipated life with his Southern flower after the war in *The Soldier's Farewell; or, The South Shall Yet Be Free* (words and music by John H. Hewitt, adapted from the French air, *Partant pour la Syrie*):

The bugle sounds upon the plain,
    Our men are gathering fast;
You would not have your friend remain
    And be among the last.
Cheer up, cheer up, my Southern flower,
    There's joy for you and me.
While right is strong and God has power,
    The South shall rise up free.
While right is strong and God has power,
    The South shall rise up free.

When by the campfire's fitful light
    Beneath the starlit sky,
I picture scenes of young delight,
    Your form shall hover nigh.
Your smile will cheer the lonely hour,
    Your eye my lodestar be,
For well I know while God has power
    The South shall rise up free!
For well I know while God has power
    The South shall rise up free!

The husband departed bravely in *Farewell, My Dearest Katy; or, The Volunteer's Farewell* (words by Dr. J. Mathews, music by Theodore von La Hache):

Our little children, Katie, take precious care of all,
I could not leave them, Katie, but at my country's call.

In future years, dear Katie, our children proud shall be
That their father fought for Freedom, Southern Rights and Liberty!

James Ryder Randall contributed his rallying song in September, 1861, calling it *There's Life in the Old Land Yet,* set to music by Edward Eaton:

By blue Patapsco's billowy dash
    The tyrant's war-shout comes,
Along with the cymbal's fitful clash,
    And the growl of his sullen drum.
We hear it! We heed it, with vengeful thrills,
    And we shall not forgive or forget;
There's faith in the streams, there's hope in the hills,
    There's life in the old land yet!
There's faith in the streams, there's hope in the hills,
    There's life in the old land yet!

Our women have hung their harps away,
    And they scowl on your brutal bands,
While the nimble poignard dares the day
    In their dear, defiant hands;
They will strip their tresses to string our bows
    E'er the Northern sun is set.
There's faith in their unrelenting woes,
    "There's life in the old land yet."
There's faith in their unrelenting woes,
    "There's life in the old land yet."

The Confederates were not, however, without their rallying songs to send the boys off in an excitable mood. *Close Up the Ranks* (addressed to soldier comrades in the field by Chaplain Cameron) said:

Are we to bend to slavish yoke?
    Close up the ranks, close up the ranks!
We'll bend when bends our Southern oak,
    Close up the ranks, close up the ranks!
On with the charge of serried steel!
    We all can die, we none can kneel,

118

By blue Pa - taps-co's bil-lowy dash The ty-rant's war shout comes, A-

long with the cymb-al's fit - ful clash, And the growl of his sul-len drum. We

hear it! We heed it, with venge-ful thrills, And we shall not for-give or for-

get; —— There's faith in the streams, there's hope in the hills, There's

life in the old land yet! —— There's faith in the streams, there's

hope in the hills, There's life in the old land yet!

There's Life in the Old Land Yet

To crouch beneath the Northern heel,
  Close up the ranks! Close up the ranks!

A Baltimorean of Southern sympathies, Earnest Halphin, composed the
words and music to *Where Is the Freeman Found:*

Come, brothers, come, come to the cannon's mouth!
There is your only home, men of the sunny South.

And *Dixie, the Land of King Cotton* (words by Capt. Hughes of Vicksburg, music by John H. Hewitt) was sung in the military operetta *The Vivandière*:

> Three cheers for our army so true,
> Three cheers for our President, too,
> May our banner triumphantly wave
> Over Dixie, the land of the brave!

Freedom's Muster Drum (words and music by John H. Hewitt) asserted:

> Then Freedom spoke in cheering strain
>   "The air, the earth, the sea are thine,
> Dash to the dust the galling chain
>   That binds a soul God made divine.
> Give to the breeze thy warlike cry,
>   And rive the helm of the hireling scum,
> Than live a slave, 'twere best to die
>   While rattling Freedom's muster drum."

The Soldier's Mission (words and music by A. W. Morse) is to

> Give thy arm the power
> To defend thy trust.

When the tide turned after Gettysburg and when the Union poured forth ever new and fresh manpower, the Confederates experienced a resurgence of patriotism, and a number of stirring songs were published. Three 1863 compositions were *Strike for the South!* (words by Carrie Bell Sinclair, music by James Pierpont):

> Strike for the South! for her weapons are bright
> And the heroes who wield them are strong;
> Let her name brightly glow on the record of fame
> And hers be the proudest in song.

The March of the Southern Men, set to an old Scottish air, and *Harp of the South, Awake!* (words by J. M. Kilgour, music by C. L. Peticolas), the chorus of which affirmed:

> Harp of the South, awake! and strike the strain once more
> Which nerved the heroes' hearts in glorious days of yore.

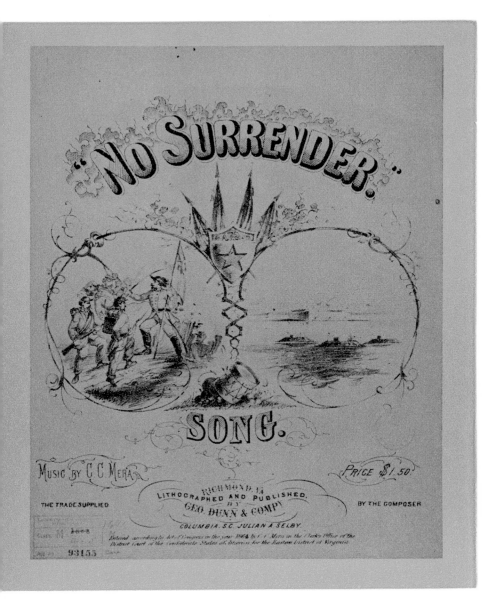

As the Civil War continued, the price of sheet music increased. Note that the Confederate imprints were copyrighted in the state of origin.

However, the song which, with the advantage of a martial tune, un-doubtedly fired the Southern heart more than any other was *The Southron's Chaunt of Defiance* (words by Catherine A. Warfield, music by A. E. Blackmar):

You can never win us back, never! never!
Though we perish on the track of your endeavor;
Though our corpses strew the earth
That smiled upon their birth,
And the blood pollutes each hearthstone forever!

We have risen to a man, stern and fearless;
Of your curses and your ban we are careless.
Every hand is on its knife,
Every gun is pruned for strife,
Every palm contains a life, high and peerless!

You have no such blood as ours for the shedding,
In the veins of cavaliers was its heading!
You have no such stately men
In your abolition den,
To march through foe and fen, nothing dreading!

The last two verses indicated that the Confederate Army, in comparison with the North's large numbers, was like David fighting against the giant Goliath but asserted the hope that, as long as God reigned above, the vic-tory would be given to the side of the right—the South.

The Southern states, though numerically inferior to the North, pos-sessed certain characteristics which made it impossible for their zeal and loyalty to be measured in terms of numbers of men. The South's aristocracy was military-minded as a result of the cavalier spirit which considered the profession of arms a noble attainment. Jefferson Davis, himself a soldier, had the best talent in the land from which to select his army officers, for he adopted the principle of transferring officers of the regular United States Army to equivalent rank and seniority in the new Confederate service and was therefore in a position to resist political pressure in organizing it.

The Southern volunteer was fighting for his home; he was imbued with the spirit of one seeking to repel an invader, and thus the struggle was personalized for every soldier. It is interesting to note in how many Confederate songs the Union soldiers are referred to as "invaders of our sacred soil."

Finally, the Southern lines of communication were centralized so that a comparatively small number of men was required to defend an extensive area of border land. With these advantages, the South successfully repelled the almost overwhelming forces of the Union for two years. Because of the superior military leadership of the Confederacy and its united determination to forestall hostile invasion, the advantage from 1861 to 1863 was *not* on the side with the heaviest battalions and greatest number of volunteers—the numerically superior North. Citizens and soldiers of such inspired patriotism did not require songs in order to stimulate service for the Confederacy.

The total number of soldiers under arms during the war has never been accurately determined. Because of the frequency of multiple enlistments in the Union Army—the same soldier might be recorded in duplicate under periods of three, six, nine, and twelve months, and one, three, and even five years—and the loss of many Confederate rolls and records, no authoritative figure has ever been compiled. However, it may be assumed that four out of nine men of military age in the North and nine out of ten in the South—nearly one-half of the 5,635,000 men in that classification in contemporary census estimates—participated during the four years of the struggle.

The most reliable estimate indicates that the number of Union Army enlistments, short- and long-term, was 2,900,000. This means that probably 1,500,000 different men served, when allowance is made for duplicate counts of those re-enlisting. This figure included 494,000 foreigners, 186,000 Negroes, and 86,000 Southern whites.

Although the official records of the adjutant general of the Confederate States, captured in the evacuation of Richmond, showed 618,000 total enlistments in the Confederate Army, a figure of about 1,000,000 would seem to be more exact. The rolls of several Southern states, including Alabama, were never found. Since the estimated white male population between the ages of eighteen and forty-five in the states at the beginning of the war was 984,475, the total figures indicate that practically every able-bodied man in the Confederacy who had reached eighteen and was under sixty years of age, the maximum age finally set in the draft, was a soldier.

Whether volunteers or draftees, these were the men who were to suffer, fight, and die for the cause with which they were willingly or unwillingly associated.

123

CHAPTER 4

The Soldier's Life in Camp and on the March

As SOON AS the novelty of military life had worn off, the recruit or draftee settled down to the routine of camp life, interrupted by maneuvers and participation in campaigns with long marches and occasional combat. While off duty he sang songs, played games, and passed the time in lighthearted abandon, broken only by spells of homesickness and loneliness.

Lacking a well-defined "cause," the majority of Union soldiers did not know definitely why they were in uniform. Some had joined the army in the first flush of patriotism, while others sought excitement and a change of scene with regular pay. No Northern male with sufficient funds to hire a substitute found it necessary to join the army. The draftees were generally unable to explain the reason for their transition from civilian to military life. Northern soldiers recognized vaguely that the nation's unity was threatened, but they were usually uninformed on the constitutional basis of the war. Indeed, the "patriotism" of the boy in blue had been stirred against the "rebels," and it seemed unnecessary to examine the question further, for he was satisfied with the current slogans—"Save the Union," "Put Down the Rebels," "Subdue the Traitors," and the like.

The Confederate soldier had more incentive to fight, for his homeland was being invaded. His was a dedication of well-defined purpose; the seceding states had taken a serious step, and their very survival was dependent upon success in battle. The appeal to his patriotism was enough reason for being in the army.

At first, war seemed glamorous, and most volunteers were tempted by the variety in the military life and the prospect of appearing heroic, as expressed in *A Soldier's Life Is the Life We Love:*

Away we march, to the bugle sounding,
Our hands are firm and our hearts are glad;
Our steps are light o'er the green turf bounding,
And happy is the life of a soldier lad.

But when from home and called to duty,
Our hopes are high and our flag's unfurled;
We bid adieu to smiles and beauty,
For a soldier's home is the wide, wide world.

We seek our foes 'mid cannon's rattle,
And when we're victors in the battle
O, then we sing to the stars above,
A soldier's life is the life we love.

Anticipation of the soldier's life was pleasing to at least one Union boy, in *Oh, I'd Be a Soger Boy* (words and music by T. H. Hinton):

Oh, I'd be a soger boy, I love to hear the rattlin' drum,
And I love to see the old flag fly and hear the burstin' bomb.

'Tis sport to see the rebels run when our hosts are marching on;
From each gleaming sword and gun flashes back the dazzling sun.

The appeal of the uniform was a universal one, indicating boldness and a promise of becoming a hero, according to *Oh, I Shall Wear a Uniform* (words and music by Father Reed):

Oh, I shall wear a uniform and march away to war,
    To bravely meet the enemy until the strife is o'er.
They say I shall be furnished arms, no legs do they provide
    Although they would of service prove if rank and file divide!

The spit and polish of the new recruits was generally short lived. Uniforms deteriorated on long marches, and exposure to rain and mud often made the wearer seem bedraggled and far from the impressive ideal.

Although the soldiers themselves may have felt great pride in the uniform, the Southerners appreciated their boys for their fine qualities rather than their handsome regalia, asserts *The Soldier's Suit of Gray* (words by Carrie Belle Sinclair, music by E. Clarke Ilsley) :

> I've seen some handsome uniforms deck'd off with buttons bright,
> And some that are so very gay they almost blind the sight;
> But of these handsome uniforms I will not sing today,
> My song is to each soldier lad who wears a suit of gray.
>
> CHORUS:
> Hurrah! hurrah! hurrah! hurrah! for Southern boys, we say,
> And God bless every soldier lad who wears a suit of gray.
>
> Brass buttons and gold lace, I know, are beautiful to view,
> And then, to tell the honest truth, I own I like them too;
> Yet should a thousand officers come crowding 'round today,
> I'd scorn them for a lad who wears a simple suit of gray!
>
> Tho' torn and faded be each coat, their buttons tarnished, too,
> I know beneath each soldier's dress a Southern heart beats true;
> We honor every gallant son who fights for us today,
> And Heaven protect the noble boys who wear the suit of gray!

"A. Growler" felt that the Confederate private soldier was being shelved by the ladies in favor of the "gold lacers," men of higher rank. He voiced his complaint in *The Officers of Dixie*, to the tune of *Dixie*:

> Let me whisper in your ear, sir,
> Something that the South should hear, sir,
> Of the war, of the war, of the war in Dixie;
> A growing curse, a burning shame, sir,
> In the chorus I will name, sir,
> Of the war, of the war, of the war in Dixie.
>
> CHORUS:
> The officers of Dixie, alone, alone!
> The honors share, the honors wear
> Throughout the land of Dixie!
> 'Tis so, 'tis so, throughout the land of Dixie!
>
> Swelling round with gold lace plenty,
> See the gay brass button gentry,
> Solomon in all his splendors
> Was scarce arrayed like these defenders.

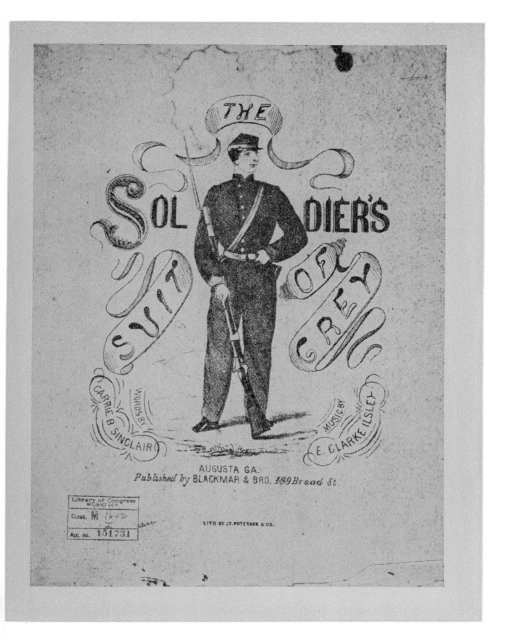

"Tho' torn and faded be each coat, their buttons tarnished, too,
I know beneath each soldier's dress a Southern heart beats true."

Should a grand soiree be given,
The braided lions take the even.
No! no! the privates are not slighted!
They can't expect to be invited!

In Dixie's land, in every way, sir,
Fuss and feathers win the day, sir,
For with all sexes, sizes and ages,
How the gold lace fever rages!

But in camp all past glory, antecedents, and former social position meant nothing. Here the soldier rubbed elbows with men from all walks of life. Camp life followed a set pattern, regulated at a relatively fast pace, as explained in *I'm Down on Double Quick* (words and music by Lindon L. Parr):

Since I've become a soldier, things have gone so very queer,
Some say that I'm a one-year, some a three-year volunteer.
With plenty of likes and dislikes, to all I have to stick;
It's nothing but salt pork, hardtack and plenty of double quick!

CHORUS:
Oh, I'm miserable, I'm miserable, to all I have to stick.
The old salt horse is passable but I'm down on the double quick!

Every morn at five precisely the Reveille will sound
And then there's such a scampering time, you have to fly around.
Before you get your breakfast, it's enough to make you sick,
To give the men an appetite, they give them double quick!

Friends, don't think that I am weary of the soldier's life I lead
For, oh, I deem it happiness for the Union cause to bleed.
Young men, if you will help us the rebs down South to lick
To old Harry we'll send traitors at a headlong double quick!

The bugler gained a reputation, through no fault of his own, for being a continual joy killer. He regulated the soldiers' lives in camp and managed to rob them of their few pleasures, often seeming to take a personal delight in doing so. From morn till eve, he continued to disturb every peaceful moment. Irving Berlin's *Oh, How I Hate to Get Up in the Morning* had its counterpart fifty-five years before World War I in *That Bugler; or, The Upidee Song* (words by D. G. Knight, music by A. E. Blackmar), a Confederate song which is best known as the modern setting to Long-fellow's poem, *Excelsior:*

> The shades of night were falling fast, Tra! la! la! Tra! la! la!
> The bugler blew his well-known blast, Tra! la! la! Tra! la! la!
> No matter, be there rain or snow,
> That bugler still is bound to blow.
>
> CHORUS:
> Upideei, dee-i-da, Upidee, Upida,
> Upideei, dee-i-da, Upidee-i-da.
>
> [*All successive verses have alternate lines of* Tra! la! la!]
>
> He saw, as in their bunks they lay,
> How soldiers spent the dawning day.
> There's too much comfort there, said he,
> And so I'll blow the "Reveille."
>
> In nice log huts he saw the light
> Of cabin fires, warm and bright,
> The sight afforded him no heat,
> And so he sounded the "Retreat."
>
> Upon the fire he spied a pot,
> Choicest viands smoking hot,
> Says he, "You shan't enjoy the stew,"
> So "Boots and Saddles" loudly blew.
>
> They scarce their half-cooked meal begin,
> Ere orderly cries out, "Fall in!"
> Then off they march through mud and rain,
> P'raps only to march back again.
>
> But soldiers, you are made to fight,
> To starve all day and march all night,
> Perchance if you get bread and meat
> That bugler will not let you eat.
>
> Oh, hasten then, that glorious day
> When buglers shall no longer play;
> When we, through Peace, shall be set free
> From "Tattoo," "Taps," and "Reveille."

Sickness inevitably became a part of camp life routine. According to

George W. Adams, the average soldier in the Union Army fell sick more than twice each year. Diarrhea and dysentery (with an average of 711 cases per 1,000 soldiers annually), malaria (with an average of 522 per 1,000 annually), and typhoid fever were common, particularly in summer; and pneumonia took its toll in winter. The high incidence of dysentery was caused by the almost constant lack of fresh vegetables and dietary balance, as well as the common practice of eating mostly fried foods.

During the course of the day, the bugler blew the doctor's call, at which time all those with ailments, real or imaginary, were summoned to report for treatment. The professional "gold-bricker" would, of course, report every day and feign a variety of ills in an effort to be relieved from duty. The favorite and universal prescription for headache, toothache, coughs, lameness, rheumatism, fever, ague—for almost any ailment—was quinine; hence, the call was also known as the quinine call. In the absence of buglers, many of the calls, particularly in large units, were sounded by the young drummers and fifers.

One of the amazing features of this war was the large number of young boys who were accepted into the ranks, in spite of the eighteen-year-old legal age limit for volunteers. Indeed, eighteen-year-olds formed the largest single age class in the Union Army. Of its total strength throughout the war, 844,891 soldiers were seventeen years old or younger, and of these, 104,987 were less than fifteen years old. Three hundred soldier boys were under thirteen years of age, and twenty-five were ten or under. Most of these youngsters were used as drummers and fifers.

In the early rush to the colors, adolescent and juvenile patriots, both Union and Confederate, obtained the required consent of their parents. Many lads joined the regiments of which their fathers or male relatives were members; this association often continued until one or the other was wounded or killed. Boys who were tall or large for their years blithely lied to recruiting officers about their ages and were gladly accepted in order to meet quotas.

Boys of sixteen or younger could enlist as musicians. Every company in the Union Army was entitled to two field musicians, or twenty to the average wartime regiment. There were 1,981 Union regiments—infantry, cavalry, and artillery—organized during the war, and, in addition, separate companies sufficient in number to constitute almost seventy more. Thus the North had 2,050 regiments, in all, accounting for over 40,000 boy musicians. Regimental bands were discontinued in favor of drummers and fifers on July 27, 1862.

A full regimental drum corps included a dozen boys. A boy could not pass muster unless he could do the "double and single drag" with variations, execute the "long roll," and imitate the rattle of musketry. When the corps, with caps set saucily at a sharp angle and the brass buttons on their red-trimmed jackets polished to blazing brightness, led a regiment in review, men in the ranks "stepped off" as though they were bound for a fair or a pleasure excursion.

The drum, together with the bugle, was called the tongue of the camp, for it regulated the pattern of camp life. Drummers became proficient, practicing from early morning until bedtime. They were the early risers, also, for at daybreak the fifers trilled, and the drummers rolled the regulation music of reveille—3 Camps, Dawn of Day, Slow and Quick Scotch, Austrian and Hessian. The drummer had to beat loud enough to awaken even the heaviest sleeper for roll call. Next came the daily sick call, which, because of its rhythm, seemed to say, "Come and get your quinine." Camp drummers were active participants in the guard-mounting exercises which were scheduled for about nine o'clock in the morning. The musicians usually practiced from one to two hours in the forenoon, with another session in the afternoon, unless there was a battalion drill, when they took part in troop maneuvers. Their next duty was at twilight dress parade, the most pleasing and spectacular event of the day. At nine o'clock they assembled again and beat the tattoo for evening roll call; fifteen minutes later taps were sounded, and the day's duties were ended.

The soldiers took a fatherly interest in the boys, who participated in all the long and forced marches. The lads were indispensable in sounding various calls in the fury of battle, and their deaths were celebrated in many plaintive songs (see Chapter V).

In addition to drummers and fifers, each regiment also had two or more "markers" who, with the adjutant and sergeant major, established the alignment in battalion drill or parade. They were usually lads who carried a light staff and fluttering banner instead of a rifle.

As in all wars, gambling was a popular pastime. Card playing—poker, twenty-one, euchre, and keno—and dice games helped soldiers pass many an hour. In 1862, gambling was so prevalent in the Confederate Army that General Lee issued an order prohibiting it. In intervals between games like cribbage and checkers, the soldier often made small trinkets out of his battle souvenirs.

Perhaps the favorite off-duty recreation, however, was singing. In camp and on the march, the soldier could while away the time in singing nonsense and sentimental tunes. On lonely picket assignments, he hummed or whistled to himself. Around the campfire, informal group singing was most popular. This phase of the soldier's life forms the subject of *Our Boys in Camp* (words by W. Dexter Smith, Jr., music by R. J. Lessur):

> Come where the tents are on the highland,
>   Come where the campfires are bright.
> Hear now the voices of our boys;
>   Hear, hear what they sing in camp tonight.
> Some are thinking of home and of mother,
>   Some of loved ones who dwell far away,
> For the fond heart, though distant and weary,
>   To the dear ones at home it will stray.

In afterwar years, this memory would be brightest in retrospect, says *The Songs We Sang upon the Old Camp Ground* (words and music by H. L. Frisbie, 1866):

> Oh, sing for me tonight those merry songs we sang
> When bright and warm the cheerful campfire blazed.
> At twilight's closing hour, with comrades gathered 'round
> We gaily sang those oft-repeated lays.
> How quickly beats my heart when comes the echoed strain,
> I listen then to catch the faintest sound.
> I never can forget those old familiar tones,
> Those songs we sang upon the old camp ground.

The soldier had a penchant for romantic ballads then popular with civilians, and they brought back these tunes upon returning from furloughs. The martial war songs were actually of little interest to the warriors except as marching songs. In camp, their thoughts turned always to home, family, and loved ones. The first lines of the songs indicate their prevailing moods.

Home Sweet Home, composed in 1823, was undoubtedly the most cherished air of both the blue and the gray. Ballads celebrating the love and beauty of many a girl were popular. *Annie Laurie* was liked by both sides, and records, diaries, and reminiscences indicate that *Sweet Alice Ben Bolt, The Hazel Dell* (1853: "In the hazel dell, my Nelly's sleeping"), by George F. Root, and *Kathleen Mavourneen* (1837) led in favor with Union soldiers. Confederates preferred *Juanita* (Spanish air which had become popular during the Mexican War: "Soft o'er the fountain"); *Annie of the Vale* (1852: "The young stars are glowing"), by J. R. Thomas; *Lilly Dale* (1852: "'Twas on a calm, still night"), by H. S. Thompson; *Sweet Evelina* (1863: "'Way down in the meadow where the lily first blows"); and *Bell Brandon* (1854: "We met 'neath the old arbor tree"), by Francis Woolcott. These melodies were widely sung in camp and on the march.

Lorena was probably the most popular sentimental ballad among Confederates, competing with *The Girl I Left Behind Me,* written before the war. *Listen to the Mocking Bird* knew no sectional barriers. A number of songs composed during the war years were enjoyed by soldiers of both camps. One of these songs, *Weeping, Sad and Lonely; or, When This Cruel War Is Over,* was so destructive to the morale of troops that it was banned. Two other Northern songs, *Just Before the Battle, Mother* and *The Vacant Chair,* were equally popular with Unionists and Confederates; the fighting man, whether his uniform was blue or gray, was a sentimentalist. Because picket duty was common to all troops, *All Quiet Along the Potomac* became a favorite song. Gospel hymns were often sung, many hymn books having been distributed by church organizations.

The songs most uniformly popular with the soldiers, however, were the so-called "nonsense rhymes." These songs of mirth and frivolity were naturally popular, for the line of a ditty of the 1860's said: "Why, soldiers, why, should we be melancholy boys, whose business 'tis to die?" The Union forces' most-sung camp song was *Co-Ca-Che-Lunk; or, The Camp War Song,* a college song first published in 1855, which had the attraction of a completely meaningless chorus:

Version One

Raise the banner, raise it high, boys!
Let it float against the sky;
"God be with us!" this our cry, boys,
Under it we'll do or die.

CHORUS:
Co-ca-che-lunk-che-lunk-che-lay-ly,
Co-ca-che-lunk-che-lunk-che-lay,
Co-ca-che-lunk-che-lunk-che-lay-ly,
Rig-a-ge-dig, and away we go!

Rebel miscreants, stand from under;
Ye who bear the traitor's name!
Every star's a bolt of thunder—
Every stripe a living flame!

Version Two

Since our muskets we have shouldered
In the cause we love the best,
Let us sing with hearty voices
As today we here do rest.

CHORUS:
Co-ca-che-lunk-che-lunk-che-lay-ly,
Co-ca-che-lunk-che-lunk-che-lay,
Co-ca-che-lunk-che-lunk-che-lay-ly,
Hi! O, Chick-a-che-lunk-che-lay.

We will fight for Freedom's honor,
Guard it from the traitor's hand,
And we'll raise its spangled banner
Over all our native land.

The Southern counterpart was *Gay and Happy* (music by Louis Winters); first sung by Texas regiments, this song attained immense popularity. It was equally popular among civilians—using the pronoun "I" as if a young girl were speaking—and many different local versions were sung.

We're the boys so gay and happy,
    Wheresoe'er we chance to be,
If at home, or on camp duty,
    'Tis the same, we're always free.

CHORUS:
Then let the Yanks say what they will,
We'll be gay and happy still;
Gay and happy, gay and happy,
We'll be gay and happy still.

We've left our homes and those we cherish
    In our own dear Texas land,
We would rather fight and perish
    Side by side and hand in hand.

We're the boys so gay and hap-py, Where-so-e'er we chance to be, If at home, or on camp du-ty, 'Tis the same, we're al-ways free. **Chorus** Then let the Yanks say what they will, We'll be gay and hap-py still; Gay and hap-py, gay and hap-py, We'll be gay and hap-py still.

Gay and Happy

Old Virginia needs assistance,
  Northern hosts invade her soil;
We'll present a firm resistance,
  Courting danger, fire and toil.

Then let drums and muskets rattle,
  Fearless as the name we bore,
We'll not leave the field of battle
  While a Yank is on our shore.

Root Hog or Die, which survives today as an American cowboy ballad with scores of verses in many versions, was a completely nonsensical popular minstrel song taken over by the Confederates. The words have been attributed to Tony Pastor, later the most famous music hall impresario in New York. The title urged the Southerner to work and fight for his life and "living." Abe Lincoln was satirized in its verses, to the great delight of Confederate soldiers, to whom he was always—deservedly, from their point of view—a bitter enemy.

> Old Abe Lincoln keeps kicking up a fuss,
> I think he'd better stop it, for he'll only make it wuss;
> We'll have our independence, I'll tell you the reason why,
> Jeff Davis will make them sing "Root hog or die."
>
> When Lincoln went to reinforce Sumter for the fight,
> He told his men to pass through the harbor in the night;
> He said to them: "Be careful, I'll tell you the reason why,
> The Southern boys are mighty bad on 'Root hog or die'."

Another Southern nonsense song was *Goober Peas,* of which A. E. Blackmar was author-composer, though copies always indicated that the tune was by "P. Nutt" and the words by "A. Pender." A goober pea is the common peanut grown throughout the South, particularly in Georgia, and because of this fact, Georgians were sometimes called "goober-grabbers." The chorus lent itself admirably to rousing group singing:

> Sitting by the roadside on a summer day,
> Chatting with my mess-mates, passing time away,
> Lying in the shadow underneath the trees,
> Goodness, how delicious, eating goober peas!
>
> CHORUS:
> Peas! Peas! Peas! Peas! eating goober peas!
> Goodness, how delicious, eating goober peas!
>
> When a horseman passes, the soldiers have a rule
> To cry out at their loudest, "Mister, here's your mule;"
> But another pleasure enchantinger than these
> Is wearing out your grinders eating goober peas!
>
> Just before the battle the Gen'ral hears a row,
> He says, "The Yanks are coming, I hear their rifles now."
> He turns around in wonder, and what d'you think he sees?
> The Georgia militia, eating goober peas!
>
> I think my song has lasted almost long enough,
> The subject's interesting, but rhymes are mighty rough;
> I wish the war was over, when free from rags and fleas,
> We'd kiss our wives and sweethearts and gobble goober peas!

Sit - ting by the road - side   on a sum - mer   day

Chat - ting with my mess - mates, pass - ing time a - way,

Ly - ing in the sha - dow   un - der - neath the   trees,

Good - ness, how de - li - cious,   eat - ing goo - ber   peas!

Chorus

Peas! Peas! Peas! Peas! eat - ing goo - ber   peas!

Good - ness, how de - li - cious, eat - ing goo - ber   peas!

Goober Peas

Even while contemplating the dangers of battle, the soldier could not always remain serious. There were men who were "invincible in peace and invisible in war," who would prefer to be absent or otherwise occupied when the firing commenced; they were perpetuated by Confederate soldiers in *Do They Miss Me in the Trench?,* to the tune of *Do They Miss Me at Home?,* an 1852 composition:

> Do they miss me in the trench, do they miss me?
> When the shells fly so quickly around?
> Do they know that I've run down the hillside
> To look for my hole in the ground?

But the shells exploded so near me,
It seemed best for me to run;
And though some laughed as I crawfished,
I could not discover the fun.

I often get up in the trenches,
When some Yankee is near out of sight,
And fire a round or two at him,
To make the boys think that I'll fight.
But when the Yanks commence shelling,
I run to my home down the hill.
I swear my legs never will stay there,
Though all may stay there who will.

I'll save myself through the dread struggle,
And when the great battle is o'er,
I'll claim my full rations of laurels
As always I've done heretofore.
I'll say that I've fought them as bravely
As the best of my comrades who fell,
And swear most roundly to all others
That I never had fears of a shell.

Desertion became common as the war progressed; the Confederate percentage of men absent without leave (A.W.O.L.) rose from 21 in December, 1861, to 56 in April, 1865. Lee's surrender of 28,000 men at Appomattox represented the "present" remnants of over 75,000 troops on his rolls. The Union percentage of desertion was always smaller because the forces were larger; from 10 in December, 1861, the percentage of absence rose steadily to 30 in April, 1865. The polite name for a deserter was "straggler."

Practical jokers were found in every camp. "Here's your mule" was a popular though meaningless expression during the 1860's, much like "Where's Elmer?" in World War I. One version of its origin was given in a Confederate diary late in 1861, as reported by Wiley:

The first I heard of it was this—Some man in the neighborhood had lost an old gray mule and was enquiring for it among the regiments. Co. B had straw in their tents to sleep on. Among them, Tom Nance, his hair was very thick on his head and his ears seemed all the larger for it. . . . Under the general excitement of the day, he laid down in his tent to sleep. Some lively fellows roving about . . . happened to look in Tom's tent and being struck with his appearance called out for the mule man—"Here's your mule." Others came to see and repeated the saying . . . and fun and yelling being the order of the day, the words soon became reechoed all over the camp and those adjoining and became a by-word everywhere . . ."

A popular comic Confederate song, *Here's Your Mule* (words and music by C. D. Benson), placed the blame on a farmer:

A farmer came to camp one day With milk and eggs to sell,
Upon a mule who oft would stray To where no one could tell;
The farmer, tired of his tramp, For hours was made a fool
By everyone he met in camp With, "Mister, here's your mule."

CHORUS:
Come on, come on, come on, old man
And don't be made a fool
By everyone you meet in camp,
With, "Mister, here's your mule."

His eggs and chickens all were gone Before the break of day;
The mule was heard of all along, That's what the soldiers say.
And still he hunted all day long, Alas, a witless fool,
Whil'st every man would sing the song Of "Mister, here's your mule."

The soldiers run in laughing mood, On mischief were intent,
They lifted muley on their back Around from tent to tent,
Through this hole and that they pushed His head, and made a rule
To shout with humerous voices all, "I say, mister, where's your mule?"

Alas! one day the mule was missed, Ah! who could tell his fate?
The farmer, like a man bereft, Searched early and searched late;
And as he passed from camp to camp With stricken face, the fool
Cried out to everyone he met, "Oh, mister, where's my mule?"

The mule was widely used as a beast of burden and for wagon trains; in mud he was agile and could traverse terrain impossible for horses. The best horses were used only by crack cavalry units, and foot soldiers found great delight in taunting the proud equestrians with this slang phrase: "Here's your mule!"

On the eve of battle and whenever the release from excitement of actual combat and the preceding activity permitted rest and recreation, particularly during the long waits at winter encampments, soldiers' thoughts turned fondly to the homefolk—wives, parents, children, sisters, brothers—and the men hoped earnestly to be spared to them through the approaching conflict and uncertain days ahead. In fact, a characteristic of the soldiers' sentimental songs was that sweethearts were outnumbered by mothers and sisters as subjects. This is explained partly by the extreme youth of many soldiers, who had not yet reached the courting stage; sisters rather than sweethearts held a place in their thoughts. The songs of sentiment, of farewell, and of battle fears were more numerous than the purely romantic soldier ballads, although they were rarely composed by soldiers.

An example of the "soldier thinking of family" type is *Can the Soldier Forget?* (words by Charles Boynton, music by George F. Root) :

> Yes, belov'd ones at home, we remember,
>   Ah, how can the soldier forget?
> All the vows that were said when we parted
>   Are sacred and dear to him yet.
> When the night throws its mantle around us,
>   We dream 'neath the heaven's starry dome
> Of the dear ones whose sweet spell has bound us
>   And whose voices shall welcome us home.
>
> CHORUS:
> Yes, belov'd ones at home, we remember,
> Ah, how can the soldier forget?
> All the vows that were said when we parted
> Are sacred and dear to us yet.

In *Dreaming of Home* (words by Louis Chapman, music by Charles Ashman), the soldier sees his mother and sister:

> Mother and sister, I am dreaming, dreaming of happy bygone days,
> Which with the joys of home were teeming o'er which my memory
>   ever strays.
> Tho' weary miles may us divide and distance keep us far apart,
> In thought I still am by thy side, for distance ne'er affects the heart.

Another soldier feels close to his family in *Tell Me, Little Twinkling Star* (words and music by G. W. H. Griffin) :

All is dark and gloomy 'round, soldiers sleeping on the ground.
All are dreaming of the past, of the joys too bright to last.
As I gaze with trembling eye on thy home far in the sky
One sweet thought will come to me; other eyes are fixed on thee.
Midnight star, oh, tell them then, I will see them once again,
When the battle strife is o'er I will meet them all once more.

Thinking of his mother, one Union soldier declares, *I Know My Mother Weeps for Me* (words and music by Charles F. Thompson):

When all the world is hushed in sleep,
O, soon may we the hour see
When mother need no longer weep.

The quantity of "lonely soldier" songs indicates the extent to which these sentiments existed in the camps.[12]

Almost every soldier, at one time or another, particularly before or after battle or when near enemy territory, "stood picket." To many, picket duty was welcome, since a soldier could be away from the noise of camp in the company of a small group of comrades—or alone. The "picket" was called the army's antenna, warning of the approach of enemy scouts. These were times for fellowship around the campfire, almost like a group picnic. Picket duty sometimes brought a different type of contact with the enemy. The feeling between individual soldiers on opposite sides was friendly, in spite of the fact that collectively they were bitter enemies.

Fraternization always existed to such an extent that officers were frequently disturbed by it. According to Wiley, because the men in both forces for the most part spoke the same language and many had mutual

---

[12] *The Soldier's Dream of Home* was the title of at least two Union songs (words by Charles Slatter, music by Felix Shelling; words by Mrs. E. O. Perrin, music by C. Hatch Smith). Other songs of this type were *The Soldier's Home* (words from Dadmun's Melodeon, music by S. A. Munson), *The Soldier's Vision* (words and music by C. Everest), in which he pictures scenes of his boyhood home, *The Volunteer's Dream of Home* (words and music by T. H. Howe), and *The Old House Far Away; or, The Dream of the Soldier* (words and music by H. T. Merrill). A soldier thinks of his family in *My Wife and Child* (written by a soldier poet, music by James W. Porter) and of his loved one in *I Am Lonely Tonight* (words and music by George W. H. Griffin), *Whisper Goodnight, Love* (words and music by Harrison Millard), and *We Parted with a Cheerful Smile* (words by William H. Morris, music by Matthias Keller). Two Confederate songs concerning this subject were *I Cannot Forget Thee* (words and music by Albin Visher) and *I Will Not Quite Forget* (words by Carrie, music by Henry Schoeller).

acquaintances or relatives on the opposing side, individual Northerners and Southerners tended to draw together. This, coupled with curiosity, war weariness, failure to comprehend clearly the issues of the conflict, and the desire to trade, made it increasingly difficult to maintain a line of demarcation between the two camps. Joint gambling, swimming, trading and "swapping," raillery, and shouting back and forth existed wherever and whenever pickets were stationed under settled conditions and encampments were located near each other.

The subject was a favorite among song writers. In *The Two Pickets* (words and music by Ossian E. Dodge), there is friendly bantering and rivalry between a Southerner and a Yankee:

SOUTH: Hello, you Yankee renegade,
　　　　You mudsill of a cricket,
　　　Take off your hat and make a bow
　　　　To a Confederate picket.

YANKEE: So you're one of the Southern bloods
　　　　That's talking 'bout secession!
　　　You look just like the fag end
　　　　Of a funeral procession!

SOUTH: Well, though for you I must confess
　　　　I have a hearty loathing,
　　　I wish we had more of your guns
　　　　And more of Yankee clothing.

YANKEE: Won't you please state to me
　　　　How's your sugar in your tea?
　　　Don't you find it rather
　　　　Troublesome and sandy?

SOUTH: Well, after all, you must confess
　　　　Although we're short of rations,
　　　We have our servants at our call,
　　　　Which gives us pride and station.

YANKEE: Well, yes, ye all for vittles wait
　　　　And so ye've lots of waiters,
　　　But why should ye be proud of that
　　　　For where's your bread and 'taters?

142

An afterwar song, *Along the Picket Line; or, "Halloo, Johnny, Halloo, Yank"* (words and music by L. L. Ross), depicts the friendliness of the pickets:

"Halloo, Johnny; halloo, Yank, Will you stop your firing now?
Come and take a drink;" Then down they'd go and meet half way
And this is what they'd do, they say. They'd trade jack knives and
     papers, too,
These Johnnies gray and Yankees blue.

The Johnnies gray tobacco grew, little had the Yankees blue,
But coffee plenty had, they say; none at all had Johnnies gray.

The memoirs of Civil War soldiers frequently contain stories of visits by opposing forces and entertainments to which the enemy were invited. "Swapping" was a particularly brisk activity in such meetings, for enemy souvenirs were prized and could not otherwise be obtained except from corpses on the battlefield after an engagement. Since Northerners often possessed items purchased from the ever present sutlers and since Union rations were apt to include "luxury" items, the Confederates were always ready to bargain for them. Northerners would occasionally transfer letters for delivery to relatives in the South and Southerners entrusted to Union soldiers letters destined for the North. Secret meetings between blood relations and ante bellum friends were often arranged through pickets. Newspapers were much in demand and would be exchanged once they were read. The information (or misinformation) they contained formed subjects for many lively discussions.

During the Rappahannock campaign in 1863, pickets were near one another across the narrow stream, and on one occasion a Yankee band came down to the river's edge and played *Dixie*. The Confederates across the stream cheered lustily and responded with *Yankee Doodle*. The Northerners applauded and played *Home Sweet Home,* in which the voices of both sides joined. This incident was described in a popular contemporary poem, *Music in Camp,* by John R. Thompson. The first exchange of many ballads could undoubtedly be traced to these meetings of "enemy" soldiers. The human element often rose above political, military, and regional considerations.

But all was not lightheartedness on picket duty. In *The Happy Picket Boy* (words and music by Richard Zellner), the youth has a premonition that he will be killed. In *Bill and I* (words and music by Frank Ward-law), two Union pickets kill a young rebel and break into tears on the discovery that he had been a friend on previous picket assignments. In *The Picket* (words by Una, music by W. C. Peters), the lad is found frozen in the snow.

The lone picket, having a monotonous job and time for private thoughts, almost automatically turned his mind to home and mother, to the comfort of the fireside, and to the prayers of the loved ones. He could easily picture the scenes in his home, made more vivid by his isolation. *On Picket Duty* (words by R. Torrey, Jr., music by Carl Lazare) depicts such a situation:

> Up and down on my lone beat I'm marching
> In silence and darkness and gloom.
> But here for the foeman I'm watching
> My heart wanders back to my home.
> I am thinking of loved ones now sleeping
> In peace, at my home by the sea,
> I am thinking of eyes that are weeping
> And hearts that are praying for me.

The soldier in *On Guard* (words by Henry M. Hunt, music by R. S. Frary) is typical:

> So guarding thus my lonely beat,
> By shadowy wood and haunted lea,
> That vision seems my view to greet
> Of her at home who prays for me.

The thoughts of a Confederate soldier on picket duty turn to his sweet-heart in another *On Guard* (words by Wallace Rowe, music of an old German melody):

> At dead of night when on my beat,
> And naught but darkness meets my view,
> Oh, then, my love, I think of thee,
> And ask if still thou'rt kind and true.
>
> Thou lov'st me yet, thou'rt still my own,
> My heart from every care is free;

It warmly throbs this wintry night,
    Because, my love, I think of thee.

The bell has struck, my watch is past,
    And now the welcome guard I see;
Good night, my love, sweet rest be thine,
    And in thy dreams still think on me.

The protection and security which knowledge of his mother's prayers give to him make the Union picket contented, happy in the knowledge that he is protecting her and the mothers of all soldiers, asserts *I'm Standing Guard* (words and music by Lieutenant S. Greig):

I'm Standing Guard

Ah, who is thinking of me now
    In cot or pallet warm,
While on my cold and aching brow
    Comes down the midnight storm?
Who wakes to mind a soldier's fate
    That nightly dangers dare?
What brother's heart is not ingrate,
    What sister breathes a prayer?

CHORUS:
Wake not, mother, sweetly sleep,
    Nor mind the soldier scarred.
God keeps the right, the wrong should weep,
    Sleep, mother, I'm standing guard.

I'm standing guard while 'round me sleep
    The braves that shield the land;
Then wakeful mother, do not weep,
    God holds them in his hand!
And proud of heart and calling they
    With honor's bright award,
Who arm for country's right and say
    Sleep mother, I'm standing guard.

To "wing" an enemy picket without cause would disgrace a soldier, hence the assignment was generally very safe. *All Quiet Along the Potomac* became one of the most popular of all war ballads, sung by soldiers and civilians alike in both North and South. The title was, for the first year of the war, the most popular stereotyped phrase telegraphed to Northern newspapers by their Washington correspondents—as familiar in its day as "all quiet on the western front" became to readers during World War I. Specifically, it referred to the stalemate after the Union defeat at Bull Run, while General McClellan was organizing and training the Army of the Potomac for the defense of Washington and the hoped-for march on Richmond. Since the march was long delayed, the correspondents could day after day wire their papers only "all quiet along the Potomac." This phrase occasioned the writing of *All Quiet Along the Potomac* (words by Lamar Fontaine, authorship often claimed by Ethel Lynn Beers, music by John H. Hewitt), published under this title as a Confederate song and under *The Picket Guard* (in several musical settings by H. Coyle, W. H.

Goodwin, J. Dayton, and David A. Warden) by the Union. The story goes that Fontaine and a good friend on picket duty stirred the campfire, revealing their position, and a Union picket fired upon them. As Fontaine determined that his friend had been killed, his eyes fell upon the headlines of a newspaper lying on the ground, "All Quiet Along the Potomac." That headline resulted in the composition of the poem, which was dedicated to "the unknown dead of the present Revolution."

All quiet along the Potomac, they say,
Except here and there a stray picket
Is shot on his beat as he walks to and fro
By a rifleman hid in a thicket.
'Tis nothing, a private or two now and then
Will not count in the news of the battle;
Not an officer lost, only one of the men
Moaning out all alone the death rattle.
"All quiet along the Potomac tonight."

"All quiet along the Potomac tonight,"
Where the soldiers lie peacefully dreaming,
And their tents in the rays of the clear autumn moon
And the rays of the campfires are gleaming.
A tremulous sight as the gentle night wind
Through the forest leaves slowly is creeping.
While the stars up above, with their glittering eyes
Keep guard o'er the army while sleeping.
"All quiet along the Potomac tonight!"

There's only the sound of the lone sentry's tread
As he tramps from the rock to the fountain,
And thinks of the two in the low trundle bed
Far away in the cot on the mountain.
His musket falls slack and his face dark and grim
Grows gentle with memories tender,
As he mutters a prayer for the children asleep
For their mother, may heaven defend her.
"All quiet along the Potomac tonight."

The moon seems to shine just as brightly as then,
That night when the love yet unspoken
Leaped up to his lips, when low murmured vows
Were pledged to be ever unbroken.

Then drawing his sleeve roughly over his eyes
He dashes off tears that are welling,
And gathers his gun closer to its place
As if to keep down the heart swelling.
"All quiet along the Potomac tonight."

Hark! Was it the night wind that rustles the leaves?
Was it the moonlight so wondrously flashing?
It looked like a rifle! "Ha, Mary, good-bye!"
And his life-blood is ebbing and plashing.
"All quiet along the Potomac tonight,"
No sound save the sound of the river;
While soft falls the dew on the face of the dead,
The picket's off duty forever.
"All quiet along the Potomac tonight!"

Napoleon's remark that "an army travels on its stomach" applied to both North and South. The quartermaster departments of each army attempted to supply adequate rations. These were of two types: regular rations for use in camps near storage depots, and field rations for use in time of battle or on long marches.

Beginning in mid–1862, the wide dispersal of troops in campaigns far from transportation arteries prevented efficient distribution, and delivery of uniform and standard rations became impossible. Soldiers passed through periods of near starvation when the breakdown of railroad systems stopped receipt of all rations. At such times it became necessary to forage for whatever could be taken from the countryside. On many a long march, soldiers far from their base of supplies literally lived off the land.

Both Confederate and Union supply centers were constant targets for raiding parties. The Southerners frequently ate particularly well following their victories, for the Northerners always possessed a greater variety and quantity of rations than they.

The food supply in the field was alternately abundant and scarce. Seldom were balanced rations available. Sometimes the men ate bread and no meat, then meat and no cereal of any kind; sometimes sugar and no coffee, then coffee and not a bit of sugar; for months nothing but wheat flour, then nothing but corn meal.

Most of the soldiers prepared their own meals on marches and in campaigns, and the inevitable frying pan was used over the campfire. The digestion of the men invariably suffered, and sick call always included many suffering from diarrhea, often in an acute form. One commander referred to the malady as "death from the frying pan." Indeed, the incidence of diarrhea was highest in the list of illnesses. Bean soup produced similar casualties, and one officer declared that "beans killed more than bullets."

The standard Union ration was pork, beans, hardtack, and coffee. Fresh vegetables other than potatoes were seldom eaten since they were rarely available. Many a meal consisted only of sow belly, coffee, and hardtack.

Hardtack was always the staple. It was a plain flour and water biscuit of a standard 3x2x½-inch size. The daily ration was nine biscuits per soldier. Most of these biscuits were too hard to be bitten into. Hardtack was heavier than ordinary biscuits, but absorbed a great deal of water, much more than an equal weight of flour, indicating that in its manufacture the chief object was to include the greatest possible nourishment concentrated in the smallest amount of space, like the modern army's dehydrated rations.

Ingenious soldiers devised various ways of disguising hardtack with fat, gravy, coffee, or soup. A particular delicacy was a piece of hardtack soaked in the drippings of bacon or salt pork. When a biscuit was dipped in coffee, a school of weevils or maggots more often than not floated on the surface. So common was the presence of these maggots that hardtack was nicknamed "worm castles."

When Union soldiers wanted a feast, they could prepare "slapjacks," pancakes of flour mixed with water and fried in fat. "Slosh" or "coosh," watered flour dropped into dirty bacon grease, enjoyed enforced popularity. Parched corn was an important item in the soldier's diet. Dried foods with nourishing content, such as desiccated compressed potatoes or vegetables and concentrated milk were first introduced during the Civil War. These were humorously termed "desecrated vegetables and consecrated milk."

The mainstay of Confederate rations was corn bread, beef, and field peas, which General Lee was said to have called "the Confederacy's best friend." Flour, salt pork, rice, sorghum molasses, coffee, and sugar were at first abundant, but later became almost nonexistent.

The monotony of army-issued rations was often broken by foraging (sometimes called "jayhawking" and "jerking") from the countryside. Virtually all memoirs of civilians in occupied territory recount the predatory forays of enemy soldiers, who were often tactless in their approach and unsparing in their assaults. Ingenuity was frequently rewarded by a single feast, which would raise the spirits of the men and prepare their stomachs once again for subsequent long periods of undistinguished and often undigestible fare.

The quartermaster wagon trains, hauled by mules, were ever in pursuit of the soldiers. Though sometimes tardy in arriving and delivering their supplies, they would always be welcomed, says *The Quartermaster's Band,* to the tune of *Tattoo:*

> Comrades will all remember when
>   The rations were all gone,
> What were our preparations then
>   To fight at morning's dawn?;
> So hungry every man was blue,
>   All deep in mis'ry stand,
> When hark! what sound now thrills us through?
>   The quartermaster's band.
>
> We oft had heard them sing before
>   And didn't like their voice;
> We now were glad they honked once more,
>   It made each man rejoice.
> Why did we then enjoy their din,
>   And cheer it?—here's the rub—
> Those long-eared mules were hauling in
>   The wagons with our grub.

Before Union forces penetrated south of Virginia and Tennessee, sutlers' vans (like a modern, though unofficial, army post exchange) offered luxuries to those who were able to pay, overcharging and profiteering outrageously. The sutler was often pictured as a skinflint, which he was, since he was often able to obtain items not otherwise available and to charge exorbitant prices.

A popular veterans' song celebrated the Union staple ration, *The Army Bean,* to the tune of the well-known hymn *Sweet By and By:*

> There's a spot that the soldiers all love,
>   The mess tent's the place that we mean,
> And the dish that we best like to see there
>   Is the old-fashioned white Army Bean.

CHORUS:
'Tis the bean that we mean,
    And we'll eat as we ne'er ate before;
The Army Bean, nice and clean,
    We'll stick to our beans evermore!

Now the bean in its primitive state
    Is a plant we have all often met;
And when cooked in the old army style,
    It has charms we can never forget.

The German is fond of sauerkraut,
    The potato is loved by the Mick,
But the soldier has long since found out
    That through life to our beans we should stick.

The Confederate soldier was constantly plagued with shortages in food, either through breakdown of the transportation system or limitation of available supplies. As usual, the higher-ups were blamed for this situation in *Short Rations* (words concocted by Ye Tragic, music gotten up by Ye Comic), which was dedicated to "the cornfed Army of Tennessee":

Our bugles had roused up the camp,
    The heavens looked dismal and dirty,
And the earth looked unpleasant and damp,
    As a beau on the wrong side of thirty.
We were taking these troubles with quiet
    When we heard from the mouths of some rash ones
That the army was all put on a diet,
    And the Board had diminished our rations!

Reduce our rations at all?
    It was difficult, yet it was done.
We had one meal a day, it was small;
    Are we now, oh! ye gods! to have none?
Oh! ye gentlemen issuing rations,
    Give at least half her own to the State,
Put a curb on your maddening passions,
    And commissaries commisserate[*sic*]!

Erewhile we had chickens and roosters
    For the fowls and pigs were ferocious;
We would send them a short Pater Nosters,

And the deed was not stamped as atrocious;
But since men have been shot for the same,
    We parch corn, it is healthier but tougher—
And chickens and pigs have got tame,
    But the horses and mules have to suffer.

The "cooties" of the Civil War were humorously called "pediculus vestimenti," and Confederates nicknamed them "graybacks," "rebels," "Zouaves," "tigers," and "Bragg's bodyguard." "No hardship, or enforced self denial of food, or rest or comfort," wrote one soldier, "is as hard to bear as the lice." These insects knew no restriction of time, place, or rank; they propagated in the soldier's clothing with amazing rapidity. It was impossible to escape them. It was said that even in camp a man could draw an entirely fresh suit from the quartermaster, go out in a field, strip, burn his old clothes, put on his new ones, come back to camp, and find as many lice as ever upon him the next morning! Washing was resorted to only as an extreme measure, but with cold water it was impossible to kill the vermin. Once every few months the soldier obtained temporary relief by boiling his clothing, using only the receptacles he possessed, often the same kettles used for cooking his coffee, soup, beans, and pork. Military terms were applied to the methods of extermination: killing lice was referred to as "fighting under the black flag"; throwing away an infested shirt was spoken of as "giving the vermin a parole"; and discarding lice by turning a garment wrong-side out was called "executing a flank movement." Most veteran fighters, however, eventually reached a state of "live and let live." The reminiscences of veterans were filled with stories of this bitter, ever present enemy, and the lice were often so numerous that ingenious soldiers devised fights between the largest. The vermin occupied a vivid place in the recollections of old soldiers, who delighted in singing *Army Bugs,* to the tune of *Sweet By and By:*

Soldiers sing of their beans and canteens,
    Of the coffee in old army cup,
Why not mention the small friends we've seen
    Always trying to chew armies up?

CHORUS:
Those firm friends, tireless friends,
    Hardly ever neglecting their hugs,

Their regard never ends,
　　How they loved us, those old army bugs!

Many veterans admitted that their most vivid memories of army life concerned the lice. The mere recall of the crawly little creatures led men to sing *The Graybacks So Tenderly Clinging,* to the tune of *Marching Through Georgia:*

There were companions on the march, as every soldier found,
With ceaseless zeal in digging deep in every spot around,
And though each hero killed a lot, still thousands more abound,
　　The graybacks so tenderly clinging.

CHORUS:
O! ho! no! no! we never can forget,
Ow-ow! ow-ow! we almost feel them yet;
The busy little grayback teeth in us so firmly set,
　　Who went with us Marching Through Georgia.

Those visitors were never big, in fact were rather small,
In silence they put in their work, no sound they made at all;
They thought it was full fun enough to hear the comrades bawl
　　While graybacks were busily biting.

And never partial were those bugs, no mortal would they spare,
No dignity could keep them off, they just bit everywhere.
And generals could not deny but what each had a share
　　Of graybacks so constantly nibbling.

The Confederate draftee, in *The Conscript,* encountered difficulties with the lice:

Oh, Weep not, conscript, weep not,
　　You're battling for the right,
Now, conscript, let me tell you,
　　Don't scratch them when they bite.
But jerk your shirt off with a flirt,
　　And catch them as they run,
Then with your nail, the bugs assail,
　　And mash them one by one.

Life in the Confederate and Union navies undoubtedly provided more

153

continued excitement than the necessarily routine life of the foot soldiers. The sailors were content to sing traditional sea chanteys and shanty ballads. However, some songs paid a tribute to their less spectacular exploits and indicated the people's pride in their navy. *Oh, Give Us A Navy of Iron* (words by D. Brainard Williamson, music by J. W. Porter) said:

> Oh, give us a navy of iron, and to man it our Yankee lads,
> And we'll conquer the world's broad ocean with our navy of ironclads.

These seamen were lauded in *The Old Flag* (words by James Mortimer, music by W. L. Hobbs):

> All honor to our gallant tars,
>   Columbia's fearless sons,
> Whose watchword is the stripes and stars,
>   Their war cry "Man the guns!"
> Their noble deeds, the voice of fame
>   To endless ages shall proclaim
> And evermore pure glory's flame
>   Will gild the Union sailor's name.

Our Boys Afloat (words by W. Dexter Smith, Jr., music by Ernest Leslie) cheered them on:

> Let cheers for all our sailors rise
>   From every loyal throat,
> God bless the darling ones we prize,
>   Our gallant boys afloat.

The sailor's life was less complicated than that of other warriors, although they had pride in their emblem, said *The Banner of the Sea* (words by D. Brainard Williamson, music by George W. Hewitt):

> Then dip it, lads, in ocean's brine
>   And give it three times three,
> And fling it out, 'mid song and shout,
>   The banner of the sea.

The watch was the main event for a sailor (*All's Well*, words by J. Gordon Emmons, music by Thomas Sullivan):

Midnight upon the placid bay, all nature seems at rest,
   The silver moonbeams lightly play upon the harbor's breast.
But, hark! From yonder ship a sound disturbs the silence
     reigning round.
   It is the frigate's midnight bell and watch proclaiming
     "All's well, all's well."

CHORUS:

All's well, the lonely watchman's cry
   Succeeds the stroke of midnight bell.
The ship is safe, no foe is nigh,
   The hour is peaceful—all's well.

Sailors who perished in ocean battles lacked a grave, affirms *They Buried Him in a Watery Grave* (words and music by J. W. Turner):

We cannot strew his turf with flowers,
For 'neath his cold bed he slumbers in the wave;
But we'll trust in God, His will is ours,
And love the sea, for 'tis his grave.

Grog, a mixture of rum and water, was served as a regular ration in the Union Navy until September 1, 1862, after which, by order of the Secretary of the Navy, spirituous liquors were to be forbidden on shipboard. In anticipation of this zero hour, Casper Schenck of the U.S.S. *Portsmouth* wrote lyrics for a song which was sung in the wardroom on the night of August 31, just before the deadline. He set it to the tune of *Come, Landlord, Fill the Flowing Bowl* and called it *Farewell to Grog:*

Come, messmates, pass the bottle 'round,
   Our time is short, remember,
For our grog must stop, and our spirits drop
   On the first day of September.

CHORUS:

For tonight we'll merry, merry be,
For tonight we'll merry, merry be,
For tonight we'll merry, merry be,
   Tomorrow we'll be sober!

155

Farewell old rye, 'tis a sad, sad word,
    But alas! it must be spoken,
The ruby cup must be given up,
    And the demijohn be broken.

All hands to splice the main brace, call,
    But splice it now in sorrow,
For the spirit-room key will be laid away
    Forever, on tomorrow.

Common soldiers, anonymous in the military mass, bore the brunt of this conflict, in spite of glory accorded men holding rank. *What Did the Privates Do?* (by P. V. Carey), sung to the tune of *Tattoo,* recalled for Grand Army of the Republic veterans the menial yet praiseworthy tasks of their army life:

Who jerked for gee, pulled steady haw,
    And whacked the army mule,
To haul hardtack and pork and beans,
    And whiskey as a rule;
Who drove the ambulance along,
    With officer's traps into,
If officers did all of this
    What did the privates do?

Memories of camp life were always pleasant, reminisced *We're Tenting on the Old Camp Ground* (words and music by J. W. Turner):

The dear old spot has many a charm
    That gives the soldier joy and pleasure;
'Mid all the scenes of war and strife,
    Old Camp, thou are the soldier's treasure.

We're tenting today on the old camp ground,
    Our hearts are light and joyous ever;
We think of home, we talk of friends,
    And happy times we've had together.

The brotherhood fostered in camp would ever remain, according to *The Song of the Soldiers* (words by Miles O'Reilly, music by Charles Van Oeckelen):

156

Comrades are known in marches many,
Comrades tried in dangers many,
Comrades bound in memories many,
　　Brothers ever let us be.
Wounds or sickness may divide us,
Marching orders may divide us,
But whatever fate betide us,
　　Brothers of the heart are we!

The camp kettle, hanging on a pole, had earned its rest at war's end, declared *The Old Camp Kettle* (words and music by C. I. Adkins):

The old camp kettle, that old iron vessel,
The kettle that hung on the pole.
It has cheered up the heart of many a weary soul,
Did that old camp kettle that hung on the pole.

And the old camp kettle that hung o'er the fire,
Has served well its mission and may well retire.
But 'twill long be remembered when we answer to the roll
'Round the old camp kettle that hung on the pole.

The canteen was always a faithful friend, according to the *Song of the Canteen* (words and music by H. Lovegrove):

Oh, my old battered friend
　　As you swing by my side,
I cannot forget
　　That we both have been tried.
And though sometimes found wanting
　　You never were seen
Attached to a coward,
　　My brave old canteen!

Always with the soldier, it became a symbol of shared friendship, as expressed in *We've Drunk from the Same Canteen* (words by Miles O'Reilly, music by James G. Clark), which, after the war, became a favorite song of Union veterans:

We've shared our blankets and tent together,

And marched and fought in all kinds of weather;
And hungry and full we've been
Had days of battle and days of rest;
But this memory I cling to and love the best,
We have drunk from the same canteen.

CHORUS:
The same canteen, my soldier friend, the same canteen,
There's never a bond, old friend, like this,
We have drunk from the same canteen.

The average soldier maintained a remarkably optimistic attitude toward his years in the war. Contacts made around the campfire in idle hours of mirth and song helped to preserve a high standard of morale and devotion to duty among soldiers. These "vocational" songs are as much a part of the story of the Civil War as are histories of military campaigns and chronicles of diplomatic discussions. In encampments of both the United Confederate Veterans and the Grand Army of the Republic throughout the last years of the century, former soldiers lustily sang of their military life, weaving anecdotes by the dozens and recalling war days, which in retrospect became glorious with remembrances of friendship and companionship.

****

CHAPTER 5

****

The Soldier in Battle

"The battle is the pay-off," Ernie Pyle's 1943 phrase, was even more true in the 1860's than in World War II. The months of preparation, winter encampments, and idleness were focused toward the brief but critical hours of actual combat. The duration of the war, the balance between victory and defeat, the fate of thousands of men, and the future of sweethearts, wives, and children were often decided in one or two days of fighting. Battles usually lasted only one day, though several of the more critical engagements—Gettysburg, Second Bull Run, Antietam, and Chickamauga, for example—continued through the second or third days.

As the hour of battle approached, the soldier, whether a veteran or an inexperienced recruit, made a determined effort to be cheerful and to maintain his courage. But the spectre of what he was to face in battle made him serious and often heartsick. His usual patriotism momentarily failed him. The war seemed futile and prolonged, the end far removed. Thoughts of absent friends, of loved ones in their distant homes, of the dangers of battle, of possible wounds, imprisonment, or death, and a thousand other depressing ideas rushed through the soldier's mind.

The most popular "melancholy" song was *Tenting on the Old Camp Ground,* written in 1862 by Walter Kittredge of New Hampshire, who, oddly enough, was never a soldier. The words he composed appealed to soldiers and civilians alike, and the song was later to become a favorite at veterans' reunions. The chorus aptly expressed the heavyheartedness of a war-weary people. The first verse ("Give us a song to cheer"), the second verse ("Thinking of days gone by"), and the third verse ("We are tired of war") seemed written expressly for the soldier facing the unknown in the morrow's battle. The final chorus, with its substitute "dying tonight" as rendered by male quartets, was full of profound and heartfelt sadness:

> We're tenting tonight on the old camp ground,
>   Give us a song to cheer
> Our weary hearts, a song of home
>   And friends we love so dear.
>
> CHORUS:
> Many are the hearts that are weary tonight,
> Wishing for the war to cease;
> Many are the hearts that are looking for the right
> To see the dawn of peace.
> Tenting tonight, tenting tonight,
> Tenting on the old Camp ground.
>
> We've been tenting tonight on the old camp ground,
>   Thinking of days gone by,
> Of the loved ones at home that gave us the hand,
>   And the tear that said "Goodbye!"
>
> We are tired of war on the old camp ground,
>   Many are dead and gone
> Of the brave and true who've left their homes,
>   Others been wounded long.
>
> We've been fighting today on the old camp ground,
>   Many are lying near;
> Some are dead, and some are dying,
>   Many are in tears.
>
> [FINAL LINES OF LAST CHORUS]:
> Dying tonight, dying tonight,
> Dying on the old camp ground.

Picturing soldiers' thoughts on the eve of an engagement, the foremost Northern composer, Chicago's George F. Root, wrote *Just Before the Battle, Mother,* which, unlike most "battle" songs, attained some popularity with the soldiers themselves. The feelings expressed were probably closer to the truth than most soldiers would admit.

THE SOLDIER'S VISION.

MUSIC AND WORDS
By
C. EVEREST.

Philadelphia LEE & WALKER 722 Chestnut St.

Hundreds of these "soldier dreaming of his return home" songs were published in the 1860's.

Just before the battle, mother,
    I am thinking most of you,
While upon the field we're watching,
    With the enemy in view.
Comrades brave are round me lying,
    Fill'd with thoughts of home and God;
For well they know that on the morrow
    Some will sleep beneath the sod.

CHORUS:
Farewell, mother, you may never
Press me to your breast again;
But oh, you'll not forget me, mother,
If I'm numbered with the slain.

Oh, I long to see you, mother,
    And the loving ones at home,
But I'll never leave our banner
    'Till in honor I can come.

Tell the traitors all around you
    That their cruel words we know,
In every battle kill our soldiers
    By the help they give the foe.

Hark! I hear the bugles sounding,
    'Tis the signal for the fight.
Now may God protect us, mother,
    As he ever does the right.
Hear the "Battle Cry of Freedom"
    How it swells upon the air,
Oh, yes, we'll rally round the standard
    Or we'll perish nobly there.

Another popular Union eve-of-battle song gave the sweetheart her share of attention in the thoughts of a young warrior. As he lay on the ground underneath the clear and starry sky, he felt that his sweetheart was thinking of him. The story is told in *The Soldier's Dream Song* (words and music by R. Stewart Taylor):

'Tis a calm and beauteous night, love,
    As my soldier couch I spread;

Where the stars are smiling down, love,
　Thro' the trees above my head;
But my thoughts are far away, love,
　Far away with home and thee;
And I know, within my heart, love,
　Thou art thinking now of me.

In the deep blue vault of heaven, love,
　Seated on its golden throne;
Well I know the glowing stars, love,
　That we mark'd and called our own.
And thro' all the lonely night, love,
　Ever turn my tho'ts to thee;
As it whispers to my heart, love,
　Thou art thinking still of me.

Ere the dawn of coming day, love,
　I may hear war's rude alarms;
And the stars of joy and hope, love,
　Set amid the clash of arms;
But in camp or bloody field, love,
　Whatsoe'er my fate may be;
Still I'll know within my heart, love,
　Thou wilt ever think of me.

Another sweetheart occupied a soldier's thoughts in *The Night before the Battle* (words by Robert Morris, music by Jean Louis):

'Twas the night before the battle,
　The moon was beaming bright,
But death's red storm would rattle
　With morning's early light.
A soldier from his bosom
　A beauteous portrait drew
And kissing it he murmured,
　"In life or death, I'm true."

A sister was the subject of *On the Eve of Battle, Sister* (words by W. Dexter Smith, Jr., music by J. A. Hills):

On the eve of battle, sister,
　I am dreaming of home

Where I passed a happy childhood
Ere my feet had learned to roam.

But moments for contemplation and dreaming were limited, for equipment and arms had to be made ready. Because of the importation of many out-of-date guns, the possessor of a truly fine rifle-barreled gun was a source of envy to his comrades. As the war progressed, more and more Enfield (English-made) rifle-muskets were issued by both North and South. These guns were muzzle-loaders, but the inclusion of a percussion cap and rifling resulted in remarkable accuracy. A "minnie ball," constructed to insure a snug fit in the rifling at the time of the explosion, was the ammunition used in Enfield rifles. The word "minnie" was a popular corruption of the surname Minié, that of the French army captain who devised the missile. Many of the wounded and dying soldiers celebrated in sentimental ballads had been wounded by "minnie balls." Enfield rifles were highly prized as the best of their type, and the high repute in which they were held by Northerners was expressed in a humorous song, *The Enfield Gun,* sung to the tune of *Cruiskeen Lawn,* an old Irish air:

Let the rebels grind their teeth,
While cowards crouch beneath,
And let Davis for money still dun;
But soon they'll fly the track,
When they hear a little crack
From a rifle-barreled Enfield gun, gun, gun!
From a rifle-barreled Enfield gun.

By June, 1862, the Federal authorities had purchased from Europe 738,000 small arms, of which about one-sixth (45,000) were Enfields, the remainder of miscellaneous types. Over 100,000 Enfield rifle-muskets were bought from England by Caleb Huse, the Confederate purchasing agent, in 1861. After each major engagement, thousands of enemy weapons were captured and pressed into use by the victorious force.

The importance of keeping ammunition dry was impressed upon all soldiers, for damp powder might mean the difference between life and death. The Southern muskets were, in general, inferior to those used by Northerners, since the blockade made European purchases increasingly difficult as the war progressed. Confederate powder was as good as that imported from England and was always plentiful throughout the war. But transportation difficulties sometimes prevented a sufficient supply at the particular location of battle when it was most needed. Rainy weather often halted the major campaigns, and protecting ammunition from the elements was essential to success in battle. Once, at Chantilly, a Southern divisional commander, General A. P. Hill, sent word to General "Stonewall" Jackson that he could not hold his position because his gunpowder was damp. Jackson replied through the messenger: "My compliments to General Hill and say that the enemy's ammunition is as wet as his and to hold his ground." A Southern song, *Boys, Keep Your Powder Dry* (words by F. H. Hodges, music by Fr. C. Mayer) used this theme:

Does a loved one home await you,
 Who wept to see you go,
Whom with a kiss imprinted,
 You left with sacred vow?
You'd come again when warfare
 And arms are all laid by,
To take her to your bosom?
 "Boys, keep your powder dry."

The foe awaits you yonder,
 He may await you here;
Have brave hearts, stand with courage,
 Be strangers, all, to fear;
And when the charge is given,
 Be ready at the cry;
Look well each to his priming:
 "Boys, keep your powder dry."

Before an encounter, each man was given a supply of ammunition. The customary individual allotment was from forty to sixty rounds, a round being a ball and enough powder for a single shot. For convenience, lead and powder for each load were wrapped in a piece of paper with the bullet at one end, the powder behind it, and the other end enclosed with a twist or a plug to hold the powder in place. When loading a gun, the soldier bit off the twisted end, dropped the cartridge into the muzzle, rammed it in, and was ready to shoot. The powder would be exploded by the spark when the trigger was pulled. Brass cartridges were used in Union breechloaders.

The day of battle was one of hard work. The men were awakened before daylight, often in the middle of the night. Drummer boys, using snare drums, sounded the "long roll" as a call to arms. The soldiers found their places in line, and officers made a last inspection, particularly of firearms and ammunition. Final directions were given regarding conduct on the battlefield—firing, movements, holding ranks in advance and retreat, and warnings not to stop to aid the wounded or plunder the dead.

To the beat of fife and drum, the regiments started through the misty dawn to the battleground. Upon arrival there was the long and tiring task of finding one's place, often made more confusing by conflicting orders and changes of plan. The men waited, sometimes for long hours, while other units were brought into position. While they waited, in suspense and silence, the soldiers promised to seek each other out at the battle's end, to give help to a wounded comrade, to gather up belongings, and to notify homefolk if a companion was killed. Many of the songs deal with these last pledges. In *Tidings Sad Must Be Conveyed* (words and music by P. Hancox), a soldier tells his comrade to notify his mother should he fall in the battle. Another says *Break It Gently to My Mother* (words by Mary A. Griffith (music by Frederick Buckley).

A thin line of soldiers called skirmishers was sent out in advance, particularly in wooded areas, and their contact with the enemy pickets was signalized by the noise of musketry. A single rifle shot rang out, followed by scattering shots; then a light rattling volley like a sudden dash of rain upon the roof or against the window; then a steady, lively, and collective popping; then the dull heavy boom of cannon as the artillery joined in the accumulating fury. This preliminary artillery duel, while soldiers silently stood in line or deployed, was often deadly, and many soldiers were killed before firing a single shot. Particularly feared was the twisting shot of the rifled cannon, which tore holes in the ranks. Then came the charge and the resistance. Usually both advancing and retreating troops fired their muskets. Overhead were shrieking shells, which, compared with those of today, were toys but nevertheless took their toll. A veteran described the sound: "Firing becomes a terrible, steady, determined angry roar, like the falling of some mighty waters. Pandemonium is turned loose; the earth seems to rock; the sun, if shining, becomes obscured by the stifling sulphurous smoke."

The soldier moved constantly forward, stopping only to load, aim, and fire. The pattern became monotonous—drop on one knee, bite off a cartridge, insert it, ram it home, rise and start forward again, take aim, and fire. He became almost oblivious to the dead and dying around him. Nearly always the defenders were behind a slight earthen breastworks and, if their position was a prepared one, an abatis (a defense of felled trees with the branches turned toward the enemy) in front of it.

As resistance increased and the attacking ranks were thinned when men fell dead or wounded, the advance was retarded; but gaps closed, and the line pushed ever onward. Meeting the enemy's lines, the combat became individual, and bayonets, muskets, rocks, and even sticks were used in hand-to-hand struggles. Presently one side or the other retreated, and the charge was over.

Several such charges and countercharges, made in quick time and pushed forward from a few hundred feet to a mile, usually determined the result of the day's fighting. After as many as sixteen to twenty hours of continued effort and tension, fighting ceased as one army or the other withdrew and both recuperated from the strife. If the battle extended into a second or third day, as at Gettysburg, the pattern of the attack was repeated over various portions of the field. The wake of the battle was a scene of ruin. Dismounted gun carriages, shattered caissons, knapsacks, haversacks, muskets, bayonets, and equipment were scattered over the field in wild confusion. Horses, dead and dying, were everywhere. Heaps of wounded or dead soldiers lay exposed and waiting for attention.

Because of the horror of the battles, with their legacies of sorrow and grief, it is easily understood why the songs of battle were usually written and sung by civilians and dealt almost exclusively with death and wounds. An unhealthy interest in death is expressed in these songs—but an undertone is the dirge for the fallen youths meeting death alone, without the comfort of mother and loved ones. The recurrence of the mother-theme is surprising; sweethearts are seldom mentioned in verses about the last moments of the dying. Every conceivable incident of the battlefield is recounted in these ballads; the predominant note is one of sorrow. Thousands of mothers never received news of their sons' deaths or even knew the location of their burial places. It was a period of anxiety, despair, and utter loneliness.

The soldier in the thick of battle could not pause to aid his wounded companions; the advance must continue, with or without commanding officers, since the success of recurrent charges determined eventual victory or defeat. Of the many songs dealing with fallen companions, two are typical. In *Comrades, Hasten to the Battle* (words by Thomas Manahan, music by George F. Root), a wounded soldier refuses the help of his fellows and urges them to go on without him:

> Comrades, hasten to the battle,
>   Leave me here alone to die;
> While the cannon roar and rattle,
>   Quickly to the conflict fly!
> For the angels dwell around me,
>   They their vigils o'er me keep;
> Hasten, hasten to the battle,
>   I would like a soldier sleep.
>
> CHORUS:
> "Comrades, hasten to the battle."
> Unto death I'll calmly bow,
> For upon the road to Heaven
> I see soldiers marching now.

The soldier in *Hasten Brothers to the Battle* (words by Theodore D. C. Miller, music by Vincent Percival) is "bleeding for his country" but urges his fellows onward:

> Hasten brothers, to the battle,
>   Loud the bugle sounds afar;
> I am weary, wounded, dying,
>   But I hear the call for war.
> Hasten brothers, do not linger,
>   Leave me here alone to die;
> Forms seraphic hover near me,
>   They will bear my soul on high.

In *Brothers, Hasten on to Battle* (words and music by Frederick Schilling), the wounded soldier urges his comrades to leave him. A soldier says *Comrades, Lay Me Gently Down* (words by W. Dexter Smith, Jr., music by Edward N. Catlin), while another wounded man asks *Is Our Banner Still Advancing?* (words by John H. Lozier, music by C. M. Currier). When a dying soldier has been given a drink from the canteen of a comrade, he breathes a prayer for his mother and then, pointing to the place where the battle is still raging, says, *Follow the Flag* (words by Rev. W. B. Slaughter, music by O. F. Barbour) and dies.

The task assigned to color-bearers was extremely difficult and dangerous. To keep the flag flying was a matter of pride and its capture by the enemy a disgrace. Consequently, men vied with each other for the honor of holding the cherished emblem aloft in the thickest of the fight. Casualties were highest among color-bearers, since the flag had to be kept at the forefront of the advance as a guide to the line of advancing soldiers. The importance of the flag is shown in the words of a commanding officer, a dying hero, who, in a Northern song, orders his men to *Lay Me Down and Save the Flag* (words and music by George F. Root):

> They arose, whose name was Legion,
>   As an overwhelming wave,
> And the battle surged its billows
>   Round a chosen few and brave;
> And they neared the sacred banner
>   With their foul and flaunting rag,
> When the dying hero shouted,
>   "Lay me down and save the flag."
>
> CHORUS:
> So he fell, the brave commander,
> Like the oak from mountain crag;
> But his last words still are ringing,
> "Lay me down and save the flag."
>
> Then they looked at one another,
>   In the speechlessness of woe,
> As each eye would ask a brother,
>   Shall we stay or shall we go?
> And again the sight was blasted
>   By the traitor's boastful rag,
> And again the word fell sternly,
>   "Lay me down and save the flag."

Other Union songs include *Leave Me and Save the Glorious Flag* (words and music by C. R. Moon) and *For God's Sake, Save the Flag* (words by Charles Haynes, music by J. E. Haynes). Lyrics of the latter are the last words of the Ninety-third Ohio Regiment flag-bearer. *Our*

Color Guard (words by Thomas J. Diehl, music by Henry Tucker) glorifies these boys:

> On, color guard, oh, noble, brave!
>   How one by one they fall!
> But not their fate nor yet their grave
>   Our brave lads can appall.
> Now from the ranks leap eagerly,
>   Like groom to meet his bride,
> A score of volunteers and see
>   Our color guard supplied.

The Old Sergeant (words and music by Will S. Hays) rallied the company around the Southern flag time and again before he expired.

A youthful Confederate died clasping to his breast the South's flag in *The Standard Bearer* (words by Major T. N. P., music by N. S. Coleman):

> A shout, a shout for Victory!
>   A cheer from the blood-red field,
> As onward dashed the serried ranks
>   The guns their death knell pealed.
> A youthful soldier spurred along
>   Before the cannon's mouth,
> Bearing aloft exultingly
>   The banner of the South!
>
> "Dost see the foe outnumbers us?"
>   A veteran calmly said;
> The youthful soldier laughed aloud
>   And gaily shook his head.
> Then onward rode him to the fray,
>   Before the cannon's mouth,
> Bearing aloft exultingly
>   The banner of the South!

Another dying Confederate soldier sees *The Flag of the Regiment* (words by Carl Veeder, music by Edward O. Eaton):

> Oh, thus may death's summons always come in triumph's hour
> And beckon us away when Freedom's fight is won,

When victory on the banner of our ranks begins to lower
And the flag of the regiment is proudly marching on!

The Dying Flag Bearer (words and music by Emma Scarr Ledsham)
charges his comrades to seek out "the friends I love best" and to:

Tell them gently how I died
    While their trembling hands you clasp,
How the shot that pierced my side
    Tore our banner from my grasp.

My young sister helped to make
    That fair flag, three years ago,
And eight times, for freedom's sake
    It and I have faced the foe.

One Willie, nearing death ("We knew that noble Willie soon would
bloom in courts above."), said, *Comrades, I Am Going Home!* (words by
Theodore D. C. Miller, music by George A. Russell):

Soon he saw our starry banner,
Floating high in ether blue,
And his bosom swelled with rapture—
He had to that flag proved true.

While the' ebon angels lingered,
Soon to touch the magic wand,
Willie's feeble shouts were ringing
For the emblem of our land.

The bugler's main battle duty was to sound a long note whenever the
enemy was near and to aid the drummer in beating the rally when the
ranks were re-forming after a charge. The death of one bugler in the blood-
stained snow is recounted in *The Bugler* (words by F. E. Weatherly, music
by Ciro Pinsuti):

The bugler paced thro' the driving snow,
By the frozen river to watch the foe;
Behind him in camp his comrades lay,
Wounded and spent from the morning's fray.
His orders ran, "When thou see'st the foe,

Three loud blasts on thy bugle blow."
These were his orders, he'd keep them well,
Gallantly, faithfully, 'till he fell.
Steady and slow, pacing the snow,
Stalwart old bugler, watching the foe!

But the bugler was shot by the enemy and:

His comrades came when the fight was past,
They found him clasping his bugle fast;
Dead at his post in the ice and snow,
His old face turned as he met the foe.
There let him rest, he shall be blest,
Gallant old bugler, bravest and best.

The "long roll" of the drums was the signal to assemble for action.
In battle, the main task of the drummer was to "beat the rally." Whenever the ranks were broken and the soldiers scattered, they would re-form
their lines under fire, guided by the drum's tattoo rising above the noise
of shot and shell. Drummer boys almost always threw away their heavy
drums in battle and seized the guns and equipment of dead comrades,
or became stretcher-bearers. One little fellow, Willie Johnson, received
a medal for heroism; he was the only drummer to bring his drum from
the field after the seven days' battle before Richmond. Because of their extreme youth (see Chapter IV), these boys formed ideal subjects for pathetic
narrative ballads; they could always be pictured as calling for their mothers
as death approached. Hence the songs presenting the last moments of the
drummer boys were designed to stir even the most stolid of hearts.

In *Little Major* (words and music by Henry C. Work), a drummer
boy is refused water by soldiers of the opposite side, who think him not
worth the bother:

At his post the "Little Major"
    Dropped his drum that battle day,
On the grass all stained with crimson
    Through that battle night he lay,
Crying, "Oh! for love of Jesus,
    Grant me but this little boon.
Can you, friend, refuse me water?
    Can you, when I die so soon?"

There are none to hear or help him,
    All his friends were early fled,
Save the forms outstretched around him
    Of the dying and the dead.
Hush! they come! There falls a footstep!
    How it makes his heart rejoice!
They will help, oh, they will save him,
    When they hear his fainting voice.

Now the lights are flashing round him,
    And he hears a loyal word,
Strangers they, whose lips pronounce it,
    Yet he trusts his voice is heard.
It is heard—Oh, God, forgive them!
    They refuse his dying prayer.
"Nothing but a wounded drummer,"
    So they say and leave him there.

See! the moon that shone above him
    Veils her face, as if in grief;
And the skies are sadly weeping,
    Shedding tear-drops of relief.
Yet to die by friends forsaken,
    With his last request denied,
This he felt his keenest anguish
    When at morn he gasped and died.

The Dying Drummer Boy (words by Mary A. Lathbury, music by E. C. Howe) calls throughout the night for his mother and finds peace with the dawn:

The night is so long and drear, mother,
And the stars are so cold and bright;
And your boy has lain on the battlefield
This long and weary night.
I've called to you o'er and o'er, mother,
'Till my voice is faint and low,
But I only hear the dying moan
And the far off river's flow.

CHORUS:
Cold is my bed for my fallen head,
Gone is my broken drum!

Oh, when will the long night end, mother,
And when will the morning come?

The *Drummer Boy of Antietam* (words and music by Albert Fleming) was buried as they found him:

Near where the stripling perished, lay the drum he so much cherished,
And the sticks he nimbly flourished, in his hands were still descried.
Ah, well-a-day, his soul had fled away.
Nevermore may they see him whom once they knew
And the soldier ears that fed on the music that he shed
No more shall hear his thrilling rat-tat-too.

On the other hand, *Little Harry, the Drummer Boy* (words and music by S. Wesley Martin) died in the fray "where loud boomed the cannon 'mid shouts of brave men and sabres in true hands did play," but his body was sent home:

'Tis one month tomorrow since Harry came home,
And his dear form we first did espy,
Enwrapped in the banner of red, white and blue
With his drum sitting silently by.
His hands on his bosom were tenderly clasped,
He had beat his last reveille call,
'Twas down with the traitor and up with the star,
He was beating when fell'd by a ball.

In the last verse, Harry was buried, as he had wished, beneath a willow with the flag of the Union wrapped around him and the drum near by.

In the Confederate *Drummer Boy of Shiloh* (words and music by Will S. Hays, sometimes attributed to E. Clarke Ilsley and dedicated to Harry Macarthy), the dying boy prays "while brave men wept like children." In the Union *Drummer Boy of Vicksburg; or, Let Him Sleep* (words and music by P. De Geer), he "passed from the earth while contending for the right." The eleven-year-old drummer boy of the First Minnesota Regiment asks, *If I Sleep, Will Mother Come?* (words and music by H. W. Luther), while Little Eddy, *The Dying Drummer Boy* (words by J. C. Koch, music by L. Grube), calls for his mother, as does *The Dying Drummer* (words by Thomas Manahan, music by Mrs. Parkhurst). Another of

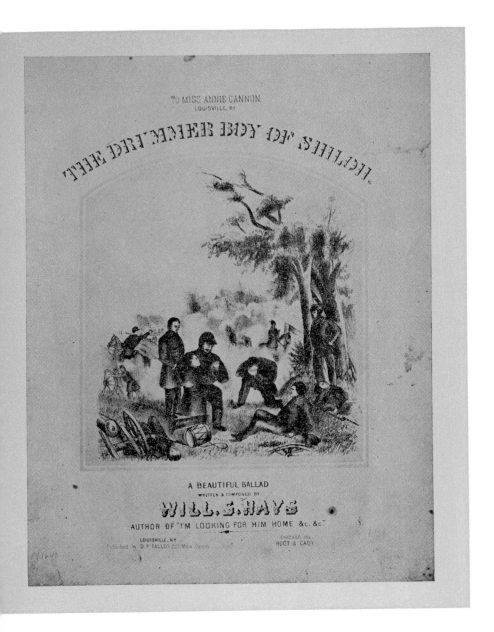

Such scenes of pathos were designed to prepare the singer for a heart-breaking experience. More than a dozen boys, both Union and Confederate, claimed to be the original subject of this famous song.

Take I pray thee this small lock-et, Broth-er sol-dier, ere I die;

Life is flick-'ring in its sock-et, And my spir-it soon will fly; I am

dy-ing, com-rade, dy-ing, Far from home and her I love, Death with

life is strong-ly vie - ing And I soon will be a - bove.

Chorus

Take this lock-et, sol-dier, broth-er, Don't for-get, give this to moth-er.

Give This to Mother

these songs is *The Drummer Boy of the National Greys* (words by Miss G. P. Burge, music by Augustus Cull).

As many a soldier lay wounded and dying, he was comforted by his comrades and often gave them some token he carried to be sent to his loved ones at home. *Give This to Mother* (words by S. W. Harding) was the final composition of Stephen C. Foster, sent to his publishers three days before his death. The speaker is a dying drummer boy:

> Take I pray thee this small locket,
> Brother soldier, ere I die;
> Life is flick'ring in its socket,
> And my spirit soon will fly:
> I am dying, comrade, dying,
> Far from home and her I love,
> Death with life is strongly vieing
> And I soon will be above.

176

The Soldier in Battle

CHORUS:
Take this locket, soldier, brother,
Don't forget, give this to mother.

A locket was also sent by the subject of *Bear This Gently to My Mother* (words by Thomas Manahan, in three musical settings by Frank M. Davis, George A. Russell, and J. E. Turner):

Bear this gently to my mother, tell her that it came from me;
'Tis the little lock she cherished, I trust it now with thee.

A ring is sent by *The Soldier to His Mother* (words by S. Fillmore Bennett, music by J. P. Webster):

You may take this little token, 'tis a ring she used to wear
And as yet it is not broken, so the love to her I bear.
Take it safely back to mother, bid her wear it now for me,
She must prize it as no other, for my love-pledge it shall be.

A dying Confederate bids his companion send a lock of his sweetheart's hair to his mother in *I've Fallen in the Battle* (words and music by A. B. Chandler):

To me at our last meeting, while trembling on my breast,
With heart all wildly beating, she gave this golden tress;
Oh, take it to her, mother, and say that ever more
My spirit shall be with her, on earth, by sea or shore.

Another Confederate soldier, dying on a blood-drenched field during the Virginia campaign, told his comrade in *Richmond on the James* (words by an Exile, music by T. E. Bayley):

Bear my good sword to my brother,
    And the badge upon my breast,
To the young and gentle sister
    That I used to love the best;
But one lock from my forehead
    Give the mother still that dreams
Of her soldier boy near Richmond,
    Near Richmond on the James.

Even decades later, when the emotions of our forebears are replaced by a more dispassionate, remote, and realistic objectivity, the high incidence of casualties and the appalling cost in human lives of the four years of conflict are still shocking. The odds were seldom as small as one in ten, and often as high as one in three, that a soldier participating in a battle would be either killed or wounded.

Statistics have never been completely accurate, but authorities usually agree that the toll on both sides approximated 700,000 lives, divided more or less equally in the proportion of 400,000 Union and 300,000 Confederate casualties. Counting all deaths attributed directly to the war, however, this may be an underestimate, and some historians assume one million, equally divided between the North and South, as a more realistic figure. This number represents approximately 2 per cent of the white population of the North and 10 per cent of that of the South. The Southern loss of human "wealth" was therefore five times as heavy as the Northern. The greater part of this toll consisted of young men between the ages of eighteen and thirty-five, men who would ordinarily have been producing the generation to succeed them. Many of these men, in a period when large families were customary, died without becoming fathers. The number of dead, together with a similarly enormous toll of wounded and missing, which has never been completely and accurately determined, caused a significant number of broken homes and depletion of young, vigorous manhood and potential families.

Available Union Army records account for a mortality total of 359,528 —110,070 killed in battle or dead of wounds, 224,586 dead of disease, and 24,872 dead in Confederate prisons. A total figure of 400,000 is therefore not unreasonable. The average death rate from disease was 53.4 per 1,000 men, twice that from combat.

Estimates of Confederate losses are even less definite, for the records of several states were destroyed and the reporting system was incomplete. The only available figures list 74,524 soldiers killed in action or dead of wounds, 59,297 dead of disease, and 25,591 dead in Union prisons. However, it is probable that there were at least 100,000 Confederate deaths from disease above the number recorded. Deaths from wounds were also more numerous than records indicate. Hence, the total figure of 300,000 does not seem excessive.

The higher incidence of casualties in Southern ranks was due to the superiority of Union weapons, the difference in basic battle tactics, and the numerical superiority of Northern troops during the final years. The charge, with or without artillery preparation, was much more frequently used by Confederates and resulted in the exposure of many more men to direct enemy gunfire. This charge, accompanied by the famous Rebel yell, was always effective in bewildering and paralyzing armies of greater numbers. The yell has been variously described as a shout "more overpowering than the cannon's roar," "a mingling of Indian whoop and wolf-howl," "the scariest sound that ever split a human ear," and "a soul-harrowing sound to hear." It was first used at the Battle of Manassas (First Bull Run) and seems to have been a spontaneous release from the fright preceding battle as well as an outpouring of triumph. Later in the war, as Southern manpower dwindled, the sheer volume of Northern opposition became overwhelming, with more Confederate casualties resulting.

Similarly, the Union's toll was multiplied rapidly in the campaigns of Grant, who, foreseeing that the end of the war would be hastened by more and more crushing and decisive engagements, sacrificed men to obtain victories. In a month of fighting in Virginia in 1864, the Union Army of the Potomac lost 70,000 men.

Single battles caused losses of thousands—killed, wounded, and missing. The missing, when counted, may have been deserters or soldiers completely disintegrated by shot, hence not identifiable. Official casualty lists of the major battles indicate why civilians, realizing that each encounter might affect their loved ones at the front, preferred songs which reflected a preoccupation with death, the dying, and the wounded and why *Weeping, Sad and Lonely, The Vacant Chair,* and *Just Before the Battle, Mother* were the most popular civilian songs of the period.

At Shiloh (a Union victory), the casualty total was over 23,000; at Antietam, 26,000. Confederate victories were similarly costly: at Chickamauga the toll was more than 34,000; at Chancellorsville, 21,000. These encounters—fought in comparatively small areas under almost hand-to-hand conditions—and the huge resultant losses are difficult to conceive when compared to battles of twentieth-century wars—with their superior and perfected weapons.

The most important and crucial engagement of the Civil War—its turning point—was Gettysburg, by reason of its strategic importance, the number of participants, and the high incidence of casualties. The three-day battle, July 1-3, 1863, involved nearly 160,000 men, with a loss of over 50,000, almost evenly divided between North and South. Seldom in military history have more casualties occurred in such a short time. In Pickett's charge alone, 10,000 soldiers were killed, wounded, or missing. At Gettysburg, Confederate regiments suffered the highest percentage of casualties in the entire war. Captain Tuttle's company, the Twenty-Sixth North Carolina Regiment, consisting of three officers and eighty-four men, lost all officers; and eighty-three men were killed or wounded. In Company F of the same regiment, consisting of three officers and eighty-eight men, every man was killed or wounded. Company C, the Eleventh North Carolina Regiment, lost two officers and thirty-four men from a total of thirty-eight.

Severe (but not fatal) wounds were even more feared than death itself, because medical staffs, limited in personnel and essential facilities, were unable to give prompt and adequate care to the thousands of men injured in each major encounter. Although field hopitals were always set up before an engagement, the rapidity with which men fell made it impossible to bring them to the medical center and give them immediate attention. As a result, many lay unattended where they fell during the battle, frequently for hours. The cries of the wounded were a part of the aftermath of battle. More than once the ground was literally stained with blood, and streams became red with blood of bathed wounds. After the Battle of Fredericksburg, the wounded lay forty-eight hours in the freezing cold before they received attention; at Gettysburg, many of the first day's wounded were not given attention until the third and final day of that battle.

Transportation presented another difficulty. Litter-bearers collected the wounded as soon as possible after major engagements. After temporary medical attention, the more seriously wounded were transported to hospitals in ambulances, which were either two- or four-wheeled vehicles called "dead carts." The two-wheelers were called "hop, step and jumps," so constructed that foreparts were either very high or very low, the wounded lying with their heels above their heads. The four-wheelers had built-in shelves or compartments, often leather-covered, with a keg of water under each. A supply of beef stock and bandages was stored under the front seat, and a stretcher was hung on each side.

According to George W. Adams, whose *Doctors in Blue* is a medical history of the Union Army, the typical wound was in the arm or leg, made by a "minnie ball" fired from a musket. Bullets from small arms accounted for 94 per cent of the total wounds, only 5.5 per cent having been caused by artillery fire and .4 per cent by sabre or bayonet.

Practically all songs concerning wounded soldiers indicate that death is inevitable, and scarcely one melody gives hope of survival. This is a singular phenomenon, perhaps explained by the fact that implications of death furnish a more pitiful song subject than hope of survival. One of the few songs expressing optimism was *Just After the Battle* (words and music by George F. Root), a companion-piece to *Just Before the Battle, Mother,* which pictures the despair and loneliness of a wounded soldier as he awaits dawn:

Still upon the field of battle,
I am lying, mother dear,
With my wounded comrades waiting
For the morning to appear.
Many sleep to waken never
In this world of strife and death,
And many more are faintly calling
With their feeble dying breath.

CHORUS:

Mother dear, your boy is wounded,
And the night is drear with pain,
But still I feel that I shall see you,
And the dear old home again.

Oh, the first great charge was fearful,
And a thousand brave men fell;
Still amid the dreadful carnage
I was safe from shot and shell.
So amid the fatal shower,
I had nearly passed the day,
When here the dreaded Minnie struck me,
And I sunk amid the fray.

Oh, the glorious cheer of triumph
When the foemen turned and fled,
Leaving us the field of battle
Strewn with dying and with dead.
Oh, the torture and the anguish
That I could not follow on,
But here among my fallen comrades
I must wait 'till morning's dawn.

The common picture of Northerner and Southerner lying wounded and dying close to one another forms the subject of *Foes and Friends* (words by Ellen H. Flagg, music by George F. Root). Each soldier, one from New Hampshire, the other from Georgia, had a wife and little girl. Each talked of his loved ones and pardoned the other before expiring:

Two soldiers, lying as they fell
Upon the reddened clay,
In daytime foes, at night in peace
Breathed there their lives away;
Brave hearts had stirred each manly breast,
Fate only, made them foes;
And lying, dying side by side
A softened feeling rose.

The dying lips the pardon breathe,
The dying hands entwine;
The last ray dies, and over all
The stars of heaven shine.
And, now, the girl with golden hair,
And she with dark eyes bright,
On Hampshire's hills, and Georgia's plain,
Were fatherless that night.

A not unusual occurrence was the discovery that the soldier had killed a relative in the opposing forces. In *Write a Letter to My Mother* (words by E. Bowers, music by P. B. Isaacs), a Confederate soldier at Bull Run discovers that he had shot his own brother in the Union forces. They speak of their home and childhood, and the dying soldier asks his brother never to tell of the tragedy:

Write a letter to my mother, send it when her boy is dead;
That he perished by his brother, not a word of that be said.

Brother, I am surely dying, keep the secret, for 'tis one
That would kill our angel mother, if she but knew what you have done.

In *Brother and the Fallen Dragoon* (words and music by J. P. Webster), a Union captain orders a rifleman to kill a lone Confederate horseman and to bring him any plunder which he might find. The rifleman snatches a locket of gold from the fallen Confederate, examines the picture within, and is shocked by the resemblance to the captain, who says:

> Ah, rifleman, fling me the locket—
> 'Tis she, my brother's young bride,
> And the fallen dragoon was her husband,
> Her soldier; 'twas heaven's decree.

Fortunate were those wounded who received medical attention, later to die in hospitals, for after each major battle hundreds of soldiers expired before medical aid could be administered. Battlefields were strewn with heaps of dead in varied postures, faces bloated and black, bodies swollen. At points of concentrated attack there were often huge piles of bodies in different states of decomposition, lying in the positions in which they fell. Corpses sometimes remained exposed for days, baking in the heat of the sun or dissolving in the rain. Burial parties experienced difficulty in enduring the sights and smells they encountered.

Wounded soldiers, after having been made temporarily comfortable by their advancing or retreating comrades, often died before aid could reach them. The retreating units were sometimes forced to leave their wounded on the field, where they did not receive attention until all of the victor's wounded had been cared for. Even then, they were often not given the same care as their captors. Walt Whitman, who was for a short time a litter-bearer and nurse, recorded his impressions of the dying and dead in *Memoranda during the War*:

> Of all the harrowing experiences, none is greater than that of the days following a heavy battle. Scores, hundreds of young men, uncomplaining, lie helpless, mangled, faint, alone, and so bleed to death or die from exhaustion, either untouched at all, or with merely the laying of them down and leaving them, when there ought to be means provided to save them.

Death on the battlefield or in hospitals held a fascination for song writers. The songs on this subject, however, were products of civilian writers who tended to glorify the conditions and surroundings of death and who placed in the mouths of the dying soldiers phrases which were somewhat stilted and often poetically phrased.

A few of the more unusual titles of the popular songs which were concerned with dying will serve to indicate their typical contents: *The Stars and Stripes Brought Me Here* (words by Mrs. S. J. Megargee, music by J. Remington Fairlamb), in which a soldier boy explains why he finds himself dying far from home; *Still He Kept Thinking* (words and music by John P. Ordway), wherein a soldier dreams of home as he dies in the Battle of the Wilderness; *Tell Him I'm Ready* (words and music by James M. Stewart), "Him" being God; *The Soldier Lay on the Tented Field* (words and music by H. S. Thompson), where the warrior's life passes in review; *There's a Cottage on the Hillside of the Noble Prairie State* (words by Minnie Moore, music by J. P. Webster), containing a vision of the home fires; *Good Night, Who Wouldn't Be a Soldier* (words by Mrs. J. W. McConihe, music by L. P. Whitney), which expresses the thought that death is worthwhile in view of the noble cause; and *Soon Within the Grave I'll Slumber* (words by Thomas Manahan, music by Frederick Widdows), which welcomes the relief which death will bring.

A very common type of song was that wherein the dying soldier talks to his comrades while awaiting death, sometimes speaking of the battle, at other times of his home.[13] As unconsciousness sets in, he often has visions of meeting his mother or sweetheart and deplores the fact that he is never to see them again.

In *Breathe It Softly to my Loved Ones* (words by W. Dexter Smith, Jr., music by John R. Thomas), the dying soldier pictures his family group:

Comrades, there are dear ones gathered
In our cottage home tonight,
Thinking of the absent soldier
And I see their faces bright.
To those loved ones, best and dearest,
Gently, boys, the story tell.
Breathe it softly, oh! so softly,
How the soldier fought and fell.

[13] The "comrades-gathered-round" type of song is exemplified by *Our Comrade Has Fallen* (words by W. T. Rossiter, music by O. M. Brewster), *Weep Not, Comrades, for Me* (words and music by George R. Cromwell), *Let Me Die, Face to the Foe* (words and music by Elbridge G. B. Holder), *Comrades, All Around Is Brightness* (words by Thomas Manahan, music by George F. Root), *Comrades, I Am Dying* (words by Thomas Manahan, music by George A. Russell), *Let Me Kiss the Dear Old Flag Once More Before I die* (words and music by Henry C. Watson), and *The Old Flag Will Triumph Yet* (words by J. E. Parker Doyle, music by J. Henry Whittemore).

The same composer was author of the words of *I'm Dying Far from Those I Love!*:

Oh! tell them in the gory fight
I bore our banner's starry folds
And battled for the Truth and Right.
What grief will rend poor Mother's heart
To hear my mournful story told!
I was her pride, and by her side
I thought to stay when she was old.

Mothers receive the major attention in all songs of wounded and dying, with a number of variations of the common theme of good-bye messages, calls for her arms and kisses, and moans for her future alone, for mothers seem to be almost universally widowed.[14]

One of the favorites in both North and South was *Who Will Care for Mother Now?* (words and music by Charles Carroll Sawyer,[15] arranged by Charles F. Thompson). The explanatory note accompanying

[14] The many variations on the "good-bye, Mother" theme are best exhibited by the titles of a few Union songs: *It Was My Mother's Voice* (words by M. A. Kidder, music by Frederick Blume), *Mother, I'll Come Home Tonight* (words by W. Dexter Smith, Jr., music by Frederick Buckley), *The Soldier to His Mother* (words by Thomas Mackellar, music by William U. Butcher), *The Dying Soldier; or, Kiss Me Goodnight, Mother* (words and music by Edward Clark), *O Pray Once More for Me, Mother* (words and music by Edwy Wells Foster), *Shall I Never See My Mother?* (words by Georgie C. Slatter, music by W. Irving Hartshorn), *Is That Mother Bending O'er Me?* (words and music by J. C. Johnson), *Mother, Oh, Sing Me To Rest* (music by Matthias Keller), *Angel Mother, I'm Coming Home* (words by W. Dexter Smith, Jr., music by M. J. Lessur), *Is It Mother's Gentle Touch?* (words by Theodore D. C. Miller, music by V. E. Marston), *It Grows Very Dark, Mother* (words and music by S. Wesley Martin), *Tell My Mother Not to Weep* (music by Charles H. Pease), *One Parting Word, Dear Mother* (words by J. Walter Montgomery, music by J. W. Porter), *On the Field of Battle, Mother* (words and music by George F. Root), *If I Sleep, Will Mother Come?* (words and music by C. A. Shaw).

[15] Charles Carroll Sawyer was born in Connecticut in 1833. At the age of twelve, his sonnets began to attract attention, but with the commencement of the war, his sentimental ballads found a place in the hearts of both Northerners and Southerners. His most popular songs—*Mother Would Comfort Me, Who Will Care for Mother Now?, Weeping, Sad and Lonely,* and *He Was Not Afraid to Die!*—sold over a million copies, a record for that time. All his songs had their basis in actual fact or incident, generally reported to him by friends. A characteristic of his work was its complete lack of sectional bias; the tenderness which the songs express was appealing to Unionists and Confederates alike, for as did almost no other war composer, he touched the hearts of all, regardless of loyalty.

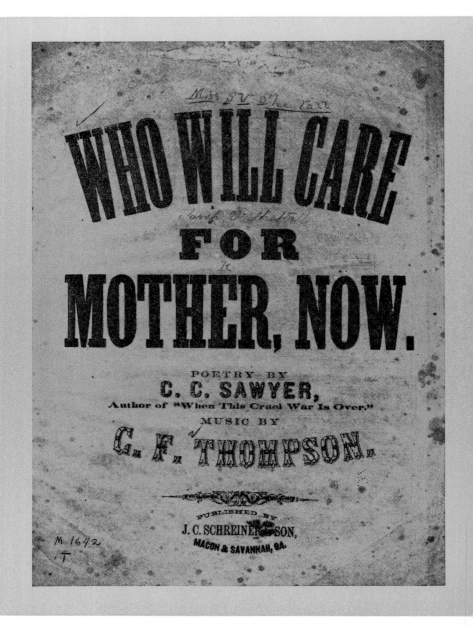

Appealing "heart" songs whose themes were equally applicable to both the North and the South were recklessly pirated. *Who Will Care for Mother Now,* a favorite of both sides, was published in full sheet music form in Georgia and as a penny broadside in Maryland, which did not secede from the Union.

WHO WILL CARE FOR MOTHER NOW.

Thompson, C.

Why am I so weak and weary?
  See how faint my heated breath,
All around to me seems darkness;
  Tell me, comrades, is this death?
Ah! how well I know your answer;
  To my fate I meekly bow,
If you'll only tell me truly,
  Who will care for mother now?

CHORUS.—Soon with angels I'll be marching,
      With bright laurels on my brow;
      I have for my country fallen,
        Who will care for mother now.

Who will comfort her in sorrow?
  Who will dry the falling tear,
Gently smooth her wrinkled forehead?
  Who will whisper words of cheer;
Even now I think I see her,
  Kneeling, praying fore me now!
Can I leave her in anguish;
  Who will care for mother now?

Let this knapsack be my pillow;
  And my mantle be the sky;
Hasten, comrades to the battle!
  I will like a soldier die.
Soon with angels I'll be marching,
  With bright laurels on my brow;
I have for my country fallen,
  Who will care for mother now?

LOUIS BONSAL,
Bookseller, Stationer and Blank Book Manufacturer.
Corner of Baltimore and Frederick Sts., Baltimore, Md.
OLD BOOKS RE-BOUND, & BLANK BOOKS MADE TO ORDER
Songs—Wholesale and Retail.

the song described a dying young man who had been the only support of an aged and sick mother for years. Hearing the surgeon tell those who were near him that he could not live, he placed his hand across his forehead and spoke these words with a trembling voice, while burning tears ran down his fevered cheeks:

Why am I so weak and weary?
    See how faint my heated breath!
All around to me seems darkness,
    Tell me, comrades, is this death?
Ah! how well I know your answer;
    To my fate I meekly bow,
If you'll only tell me truly,
    Who will care for mother now?

CHORUS:
Soon with angels I'll be marching
With bright laurels on my brow,
I have for my country fallen,
Who will care for mother now?

Who will comfort her in sorrow?
    Who will dry the falling tear?
Gently smooth her wrinkled forehead?
    Who will whisper words of cheer?
Even now I think I see her,
    Kneeling, praying for me, how
Can I leave her in her anguish?
    Who will care for mother now?

The question was answered in a number of songs. A soldier comrade promises to take the fallen soldier's place in *I Will Care for Mother Now* (words by Thomas Manahan, music by Samuel L. Condé):

Comrade, I will guard thy mother,
    She shall be my fondest care;
I will be to thee a brother
    While thou art an angel there.
Let no sorrows fill thy bosom,
    Let no sadness shade thy brow;
Let thy spirit calmly slumber,
    I will care for mother now.

Friends will comfort her, the soldier is assured in *Kind Friends Are Near Her* (words by Ednor Rossiter, music by B. Frank Walters):

> Friends will be near her, angels will come
> To guard and cheer her when you are gone.

while *Do Not Grieve for Thy Dear Mother* (words and music by James W. Johnson) promises:

> We will comfort her in sorrow while sitting by her side,
> We will tell her how you perished, how you like a soldier died.

An even brighter assurance is given in *Loyal Hearts Will Gather Round Her* (words by Norris R. Norton, music by C. M. C.):

> Weep not, brave one, for your mother, for the battle is not lost,
> And the Cause for which you're dying will repay her all the cost.
> God is with her though you are not, He will soothe her throbbing brow,
> And throughout the coming future, He will care for mother now.

Heaven's solicitude is also expressed in *He's Watching O'er My Mother* (words by M. A. Geuville, music by Ferdinand Mayer) and *Christ Will Care for Mother Now* (words by W. H. R., music by J. F. W.).

In *Dying on the Battlefield* (words and music by Josephine Braham), the soldier calls:

> Mother, mother, not another can thy holy place supply,
> I am pining for the twining of thy arms once ere I die.

A dying Confederate soldier says he must pass on before the victory in *Kiss Me Before I Die, Mother* (words by Joseph M. Goff, music by E. Clarke Ilsley):

> Kiss me before I die, Mother, I would have lived to see
> Our fair land free, my Mother, from this base tyranny.

The dying Union soldier says *Mother Kissed Me in My Dream* (words and music by John R. Thomas):

Comrades, tell her, when you write,
    That I did my duty well;
Say that when the battle raged,
    Fighting, in the van I fell;
Tell her, too, when on my bed
    Slowly ebbed my being's stream,
How I knew no peace until
    Mother kissed me in my dream.

Another soldier entreats (words by C. A. Vosburgh, music by Jabez Burns):

Tell Mother I Die Happy, that for me she must not weep,
Tell her how I longed to kiss her ere I sank in death to sleep.

The Confederate *Dying Volunteer* (words by James C. Beckel, music by A. E. A. Muse) had followed his mother's admonition to be true to the flag, although life might be the forfeit:

Ere life's pulse is stilled, and the cold chill of death
Creeps o'er my heart, I would see thee once more!
Fond words of farewell with thy very last breath
I'd whisper to thee from eternity's shore.

Another soldier says *Kiss Me, Mother, Ere I'm Dead* (words by C. W. S., music by Matthias Keller):

Fold your arms again around me,
    Press against my aching head,
Sing the lullaby you sang to me;
    Kiss me, mother, ere I'm dead.

While Mother garnered the major part of attention, others came in for some occasional consideration. Sweethearts were thought of in *The Soldier's Last Message* (words and music by W. L. Pierce) and in *I've Been Dreaming of You, Jessie* (words by L. Hattie Aldrich, music by William S. Pitts). The family is a subject of worry in *Who'll Protect My Children Now?* (words by Fanny Crosby, music by Hubert P. Main); the wife of a soldier killed at Shiloh in *The Soldier's Orphan Bride* (words by Mrs. H. Plout, music by Ch. Mathias); and a brother in *Farewell, Dearest Brother* (words by Mr. Copley, music by N. B. Hollister). Fathers were in general neglected, except in *O, Could I See My Father* (words and music by J. W. Turner) and *Kiss Me, Father, Ere I Die* (words and music by T. R. Walker):

> Father, I have done my duty in the camp and 'mid the strife;
> Soon I'll seal my deep devotion to my country with my life.
> But it soothes my dying moments when I know that you are by,
> Put your loving arms around me; kiss me, father, ere I die.

The report of the surgeon general of the Union Army listed 1,057,423 cases treated in general hospitals alone from the earliest days in 1861 until July 1, 1865. Confederate statistics are not available, but the number would possibly be comparatively as great. The halls and wards of hospitals behind the lines were scenes of anguish, pain, and loneliness. Because of the shortage of male nurses, civilian women of the neighborhoods near the evacuation and general hospitals would often form the major nursing staffs. Hence the many songs of the "for-his-mother" theme, when dying soldiers found comfort in the presence of women whom, in their delirium, they mistook for their own mothers. The loneliness of the wounded or dying soldier as he lay in pain far from home and loved ones, accepting the ministrations of a volunteer, was hard to bear. A Union organization, *The Christian Commission* (words by Robert Morris, music by Alfred Delaney), performed many good works:

> The mission of the Christian band who bathe the brow and clasp
>   the hand
> And whisper hope in accents bland, Oh! 'tis a holy cause!
>
> They hear the battle's awful roar, but when the dreadful din is o'er
> How grateful is the task to pour oil upon gaping wounds.
>
> But see, a hand is beckoning on, a failing voice is heard to moan,
> Another life is nearly done, a wounded soldier calls.

These volunteers listened to many dying messages, promising to convey them to the loved ones. Volunteer women are praised in *Our Lady of the Hospital* (words by Miles O'Reilly, music by Harrison Millard):

The ward is silent again as our lady resumes her place
    And I see as I watch her a patient pain
That is pitiful in her face.
    Lily of beauty, too bright for a camp,
Oh, saint that ever our sorrows will share!
    Now I see by the light of the shaded lamp
Tears fall on the page of her prayer.

The soldier who died in friendly hands and who was tenderly cared
for was the subject of one of the most well-beloved and popular Confederate poems, *Somebody's Darling,* by Marie LaCoste, set to music by both
Southern and Northern composers:

Into the ward of the clean white-washed halls
Where the dead slept and the dying lay;
Wounded by bayonets, sabres and balls,
Somebody's darling was borne one day.
Somebody's darling, so young and so brave,
Wearing still on his sweet, yet pale face,
Soon to be hid in the dust of the grave,
The lingering light of his boyhood's grace.

CHORUS:
Somebody's darling, somebody's pride.
Who'll tell his mother where her boy died?

Matted and damp are his tresses of gold,
Kissing the snow of that fair young brow;
Pale are the lips of most delicate mould,
Somebody's darling is dying now.
Back from his beautiful purple-veined brow,
Brush off the wand'ring waves of gold;
Cross his white hands on his broad bosom now,
Somebody's darling is still and cold.

Give him a kiss, but for Somebody's sake,
Murmur a prayer for him, soft and low;
One little curl from its golden mates take,
Somebody's pride they were once, you know;
Somebody's warm hand has oft rested there,
Was it a mother's so soft and white?

192

Or have the lips of a sister so fair,
Ever been bathed in their waves of light?

Somebody's watching and waiting for him,
Yearning to hold him again to her heart;
Yet there he lies with his blue eyes so dim,
And purple child-like lips half apart.
Tenderly bury the fair, unknown dead,
Pausing to drop on his grave a tear;
Carve on the wooden slab over his head,
Somebody's darling is slumbering here.

This poem attracted more composers than any other single song of the Civil War. The most famous Confederate version, the original, was composed by John H. Hewitt; another Southern setting was by A. C. Matheson. Union versions were by A. J. Abbott, Mrs. E. K. Crawford, William Cumming, C. Everest and Leon C. Weld, and, under the title *Somebody's Darling Slumbers Here,* by John P. Ordway and C. R. Moon. G. G. Goodfellow titled his variation *He's Somebody's Darling:*

Close the eyes drooping 'neath death's heavy dew,
He's somebody's darling, God only knows who.

Sad eyes are watching, tearfully true,
He's somebody's darling, God only knows who.

A common occurrence was identification, by the delirious dying soldier, of the watching woman with his mother, and this is noted in several songs. *Is That My Mother?* (words and music by J. R. Stevenson) assures the absent mothers that their sons are cared for:

Oh, women in your cheerless homes; oh, women wild with woe,
There's many a motherly footfall here, where your kind steps would go,
And many a soldier boy has died thinking his mother by his side.

The substitution of the stranger for the mother is treated in *Is That Mother Bending O'er Me?* (words and music by M. G. Bisbee), *Be My Mother 'Till I Die* (words and music by Elmer Ruan Coates), and *Mother, Come, Your Boy is Dying* (words by John L. Zieber, music by Rudolph Wittig). The soldier dies happy in *Oh, Take Me Home to Die* (words by J. Harry Hayward, music by Thomas D. Sullivan):

With tearful eyes and trembling voice, the maid with tenderness
    obeyed,
And as the hymn she softly sang, the soldier closed his eyes and
    prayed.
He slept. A smile then lit his face as waking from a dream of bliss
"My maid," he said, "I have been home and felt my mother's kiss."

Another soldier gives a parting message to the stranger in *Kiss Me Good-bye for Mother* (words by M. J. Million, music by William S. Pitts):

Oh, strive to soothe her anguish when she shall learn my death,
And tell her how I whispered her name with fleeting breath.
And since amid the battle thou art beside me here,
Kiss me good-bye for mother, my sinking heart will cheer.

Tell her I died a soldier where death was flying fast,
And kiss me. Tell my mother good-bye, ere life has passed.

Occasionally a dying soldier was fortunate enough to be with his mother or sweetheart who had sought him out in the hospital or on the field. One Union mother is with her boy in *Is That Mother Bending O'er Me?* (set to music by Charles H. Greene, J. C. Johnson, and Ferdinand Mayer):

Is that mother bending o'er me
    As she sang my cradle hymn?
Kneeling there in tears before me,
    Say, my sight is growing dim.
Comes she from the old home lowly,
    Out among the northern hills,
To her pet boy dying slowly
    Of war's battle wounds and ills?

Yes, my boy, it is your mother,
    Came I from our northern hills
To my pet boy, dying slowly,
    Of war's battle wounds and ills.

Stephen Foster, in 1863, composed a song on the death of a young lad. In *For the Dear Old Flag I Die* (words by George Cooper), "the last words of a brave little drummer boy who was fatally wounded at the Battle of

Gettysburg," it is not made clear whether the mother visited a hospital to see her dying boy or whether he was sent home wounded. However, after seeing the usual angel band and hearing heavenly voices calling him, he dies with her kiss upon his lips:

> For the dear old flag I die,
>   Said the wounded drummer boy;
> "Mother, press your lips to mine;
>   O, they bring me peace and joy!
> 'Tis the last time on the earth
>   I shall ever see your face,
> Mother, take me to your heart,
>   Let me die in your embrace."
>
> CHORUS:
> For the dear old flag I die,
> Mother, dry your weeping eye;
> For the honor of our land
> And the dear old flag, I die.

A *Dying Soldier Boy* (words and music by J. T. Wamelink), wounded at Fredericksburg, expires in the arms of his mother in the Patent Office Hospital at Washington; the mother of a twenty-three-year-old finds her boy in a hospital in *I Know My Mother's Hand* (words by W. Dexter Smith, Jr., music by Henry Tucker):

> I have prayed she might be near me
>   Ere I seek that other land,
> And I feel she is beside me,
>   For I know my mother's hand.

Still another soldier boy dies in his mother's arms in a hospital in *Kiss Me Goodnight, Mother* (words and music by H. S. Thompson).

A sweetheart finds her lover on the battle plain in the Confederate *The Dying Soldier; or, The Moon Rose O'er the Plain:*

> A maiden sought that place of death
>   And gazing round the scene,
> She caught a faintly pressing breath
>   And knelt upon the green.

"Oh, Mary, dear, why art thou here?"
    Cried one she bended o'er,
"Our friends have fled, our freedom's dead,
    It is our home no more;
Then Mary, dearest Mary, fly,
    And leave, oh, leave me here to die."

A Southern matron makes the last moments of a dying Union soldier, lying under the willow tree of her plantation home, more comfortable by saying *Let Me Kiss Him for His Mother* (words and music by John P. Ordway):

Let me kiss him for his mo-ther, Let me kiss his youth-ful brow; I will love him for his mo-ther, And seek her bless-ing now; Kind friends have smoothed his pil-low, Have watched his ev-'ry care, Be — neath the weep-ing wil-low, O, lay him gent-ly there.

Chorus

Sleep, dear-est, sleep, I love you as a bro-ther;

Kind friends a-round you weep, I've kissed you for your mo-ther.

Let Me Kiss Him for His Mother

196

Let me kiss him for his mother,
　　Let me kiss his youthful brow;
I will love him for his mother,
　　And seek her blessing now;
Kind friends have smoothed his pillow,
　　Have watched his every care,
Beneath the weeping willow,
　　O, lay him gently there.

CHORUS:
Sleep, dearest, sleep,
　　I love you as a brother;
Kind friends around you weep,
　　I've kissed you for your mother.

Let me kiss him for his mother,
　　What though left a lone stranger here;
She has loved him as no other,
　　I feel her blessing near.
Though cold that form lies sleeping,
　　Sweet angels watch around;
Dear friends are near thee, weeping,
　　O, lay him gently down.

Let me kiss him for his mother,
　　Or perchance a fond sister dear;
If a father or a brother,
　　I know their blessing's here.
Then kiss him for his mother,
　　'Twill soothe her after-years;
Farewell, dear stranger brother,
　　Our requiem, our tears.

Charles Carroll Sawyer based *Mother Would Comfort Me* on an actual incident. A soldier from a New York regiment had been severely wounded and taken prisoner at Gettysburg. He was placed in a Southern hospital, and when he was finally told that nothing more could be done for him, he sadly said these last words:

Wounded and sorrowful, far from my home,
Sick among strangers, uncared for, unknown;
Even the birds that used sweetly to sing

197

Are silent and swiftly have taken the wing.
No one but Mother can cheer me today,
No one for me could so fervently pray,
None to console me, no kind friend is near—
Mother would comfort me if she were here.

CHORUS:
Gently her hand o'er my forehead she'd press,
Trying to free me from pain or distress;
Kindly she'd say, "Be of good cheer,
Mother will comfort you, Mother is here."

If she were with me, I soon would forget
My pain and my sorrow, no more would I fret;
One kiss from her lips or one look from her eye
Would make me contented and willing to die!
Gently her hand o'er my forehead she'd press,
Trying to free me from pain and distress;
Kindly she'd say to me, "Be of good cheer,
Mother will comfort you, mother is here."

Cheerfully, faithfully, mother would stay
Always beside me by night and by day;
If I should murmur or wish to complain;
Her gentle voice would soon calm me again.
Sweetly a mother's love shines like a star,
Brightest in darkness, when daylight's afar;
In clouds or in sunshine, pleasures or pain,
Mother's affection is ever the same.

This song was published in both the North and South.

The aggregate number of men in both armies who were crippled or permanently disabled was about 400,000. In the Union Army alone there were 235,583 soldiers treated for gunshot wounds. Delays in collecting the wounded increased the development of gangrene and subsequent amputation of limbs. When the wounded were eventually brought to field hospitals, emergency operations and treatment were often undertaken with only the crudest facilities. Practically all contemporary memoirs mention the stinking stacks of fingers, feet, legs, and arms outside field hospitals, for amputation was very often the only means of saving life. Anesthesia and disinfectants were seldom used, and suffering was therefore acute.

A number of songs about amputees or the blind are included among the "home-coming" songs in Chapter X. However, *Good-bye, Old Arm* (words by General W. H. Hayward, music by Philip Phillips) concerns a Union soldier in a hospital at Nashville who awoke to find that his right arm had been amputated. With his left hand he lifted the cloth and found nothing but a gory stump. "Where's my arm?" he cried, "Get my arm. I want to see it once more, my strong right arm." They brought it to him and, as he took hold of the cold, clammy fingers he addressed it with tearful earnestness:

> Good-bye, old arm, that strong right arm,
> 'Twas once my pride to wield.
> 'Twill never bear the sword again
> My country's flag to shield.

"Good-bye, old arm, we have been a long time together. We must part now. You will never fire another carbine nor swing another sabre," he said, and the tears rolled down his cheeks. He then announced to those standing near, "Understand, I don't regret its loss. It has been torn from my body that not one state should be torn from this glorious Union."

The Empty Sleeve (words by Mrs. P. A. Hanaford) was set to music by both Henry Badger and Rev. J. W. Dadmun and serves to glorify the amputees:

> That empty sleeve, it is a badge of bravery and honor,
> It whispers of the dear old flag and tells who saved our banner.
> Three hearty cheers for those who lost an arm in freedom's fray,
> And bear about an empty sleeve but a patriot's heart today.

Military funerals were rare at the front, and those held were mainly for officers, after the masses of dead soldiers had been buried. Occasionally the next of kin lived near enough to be summoned. Such ceremonies were more common during the long periods of inactivity in camp. A popular Confederate song by Caroline Norton, an English noblewoman, outlined in martial strains, complete with drum and bugle effects for piano, *The Officer's Funeral*:

> Hark! to the shrill trumpet calling,
> It pierceth the soft summer air;
> Tears from each comrade are falling,

For the widow and orphan are there.
The bayonets earthward are turning,
And the drum's muffled breath rolls around;
But he hears not the voice of their mourning,
Nor awakes to the bugle's sound.

Unmarked graves were common. More often than not the body of the soldier was unceremoniously dumped into a large trench dug by a burial detail. Haste was necessary before the stench of decay and decomposition became unbearable. When single bodies were located, they would sometimes be buried in lone graves on the spot where they fell. Soldiers of those times possessed no identification discs, and notification of families depended upon the finding of the body by a comrade or checking of the rolls by a careful and humane adjutant who took the trouble to notify the next of kin. A Union colonel wrote the mourning family, "You will always have these cheering words to console you—*He Was Not Afraid to Die!*" (words and music by Charles Carroll Sawyer):

Like a true and faithful soldier
He obeyed our country's call;
Vowing to protect its banner,
Or in battle proudly fall;
Noble, cheerful, brave and fearless,
When most needed, ever nigh,
Always living as a Christian,
"He was not afraid to die."

To his wounded, sick companions
He would tell sweet words of cheer;
Softly bathe their heated foreheads
'Till death's chariot drew near;
Tell them of a land where ne'er is
Heard the cruel battle cry;
Comfort them and tell them "they should never
Be afraid to die."

If a unit was almost entirely wiped out, the chances were few that families would ever know the circumstances of death and the location of the final resting place. In case of rapid retreat, the enemy would often give attention only to burial of their own dead. In spite of repeated warnings and the infliction of penalties, the dead were almost invariably stripped of their valuables, and this not necessarily by the enemy. One such marauding incident is told in *O, Touch Not My Sister's Picture; or, The Confession of a Rebel Prisoner* (words by Mrs. E. S. Kellogg, music by T. Martin Towne):

On the bloody field of battle one dark night with stealthy tread
I was prowling round for plunder 'mid the dying and the dead.
As I roughly seized a locket pressed upon a throbbing breast,
Words of pleading faintly uttered sought my purpose to arrest.

CHORUS:
Oh, touch not my sister's picture,
Let it lie upon my heart.
With the parting kiss I promised
I would never with it part.

'Tis my dearest earthly treasure but to you of little worth.
Would you rob a fellow-soldier, dying on the cold, damp earth?

Personal papers disappeared, together with items desirable as souvenirs; hence the large number of unidentified dead.

If a soldier was killed in a light skirmish, he might be buried by his fellows, who would write the appropriate letter and send mementos to the wife or mother. The tributes of his comrades at the bier of a hero was the subject of a Southern song, *The Soldier's Grave* (words by D. Ottolengui, music by Hermann L. Schreiner):

With hearts full of grief we stood round his bier,
And each soldier's eye was moist with a tear;
And with sad, solemn step we marched to his grave
And o'er our brave brother our flag we did wave.
Yes, slowly and sadly, we waved a farewell,
Though his spirit already in heavenly realms did dwell;
But his body we tearfully lowered 'neath there,
And the heart of the soldier did send forth a prayer.

The soldier would often be buried with the flag as a winding sheet. One Union boy's dying words were *Wrap the Flag Around Me, Boys* (words and music by R. Stewart Taylor):

O, wrap the flag around me, boys,
    To die were far more sweet,
With freedom's starry emblem, boys,
    To be my winding sheet.
In life I lov'd to see it wave,
    And follow where it led,
And now my eyes grow dim, my hands
    Would clasp its last bright shred.

The loving care exercised by a dead soldier's comrades was expressed in *Softly, Now Tenderly, Lift Him with Care!* (words and music by C. S. Harrington):

Softly, now tenderly, lift him with care,
    This is a hero whose pale form ye bear.
Raise that right arm of his up to his side
    Look here, that's where the ball struck when he died.

Brush back the hair from his pain-moistened brow,
    Cold enough, still enough, white enough now.
Lay his cap o'er it gently, that's right,
    Cover his dead eyes away from the light.

Loosen his sword belt; there, take it away,
    No blade is sheathed in the scabbard today.
Here, throw this flag o'er his poor wounded breast,
    Wrapped in its folds, we will lay him to rest.

Other songs of this type were *We Laid the Soldier Down to Rest* (words by W. Dexter Smith, Jr., music by Henry Cromwell) and *Bury Me at Sunset* (words by Frederick E. Arnold, music by Frank Wilder).

Soldiers could not be expected to brood upon the death of a fallen comrade, for partings became repetitious as the war advanced, and casualties increased. However, there was always *A Tear for the Comrade that's Gone* (words in one version by Captain T. F. Winthrop, music by James R. Murray; another variant setting by A. J. Abbey):

Together we've stood in the thick of the fray,
    Together we've stemmed the red tide.
He was true to the laws he had sworn to obey,
    For the flag of his love he has died.
No more shall our bugle his brave heart cheer on

Or "Reveille" wake him at dawn.
Let us give as a tribute a soldier's last boon,
A tear for the comrade that's gone.

Sheer physical exhaustion after combat was quickly followed by a mental letdown, described thus by one veteran:

> The higher a bird flies into the air the lower must be its descent back to the earth again. So the reaction and collapse occur after the wild excitement and tumult of the battle. In the engagement men are stirred up into madness, to the utmost fury; they are beside themselves in their frenzy. The awful noises of musketry and cannon, the swiftly moving cavalry, the charging hosts, the varying, shifting phases of the fight, with defeat or victory all the while trembling in the balances, wounds, blood, deaths, hurrahs, all together rouse the soul into a tempest, the like of which is unknown anywhere else. When the bloody work is done, the descent of the soul into weakness, gloom and despair is swift and sudden.

However, patriotism reassured the soldiers. The relief felt at the victory and the fact that the flag still waved was expressed in *After the Battle; or, Fling Out the Flag Once More* (words by H. Peterson, music by C. W. Heywood):

Then fling the flag once more
    Against the Southern sky!
Its stripes all stained with gore,
    Its stars with crimson dye;
For never in our sight
    Shone Heaven's auroral gleams,
As in this hour of night,
    Our country's banner streams!

The sight of dead or wounded comrades and the carnage of the battle-field infected victorious and defeated alike with a deep and abiding sickness of spirit. If the battle ended in defeat, retreat and disappointment caused dejection among the tired soldiers. If victorious, soldiers sought relief from the recent strain and tension in the sleep of exhaustion, while patrols were set up and campfires lighted.

At such times, as always, thoughts turned to home and loved ones.

In the stupor of thorough fatigue, the soldier found escape from the unpleasant and bloody world of reality. Edward O. "Ned" Eaton, one of Blackmar's star song writers, pictured the dreams of a Confederate soldier on watch on the banks of the Tennessee River in *I Dream of Thee; or, By the Camp Fire's Lonely Watch:*

> By the campfire's lonely watch,
>   By the mountain's granite side,
> Where the brook glides soft and free—
>   I dream of thee! I dream of thee!
> When the last farewell was spoken,
>   When I took the last love token,
> Did I think how hard 'twould be
>   To be severed thus from thee.
> From thee! from thee!
>   To be severed thus from thee!

In *I Cannot Leave the Battlefield* (words by W. Dexter Smith, Jr., music by Matthias Keller), a Union song, the soldier tells his beloved that he thinks constantly of her but cannot return home until victory is assured:

> I stand where falls the deadly rain
>   Where brave men proudly die,
> That our old flag may float again
>   Triumphant in the sky.
> Where in the land the gleaming steel
>   Is flashing at the van,
> Where gallant legions proudly wheel
>   To die as heroes can.
>
> CHORUS:
> When victory shall crown with light
> Our banner of the air,
> I'll seek my home with true delight
> To dwell in sweet joy there.

Military men testify to sentiments of deep fellowship which affect soldiers after they have faced dangers together. Psychologists would explain this as a common need for security. The Confederate *Camp Fire Song* (words by Charles Lever, music by Edward O. Eaton), also issued under the title *When the Battle Is O'er,* shows this relief:

The Soldier in Battle

When the battle is o'er and the sounds of fight
    Have closed with the closing day,
How happy around the watch fire's light
    To chat the long hours away.
To chat the long hours away, my boy,
    And talk of the days to come,
Or better still, and a purer joy,
    To think of our far-off home.

CHORUS:

We'll chat the long hours away, my boy,
    And talk of the days to come,
Or better still, and a purer joy,
    To think of our far-off home.

And those who know each other not,
    Their hands together steal
Each thinks of some long hallowed spot
    And all like brothers feel.
Such holy thoughts to all are given,
    The lowliest has his parts,
The love of home, like love of heaven,
    Is woven in our hearts.

Homesickness was almost as infectious as disease. Tired of war, the soldier could only dream of the uncertain future and assure his loved one that she was ever near him in his thoughts and his mother that her prayers reached and comforted him. But with the passing of the mood, he again became the soldier-civilian, adapting himself to the military life. The majority of soldiers felt no genuine hatred for the opposition forces; to them, fighting was a distasteful task to be endured in order that the war might be finished sooner.

An aftermath of each major engagement was the herding of captives into stockades for transport to prisons behind the lines. The fate of the captured soldier was even more uncertain than that of one wounded, for he was far from home and at the mercy of enemies, with no definite date for, and little possibility of, release or exchange. The prisoner could only hope and pray. His days were always beset with difficulties and suffering, whether he was Union or Confederate, whether he was in one of the large Southern stockades or in one of the more numerous smaller Northern enclosures. Tales of endured sufferings were circulated freely and resulted in increased hatred of the opposition. The recorded facts do not indicate that the Union captives received any more severe treatment from the Southerners than the Confederate prisoners received from the Northerners. The proportion of recorded deaths in enemy prisons was about equal: 25,591 Confederate and 24,872 Union men, about one-tenth of all soldiers imprisoned on each side. During the war, 220,000 Confederates were held in Union prisons and 270,000 Northern soldiers in Southern prisons.

At the beginning of the war, the official attitude of the North was that those Secessionists in arms against the United States were to be considered mutinous rebels, which complicated the problem of their exchange or parole as prisoners of war in the usual sense. Lincoln's government for a long time refused to make any agreement for exchange, since such an accord would recognize the independent government of the Confederacy. Furthermore, each returned prisoner would swell Southern manpower, which was sorely needed. As a result, hundreds of prisoners suffered in overcrowded prisons while the negotiations lagged. Somewhat regular exchanges were made until late in 1863 on humane rather than legal grounds. But after Grant terminated exchanges when he became general of the armies, the average prisoner lived out the war in misery, his only hope being the final cessation of hostilities or release by his conquering comrades.

George F. Root was the composer of the most famous prison song; indeed, his *Tramp, Tramp, Tramp; or, The Prisoner's Hope* became one of the twelve most popular songs of the war and one which has outlived the circumstances of its composition and is still sung by persons who know nothing of its war connotation. It expressed perfectly the element of hope and anticipated joy when liberation would come and the war would be over for the languishing captives:

> In the prison cell I sit, thinking, mother dear, of you
> And the bright and happy home so far away,
> And the tears they fill my eyes 'spite of all that I can do,
> Though I try to cheer my comrades and be gay.
>
> CHORUS:
> Tramp, tramp, tramp, the boys are marching,
> Cheer up, comrades, they will come;

And beneath the starry flag we will breathe the air again
Of the freeland in our own beloved home.

In the battle front we stood when their fiercest charge they made,
     And they swept us off a hundred men or more,
But before we reached their lines, they were beaten back dismayed,
     And we heard the cry of victory o'er and o'er.

So within the prison cell, we are waiting for the day
     That shall come to open wide the iron door;
And the hollow eye grows bright and the poor heart almost gay
     As we think of seeing home and friends once more.

The prisoner in *The Prisoner of War* (words and music by George A. Russell) was still loyal to the Union:

Oh! my country, no estranging
     Can make me your cause forego;
Though a prisoner still unchanging,
     I am with you, weal or woe.

One of the hardships endured by Union captives was the scanty rations which sometimes brought them close to starvation. There was good reason for this scarcity, since in the later war years the supply of foodstuffs in the South was so short that the Confederate soldiers fared no better than their prisoners. Thin soup, a piece of hardtack, and an occasional bit of spoiled meat was the usual fare. Starvation and dysentery reduced the men to the state of half-naked savages. They were described by a Northerner who had been in nine Confederate prisons as follows:

> It was easy by the expression of their faces alone, to distinguish the 'fresh fish' from the old prisoners. Those of the latter had a starved, hopeless look, that must have been seen to be realized. Long confinement and starvation have the effect of deadening the finer feelings ... All the selfish propensities are developed. The mind becomes gangrened. Long brooding over the deplorable situation, with hunger constantly gnawing at the vitals, gradually saps away all that is noble and God-like, leaving active only the animal nature.

This suffering of Union prisoners grew chiefly out of two factors—the breakdown of transportation and the Southerners' lack of foodstuffs even sufficient to feed their own soldiers in the field. When news of this suffering spread, the North cut Confederate prisoners' rations of food and clothing and forbade the receipt of boxes from relatives in the enemy states as a retaliatory measure.

On December 1, 1864, there were almost 13,000 graves at the Andersonville, Georgia, prison. Between its opening in February, 1864, and April, 1865, 49,485 Union prisoners were received at this prison. Of this number 12,926 died. Prison Commandant Henry Wirz was tried by the victors after the war, found guilty of gross and criminal neglect, and hanged on November 10, 1865. George Root could hardly have been expected to remain silent in the face of the disturbing reports of malnutrition and death, and he lamented the fact that so many men should be *Starved in Prison*:

> Had they fallen in the battle,
>   With the old flag waving high,
> We should mourn, but not in anguish,
>   For the soldier thus would die.
> But the dear boys starved in prison,
>   Helpless, friendless and alone,
> While the haughty rebel leaders
>   Heard unmoved each dying groan.
>
> CHORUS:
> Yes, they starved in pens and prisons,
> Helpless, friendless and alone,
> And their woe can ne'er be spoken
> Nor their agony be known.
>
> Had they died in ward or sickroom
>   Nursed with but a soldier's care,
> We should grieve, but still be thankful
>   That a human heart was there.
> But the dear boys starved in prison,
>   Helpless, friendless and alone,
> While the heartless rebel leaders
>   Heard unmoved each dying groan.
>
> Oh! the thought so sad comes o'er us
>   In this hour of joy and pride,

That the hearts we loved so fondly
    Might be beating by our side;
But the dear boys starved in prison,
    Helpless, friendless and alone,
While the cruel rebel leaders
    Heard unmoved each dying groan.

The song is filled with righteous indignation and condemnation, but the recurrent phrase

While the haughty (heartless, cruel) rebel leaders
Heard unmoved each dying groan

is obviously unjust in view of the South's shortage of food.

In Andersonville, as in other prisons, the enclosure had a small fence or ditch inside the outer pine board fence, which was generally about twelve feet high. Three feet inside this ditch, or second fence, was the "dead line," so called because a prisoner passing it would be shot by the guards without warning. It was not uncommon for desperate and hungry prisoners to cross this dead line in the hope that they might escape or that they might end their sufferings by being killed. *We Can Never Forget It; or, The Memories of Andersonville Prison Pens* (words and music by Henry Tucker) described this dead line and the sufferings and privations which were a usual part of the prisoner's lot:

We can never forget it,
    Through the many years to come,
How we lingered, starved and waited
    In the prison far from home.
How at night we longed for morning
    And the morning brought despair
As we breathed the poisonous vapors
    Of the vile and stagnant air.

CHORUS:
Freezing, starving, living death!
Father, can they know at home?
Oh, we can never forget it
In all the years to come.

How we suffered in our weakness,

Freezing, starving, none can tell.
Staggering near the fateful "dead line"
  Where so many gladly fell.
Gazing into ghastly faces
  When all joy and hope had fled
Longing, dying 'fore the firelight
  With no shelter, clothes or bed.

Oh, we never can forget it,
  No, that prison pen so bare
Where we watched in weary silence
  For our scanty, wretched fare.
For the loathsome, rancid bacon
  And the bitter mouldy bread
That we clutched with bloodless fingers
  Like the fingers of the dead.

Libby, an officers' prison in Richmond, had formerly been an old fac-
tory. No furniture was ever placed in it, and the men slept on the floors.
One tap provided water for both drinking and washing. Because the prison
was located in the Confederate capital, the prisoners housed there were
particularly badly treated and, together with Andersonville, its name came
to be synonymous with intense suffering. A Union prisoner, D. L. Atkin-
son, held captive nine months in Libby, was the author and composer of
A Voice from Libby:

CHORUS:
Mother dear, I know you'd greet
Your long lost son with welcome sweet;
But all I ask should e'er we meet,
Oh, mother, give me enough to eat!

Starved to death, oh, mother dear,
Would Will and Harry and you were here;
Ah, no! not here to starving lie,
But only to kiss me ere I die.

Another soldier in Libby Prison tells of his misery in *The Richmond
Prisoner* (words and music by George C. Deming):

The night is dark and chilling falls the rain.

The sad wind moans around my prison bars;
No fire, no light to ease my weary pain,
I lie and watch the silent, flitting stars.
The sentries guard my grating prison door,
Though to death's iron gate I now have come,
Longing to see the dear old flag once more,
And rest within my happy Northern home.

CHORUS:
Sighing and sobbing by my prison door,
I dream of forms that ne'er to me can come;
Longing to see the dear old flag once more,
And rest within my happy Northern home.

Confederate captives imprisoned in the North fared little better. Their condition was not caused by lack of food, but resulted from the officers in charge being disinterested and lazy. They were usually men of second-rate ability, for those of outstanding capabilities could not be spared from the front to undertake such commands. The rigors of the Northern winter brought death to many Southerners, who possessed only lightweight clothing and who were already undernourished when captured during that last year of the war.

Death was often preferable to captivity. One Confederate soldier who had been reported killed in the Battle of Shiloh wanted his mother to think him dead rather than suffering in prison, in *The Southern Captive* (words by Sam Houston, Jr., music by F. W. Smith):

No, they tell her that I'm sleeping,
    'Neath the turf on Shiloh's plain,
That she ne'er will see her wand'rer,
    Never on this earth again.
Oh! my poor heart sinks within me
    As the months roll slowly by
And it seems in this cold Northland,
    A lone captive I must die.

Camp Douglas was a large Union prison on the site of the first University of Chicago building on Thirty-first Street, then a rural area. During one month when 3,500 prisoners were confined there, 10 per cent of the inmates died, a mortality rate not exceeded by any other prison in either North or South. An anonymous Confederate prisoner expressed the hopeless monotony of confinement in *Camp Douglas by the Lake,* to the tune of *Cottage by the Sea,* a song popular in the 1850's.

> Exiles from our homes, we sorrow
> O'er the present's darkening gloom;
> Well we know that with the morrow
> We'll wake to feel the same hard doom.
>
> CHORUS:
> Here, old Michigan before us,
> Moaning waves that ever break,
> Chanting still the one sad chorus
> At Camp Douglas by the Lake.
>
> I dread the night's uneasy slumber,
> Hate the day that bids me wake,
> Another of that dreary number
> At Camp Douglas by the Lake.

Johnson's Island, Ohio, on the banks of Lake Erie, about three miles from Sandusky, was a prison for Confederate officers, sometimes called "the St. Helena of America." On February 1, 1864, 2,617 men were imprisoned there. Because of its proximity to the water, many of the prisoners contracted pneumonia, and the death toll was high. At one time six Confederate generals were held there, including the famous Missourian "Jeff" Thompson. In *The Prisoner's Lament,* two comrades, one from Missouri (W. D. Clarkson, author of the words) and the other a doctor from Tennessee (D. Becker, the composer), express their aching loneliness:

> My home is on a sea-girt isle,
> Far, far away from thee
> Where thy dear form, thy blissful smile,
> I never, never see.
> I rest beneath a Northern sky,
> A sky to me so drear;
> I think of thee, dear one, and sigh
> Alone upon Lake Erie.
> Alone, alone, alone upon Lake Erie.
>
> The winds that waft to others joy

The Soldier in Battle

But mock me with their breath,
They waft a perfume to destroy,
They sing a song of death.
The waves that dash against the shore
Keep angry watch at night,
They watch beneath my prison door,
Are always in my sight.
Alone, alone, alone upon Lake Erie.

Prisoners literally kept themselves alive by hopes for their liberation. George Root composed a sequel to *Tramp, Tramp, Tramp* and titled it

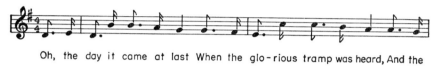

Oh, the day it came at last When the glo-rious tramp was heard, And the

boys came march-ing fif-ty-thou-sand strong; And we grasp'd each oth-er's hands, Tho' we

ut-ter'd not a word As the boom-ing of our can-non roll'd a-long.

On, on, on, the boys came march-ing, Like a grand ma-jes-tic sea, And they

dash'd a-way the guard from the heav-y i-ron door, And we

stood be-neath the star-ry ban-ner, free!

On, On, On, the Boys Came Marching

213

On, On, On, the Boys Came Marching, based on the liberation of Union prisoners by Sherman's army:

Oh, the day it came at last
When the glorious tramp was heard,
And the boys came marching fifty-thousand strong;
And we grasped each other's hand,
Tho' we uttered not a word
As the booming of our cannon rolled along.

CHORUS:
On, on, on, the boys came marching,
Like a grand majestic sea,
And they dashed away the guard from the heavy iron door,
And we stood beneath the starry banner, free!

Oh, the feeblest heart grew strong
And the most despondent sure,
When we heard the thrilling sounds we loved so well,
For we knew that want and woe
We no longer should endure,
When the hosts of freedom reached our prison cell.

Oh, the war is over now
And we're safe at home again,
And the cause we starved and suffered for is won;
But we never can forget
'Mid our woe and 'mid our pain
How the glorious Union men came tramping on!

The same idea was the subject of *The Prisoner's Release; or, The Dear Old Flag Has Come* (words and music by Eastburn, pseudonym of J. E. Winner):

Now the bugle's thrilling blast and the distant cannon's boom,
    As they break upon the hopeful prisoner's ear,
And the marching of the men as with measured tramp they come
    Tell his saddened heart release is drawing near.

Now the heavy bolts are drawn, now the door is open thrown
    And the glowing sunlight gilds the prison floor.
Many faces, pale and wan, many wasted forms are shown
    Weeping tears of joy to see their friends once more.

The story of prison life, treatment of captives, and attempted negotiations for exchange is a long and sorrowful one. Even though both North and South often had difficulty in providing for their own fighting troops, with resultant neglect of the enemy prisoners, treatment of captives could have been much more humane. The death list of over 50,000 men is a sad reflection on the neglect of the commanders responsible for the administration of prisons.

Debate on the treatment of prisoners continued long after the war's end. A flood of memoirs by veterans, who vividly and emotionally described their prison experiences, continued to stir up both hatred and pity, and such stories were capitalized upon by "patriotic" societies seeking pensions. James Truslow Adams called the prison controversy "one of the unhappy legacies of the war."

The battle was indeed "the pay-off." Conservative estimates indicate that over 75 per cent of all soldiers in both armies participated at one time or another in combat. Thus over two million men fought in the 2,261 engagements important enough to be considered battles and in the additional 4,000 skirmishes and minor encounters. Many soldiers took part in scores of major conflicts; thousands served throughout campaigns where battles were continuous occurrences. It was not at all unusual for twenty or thirty thousand troops to be locked in combat at one time and in one place. The frequency of these huge and costly battles made the stories of wounded and dying men ever fresh, and dreaded by the folks at home.

****

CHAPTER 6

****

The Folks at Home

PATRIOTISM AND THE CALL to the colors gave rise to stirring compositions, always martial and sometimes melodious. The glory and heroism of serving one's country were described in hundreds of songs. However, another side of the war was expressed in the music of sorrow, grief, and misery—in songs showing the human element, loneliness, anxiety, and personal emotion of those who stayed at home. Mothers, wives, and sweethearts did not share in the glories of war but, instead, endured the anguish of aching hearts. Sentimental ballads of the period were the expression of these feelings, and the pattern which they followed was a true reflection of the times.

Development of the manufacture of upright pianos in the first half of the nineteenth century had by the 1860's reduced their cost. As a result, ownership of a piano became one of the measures of middle-class financial success. Topped with a fringed silk scarf, it occupied the place of honor in the parlor or "front room," the walls of which were generally lined with family portraits. "Music lessons" became for the first time an accepted part of the family training. After dinner or during an evening of sociability, every young lady of culture and refinement was expected to play or sing for the guests or assembled family. This was the period of the florid musical passage, of the elaborate piano solo with crescendos, arpeggios, and trills; it was also the heyday of the parlor "concert," which included recitations, duets, and quartets. Family or neighborhood groups could usually contribute to a well-balanced and varied program, with all members participating individually in solos and collectively in ensembles.

216

The music with which the parlor performers, both Northern and Southern, entertained in the evenings varied between the two extremes of acute melancholia and spirited, bright marches, quicksteps, polkas, waltzes, and galops. Each military leader and hero and every stirring event was celebrated on the piano. Confederate publishers poured out solos lauding leaders of the moment. Lee and Jackson were particularly favored; the latter was honored by *Stonewall Jackson's Grand March, Stonewall's Victory March, Stonewall Lancer's Quadrille, Stonewall Quickstep,* and the *Jackson Galop,* to name only a few. A general like Beauregard had quicksteps, marches, and quadrilles dedicated to and named for him. Oddly enough, the North rarely celebrated its heroes' fame to this extent, perhaps because the Union generals were not personally loved as were the Confederate leaders.

The various dance compositions for piano were labeled with patriotic titles, all indicative of the feelings of the time. Southerners danced or listened to the strains of the *Secession Quickstep, Stars and Bars Polka, Contraband Schottische, Bonnie Blue Flag Quickstep, Southern Rights March, Volunteer Waltz,* and *Never Surrender Quickstep.* Titles were often dedicated to local or famed military units, like *The Madison Rifle's March, Crescent City Guard's Quickstep, The Washington Artillery Polka,* and *The Bayou City Zouave Quadrille.* Triumphant victories lent their names to compositions like *The Manassas Quickstep* and *The Shiloh Victory Polka.* Unionists, less patriotic in the naming of the music to which they danced, limited themselves to titles such as *The Emancipation Quickstep, Gunboat Quickstep,* and *The Young Recruit Galop.*

The most accomplished and virtuoso pianists performed publicly at the many fund-raising civilian benefits and patriotic entertainments. For these larger audiences, as well as for family groups, special arrangements of beloved songs, such as *The Bonnie Blue Flag* and *The Marseillaise* were particularly effective in the South. Transcriptions of coloratura soprano arias from the Italian operas were in the repertoire of every performer.

One of the most popular types of "show pieces" was the solo descriptive of a particular military event. A piano series widely purchased throughout the North was titled *Pictures of the War.* In these compositions celebrating Union victories, one could hear the roar of the cannons through the many bass and left-hand chords in double fortissimo; the whistling of bullets in the air through arpeggios and glissandos; the advances of troops through stirring march strains; and the lull after the battle through passages played in double pianissimo, with drum and bugle effects.

Florid piano selections included descriptions of the Battle of Roanoke Island, "the story of an eye witness musically portrayed"; the Battle of Shiloh, "musically photographed"; Beauregard's Retreat from Shiloh, "arranged with a running accompaniment"; and The Battle, "descriptive fantasia in three parts—the night before the battle and dreams of home, grand march, and attack and battle."

Confederates purchased a series issued by Werstein and Halsey of New Orleans, musically describing such events as the fall of Fort Sumter, Manassas (First Bull Run), Big Bethel, Stuart's ride, Chancellorsville, Sharpsburg (Antietam), the Merrimac *vs.* the Monitor, and Morgan's Kentucky raids.

In Memory of the Confederate Dead; A Requiem, composed by Jules C. Meininger, included the following descriptive notes:

> The most superficial player will understand that a requiem demands very different treatment from any other composition, but the author thinks it appropriate to give his ideas in composing. The Adagio Solemento, p. 3, conveys the news of a hero's death in the midst of battle; the Largo, pages 4 and 5, suggests the removal of the body off the field; the Pomposo, page 6, the progression to a church or chapel near by; the Religioso, pages 7 and 8, the services at the chapel, with tolling bells and choral lamentation; the Brilliant, page 9, the wild grief on the way to the grave; and the Andante, the lowering of the body into the tomb, and the departure of the people, as the music slowly dies away.

The poetry of this period concerned itself with narratives of the battle-field, appeals to patriotism, verses of commemoration, and demure love lyrics. In many a poem of sentiment, fair maidens were pictured wasting away from strange afflictions, frailty being in vogue as the height of lady-like behavior. Beautiful maidens slept in graves under the spreading branches of willow trees in green and verdant dales, and their tombs became the scenes of pilgrimages by mourning lovers who never forgot their loved ones and who poured out their never lessening grief over the tall grass and weeds choking the graves themselves. These lovers had frequently never recovered from the first numbing grief over the untimely deaths of their sweethearts. Many of the lyrics were borrowed, in form as well as in spirit, from the English, Scottish, and Irish sentimental ballads of the day, since international copyright had not been established.

Ballad writers assiduously set themselves to celebrating the frailties of maidens of every name and nationality. "Bonnie" and "gentle" seemed to fit all creatures celebrated in song and poem. The offerings of one prominent publisher of each region will serve to show the extent of these "name" ballads. A. E. Blackmar and Brothers, the South's leading house, in 1863, listed such titles as *Blanche Alpen, Blue-Eyed Nell, Bonnie Eloise, Bonny Jean, Carrie Bell, Darling Little Nell, Darling Nellie Gray, Gentle Nettie Moore, Katy Darling,* and *Lillie Terrell*. Ditson and Company of Boston, in the same year, listed *Bonny Mary, Gentle Annie Ray, Gentle Bessie, Kathleen Aroon, Katie Lee, Little Nell, Marietta Mine, Minnie Bell, Minnie Dill, Minnie Grey,* and *Vesta Moore*. These imaginary ladies were much beloved and were sung about whenever a sombre and melancholy mood called for such a ballad.

Music of sentiment expressed the culmination of American romanticism. Today the songs seem dated and artificial, yet in their contemporary setting they were moving and genuine. Their acceptance, like musical successes of the present day, proved that literary worth has little connection with popular appeal.

The songs of sentiment as sung by civilians of the 1860's, then, were expressions of their lives. As in all wars, women experienced a well-defined cycle of emotion. They first said good-bye and, in parting, wished son, brother, husband, or sweetheart well. The mother breathed a prayer for her son's safety, the sister promised to care for the mother, and the sweetheart vowed eternal fidelity. As the months passed, the women's loneliness increased, and, overshadowing all, was dread of being notified of wounds or death. Because of the enormous and staggering casualties in dead, missing, and wounded men, the women had good reason for constant anxiety; hence, prayers for safety were many and varied. The loneliness of lovers was expressed in scores of "sweetheart" songs. Over all was the hopelessness of counting upon any future happiness. Sectionalism disappeared in these songs, for geographical boundaries and war aims could not prevail against human feelings.

Many of the departure songs have been included in Chapter III. In most of these, the farewells were marked by an outward display of bravado. But, with the long stretch of loneliness facing them, it was difficult always to be brave. In *The Only Son Is Going Now* (words and music by Mrs. J. S. Reed), a sister realizes that home will be drear without her volunteer brother:

> Tomorrow are you going, dear,
> Oh! how I dread the hour to come
> To say goodbye to one so near,
> 'Tis sad indeed, the only son.
> Our poor aged parents feel so bad
> To part with you, their only lad,
> You who have always lived at home
> And been so good and kind a son.
>
> CHORUS:
> The only son is going now,
>   The only one we had to love,
> Oh, God, on him and us bestow
>   Happiness in the world above.

We Shall Miss You, Dearest Brother (words by Charles Haynes, music by Edward Haynes) follows the same line of thought.

Song writers seem to have considered the partings of sweethearts as most worthy of their attention. The fear that the soldier lover might not return was always present, as in *He Has Gone and I Have Sent Him* (words and music by Madame C. Rive):

> He has gone and I have sent him;
>   Think you I would bid him stay,
> Leaving craven-like to others
>   All the burden of the day?
> All the burden? Nay, the triumph!
>   Is it hard to understand?
> All the joy that thrills the hero
>   Battling for his native land?
>
> He is gone and I have sent him,
>   Not without a thought of pain
> For I know the war's dread chances
>   And we may not meet again.
> Life itself is but a lending
>   He that gave perchance may take
> If it be so, I will bear it
>   Meekly for my country's sake.

The Folks at Home

The sadness of parting was accompanied by flying flags, flashing swords, and marching feet. Each maiden was tearfully proud of *Her Own Brave Volunteer,* to be sung to the tune of the old English song *Soldier's Tear,* by Alexander Lee:

> Beside the road she stood,
>   With dim and tearful eyes,
> And around her rolled the noisy drums
>   And the shouting people's cries.
> She only heard a well-known step,
>   A whisper trembling near,
> But she knew that he was marching by,
>   Her own brave volunteer!
>
> Oh, what to her the glare
>   Of flags and flashing swords?
> Her gentle heart could only feel
>   His last, his farewell words;
> "Kind Heaven," he said, "my darling one,
>   Will guard me there as here,
> And if I fall, remember me,
>   Your own brave volunteer!"
>
> Oh, strong is woman's love
>   And strong her patriot's will;
> Her tears may fall, her heart may break,
>   She loves her country still!
> With such a loyal soul behind,
>   What man could yield to fear?
> What soldier would not live and die
>   Her own brave volunteer?

The Volunteer's Farewell (music by J. A. Butterfield) expresses his grief in departing, but he feels that:

> The memory of those happy days from me can ne'er depart,
> But like a halo its bright rays will linger round my heart.

In the chorus he becomes very brave and says to his loved one:

> Then still the grief within my heart
>   And let us say adieu,

For though we thus are forced to part,
    I oft shall think of you.

In 1863, Stephen Foster composed a ballad which attained a high degree of popularity in music halls. A departing soldier promises to return to his loved one *When This Dreadful War Is Ended* (words by George Cooper):

When this dreadful war is ended,
    I will come again to you,
Tell me, dearest, ere we sever,
    Tell me, tell me, you'll be true.
Though to other scenes I wander,
    Still your mem'ry pure and bright
In my heart will ever linger,
    Shining with undying light;
Do not weep, love, sit beside me,
    Whisper gentle words of cheer,
Be not mournful now, my darling,
    Let me kiss away each tear.

CHORUS:
How happy I will feel if I but know
That you'll contented be.
I'll never, never have one pang of woe,
While you are true to me.

On the gory field of battle
    Your sweet voice will nerve my hand,
And when weary, sad or wounded,
    Your fair image near me stand.
In my visions, like some angel,
    You will turn my grief to bliss;
On my pale and fevered forehead
    I will often feel your kiss.
Our dear native land's in danger
    And we'll calmly bide the time
'Till this dreadful war is over
    And the bells of peace shall chime.

When this dreadful war is ended

222

(Soon I hope the day will come),
Love's own star will lead my footsteps
   Safely back to you and home.
Oh! what joy again to meet you
   When the threat'ning storm is past
And the flag our foes have planted
   Flies in shreds upon the blast.
Farewell! farewell! blest and dearest,
   Do not let your heart repine,
Though the sky may now be gloomy,
   Soon the sun will brightly shine.

Other sweetheart-parting songs were *Then Brush Away Each Dripping Tear; or, Thou Would'st Not Have Me Stay* (words and music by James W. Johnson), *One More Kiss and Then Good-Bye* (words by H. S. Cornwall, music by E. C. Phelps), *The Trumpet of War Now Is Calling* (words by Lieutenant Robert McWade, music by Emile G. Sirret), *Wait Love, Until the War Is Over* (words and music by T. M. Todd), and *The Parting; or, The Soldier's Farewell* (words and music by Dr. William J. Wetmore).

A unique song by Stephen Foster—unique because the melody is more lilting and the lyric more amusing than most of his ballads—shows how Norah trapped her Larry into marriage as he said farewell in *Larry's Good-bye* (words by George Cooper):

Brave Larry went up to his darling,
   To bid her a speedy good-bye,
When bound where the cannon was snarling,
   The fortunes of battle to try.
Sweet Norah, he said, don't be weeping,
   I soon will come back to your side,
With all your fond love in my keeping;
   And make you my beautiful bride, Norah,
   And make you my beautiful bride.

A thousand times Larry did kiss her,
   Before he was willing to go,
For now he just felt how he'd miss her
   When fronting the ranks of the foe.
My heart will be ever the same, dear,

So Norah, he whispered, don't sigh,
  I soon will have money and fame, dear,
    And then a nice farm we will buy.

Fair Norah through teardrops was blushing
    And spoke between sobbings and sighs,
As backward her glossy curls pushing,
    She timidly looked in his eyes.
Dear Larry, you say that you're going
    To wed when you come home from the war,
I'm afraid you'll be killed, there's no knowing,
    Now could we not marry before?
    Now could we not marry before?

Now Larry, how could he refuse her?
    He saw that he might as well wed,
For if he was killed he would lose her,
    So unto fair Norah he said:
Mavourneen, it's true you've been saying,
    And where there's a will there's a way.
I see there's no use in delaying,
    I'll wed you this very same day.

Once the excitement of departure was over, the agony of waiting commenced. Letters from the camps and bivouacs were few and far between, and receipt of the scraps of paper only increased the pain of separation. By far the most popular sweetheart "separation" song in both the North and the South was *Weeping, Sad and Lonely,* sometimes called *When This Cruel War Is Over,* a ballad so mournful that generals were forced to forbid their troops to sing it, yet so popular that its sale approached a million copies, uncommon in those days. Its rhythm is that of the typical ballad, and the chorus is perfectly adapted to male quartet singing. Almost equally popular in the South, it was without question the most appealing and touching of the many sentimental ballads of the war years. The song was sung by Southerners with substitutions of certain words in the first verse—"gray" for "blue" in the sixth line and "ne'er go astray" for "ever to be true" in the eighth line. The fourth verse, with its reference to the stars and stripes, was omitted by Confederates, and a verse referring to Southern boys was substituted. If any single song may be said to have expressed the emotions of millions in the 1860's, it was *Weep-*

ing, Sad and Lonely, "subscribed to the sorrowing hearts at home" (words by Charles Carroll Sawyer, music by Henry Tucker):

Dearest love, do you remember
When we last did meet?
How you told me that you loved me,
Kneeling at my feet?
Oh, how proud you stood before me
In your suit of blue (gray)
When you vowed to me and country
Ever to be true. (ne'er to go astray)

CHORUS:

Weeping, sad and lonely, Hopes and fears how vain!
When this cruel war is over, Praying that we meet again!

If amid the din of battle,
Nobly you should fall,
Far away from those who love you,
None to hear you call.
Who would whisper words of comfort,
Who would soothe your pain?
Ah! and many cruel fancies
Ever in my brain.

When the summer breeze is sighing
Mournfully along;
Or when autumn leaves are falling,
Sadly breathes the song.
Oft in dreams I see thee lying
On the battle-plain,
Lonely, wounded, even dying,
Calling, but in vain.

But our country called you, darling,
Angels cheer your way;
While our nation's sons are fighting,
We can only pray.
Nobly strike for God and liberty,
Let all nations see
How we love the starry banner,
Emblem of the free.

[*Southern version of above verse*]
But our country called you, loved one;
Angels guide your way;
While our "Southern boys" are fighting,
We can only pray.
When you strike for God and freedom,
Let all nations see
How you love our Southern banner,
Emblem of the free.

In the companion song *I Remember the Hour* (words by Charles Carroll Sawyer, music by G. F. Thompson), which is neither poetically nor musically as appealing, the soldier lover assures the flower of his heart that he remembers those vows mentioned in the first verse of the previous song:

I remember the hour when sadly we parted,
The tears on your pale cheek glist'ning like dew,
When clasped in your arms almost broken-hearted,
I swore by the bright sky I'd ever be true.
     True to the love that nothing could sever,
     And true to the flag of my country forever.

CHORUS:
Then weep not, love, oh, weep not!
Think not our hopes are vain,
For when this fatal war is over
We will surely meet again.

The replies to this song were many, each expressing the same hope for the future. A Union *When This War Is Over I Will Come Back to Thee* (words by M. A. Geuville, music by Ferdinand Mayer) echoed the hope of an eventual return in answer to the beloved's prayer:

Peace, peace, to thee, loved one,
     Thy prayers will answer'd be;
For when this war is over
     I will come back to thee.

Alice Hawthorne (pseudonym of Septimus Winner) answered in *Yes, I Would the War Were Over*:

Yes, I would the war were over,
    Would the cruel work were done,
With our country re-united
    And the many states in one.

Another Northerner, Lieutenant Sherman Greig, in *Yes, Darling, Sadly I Remember,* urged:

Country still to us doth call, love,
    Fight we still nor ask the why;
Weep for those that fear to fall, love,
    But smile for those that die.

But not all the answers expressed optimistic hope for a reunion; the more realistic in tone expressed pessimism regarding the possibility of any future earthly meeting, as in a Southern *Answer to When This Cruel War Is Over* (words by John H. Hewitt, music by Hermann L. Schreiner), titled *When Upon the Field of Glory:*

When upon the field of glory,
    'Mid the battle cry,
And the smoke of cannon curling
    Round the mountain high;
Then sweet mem'ries will come o'er me,
    Painting home and thee . . .
Nerving me to deeds of daring,
    Struggling to be free.

CHORUS:
Weep no longer, dearest,
Tears are now in vain.
When this cruel war is over,
In Heav'n we'll meet again.

When the bullet swiftly flying
    Thro' the murky air,
Hits its mark, my sorrowed bosom,
    Leaving death's pang there;
Then my thoughts on thee will turn, love,
    While I prostrate lie.

227

My pale lips shall breathe "God bless thee—
For our cause I die!"

When up-on the field of glo - ry, 'Mid the bat - tle cry,

And the smoke of can-non curl - ing Round the moun-tain high;

Then sweet mem-'ries will come o'er me, Paint-ing home and thee...

Nerv-ing me to deeds of dar - ing, Strug-gling to be free.

Chorus

Weep no long-er, dear - est, Tears are now in vain.——

When this cru-el war is o - ver, In Heav'n we'll meet a-gain.

When Upon the Field of Glory

All sweethearts were sad and lonely. The girl in *Johnny Is Gone for a Soldier* (words and music by Septimus Winner) was full of tears:

I trace these gardens o'er and o'er
And meditate on each sweet flower,
Thinking of each happy hour.
Oh, Johnny is gone for a soldier.

I wish I was on yonder hill,
For there I'd sit and cry my fill
So every tear might turn a mill.
Oh, Johnny is gone for a soldier.

Willie's loved one, in *Willie Has Gone to the War* (words by George Cooper, music by Stephen C. Foster), in her wanderings through the meadows and woods, is continually reminded that he is gone; the bluebird, the wild bee, the brook, and the flowers all tell the same story:

The bluebird is singing his lay
    To all the sweet flow'rs of the dale,
The wild bee is roaming at play,
    And soft is the sigh of the gale;
I stray by the brookside alone,
    Where oft we have wandered before,
And weep for my lov'd one, my own,
    My Willie has gone to the war!

CHORUS:
Willie has gone to the war, Willie,
Willie, my loved one, my own;
Willie has gone to the war, Willie,
Willie, my lov'd one, is gone!

The sweetheart in *Oh, I Wish This War Was Over* (words and music by Will S. Hays) expressed the feelings of all maidens who hoped for the return of their soldier lovers:

My Johnny's in the army and never has been slain!
And once he came to see me but he went back again.
And often have I missed him and sighed for him to come.
Oh, I wish this war was over and my Johnny would come home!

CHORUS:
Why don't they cease their fighting
And stop the fife and drum!
Oh, I wish the war was over
And my Johnny would come home!

Oh, won't we girls be happy when all the boys are free!
And peace is in the country, our sweethearts then to see!

Oh, won't I run to meet him, no more from me to roam!
Oh, I wish this war was over and my Johnny would come home!

The girl in *Oh, I Wish the War Were Over* (words by John K. Holmes, music by Charles Manvers) expressed this typical thought:

Oh, I wish the war were over,
    And my lover would return,
For this long and weary waiting,
    Is a lesson hard to learn.
When I call to mind the heroes sleeping
    Where the field was won,
All my fears and tears are mingled
    Lest he will not, will not, come.

In *The Soldier's Wife; or, The Brave Deserve the Fair* (words by Lieutenant Colonel Addison, music by George Barker), the impoverished father whose son had been rejected by his sweetheart's wealthy parents read that his boy had been valorous in battle and would thus be able to obtain favor. Several other sweetheart songs were *My Love Is on the Battlefield* (words by Robert Morris, music by Alfred Delaney), *Soon This Weary War'll Be Over* (words and music by Henry Fontrill), *My Jamie's on the Battlefield* (words by Mrs. M. A. Kidder, music by Mrs. E. A. Parkhurst), and *When Will He Come Back to Me?* (words and music by Henry C. Watson).

Wives, of course, were not immune to the ever prevailing loneliness. In *Baby Sleep, Shadows Creep: Cradle Song of the Soldier's Wife* (words by Helen Cowper Elliott, music by Theodore T. Barker), the mother crooned to her baby:

Where the campfires gleam and quiver,
Far away beside the river,
Father thinks of thee, I know, I know.

The wife in *Out in this Terrible War* (words by Mary W. Janvrin, music by H. T. Merrill) mused:

I am alone by the hearthstone,
    But my heart goes roving afar,

Counting over its treasures,
   Out in this terrible war.

Two wives were proud of their husbands and wished them back, in spite of their shortcomings. In *Oh, Send My Old Man Home Again* (words by Mattie Bell, music by Herman Knake), the wife missed her husband:

Oh, send my old man back again
His home is lonely now.
I miss his dear old freckled face,
His smooth and shining brow.
I long to hear his heavy tread;
Oh dear, when shall I see
His noble form walk in the door
With a patch upon his knee?

CHORUS:
Oh, send him home to me, I pray,
   I'll check the falling tear.
All dark and dreary seems the world
   Without my old man here!

I miss his dear and hearty kiss
When he comes from the shop
With his old hat back of his head
With the button on the top.
And evening, when we'd try to sing
So loudly would he shout
The dear man could not sing a note,
He always put me out.

The wife in *Oh, My Old Man Has Gone to the War* (composed by a war widow) thought her husband would end up as a brigadier, though he began service as a substitute private:

Oh, my old man has gone to war,
He's gone and left me here.
Oh, my old man has gone to war
For to be a brigadier.
With a fife and a drum and a sergeant bold
I saw him march away.

He's gone to fight for a substitute
'Way down in Georg-i-a.

If he gets shot to death some day,
A widow I will be.
I'll wrap myself in a winding sheet
And live in a nun-ne-ree.
He'll haunt my bed in an ambulance
Like a goblin fusileer
Oh, my old man has gone to war
For to be a brigadier.

Mothers, too, felt the aching void of their sons' absences. Many a
mother was saying, *I Dreamed My Boy Was Home Again* (words and
music by Charles Carroll Sawyer):

Lonely, weary, broken-hearted,
    As I laid me down to sleep,
Thinking of the day we parted,
    When you told me not to weep.
Soon I dreamed that peaceful angels
    Hovered o'er the battle plain,
Singing songs of joy and gladness
    And my boy was home again.

CHORUS:
How well I know such thoughts of joy,
Such dreams of bliss are vain;
My heart is sad, my tears will flow
Until my boy is home again.

But the dream is past and with it
    All my happiness is gone;
Cheerful thoughts of joy have vanished,
    I must still in sorrow mourn.
Soon may peace with all its blessings
    Our unhappy land reclaim;
Then my tears will cease their flowing
    And my boy be home again.

Other mothers were lonely in *On Such a Night as This* (words by
L. Hattie S. Aldrich, music by William S. Pitts), *Poor Mother, Willie's*

The Folks at Home

Gone (words and music by Theodore F. Seward), *When Will My Darling Boy Return?* (words by E. S. Kellog, music by T. Martin Towne), and *Mother, When the War Is Over* (words and music by J. W. Turner).

Fathers came in for their share of attention in *Our Veteran Fathers* (words by James Kingsley, music by N. B. W.):

We are thinking tonight of our fathers so dear
    Far away on the dread battlefield,
And wish we could cheer their campfire so drear,
    But that wish we cannot yield.
We'll look and pray for their speedy return,
Then how happy and joyous we'll be!
Then the war will be ended and love's altar burn
    With the incense of sweet Liberty!

A brother was sorely missed by his sister in *Brother, When Will You Come Back?* (words and music by E. W. Locke):

The cold winds of winter sweep down from the hills,
With wailing more dismal than ever before;
We think of the blast that our soldier boy chills,
And sigh to divide him our basket and store.
We know that but little he heeds his hard lot,
His long weary marches, his coarse scanty fare;
The cannon's loud thunder, the death-dealing shot,
But nerve him to suffer, to do and to dare.

CHORUS:
Brother, dear brother! When will you come back—
Back to the hearts ever loving and true?
    While our campfires are burning
    Our fond hearts are yearning.
Brother! we're praying for you.

"The soldier's thoughts, like a carrier dove, to his own loved home return," said *The Girls At Home* (words and music by Henry C. Work). Thoughts from home, wafted far away, were received by the fighting man wherever he might be. *Never Forget the Dear Ones* (words and music by George F. Root), admonished one soldier:

Ever their hearts are turning to thee when far away;
Their love, so pure and tender, goes with thee on thy way
In camp or field or fortress or 'mid the ocean's foam.
Never forget the dear ones that cluster round thy home.

Another soldier reminded his comrades that *They Pray for Us at Home* (words by Ednor Rossiter, music by B. Frank Walters):

They pray for us at home, at morning's early light,
They pray for us at noon, and in the silent night.

Servicemen recognized the grief at home, lamenting that *At Home Our Friends Are Dying* (words by Virginia Rhodes Moser, music by Colonel W. J. Landram):

There, the wife and mother, sister, children dear,
Bear alone their sorrow, shed unchecked the tear.
'Tis there they pine in sadness beneath their pain and care;
At home they're slowly dying and we, alas, not there.

Assurance that the soldier's thoughts turned homeward was given in *The Soldier's Loved Ones* (words by W. W. Montgomery, music by J. Henry Whittemore)—"Loved ones, oft he thinks of thee at home"—and in the Confederate *Yes, We Think of Thee at Home* (words by John H. Hewitt, music by E. Clarke Ilsley).

Those at home, in addition to their regular duties, made socks and uniforms for their men, as their small contribution to the cause. *The Knitting Song* (words and music by Albert M. Hubbard) was dedicated to the patriotic ladies of the North and indicated that each click of the needles was a prayer:

Knit, knit, knit for our Northern soldiers brave,
    Knit, knit, knit, while the stars and stripes they wave;
While they the rebels in battle meet
    Be yours to fashion with fingers fleet
The nice warm socks for the weary feet.
    Knit, knit, knit!

CHORUS:
For our boys on Southern hills,

234

Our boys in Southern vales
By the woods and streams of Dixie's land
Are feeling the wintry gales.

Knit, knit, knit, narrow and widen the seam
Knit, knit, knit, 'till the flying needles gleam;
Knit 'till the mitten lies complete
Knit 'till the socks for the weary feet
The eye of each patient soldier greet.
Knit, knit, knit.

And those *Picking Lint* (words and music by J. W. Barker) thought of
the heroes and worked even harder:

Plying the busy fingers over the vestments old
Not with the weary needle, not for some grains of gold.
Thinking of fading heroes out in the dreary night,
Smitten in freedom's battle, first in the gallant fight.
Oh, bright are the jewels from love's deep mint!
God bless the fingers while picking the lint.

Quicker the blood is flowing, hundreds were slain today,
And every warm pulsation is stealing life away.
A hundred threads a minute, a hundred drops of gore,
The sad and thrilling measure we never learned before.
The shadows are weaving a silver tint,
God bless the fingers while picking the lint.

The threads of linen and cotton, broken into small pieces, were used as
bandages.

But even perils of war could not prevent the singing of love ballads.
Subjects of genuine love songs were far removed from the smoke of the
battlefield. Perhaps sung more than any other was *Lorena*. The Northern
author, Rev. H. D. L. Webster, a Massachusetts Universalist preacher, had
been disappointed in love some years before; and his poem, written in
1857, was the expression of his broken heart. The object of his affection,
Lorena, refused to starve on a preacher's salary and subsequently married
a lawyer who later became chief justice in Ohio. The extent of his devotion is realized when one reads that the lover had not even seen Lorena
for one hundred months. The music was composed by the author's brother,

Joseph P. Webster, who was later to write the music of the hymn *Sweet By and By* and of many war songs. The complete song contains six verses.

> The years creep slowly by, Lorena;
>   The snow is on the grass again;
> The sun's low down the sky, Lorena,
>   The frost gleams where the flowers have been.
> But the heart throbs on as warmly now
>   As when the summer days were nigh,
> Oh! the sun can never dip so low
>   Adown affection's cloudless sky.
>
> A hundred months have passed, Lorena,
>   Since last I held that hand in mine,
> And felt the pulse beat fast, Lorena,
>   Though mine beat faster far than thine.
> A hundred months—'twas flow'ry May
>   When up the hilly slope we climbed,
> To watch the dying of the day
>   And hear the distant churchbells chime.
>
> We loved each other then, Lorena,
>   More than we ever dared to tell;
> And what we might have been, Lorena,
>   Had but our loving prospered well!
> But then, 'tis past; the years have gone,
>   I'll not call upon their shadowy forms;
> I'll say to them, lost years, sleep on,
>   Sleep on, nor heed life's pelting storms.

As an author and composer team, they also published *Paul Vane; or, Lorena's Reply,* in which the lady admitted that the years were creeping slowly by, but that the memory of the old-time love was still sweet to her and made summer in her heart:

> The years are creeping slowly by, dear Paul,
>   The winters come and go;
> The wind sweeps past with mournful cry, dear Paul,
>   And pelts my face with snow;
> But there's no snow upon the heart, dear Paul,
>   'Tis summer always there,

Those early loves throw sunshine over all,
   And sweeten memories dear.

I've kept you ever in my heart, dear Paul,
   Thro' years of good and ill;
Our souls could not be torn apart, dear Paul,
   They're bound together still.
I never knew how dear you were to me,
   'Till I was left alone;
I thought my poor heart would break the day
   They told me you were gone.

Almost as popular, and expressing similar sentiments, was a song titled *Imogen* written and composed by General J. B. Magruder, dapper Confederate commander of Texas, who was called "Prince John." It was unique in glorifying a wife rather than the usual sweetheart:

CHORUS:
Then fear not, my Imogen, thou'rt dearer than life!
The heart of the soldier is the home of the wife, Imogen.

Thy steed is impatient his mistress to bear, Imogen,
Home to her lover on the prairie afar, Imogen,
Belov'd as a maiden, adored as a wife,
Thou shalt be forever the star of my life.

When a poem attained some popularity, it was not unusual for different publishers to issue the same music with variations of the original words. One very popular Confederate love ballad, *Wait 'till the War, Love, Is Over* (music by J. W. Burton), had two versions—one by A. J. Andrews, the other by Paul Mordaunt:

'Twas gentle spring, the flowers were bright,
The bird's sweet song was lovely;
I wandered in the moon's pale light
With the maid I loved so dearly.
Her face was fair with smiles to me,
With joy my heart ran over,
To hear her sweet voice say to me,
"Wait 'till the war, love, is over."

237

Three other Confederate love songs were *Dreaming of Thee* (words by John D. Bruns, music by John H. Hewitt), *I Am Dreaming Still of Thee* (words and music by Frederick Buckley), and *Her Bright Smile Haunts Me Still* (words by Joseph E. Carpenter, music by William T. Wrighton).

Unattached maidens at home felt that to marry a soldier was the greatest of all possible good fortune, and the uniform continued to dazzle most young girls. The soldier was the only man to marry, and the girl should wait, if necessary, affirmed *We Are the Gay and Happy Suckers of the State of Illinois* (words and music by J. P. Webster):

Those at home, be gay and happy,
    Show that you have woman's pride,
Never wed a homesick coward,
    Wait and be a soldier's bride.

Gay and happy, sweet they answer,
    None but fools will marry now;
Valiant men have all enlisted,
    Unto cowards we'll not bow.

We're the girls that's gay and happy,
    Waiting for the end of strife;
Rather share a soldier's ration
    Than to be a coward's wife.

For the gay and for the happy
    We're as constant as the dove,
But the man who dares not soldier
    Ne'er can obtain our love.

One mother, in *Shoulder Straps; or, Love versus Greenbacks* (words by G. Douglas Brewerton, music by Mrs. Fannie Brewerton), explained the meaning of the varied insignia to her marriageable daughter:

Now listen, my daughter, and wisely take heed;
The income and strap of a beau are agreed.
Though you dance with a leaf and flirt with a bar,
Reserve your best smile for the eagle and star.

A second lieutenant, she continued, might still be in debt for the clothes he wore out as a West Point Cadet. The first lieutenant had a small pension; the captain received better pay and rations. A major had golden leaves; but the lieutenant colonel had silver. Finally, the colonel:

> Then over the forest and 'neath the bright stars,
> The eagle soars lord of the leaves and the bars.

But the general is, above all, the best:

> To catch some old General, then make him afraid,
> You won't be the first to command a brigade!

The daughter, after listening, decided rank was not important, and said:

> I've heard you, dear mother, and thought it all o'er;
> My heart's with the lover who went to the war;
> You know the poor boy has not even a bar,
> But I'd rather be his than the bride of a star!

A gay and light song (words by Thomas Haynes Bayly) was published in the South as *The Captain with His Whiskers* (music by G. L. Peticolas) and in the North as *The Captain's Sly Glance, and Oh, They Marched Through the Town* (music by William J. Wetmore, with another Union version set to music by Guillaume Gervaise under the title *The Captain*):

> As they marched thro' the town, with their banners so gay,
> I ran to the window to hear the band play.
> I peeped thro' the blinds very cautiously then
> Lest the neighbors should say I was looking at the men.
> Oh! I heard the drums beat and the music so sweet,
> But my eyes at the time caught a much greater treat.
> The troops were the finest I ever did see,
> And the Captain with the whiskers took a slight glance at me.
>
> We met at the ball; I of course thought 'twas right
> To pretend that we never had met 'till that night.
> But he knew me at once I perceived by his glance,
> And I hung down my head when he asked me to dance.

Oh, he sat by my side at the end of the set
And the sweet words he spoke I shall never forget.
For my heart was enlisted and could not get free
As the Captain with his whiskers took a sly glance at me.

But he marched from the town and I saw him no more,
Yet I think of him oft and the whiskers he wore.
I dream all the night and I talk all the day
Of the love of a Captain who went far away.
I remember with superabundant delight
When we met in the street and we danced all the night,
And keep in my mind how my heart jumped with glee
As the Captain with his whiskers took a sly glance at me.

But there's hope—for a friend just ten minutes ago
Said the Captain's returned from the war, and I know
He'll be searching for me with considerable zest
And when I am found—but, oh, you know the rest!
Perhaps he is here, let me look 'round the house,
Keep still every one of you, still as a mouse!
For if the dear creature is here, he will be
With his whiskers a-taking a sly glance at me.

One girl looked forward to the time *When My Soldier Is Married to Me* (words and music by Addie Livingstone):

He says at the sound of the drum
    He must leave me and hurry away;
But I wish that the time it was done
    He would live upon love and half pay.
Promotion is certain, he vowed,
    But the thought must the bravest alarm
To think that she does get a spouse
    That is minus a leg or an arm.
Still while there are stars in the sky
    My love says he faithful will be,
And crosses will come bye and bye
    When my soldier is married to me!

In both the North and the South, lonely families and sweethearts—aware of the precarious lives their boys were living, ever dreading the receipt of bad news, always wondering where their loved ones were resting or fighting, and not knowing whether at any moment they had perhaps fallen and were already dead—could only pray for God's protection. The "aching void in every heart" was expressed musically by sisters, sweethearts, and mothers; these are the songs of deepest sincerity and feeling.

Mothers seemed to bear the brunt of loneliness, always praying for the safety and protection of their sons. Though one mother seldom knew where her son marched—his earthly toil might be over—she still stoutly prayed, *God Bless My Boy Tonight* (words by Thomas H. Rodgers, music by H. Lovegrove):

Two years ago he marched away,
    The war light glittering in his eye;
No terror shook his soul that day,
    No faltering marked his brief goodbye;
He promised then to think of me
    Whene'er he saw the moon's pale light.
May all good angels hold him free
    From harm: God bless my boy tonight!

CHORUS:
O, breeze that fans my throbbing brow,
O, birds that fade in noiseless flight,
Speed, speed and whisper to him now
These words: God bless my boy tonight!

There was no way of knowing what was happening, according to *Our Brave Boys in Blue* (words and music by William S. Pitts):

Far from their homes tonight, mother dear,
    Many a brave boy is sad;
Within the prison cell lonely, sad and drear
    With no one to cheer or make them glad.
But mother, we can pray for the brave boys tonight,
    Our heroes noble and true,
That morning, noon and night God will hear their cries
    And save the brave boys in blue.

One mother prayed thus for her son in battle (*A Mother's Prayer,* words and music by Otto Sutro):

Father! in the battle fray, shelter his dear head, I pray,
Nerve his young arm with the might of justice, liberty and right.
Where the red hail deadliest falls, where stern duty loudly calls,
Where the strife is fierce and wild, Father, guard, oh, guard my child.

Often in my troubled sleep, waking, wearily to weep,
Often dreaming he is near, calming every anxious fear—
Often startled by the flash of hostile swords that meet and clash,
'Til the cannon's smoke and roar hide him from my eyes once more.

The all-pervading hopelessness was expressed in *Our Boy Is a Warrior Now* (words and music by E. G. B. Holder):

Will this dread strife never end
    'Twixt brothers dear and kindred so near?
Will our hearts ne'er cease to ache
    With cruel doubts and anxious fear
For brave hearts who have left their homes
    Who have forsaken the pen and the plow
To fight for country and her rights
    With our boy that's a warrior now?

I Cannot Bid Thee Go, My Boy (words by Josie, music by E. G. B. Holder) defines woman's role at home:

Our task should be to cheer them on
    In duty's rugged road,
In humble faith to pray for them
    And ask the care of God
On husbands, fathers, brothers, sons
    Who nobly in the fight
Beneath their own loved starry flag
    Are battling for the right.

Other mothers' prayers were *No, I'll Not Forget You, Darling*, an answer to *Just Before the Battle, Mother* (words by Ella, music by S. Wesley Martin); *We May Meet Again in Gladness* (words and music by E. A. Samuels); and *The Patriot Mother's Prayer: "Protect My Boy"* (words and music by J. P. Webster).

Families gathered round the fireside, "even though it be summer time, forgetting the midnight chime," and talk of their heroic lads was marked by a fear of impending tragedy, for many brave boys must fall, asserted *Brave Boys Are They* (words and music by Henry C. Work), which was dedicated "to the sisters of our volunteers":

Heavily falls the rain;
  Wild are the breezes tonight;
But 'neath the roof, the hours as they fly
  Are happy and calm and bright.
Gathering 'round our fireside,
  Tho' it be summer time,
We sit and talk of brothers abroad,
  Forgetting the midnight chime.

CHORUS:
Brave boys are they!
Gone at their country's call;
And yet, and yet, we cannot forget
That many brave boys must fall.

May the bright wings of love
  Guard them wherever they roam;
The time has come when brothers must fight,
  And sisters pray at home.
Oh! the dread field of battle
  Soon to be strewn with graves!
If brothers fall, then bury them where
  Our banner in triumph waves.

Northern maids sitting by their cottage doors at twilight had heavy and desolate hearts as they prayed and sang the *Vesper Song for Our Volunteers' Sisters* (words and music by R. Stewart Taylor):

We are sitting by the cottage door, brother,
  In the hush of the twilight's spell;
We are gathered as in days of yore, brother,
  With a song bidding day farewell.
But there's a vacant place in our circle so dear,
  And our song has lost its wanton glee;
And there's an aching void in every heart, brother,
  As we murmur a prayer for thee.

In *Pray Maiden, Pray* (words by A. W. Kercheval, music by A. J. Turner), a Southern girl prays for the safety of her loved one on the eve of battle:

Maiden, pray for thy lover now,
 Thro' all this starry night,
Heaven prove auspicious to thy vow,
 For with tomorrow's dawning light
We meet the foe in deadly fight.
 Pray, maiden pray!

for the banner which "foeman's shot and steel defy," for victory on the morrow when the Southern cross may wave "in triumph floating o'er the brave who strike for freedom or the grave," and for the eventual successful end of the war "to win our glorious fight for home, for freedom and the right." A Confederate sister cries, *Oh, Bring My Brother Back to Me* (words and music by C. Nordendorf):

Bring back, bring back, I pray,
When our fair South is free,
My own, my darling brother,
Oh, bring him back to me!

A sister, no more hearing her brother's step at the gate but thinking of his "smiling healthful glee," prayed, *Bring My Brother Back to Me* (words by George Cooper, music by Stephen C. Foster):

Bring my brother back to me,
 When this war is done,
Give us all the joys we shared
 Ere it had begun.
O, bring my brother back to me
 Never more to stray.
This is all my earnest prayer
 Thro' the weary day.

All the house is lonely now,
 And my voice no more
In the pleasant summer eves
 Greets him at the door.

Never more I hear his step
  By the garden gate,
While I sit in anxious tears
  Knowing not his fate.

The *Song of Our Country's Daughters* (words by Miss M. E. Blair, music by E. Millet) expressed well the common feeling of the home folks:

Oh, brothers, brave and tender;
  Oh, fathers, strong and true
In all the battle's storm and splendor,
  All our hearts go forth to you.

Other prayers for the soldier boys were *God Grant Our Soldier's Safe Return* (words and music by Ossian E. Dodge), *The Blue-eyed Soldier Boy* (words by Jennie Caulfield, music by Herman Knake), and *A Prayer for the Absent* (words by Helene Osgood, music by J. Gaspard Maeder).

In the early years of the war, regular furloughs were given to the soldiers of both forces, particularly after battles or between major campaigns. These rest periods were to be considered borrowed time, for the soldier must always return to the fight, perhaps never again to visit his home. But while he was in the family circle, joyfulness, bliss, and tranquillity reigned in *The Soldier's Home* (words by George Cooper, music by Stephen C. Foster):

The weary soldier reaches home at pleasant eventide,
He fondly kisses those he loves, all gathering by his side;
His gentle wife is ling'ring near, his boy is on his knee,
Beguiling evening's tranquil joys with childhood's prattling glee.

CHORUS:
How happy is the soldier to be once more at home!
But sorrow falls on those he loves when parting time has come.

The joy of being in the home circle was expressed in *Home on Furlough* (words by Hattie S. Aldrich, music by William S. Pitts):

Here back in dear New England and in my home once more,
Beside me is my dearest, my darling Leonore;

THE SINGING SIXTIES

I hear her joyous laughter, her footsteps as of yore,
I hear her blithe voice singing the olden songs once more.
I hear the prelude straying to echo 'mid the trees,
I see her fingers playing the old piano keys.

The soldier on leave was showered with honors, kindnesses, and attentions. Although he was sometimes asked to relate tales of bloodshed out of mere curiosity, more often the questioner wanted to understand the hardship which the loved one had undergone. To her brother, who had been reported dead and whom she thought never to see again, a sister directs the request *Brother, Tell Me Of the Battle* (words by Thomas Manahan, music by George F. Root):

Brother, tell me of the battle,
How the soldiers fought and fell;
Tell me of the weary marches,
She who loves will listen well.
Brother, draw thee close beside me,
Lay your head upon my breast;
While you're telling of the battle
Let your fevered forehead rest.

Brother, tell me of the battle,
I can bear to hear it now;
Lay your head upon my bosom,
Let me soothe your fevered brow.
Tell me, are you badly wounded?
Did we win the deadly fight?
Did the vict'ry crown our banner?
Did you put the foe to flight?

Neighbors would attempt to glean possible news of relatives from those soldiers who were at home: Had they seen them? Were they wounded? Or slain? How did they behave in battle? Any bit of information was welcome. A distracted and careworn sister asks "a weary soldier from the rude and stirring wars," *Was My Brother in the Battle?* (words and music by Stephen C. Foster):

Tell me, tell me, weary soldier from the rude and stirring wars,
Was my brother in the battle where you gained those noble scars?
He was ever brave and valiant, and I know he never fled:

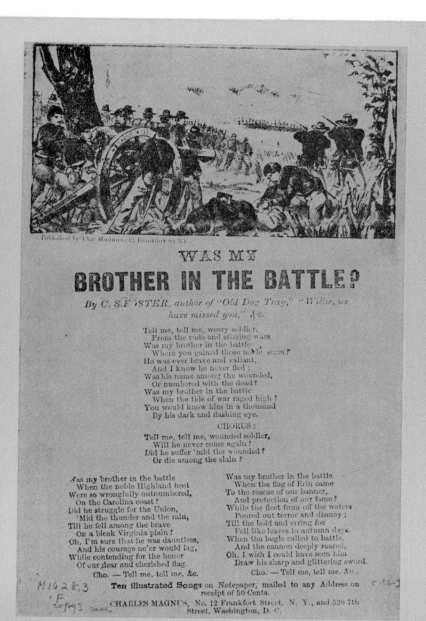

The lyrics of many of the most popular Civil War songs were printed on cheap paper broadsides selling for a penny. If an illustration was used, the paper was of a better quality and the price became five cents.

Was his name among the wounded or numbered with the dead?
Was my brother in the battle when the tide of war ran high?
You would know him in a thousand by his dark and flashing eye.
Tell me, tell me, weary soldier, will he never come again,
Did he suffer 'mid the wounded or die among the slain?

In *Tell Me of My Darling Boy* (words and music by Harry Buckline),
one mother wanted to know how her son was faring. Another had a son
who was evidently a practical joker, and since he was completely changed
in appearance—"bronzed, tanned and bearded"—he decided to capitalize
on the fact that his mother failed to recognize him when she, thinking
him a stranger, cried, *Oh, Come You from the Battlefield?* (words and
music by George F. Root):

MOTHER:
"O, come you from the battlefield, and soldier can you tell
About the gallant twentieth and who are safe and well?
Oh, soldier! say my son is safe, for he is all my care,
And you shall have a mother's thanks, a widowed mother's prayer."

SOLDIER:
"Oh, I've come from the battlefield, I've come right from the war,
And well I know the Twentieth, and gallant lads all there.
From colonel down to rank and file, I know my comrades well,
And news I've brought for you, good dame, your Robert bade me tell."

He tells her a tall tale of her son's heroism, resulting in a medal and a
pension, and of how often he spoke of her. When she asked if he would
be home soon, he said, "Did you say soon? Well, he is home, keep cool,
old dame, he's here!" and revealed himself.

The unpleasant task of breaking the news of death to a family often
fell to soldier friends from the same town; often this obligation included
a description of the conditions of death and the delivering of the soldier's
farewell message, as in *Dear Mother, the Battle Is Over* (words and music
by Henry Fontrill):

Dear mother, the battle is over,
    We've buried our dead where they fell;
The hardest of duties is finished,
    And now I've a sad tale to tell.
Dear mother, your heart will be breaking

With grief, for the spirit that's fled.
Oh, mother, God help you to bear it,
 For Willie, your darling, is dead!

CHORUS:
He will no more hear the sound of battle,
For he's singing with the angels now;
And flowers immortal are twining
In beauty around his fair brow.

Not all home-comings were happy. The wounded soldier's most frequent request was that he be sent home to die surrounded by his family. Many were the men maimed, diseased, or broken in health who returned to pass their remaining days (or, more tragically, long endless years) with their families, where they would receive loving care. One such soldier returned in *Brother's Fainting at the Door* (words by E. Bowers, music by P. B. Isaacs):

Yonder comes a weary soldier,
 With falt'ring steps across the moor;
Memories of the past steal o'er me,
 He totters to the cottage door.
Look, my heart cannot deceive me!
 'Tis one we deemed on earth no more.
Call mother, haste, do not tarry,
 For brother's fainting at the door.

CHORUS:
Kindly greet the weary soldier, words of comfort may restore;
You may have an absent brother, fainting at a stranger's door.

One delirious dying soldier did not realize that "one short year would crush the hopes that soared so high" and that he would be broken in spirit and body as he returned, saying, *Dear Mother, I've Come Home to Die* (words by E. Bowers, music by Henry Tucker), published in both North and South:

Dear mother, I remember well
 The parting kiss you gave me,
When merry rang the village bell,
 My heart was full of joy and glee;

249

I did not dream that one short year
   Would crush the hopes that soared so high!
Oh, mother dear, draw near to me,
   Dear mother, I've come home to die.

CHORUS:
Call sister, brother, to my side,
And take your soldier's last good-bye.
Oh, mother dear, draw near to me;
Dear mother, I've come home to die.

His mother welcomed him in a reply titled *My Boy, How Can I See You Die?* (words by Louis Barrow, music by Henry Tucker):

My darling boy, I little thought
   When last I heard your merry tone
And finally kissed your noble brow
   That death would claim you as his own.
With breaking heart, I bade you go, my boy,
   And weeping, breathed a sad goodbye;
You told me that you'd soon return.
   You have, but oh, you've come to die.

CHORUS:
Home to die, home to die!
My boy, how can I see you die!

Other "home-to-die" songs were *The Soldier's Request; or, Take Me Home to Die* (words by Mrs. Clara Eastland, music by J. A. Butterfield) and *I'm Coming Home to Die* (words and music by Ossian E. Dodge).

Many soldiers failed to return from the front, and receipt of the news of death required as much fortitude as could possibly be summoned. Southern and Northern families alike shared the experience of loneliness and emptiness of heart—the tragic, immeasurable legacy of war.

By far the most popular song of death, and one of the few to endure, was *The Vacant Chair,* beloved by both Confederates and Unionists. Its subject was a young eighteen-year-old soldier, John William Grout of Worcester, Massachusetts, who was killed at Ball's Bluff in October, 1861, and who had expected to have his first furlough on Thanksgiving Day, November 28. At the dinner table on that day his chair, in its usual place, was left unoccupied; and one of the guests, Henry S. Washburn, was so moved that he wrote the poem in honor of Willie. Set to music by George

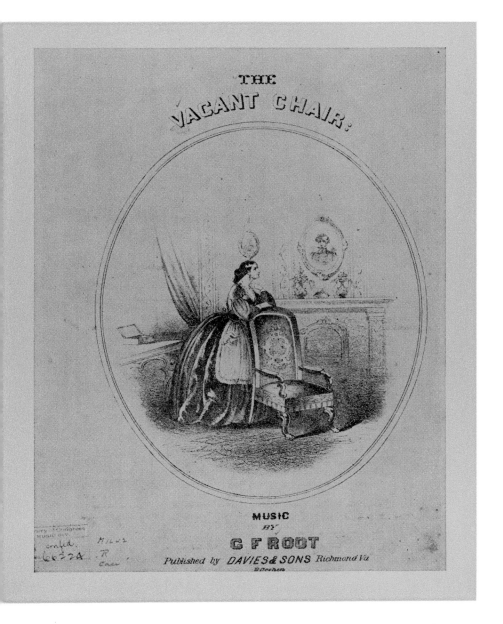

The illustration on this Confederate copy of a famous Union song disregards its words, for the chair was originally at the dinner table, and the dead soldier was an eighteen-year-old lad.

F. Root early in 1862, the poem became one of the most familiar ballads of the war, a favorite in both North and South. The song's popularity was due both to the fact that it was written early in the war when the dreadful slaughter had scarcely begun and that it expressed a common situation and sincere emotion. In over half a million homes *The Vacant Chair* was a familiar tune:

> We shall meet but we shall miss him,
>   There will be one vacant chair;
> We shall linger to caress him
>   While we breathe our evening prayer.
> When a year ago we gathered
>   Joy was in the mild blue eye,
> But a golden cord is severed
>   And our hopes in ruin lie.

> CHORUS:
> We shall meet, but we shall miss him,
> There will be one vacant chair;
> We shall linger to caress him
> When we breathe our evening prayer.

> At our fireside, sad and lonely,
>   Often will the bosom swell
> At remembrance of the story
>   How our noble Willie fell;
> How he strove to bear our banner
>   Thro' the thickest of the fight
> And upheld our country's honor
>   In the strength of manhood's might.

> True they tell us wreaths of glory
>   Evermore will deck his brow,
> But this soothes the anguish only
>   Sweeping o'er our heartstrings now.
> Sleep today, O early fallen,
>   In thy green and narrow bed,
> Dirges from the pine and cypress
>   Mingle with the tears we shed.

The symbol of the vacant chair became popular, but in spite of imitations, the original song was never supplanted in favor. *Sleeping in the Valley* (words and music by A. J. Abbey) contained a vacant chair:

Still that vacant chair is sitting in its old familiar place,
But the one we love is missing, as his form we there can trace.

G. R. Lampard composed the words and music to:

There's a Dear Vacant Chair by the Hearthstone
    Where so nobly our Willie once sat.
In the pride of his youth we have parted,
    The day I shall never forget.
The chair by the fireside is sitting
    Where once all were happy with glee,
But now one is missed from our number
    By the hearthstone, so lonely to me.

Oh, We Miss You at Home (words and music by H. H. Hawley) also
used this subject:

Oh, we miss you at home, yes, we miss you
    When the family board we surround,
Where smiles were oft met by kind glances
    And social joy used to abound.
But now there's a chair that is vacant
    Though it stands in its place as of old,
And we cherish the name of its owner
    With affection that ne'er can grow cold.

A Confederate song, *Kiss Me Before I Die, Mother* (words by Joseph M.
Goff, music by E. Clarke Ilsley), refers to the vacant chair:

Beside our hearthside, Mother,
    Will stand a vacant chair;
There's one beyond the stars, Mother,
    I go to claim it there.

Mothers scanned the published casualty lists in fear and trembling,
for in those days official notification of death was often slow in arriving.
A dying soldier in *O, Search Ye Well the Lists, Mother* (words and music
by W. O. Fiske) knew his mother would eventually read his name:

Oh, search ye well the lists, dear Mother,
    You will find your darling's name therein,
Who fighting for his country's honor
    Fell amid the battle's din.
Oh, weep not for your boy, dear Mother,
    No prouder death than mine could be!
I die that others may be happy,
    I die for country and for thee.

A Southern child who could not read sensed that something was wrong and asked, *Mother, Is the Battle Over?* (words and music by Joseph H. Denck, another setting by Benedict Roefs):

Mother, is the battle over?
Thousands have been killed they say.
Is my father coming? Tell me,
Have the Southrons gained the day?
Is he well or is he wounded?
Mother, do you think he's slain?
If you know, I pray you tell me,
Will my father come again?

Mother, dear, you're always sighing
Since you last the papers read.
Tell me why you now are crying,
Why that cap is on your head?
Ah! I see you cannot tell me,
Father's one among the slain.
Although he loved us very dearly,
He will never come again.

The mother in *My Darling Boy Is Slain* (words and music by G. P. Graff) knew her boy was dead:

Whisper low, say not he's dead,
    'Twill only give me pain,
To know my only hope has fled,
    My darling boy is slain.

The report of *Missing* (words and music by A. A. Hopkins) was even more difficult to bear, for there was nothing to console those left behind:

Missing is all, and how little to mark
The lost link from a living home chain!
'Tis a brief little word
But it quenches hope's spark
And some hearts must wander through life in the dark
With "missing" for aye their refrain.

Even though there was *Only One Man Killed Today* (words from *Harper's Weekly*, music by Guy F. North), still the news brought grief:

There are tears and sobs in the little brown house
    On the hillside slope today.
Though the sunlight gleams from the outer world
    There clouds drift cold and gray.
Only one man killed, so the tidings read,
Our loss was trifling, we triumphed, 'twas said;
And only here in the home on the hill
Did the words breathe aught but of triumph still.
Only one man killed, so we read full oft
    And rejoiced that the loss on our side was small,
Forgetting meanwhile that some loving heart
    Felt all the force of that murderous ball.
Only one man killed, comes again and again;
One hero more 'mong the martyred slain,
Only one man killed carries sorrow for life
To those whose darlings fall in the strife.

There was no relief from the sorrow of those at home when *Our Two-Year Boys* (words and music by Lewis Stecher) failed to return:

Our two-year boys, where are they?
    Alas, but few are left.
Their scattered graves speak silently
    Of those who are bereft.
Mother, father, sister—
    All their sorrows all must bear.
In heaven among the great and good,
    Our two-year boys are there.

Mourning continued at the grave for *Our Soldier* (words by E. B. Dewing, music by J. P. Webster):

255

We have laid him to rest
On the earth's silent breast,
   And the night winds still echo his knell.
Oh, we loved Willie dear
And the last welling tear
   Shall be shed where our hero sleeps well.

Sorrowing extended to the faraway graves, stated *Our Boys Are All Gone to the War* (words and music by George P. Graff):

Our boys are all gone to the war,
This cruel and terrible war!
They have left us to mourn
For many dear ones that are buried away so far.

Mothers experienced greatest heartache; they sorrowed when they bade farewell to their youngest, and they continued to grieve long after death had taken their loved ones. The grave of *The Southern Soldier Boy* (words by Father Abram J. Ryan, music by W. Ludden) was in the heart of one Confederate mother:

Young as the youngest who donned the gray,
   True as the truest who wore it,
Brave as the bravest he marched away,
Hot tears on the cheeks of his mother lay.
Triumphant waved our flag one day,
   He fell in the front before it.

CHORUS:
A grave in the wood with the grass o'ergrown,
A grave in the heart of his mother,
His clay in the one, lifeless and lone,
But his memory lives in the other.

Mourning would continue for *The Son Who Was His Mother's Pride* (words by Robert Morris, music by Alfred Delaney):

The son who was his mother's pride,
   The joy of all who met him,
Whose voice thrilled like a trumpet peal,
   Oh, how can we forget him!

Young as the young-est who donned the gray, True as the tru-est who wore it,

Brave as the brav-est he marched a-way, Hot tears on the cheeks of his

moth-er lay. Tri - umph - ant waved our flag one day, He

Chorus

fell in the front be - fore it. A grave in the wood with the

grass o'er-grown, A grave in the heart of his moth - er, His

clay in the one, life-less and lone. But his mem'ry lives in the oth-er.

The Southern Soldier Boy

Many a mother had a foreboding that her boy was among the dead, according to *Where Is My Boy Tonight?* (words from the *Ladies Repository*, music by J. Henry Whittemore):

> I feel but I cannot tell why
>   That fallen he has in the fight,
> That God has promoted my boy
>   And tempered my soul tonight.

The Confederate woman who daily visited the green fields which were once a battleground was *The Mother of the Soldier Boy* (words by Thomas H. Bayly, music by Hermann L. Schreiner):

Why daily goes yon matron forth,
As 'twere to trace the dead?
No stain of gore is on the earth,
On flowers and grass we tread!
Tho' summer, fields are green again,
And crystal waters glide;
Yet this was once a battle plain,
Here brave men fought and died.

Her only son had fallen there,
To sometime bring relief
Unmarked, she passes with despair,
Still recent seems her grief;
Since then, though many suns have shone,
The matron dreams of joy
And daily wanders forth alone
To seek her soldier boy.

Some solace was found in the nearness of the graves, indicated in *His Pleasant Grave* (words by Mrs. Elizabeth A. C. Akers, music by Elliott C. Howe), *Our Dead Soldier Boy* (words by Henry Morford, music by John Mahon), *Why Do I Weep Beside Thy Grave?* (words by Thomas B. Long, music by J. C. Meininger), and *He Is Sleeping, Sweetly Sleeping* (words and music by O. P. Sweet).

Wives, too, bore their share of the general sorrow. *The Soldier's Widow* (words and music by H. T. Merrill) promised to be brave:

I'm alone, all alone, 'mid the cares of this life
And my heart almost breaks when I think of the strife.
But I'll cheerfully bear all the trials that come
For he suffered and died for our dear happy home.

CHORUS:
Oh, how sad 'tis to die for our country so dear
But how sad 'tis to part from the one who's so near.
But I'll murmur not a word though it's hard to bear the rod.
For our country he died in the fear of his God.

Everyone comforted *The Soldier's Wife* (words and music by George P. Graff):

> My soldier sleeps, he sweetly sleeps,
> While the angels watch me in my strife.
> They are praying, they are praying,
> Praying for the soldier's wife.

Sisters shared in the suffering. One was now all alone, in *My Only Brother's Gone* (words by Willie Ware, music by Matthias Keller):

> He went to join our mother,
>   Our generous father, too,
> In lands beyond the starlight
>   Where all is good and true.
> They wrapped him in the banner
>   He loved so fondly well,
> And laid him 'neath the clover
>   Upon the spot he fell.

After the initial blow, only memories remained—and sometimes an item of clothing, a sword, or a badge as a souvenir. A wife voices her realization that *He Will Not Come Again* (words by Randal Weber, music by Henry Weber):

> I have the sword he nobly held
>   When death his captor came,
> Its shining blade repeats the sound,
>   "He will not come again."

One mother had *The Sword That My Brave Boy Wore* (words and music by James G. Clark). *The Badge My Soldier Wore* (words by Dexter Smith, music by Jean Foster) was cherished:

> 'Tis a bit of faded ribbon
> Hanging on the shadowed wall,
> Where the sunshine never falleth
> To dispel the heavy pall.
> But a ribbon, yet I cherish

259

That lone relic more than gold!
And the world has naught to tempt me
To give up that badge of old

Soiled and torn and faded ribbon,
Hanging on the chamber wall,
Of a sweet and blissful vision
What sad memories you recall!
Yet until I stand beside him
On the green and peaceful shore
I shall cherish, nearer, dearer,
That old badge my soldier wore.

The jackets, whether blue or gray, had often been exchanged for "death's white robes." The Northern mother's brave lad slept in an unmarked grave; she longed to hear his footfall and see him coming o'er the hill, in *The Faded Coat of Blue; or, The Nameless Grave* (words and music by J. H. McNaughton):

My brave lad he sleeps in his faded coat of blue,
    In a lonely grave unknown lies the heart that beat so true;
He sank faint and hungry among the famished brave,
    And they laid him sad and lonely within his nameless grave.

CHORUS:
No more the bugle calls the weary one,
    Rest, noble spirit, in thy grave unknown.
I'll find you, and know you, among the good and true
    When a robe of white is giv'n for the faded coat of blue.

Southern parents sent their boy away to defend his homeland in a spotless jacket of gray, but his life blood oozed out on it, soiled and tattered as it was; now they had, for memory, only *The Faded Gray Jacket; or, Fold It Up Carefully* (words by Mrs. C. A. Ball, music by Charlie Ward):

Fold it up carefully, lay it aside,
    Tenderly touch it, look on it with pride;
For dear must it be to our hearts evermore,
    The jacket of gray our loved soldier boy wore.
Can we ever forget when he joined the brave band
    Who rose in defence of our dear Southern land,

And in his bright youth hurried on to the fray,
    How proudly he donned it, the jacket of gray?

CHORUS:
Fold it up carefully, lay it aside,
Tenderly touch it, look on it with pride;
For dear it must be to our hearts evermore,
The jacket of gray our loved soldier boy wore.

A Confederate wife had only *The Coat of Faded Gray* (words by G. W. Harris, music by H. M. Hall) as she waited for death in loneliness:

The breezes through the lowly door
    Swing mute a coat of faded gray,
A tattered relic of the fray,
    A threadbare coat of faded gray.
'Tis hanging on the rough log wall,
    Near to the foot of a widow's bed,
By a white plume and well-worn shawl,
    His gift the happy morn they wed;
By the wee slip their dead child wore.

And all she craves is here to die,
    To part from these and pass away,
To join her loves eternally,
    That wore the slip, the coat of gray;
The shell-torn relic of the fray,
    Her soldier's coat of faded gray.

The mourning would ever endure, and solace was found only in the fact that the cause was worthwhile, opined *What Will They Tell Our Children When This Sad War Is O'er?* (words by Jennie S. Frodsham, music by John W. Hobbs):

What will they tell the mourners,
    Throughout the land now found,
The mothers, wives, whose hearts and lives
    In husbands, sons were bound?
They'll urge them place in God their trust,
    Bid orphans' tears be dried,
And mourn no more those gone before
    And who for Freedom died!

261

As the sorrowful losses continued, it was necessary for life to go on; but occasional lapses into grief were unavoidable, expressed *Oh, Let Me Shed One Silent Tear* (words by F. H. Norton, music by John R. Thomas):

Oh, deem me not of craven heart
    Nor think I've lost the patriot's pride,
Because I have not gained the art
    My tears for friendship yet to hide;
I love my country while I weep,
    I pray her sons may all things dare,
But still the mem'ry will not sleep
    That I have dear friends fighting there!

CHORUS:
O, let me shed one silent tear
To ease my sorrowing heart from pain;
One tribute to the friends so dear,
And then I will be brave again!

Later, as the end of fighting drew near and the time approached when troops would be coming home, the old sorrow revived for *The Unreturning Braves* (words by William H. Cook, music by Phil Harmonic, pseud.):

O, my heart is filled with love
For the unreturning braves,
For the weeping mother's dear and only son;
Who are silent sleeping now
Far away in unknown graves,
Though glory hovers o'er the race they've won.

As we look toward the South,
Our eyes well up with tears,
For we know the loved ones there will never come.
Oh, how happy we would be
In the peaceful coming years
Could they join with us around the hearth at home.

These boys were far away in unknown graves, *Sleeping for the Flag* (words and music by Henry C. Work):

When our boys come home in triumph, brother,
    With the laurels they shall gain,
When we go to give them welcome, brother,
    We shall look for you in vain.
We shall wait for your returning, brother,
    Though we know it cannot be,
For your comrades left you sleeping, brother,
    Underneath a Southern tree.

CHORUS:
Sleeping to waken
    In this weary world no more;
Sleeping for your true loved country, brother,
    Sleeping for the flag you bore.

The sole consolation was that *We Shall Meet Him Bye and Bye* (words
by H. A. Lockwood, music by C. T. Lockwood):

Heavenly Father, once more bless us,
    Give us peace, our country save.
Is our boy no more to see us?
    Must he fill a Southern grave?
No, oh, no, we'll not believe it!
    Then away this heavy sigh,
And we'll calmly wait his coming;
    We shall meet him bye and bye.

A postwar song, *Gone Where the Woodbine Twineth* (words and
music by Apsley Street, pseudonym of Septimus Winner), published in
1870, became the most well known mourning song of the Civil War
period, eventually equaling *The Vacant Chair* in popularity.

Feelings of anxiety and sorrow quite logically led to a consecration
of self and loved ones to the cause and to petitions to the Deity for victory
to be given the side of the right.

The North asked blessings upon the recruits. *God Save the Volunteers,*
to the tune of *America,* said:

God save that noble band
Fighting for fatherland,
True heroes all!

Keep their faith pure and bright,
Uphold them by Thy might,
While they contend for right,
And if they fall—

Do Thou their souls receive,
Comfort the hearts that grieve,
Wipe every tear;
Bid all on Thee depend,
Each lonely hearth attend;
Be Thou the orphan's friend,
Conquering fear!

Also to the tune of *America,* Southern patriots petitioned, *God Bless Our Southern Land:*

God bless our Southern land,
God save our sea-girt land,
And make us free.
With justice for our shield,
May we on battle field
Never to foemen yield
Our liberty.

O Lord, our God, arise,
Scatter our enemies,
And make them fall!
And when, with peace restored,
Each man lays by the sword,
May he with joy record
Thy mercies all.

A verse of the Union *God Bless Our Brave Young Volunteers* (words and music by George F. Root), after recounting how the young boys had left their anvils, looms, and plows, begged God for their protection:

May He protect them in the strife
Whose powers can quell our rising fears
Oh, may He guard each precious life
And bless our brave young volunteers.

Farewell, true hearts, our prayers shall be

Where'er the starry flag appears,
That He who made our fathers free
May bless our brave young volunteers.

The nearest approach to a Confederate anthem which possessed the religious qualities necessary in a poem of consecration to a cause—expressing a high and worthy purpose, faith in Divine protection, belief in the rightness of the struggle, and devotion to the bitter end—was *God Save the South! A National Hymn* (words by Earnest Halphin, music by Charles W. A. Ellerbrock; same title also with words by George H. Miles, music by C. T. De Coeniel). The lyrics by Earnest Halphin entreated:

God save the South,
God save the South,
Her altars and firesides,
God save the South!
Now that the war is nigh,
Now that we arm to die,
Chanting our battle-cry:
Freedom or Death!

CHORUS:
Now that the war is nigh,
Now that we arm to die,
Chanting the battle-cry:
Freedom or Death.
Chanting the battle-cry:
Freedom or Death!

God made the right
Stronger than might;
Millions would trample us
Down in their pride.
Lay Thou their legions low,
Roll back the ruthless foe,
Let the proud spoiler know
God's on our side.

This was one of the first songs published in the South during the war. A similar hymn was *God Save the Southern Land* (words and music adapted from an English ballad by Chaplain Cameron).

God save the South, God save the South, Her
al - tars and fire - sides, God save the South!
Now that the war is nigh, Now that we arm to die,
Chant - ing our bat - tle—cry: Free - dom or Death!
Chorus
Now that the war is nigh, Now that we arm to die,
Chant - ing the bat - tle - cry: Free - dom or Death.
Chant - ing the bat - tle—cry: Free - dom or Death!

God Save the South! A National Hymn

The Union's prayers for a reunited nation found expression in a song which combined the dignity of a hymn with the stateliness of a patriotic air, *God Save the Nation, a Battle Hymn* (words by Theodore Tilton, music by Henry C. Work):

Thou who ordainest for the land's salvation,
Famine and fire and sword and lamentation,

Now unto Thee we lift our supplication,
God save the nation, God save the nation.

These songs of sentiment stand as an enduring record of the mental
suffering which overwhelmed soldiers and civilians alike. To us, they may
seem platitudinous, mawkish, or moody, but it is well to remember that
the human heart has remained unaltered since 1861 regardless of changes
in literary tastes. From these songs we may reconstruct a picture of the
life during those days a century ago.

****

CHAPTER 7

****

The Negro and the Contraband

Part i: ROADS TO FREEDOM

ALTHOUGH THE North entered into hostilities as the only means of preserving the Union, the abolition of slavery soon became an obvious objective. However, during the first two years of the struggle, Lincoln continued to insist that slavery was not one of the issues. Not only would an emancipation proclamation unite the South into a determined unit, but it might prejudice Northerners who did not object to slavery in the Southern states. Moreover, such a policy at that time might have led several border states, among them West Virginia, Kentucky, and Missouri, to abandon the Union. Consequently, the President steered a safe course, concentrating his efforts on holding the Southern states within the Union.

As evidence of the fact that many in the Federal Army did not consider slavery an issue, the famous Hutchinson family was drummed out of a camp along the Potomac early in 1862 for singing abolitionist songs to the soldiers, and the *Washington Star* protested editorially against turning the camps into "arenas for political pow-wowing."

Kingdom Coming, Henry Clay Work's first song of the Negro,[16] was written before the slave question assumed its subsequent importance and therefore contains no reference to Negro freedom. Its Northern author and composer seized upon the common incident of a Confederate's being forced to flee in haste before the Union advance. He saw the humor of

[16] Songs of the Negro by Henry Clay Work, included in this chapter, were the best written by a Northerner. His interest in this subject was due to an unhappy childhood, when his father had been imprisoned in Illinois for strong antislavery views.

Say, dar-kies, hab you seen de mas-sa Wid de muff-stas on his face, Go

'long de road some-time dis morn-in' Like he gwine to leab de place? He

seen a smoke way up de rib-ber, Whar de Lin-kum gum-boats lay; He

Chorus

took his hat an lef' ber-ry sud-den, An I spec he's run a-way! De

mas-sa run, ha! ha! De dar-kies stay, ho! ho! It

mus' be now de king-dom com-in' An de year ob Ju-bi-lo!

Kingdom Coming

the situation and placed his words in the mouth of a Negro. The plantation was evidently on the Mississippi, since the master saw the smoke from the Union gunboats, and the slaves had a merry time when their three-hundred-pound master fled, in *Kingdom Coming:*

Say, darkies, hab you seen de massa
Wid de muffstas on his face,
Go 'long de road sometime dis mornin'
Like he gwine to leab de place?
He seen a smoke way up de ribber,
Whar de Linkum gumboats lay;

He took his hat an lef' berry sudden,
An I spec he's run away!

CHORUS:
De massa run, ha! ha!
De darkies stay, ho! ho!
It mus' be now de kingdom comin'
An de year ob Jubilo!

De darkeys feel so lonesome libin'
In de loghouse on de lawn;
Dey move dar tings to massa's parlor
For to keep it while he's gone.
Dar's wine an' cider in de kitchen,
An' de darkeys dey'll hab some;
I spose dey'll all be confiscated
When de Linkum sojers come.

The flight of the masters as the Army of the Potomac advanced into
Virginia was the subject of *Ole Uncle Abrum's Comin'* (words and music
by A. C. D. Sandie):

A nigger is a nigger
So long as massa stay;
But isn't nary nigger
When de massa runned away.
So git into de parlor
As fast as yer can,
And set upon de sofy
Wid yer feet on de divan.

CHORUS:
Hail, hail, hail dis day ob de jubilee
Oh, my ole massa's runned away an' lef' his niggers free!

We'll shut up all de cabins
Wid a lock on ebery door,
And be gemmen in de mansion
Wid de carpets on de floor.
So lay aside dat banjo
Dat music'll nebber do
We'll play on de piany
And we'll dance de Lancers, too!

Ole Massa on His Trabbels Gone (words by John Greenleaf Whittier, music by S. K. Whiting) also used the situation as subject:

> Ole massa on his trabbels gone,
>   He leabe de land behind.
> De Lord's breaf blow him furder on
>   Like corn shucks on de wind!
> We own de hoe, we own de plow,
>   We own de hands dat hold;
> We sell de pig, we sell de cow,
>   But nebber chile be sold!

Nicodemus Johnson's master was a Union man who left his plantation to join the Northern forces:

> My master was a Union man
>   And he did not like secession
> And so he had to leave the old plantation.
>   I thought to stay behind him there,
> 'Twould be an aggravation,
>   Oh, ho, ho, to Nicodemus Johnson.

Many Negroes in the most northern Confederate states believed that if they could escape inside Union lines they would be safe and free. The problem of fugitive slaves was defined by an order of General B. F. Butler at Fortress Monroe, Virginia, on May 24, 1861, in which he declared them to be contraband of war. All "contrabands" escaping through the lines were put to work, paid, and set free; or, if their masters were loyal to the Union, the owners were paid for their services. This idea appealed to the slaves, who began to flock into every Union camp. Butler's order is the subject of *I'se on de Way* (words and music by Wurzel [George F. Root]):

> Ole Ben, so grand, sez we contraband
> And first we work on de forticashum.
> Now we cum for to shoulder de gun;
> Oh, I'se on de way.

Many were the songs in dialect, although almost entirely the work of Union composers, honoring the contraband. *The Old Contraband* (words by John L. Zieber, music by Rudolph Wittig) was off for the North:

I'se a contraband from de ole plantation,
I think I hab worked out my own salvation.
I'se a citizen now ob dis glorious nation.
Freedom, freedom, de ole slave is free!
Den hurrah, den hurrah, I am a slave no longer,
Den away, den away to de land ob de free.

while Dan D. Emmett's *The Black Brigade* showed their eagerness to "jine the Union":

There's somethin' wrong a-brewin',
    Gwine ter jine the Union!
There's somethin' wrong a-brewin',
    Here we go!
We're on de brink of ruin,
    Gwine ter jine the Union!
Ah, ah, ah, ah!
    Der boys from Lincoln land.

The Negroes ran for *The Other Side of Dixie* (words by Sol Sharpstick, music by Willie Willieson):

The war has come and these darkies will fight,
Fight away for the North and the Union Right!
    Get out of the way, get out of the way,
    Get out of the way to Union land.
Let ole massa pick and hoe de cotton,
Leave ole missus all forgotten.

CHORUS:
Run for the North of Dixie, hurrah! get away!
T'other side o' Dixie for the Union.
Darkies all fight away, fight away,
Contraband o' war, oh, yes! fight away!

One Negro welcomed his new status when he was called *The Intelligent Contraband* (words and music by Charles Pettengill):

I'se de happiest darkey whatever you did see,
I'se been so ever since I heard

272

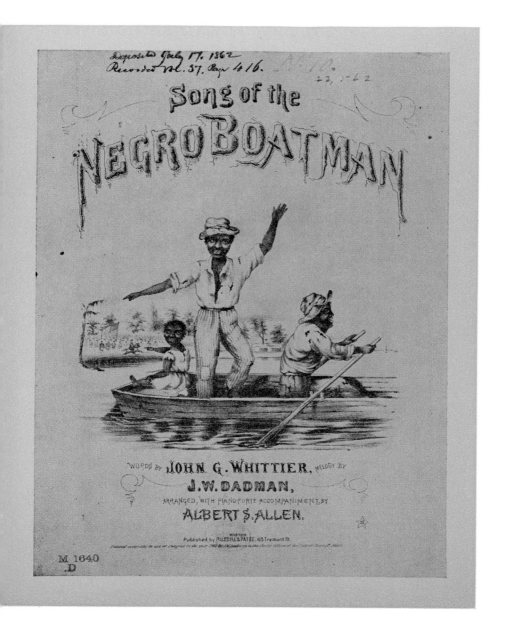

Most Northern illustrators of contraband or liberated slaves followed the "pickaninny" pattern, as on this pre-Emancipation Proclamation title page.

Dat I was to be free!
I was born way down in Dixie's land
Where dey used to call me Sam.
By golly, now de white folks say
I'm a 'telligent contraband.

The opposite view was expressed in *Contraband Now* (words and music by Frank Wardlaw):

Uncle Sambo's a'gwine to be righted,
    Uncle Sambo's a'gwine to be free;
An' dey say dat dis darkey's delighted
    Because you white folks can't agree.
Oh, dey say dat dis darkey's in clober,
    But 'deed, I don't see it nohow;
Uncle Sambo's best days are all ober,
    He's only a contraband now.

Major General David Hunter, who had become an ardent Abolitionist, carried the idea of employing black labor one step farther. Charged with the duty of holding the entire seacoast of Georgia, South Carolina, and Florida with less than 10,000 allotted men and unable to obtain reinforcements from the Washington government in early 1862, he calmly announced his intention of forming a Negro regiment to aid him. When he was called before a Congressional committee to explain this action, he said, "No regiment of fugitive slaves has been or is being organized in this department. There is, however, a fine regiment of loyal persons whose late masters are fugitive rebels, men who everywhere fly before the appearance of the National flag, leaving their loyal and unhappy servants behind them to shift as best they can for themselves." Hunter's success was celebrated in *Old Abe Has Gone and Did It, Boys* (words by S. Fillmore Bennett, music by J. P. Webster):

But McClellan thought de way was to let de niggers stay
    Diggin' trenches for de rebels in de sun,
While de Yankee sojers work wid de shobel and de dirt
    When dey ought to use de sabre and de gun.

Massa Hunter did contend dat de Government depend
    On de nigger wid his pickax and his spade;

Dat de Yankee boys could fight but dey's nebber tink it right
   For to take up diggin' ditches as a trade.

The work these contrabands did was hailed in *To Canaan:*

What troop is this that follows, all armed with picks and spades?
These are the swarthy bondsmen, the iron-skinned brigades!
They'll pick up freedom's breastwork, they'll scoop out rebel graves.
Who then will be their owner and march them off for slaves?

The Confiscation Act, passed by the Union Congress on July 17, 1862, which freed all slaves who had escaped from Confederate masters, stated "that the President of the United States is authorized to employ as many persons of African descent as he may deem necessary and proper for the suppression of the rebellion, and for this purpose he may organize and use them in such manner as he may judge best for the public welfare." For the most part the Negroes were enthusiastic about becoming fighting men. *We's A-Gwine to Fight* (words by Charles Haynes, music by J. E. Haynes) proclaimed:

When rotten shot begins to fall and massa am knocked down
I know de Lord am comin' for to do de ting up brown.
Oh, darkies, ain't yer heard it, de ting's a-comin' right.
Ole Massa Abe hab spoken it and we'se a-gwine ter fight!

while *De Darkies' Rallying Song* (words by J. O'Conner, music by J. P. Jones) indicated the Negroes' loyalty:

Ole massa now must hide him head
   While we can face de light,
For Fader Abe, God bless him!
   Said dat darkies all may fight.
So in de battlefield we'll stand
   To let de white folks know
Dat bullets fired by darkies' hands
   Can lay de rebels low.

CHORUS:
We go, we go, to strike a blow
For de old red, white and blue;

To help de Yankees in de fight,
For dey fight for me and you.

They would all *Make Ole Massa Hum* (words by Charles Haynes, music by J. E. Haynes):

Oh, darkies, hain't yer seen it,
  The glorious day hab come
When we'se a-gwine to hab de land
  And make old massa hum.
Old Abe hab done and said it,
  He say de ting what's right;
He sure spoken de big word,
  What means dat we shall fight!

That "confiscation" would eventually lead to emancipation was the message in *The Negro Emancipation Song* (words by S. Fillmore Bennett, music by J. P. Webster):

Massa say de Linkum folks make de confiscation,
  Dat was what it am, I think, den he cussed de nation.
Didn't hear quite all he said while his tongue was runnin'
  But I 'spect it mean de day of 'mancipation comin'.

The Conference Committee of the Senate and House of Representatives inserted one very important amendment in the Conscription Act when it was before them. Senator Wilson announced to them his firm resolution that no slave should serve the government for one moment as a slave, and it was provided that the drafted or enlisted slave should be free the instant he entered service. This fact was heralded in *No Slave Beneath That Starry Flag* (words by Rev. George Lansing Taylor, music by Mrs. Parkhurst):

No slave beneath that starry flag,
  The emblem of the free!
No fettered hand shall wield the brand
  That smites for liberty!
No tramp of servile armies
  Shall shame Columbia's shore,
For he who fights for freedom's right
  Is free forevermore!

The Union experiment of arming Negroes was generally considered successful, and more and more Negro regiments were formed of these willing workers. Stephen Foster pictured this enthusiastic "jinin'" in *A Soldier in de Colored Brigade* (words by George Cooper):

> Old Uncle Abram wants us and we're coming right along,
> I tell you what it is, we're gwine to muster mighty strong;
> Then fare you well, my honey dear! now don't you be afraid;
> I'se bound to be a soldier in de Colored Brigade!
>
> CHORUS:
> A soldier! A soldier in de darkey Brigade!
> I'se bound to be a soldier in de Colored Brigade.
>
> Wid musket on my shoulder and wid banjo in my hand,
> For Union and de Constitution as it was, I stand;
> Now some folks tink de darkey for dis fighting wasn't made;
> We'll show dem what's de matter in de Colored Brigade.
>
> CHORUS:
> De matter! De matter in de darkey Brigade!
> We'll show dem what's de matter in de Colored Brigade.

Dey Said We Wouldn't Fight (words by Mrs. M. A. Kidder, music by Mrs. Parkhurst), but they were certainly wrong:

> Dey said we wouldn't fight
> 'Cause we'se born so awful black,
> 'Cause we'se lazy from de cranum to de toes;
> But dey'll find dese darkies some
> When de rebel soldiers come
> If dey'll keep us well in powder for de foes.
>
> Oh, we'se fightin' for de flag
> Dat is floatin' oberhead,
> And we'se left our pickaninnies home to cry;
> But we'll nebber leab de field
> 'Til we make de rebels yield
> And we'se dreadful sure to do it bye an' bye.

Negroes were proud to have a hand in the strife, though they planned to go back to *The Old Plantation* (words by Stephen K. Glover, music by William Horton) afterwards:

Once I was a chattel on de ole plantation
    Like de horses, oxen and de lamb;
Now I is a citizen ob a mighty nation
    Serving in de ranks of Uncle Sam.
Massa when him lef' us, he felt certain sure
    De darkies lob him like de life,
But de blindness lef' us since we know de cure.
    De darkies has a hand in de strife.

CHORUS:
Hurrah for Uncle Sam! We're gwine ter fight
And sab de honor ob de nation.
When de war am ober and de sun shine bright,
We'll settle on de ole plantation.

Anyone who objected to *Sambo's Right to Be Kilt* (words by Miles O'Reilly, music by Samuel Lover) would certainly be shown that he was wrong:

The men who object to Sambo
    Should take his place and fight;
And its better to have a nigger's hue
    Than a liver that's weak and white.
Though Sambo's black as the ace of spades
    His fingers a trigger can pull,
And his eye runs straight on the barrel sight
    From under its thatch of wool.

The contraband's enthusiasm and eagerness to "jine and fight for Uncle Sam and Massa Linkum" were nowhere better illustrated than in *Babylon's Fallen* (words and music by Henry C. Work), the sequel to *Kingdom Coming,* in which the former slaves were able to capture their former master, a colonel:

Don't you see de black clouds
Risin' ober yonder,
Where de Massa's ole plantation am?
Nebber you be frightened,
Dem is only darkies
Come to jine and fight for Uncle Sam.

CHORUS:

Look out, dar, now, we's a-gwine to shoot!
Look out, dar, don't you understand?
Babylon is fallen! Babylon is fallen!
An' we'se a-gwine to occupy de land.

Massa was de Kernel
In de Rebel army,
Eber since he went an' run away;
But his lubley darkeys,
Dey has been a-watchin'
An' dey take him pris'ner t'udder day.

The kind of maltreatment from which some of these Negro contraband enlisters had fled was indicated by stanzas from *We Are Coming from the Cotton Fields* (words by J. C——n, music by J. C. Wallace):

We will leave our chains behind us, boys,
    The prison and the racks;
And we'll hide beneath a soldier's coat
    The scars upon our backs;
And we'll teach the world a lesson soon,
    If taken by the hand,
How the night shall come before 'tis noon
    Upon old Pharoah's land.

By the heavy chains that bound our hands
    Thro' centuries of wrong,
We have learned the hard-bought lesson well;
    How to suffer and be strong;
And we only ask the power to show
    What freedom does for man,
And we'll give a sign to friend and foe
    As none beside us can.

Many persons thought that to put arms into the hands of the Negro soldier might simply be a means of arming the Confederates. Even though the right to employ Negroes was recognized, was it expedient? Would they make good fighters? Would the use of Negroes embitter the Confederates and spur them to even greater effort? All of these and similar questions were answered by the activities of the Negro regiments themselves, figuring prominently at Port Hudson, Fort Pillow, Brice's Cross Roads, and The Crater. *The American Freedmen* (words by Henry O'Rielly, music by John M. Loretz, Jr.) more than proved their mettle:

> Freedmen's blood flowed red in battle
> By the side of white men true,
> All battling for freedom and Union
> And clad in the loyal blue.

> At old Carolina's harbors,
> Port Hudson's crimson plain,
> In Ollustee's fatal forest,
> At Pillow foully slain;
> At Richmond's towering ramparts
> Where treason fierce held sway,
> The valiant freedmen's flowing blood
> Bedewed the victor's way.

Northerners realized that the successful prosecution of the war might eventually require the unlimited employment of Negro troops.

Before the close of the conflict, over 185,000 Negroes had been regularly enlisted in the Union armies and the total Negro casualties reached nearly 70,000. Almost 30,000 or one in six, were killed. The last volleys of the war were fired by the Sixty-second U. S. Colored Infantry on May 13, 1865, at Palo Pinto, Texas, between White's Ranche and Chico Strait; the last soldier wounded in the war was Sergeant Crockett, a Negro.

> We clothed him in the loyal blue,
>   Put in his hand a sabre,
> And bade him strike for freedom too;
>   Free soil, free men, free labor

explains *Protect the Freedman* (words by Luke Collins, music by J. P. Webster).

Negroes always felt that Lincoln was their friend. The Northerners soon realized the futility of attempting to crush the "rebellion" while ignoring its underlying cause. Even if the Southern states eventually returned to the Union, the institution of slavery would remain a source of continued misunderstanding until it was eradicated.

The issuance, on September 22, 1862, of the Preliminary Emancipation

Proclamation, promising to free all slaves in the states still "in rebellion" on the first of January, 1863, stimulated enlistment of contraband Negroes in the Union Army. Though care was taken to keep news of the war from them, the slaves, except in the deep South, were generally informed of the progress of events. There seemed to be an underground news agency. Many Negroes prayed earnestly, though secretly, for the success of the Northern armies of Father (or Uncle) Abe, as Lincoln was called.

The hope engendered by this September proclamation formed the subject of *Cuffee's War Song,* also titled *Away Goes Cuffee; or, Hooray for Sixty-three* (words and music by L. B. Starkweather):

Abram Linkon las' September
Told de Souf 'less you surrender
Afore de las' of next December,
Away goes Cuffee!

CHORUS:
For de cannon may boom when dey fight a big battle,
But de darkeys no more is de sheep and de cattle.
For freedom's watchman has sprung his rattle,
Hooray for sixty-three!

The promise of freedom was a signal for furtive but none the less ardent rejoicing and thanksgiving, when it was actually an impending reality and not merely an anticipatory hope that *De Day of Liberty's Comin'* (words and music by George F. Root):

Darkeys, don't you see de light,
    De day ob liberty's comin', comin',
Almost gone de gloomy night,
    De day ob liberty's comin'.
High ho! de darkeys sing,
    Loud, loud, dar voices ring.
Good news de Lord He bring,
    "Now let my people go."

CHORUS:
Just you look and see dat light!
De day ob liberty's comin', comin',
Almost gone de gloomy night,
De day ob liberty's comin'.

This day of liberty (or Jubilee, sometimes called Jubilo) was at hand; in fact, you could almost "sniff it in the air." The "massa" and "missus" are already awful blue about it and will be ravin' mad when they find its comin' true; "darkies" everywhere will have a big skedaddle, for *Sixty-three Is the Jubilee* (words by J. L. Greene, music by D. A. French):

> Oh, darkeys, hab ye heard it, hab ye heard de joyful news?
>> Uncle Abra'm's gwine to free us and he'll send us where we chuse;
> For de jubilee is comin', don't ye sniff it in de air?
>> And sixty-three is the Jubilee for de darkeys eberywhere.

After years of waiting, the dawning of freedom was near. One Nicodemus, a slave, had been buried long ago in the trunk of an old hollow tree and had charged that he be awakened at the first break of the day of Jubilee; now it was time to *Wake, Nicodemus* (words and music by Henry C. Work):

> Nicodemus, the slave, was of African birth,
>> And was bought for a bagful of gold;
> He was reckon'd as part of the salt of the earth,
>> But he died years ago, very old.
> 'Twas his last sad request as we laid him away
>> In the trunk of an old hollow tree,
> "Wake me up," was his charge, "at the first break of day,
>> Wake me up for the great Jubilee!"

CHORUS:

> The "good time coming" is almost here!
> It was long, long, long on the way!
> Now run and tell Elijah to hurry up Pomp
> And meet us at the gum-tree down in the swamp,
> To wake Nicodemus today.

The Emancipation Proclamation, issued on January 1, 1863, freed slaves only where the decree could be put into effect. Even Lincoln's cabinet considered it unwise and impracticable. They failed to support him in this as a war measure, but the act introduced into the Union cause a new moral aim which spurred enlistments and enthusiasm and prevented intervention by foreign countries.

Northerners were naturally convinced that the slaves themselves desired and welcomed their new freedom. Songs of Union origin depict the joy with which Negroes heard the news that they were at last free. The Lord who helped the Red Sea waves is just as strong now as He was then, for He simply said the word, and whereas last night we were slaves, today we're the Lord's freemen, explained *The Contraband of Port Royal* (words by John Greenleaf Whittier,[17] music by Ferdinand Mayer), also published as *The Contraband's Jubilee* (music by A. J. Higgins):

Oh, praise an' tanks! De Lord he come
To set de people free!
An' massa tink it day ob doom,
An' we ob jubilee.
De Lord dat heap de Red Sea waves
He jus' as 'trong as den;
He say de word: we las' night slaves,
Today, de Lord's freemen.

CHORUS:
De yam will grow, de cotton blow,
We'll hab de rice an' corn;
Oh, nebber you fear if nebber you hear
De driver blow his horn!

We know de promise nebber fail,
An' nebber lie de Word;
So, like de 'postles in de jail,
We waited for de Lord.
And now He open ebery door
An' trow away de key.
We tink we lub Him so before,
We lub Him better free!

One former slave hailed the proclamation by shouting *Uncle Abraham, Bully for You!* (words and music by G. R. Lampard):

[17] Whittier's most famous Abolitionist poem was *We Wait Beneath the Furnace Blast*, set to music by John W. Hutchinson. It was the cause of the Hutchinson Family Quartette's being denied access to camps of the Army of the Potomac by General McClellan and became known as "the prohibited song." It was also set to music by W. O. Perkins and T. Martin Towne.

Ho, the glorious proclamation
　　Sounding grandly o'er the land,
Speaking to a joyful nation
　　Of her jubilee at hand.
Sounding to the nigger drivers
　　Like the judgment tempest blast,
For our Uncle Abram's dander
　　Is completely riz at last.

Sentiments toward the former master and overseer were shown in *When Will Dis Cruel War Be Ober?* (words and music by Frank Howard):

Oh, de time for de 'mancipation's come, I'm told
　　We're all gwine for sogers soon.
We will leab our old massas 'way out in de cold
　　For to mow and to hoe all alone.
Let de darkey's place de oberseer now fill
　　While we shoulder up de gun
And so gib our rebel massas some of Father Abram's pills
　　For de dark 'mancipation time has come.

CHORUS:

Den let's shout, shout, shout
And make dem cussed traitors run;
Let dem know what good Union men are we;
We'll make our ole massas wish
Dis war had ne'er begun,
'Case we'll 'mancipated be.

Other Union authors expressed themselves in higher moral tones. To the strains of *John Brown's Body*, Edna Dean Proctor wrote *The President's Proclamation*:

John Brown died on a scaffold for the slave;
Dark was the hour when we dug his hallowed grave;
Now God avenges the life he gladly gave,
Freedom reigns today!

CHORUS:

Glory, glory, hallelujah!

Glory, glory, hallelujah!
Glory, glory, hallelujah!
Freedom reigns today!

John Brown sowed and his harvesters are we;
Honor to him who has made the bondmen free!
Loved evermore shall our noble Ruler be—
Freedom reigns today!

John Brown's body lies a-mouldering in the grave!
Bright o'er the sod let the starry banner wave;
Lo! for the millions he perilled all to save—
Freedom reigns today!

Justice has Stricken the Chains from the Slave (words and music by A. C. Gutterman):

Never again shall the black desolation
    Blight our fair land with its pestilent breath.
Slavery dies; yes, the foul degradation
    Rise in the throes of a merited death.

Slavery has found its tomb, according to *The Contraband's Song of Freedom* (words and music by Eastburn, pseud. of Septimus Winner):

Now the captive's chains are severed
    And the handcuffs rent in twain;
Now the lash lies by unheeded,
    Never to be used again.
Shout aloud the glad hosanna,
Spread abroad the happy tidings,
Slavery has found its tomb.

The South didn't like it at all, opined *The Old Chieftain* (words and music by Edwin Henry):

The proclamation, the last and the best,
Is liked first-rate both east and west;
But Richmond gets quite red in the face
To learn of the niggers' day of grace.

285

Uncle Joe, a slave for ninety years, is ready and willing to die after having drawn a breath of freedom. He comes home singing his own version of a famous song, in *Uncle Joe's "Hail Columbia"* (words and music by Henry C. Work):

Uncle Joe comes home a-singing, Hail Columby!
Glorious times de Lord is bringin'—Now let me die.
Fling de chains into de ribber, lay de burden by;
Dar is one who will deliber—Now let me die.

CHORUS:
Ring de bells in eb'ry steeple!
Raise de flag on high!
De Lord has come to sabe his people—
Now let me die.

Bressed days, I lib to see dem, Hail Columby!
I hab drawn a breff of freedom—Now let me die.
Ninety years I bore de burden, den He heard my cry;
Standin' on de banks ob Jordan—Now let me die.

In order to hasten a Union where all men would be free, former slaves should join Massa Linkum's camp, urged *De Darkies' Rally* (words and music by W. W. Partridge):

Old Massa Linkum he's de man,
Tur break up dat ole wicked clan,
Who tink no rights to Nig's belong
But lib a slave de whole life long.

CHORUS:
Den come on all ye Darkies into Massa Linkum's camp,
    Whar we're all bound to go,
An' we'll meet our ole Massas an' we'll conquer dem or die,
    Dat we must do, you know;
We are all fur de Union ob Norf and Soufern States,
But not hab de Union like it hab been before;
Hab a Union ob freedom ober all our blessed lan',
    But wid slavery no more.

The last verse indicated that the freed slave, after the war, would like to work again for his master—for pay.

286

The Negro and the Contraband

To many slaves, freedom meant little as long as the war continued; thus more and more Negroes sought to become contrabands in order to hasten the day of final peace. Ole Shady, for one, could not wait any longer, so he set out for the North, "where de good folks say dat white wheat bread an' a dollar a day are a-comin'." His wife and baby had already fled to lower Canaday, and he was off to join them in *The Song of the Contraband; or, Day of Jubilee,* sometimes called *Ole Shady*:

> Oh! yah! yah! darkies, laugh wid me
> For de white folks say Ole Shady's free,
> So don't you see dat de jubilee
> Is a-comin', comin', hail mighty day.
>
> CHORUS:
> Den away, away, for I can't wait any longer,
> Hooray, hooray, I'm goin' home.
>
> Goodbye, hard work wid never any pay,
> I'se gwine up North where de good folks say
> Dat white wheat bread an' a dollar a day
> Are comin', comin', hail mighty day!
>
> Oh, I've got a wife and I've got a baby
> Livin' up yonder in Lower Canaday,
> Won't dey laugh when dey see Ole Shady
> A-comin', comin', hail mighty day!

The verses were said to have been written by a Negro slave, D. Blakely Durant, nicknamed Old Shady, who served as a cook at Union headquarters during the siege of Vicksburg; the music was composed by a clergyman, Benjamin R. Hanby, who had previously written *Darling Nelly Gray*.

The prospect of receiving wages appealed to the imagination of the colored man. Many times the overly enthusiastic Negro pictured himself as owner of a vast plantation. He envisioned himself with little work to do, with all the comforts to which he had been accustomed, but with the addition of a salary. His delusion went still farther; he sometimes felt that he was entitled to live with and be supported by his late master without any obligation to work!

Many Unionists felt that the condition of the freed Negro should be improved. According to a verse in *Old Abe Has Gone and Did It, Boys* (words by S. Fillmore Bennett, music by J. P. Webster):

> I 'spose de white folks know dat ole Massa Collyer go
>> For to teach de niggers how to write and read;
> But dat Stanley, Linkum's man, to de people did contend
>> Dat of such a ting we niggers hab no need.

An 1865 song, *That's What the Niggers Then Will Do* (words by Tom Russell, music by George H. Barton) indicated the eagerness of the Negroes to improve their station:

> This war has been a mighty institution for us niggers,
> It gave us a chance to show what we can do.
> The good work has begun; if they only will keep at it
> The niggers will be faithful and be true.
> We have proved that we can fight,
> Let us learn to read and write.
> We doesn't want to hold no place of trust.
> You have freed us from our pen;
> All we want is to be men.

Lest the joy of the Negro be thought unanimous, two songs expressed some doubt about all the fuss. *Young Eph's Lament* (words and music by J. B. Murphy) asked:

> Oh, whar will I go if dis war breaks de country up,
> And de darkies hab to scatter around?
> Dis dam Babolition, 'Mancipation and Secession
> Are a-going to run de nigger in de ground!

One Negro said, "a nigger will be a nigger," *Dat's My Philosophy* (words and music by Edward Berry):

> But I would like to see the white folks make their quarrels up,
>> And let the niggers be,
> For slave or free, a nigger will be a nigger,
>> Dat's my philosophy.

One of the most disgraceful aspects of the Reconstruction period which followed the war was the treatment of the freed Negroes by Northerners and carpetbaggers. The dream of equality did not come true.

Part 2: DIXIE IS MY HOME

Many slaves accompanied their Confederate officer-masters during the first year of the war. When members of slaveholding families enlisted in 1861, they frequently took with them favored and loyal slaves of the household as personal servants. The usual practice was for a single slave to minister to the needs of his own master or to a group of from four to eight officers. The duties of these Negroes consisted mainly of cooking, washing, and cleaning quarters. Thus the Negro in *Oh, Massa's Gwine to Washington* (words by Edmund Kirke, music by Charles S. Brainard) sings:

Hark! darkies, hark! it am de drum
Dat calls ole Massa 'way from hum,
Wid powder-pouch and loaded gun
To drive old Abe from Washington.

Dis darky know what Massa do,
He take him 'long to black him shoe,
To black him shoe and tote him gun,
When he am 'way to Washington.

Those attached to cavalry companies were required to look after their masters' horses. In addition, the Negroes frequently added a touch of gaiety to camp life.

During the battle, the servant usually remained in the rear, out of reach of enemy shells. A story is told of an officer who, before going into battle, ordered his Negro servant to watch his tent and take care of his property. The skirmish over, this officer was annoyed to discover that the Negro had deserted his post for the woods. On his later return, when the master threatened to chastise him, the slave said, "Massa, you done tol' me to take care of your property, and *dis* property," touching his breast, "is wurf fifteen hundred dollars and I done took care of it." When the fighting was ended, the servant would load himself with canteens and haversacks and set out in search of his master. If the latter was wounded, the servant carried him to shelter and sought medical assistance; if he was killed, the slave made arrangements for burial or took the body home. Such an incident is pictured in *The Worst of War:*

289

When my young master went to war
  He carried me wid him too;
And dough I never fired a shot
  Dere was plenty else to do.

He wore de sword an' buttons an' spurs,
  An' none was so brave as he;
But never so hard a thing did he do
  As the thing he lef' for me.

Where a storm of leaden hail fell
  He got a ball in his heart;
He died wid a smile on his face,
  But mine was de harder part.

I led his horse back home where dey sat
  Expectin' him—an' I saw
Mistis' an' Master's hearts when dey broke—
  An' dat was de worst of de war.

During the second and third years of the war, the use of Negroes as servants was abandoned because of the scarcity of provisions and the need of slave labor at home.

Many Negroes were used by the Confederacy in the construction of fortifications along the seacoast and river areas and at other strategic points. At first, planters responded generously to government calls for laborers; but in the second year it was often necessary to introduce impressment, and in 1864 levies became a general rule. In February, 1864, a Confederate law was passed authorizing the Secretary of War to conscript 20,000 Negroes for military labor. The " 'pressin' agent," who was sent around to collect the required workers, was dreaded by masters and slaves alike.

When the Confederacy was first created, there was a disposition in some quarters to take free men of color into Southern armies. A regiment was organized in New Orleans, but it was not accepted for service. In 1863, a proposal to arm slaves was launched by the press, but after a brief discussion the subject was dropped. In January, 1864, when manpower was at its lowest ebb, General Patrick Cleburne revived the question by advocating the enlistment of a large force of slaves and offering them freedom as a reward for faithful service, but President Davis ordered discussion of the matter closed.

As the reserve of Southern manpower dwindled, sentiment favoring the enlistment of Negroes increased. In November, 1864, Davis intimated a willingness to consider limited use of Negroes in the ranks; he wished to authorize the purchase from their owners of 40,000 slaves to be used as army cooks, teamsters, and labor troops. But the states felt that only they could legislate the domestic institution of slavery. The Governor of Virginia, William Smith, urged his legislature to arm the slaves for the state's defense and give them freedom. Citing the fact that almost 200,000 Negro soldiers were already in the Union Army at that time, the Governor asked, "Can we hesitate, can we doubt, when the question is whether the enemy shall use our slaves against us or we use them against him; when the question may be liberty and independence on the one hand or our subjugation and utter ruin on the other?" In January, General Lee spoke out clearly for arming the slaves, "accompanied by a well-digested plan of gradual and general emancipation."

Finally, in March, 1865, the Confederate Congress passed a law authorizing President Davis to call for as many as 300,000 slaves to serve as soldiers. A few companies were hurriedly organized, but the war came to an end before they could be used. Negroes who fought for the North aroused Southern ire; the average Confederate saw in the arming of the blacks the fruition of oft-repeated Yankee efforts to incite slave insurrections and to establish racial equality. Ideas of the Negroes as contrabands of war represented a reversal of the Southerners' entire way of life. When whites and blacks met on the field of battle, the results were often horrible.

Many Northerners believed that if the slaves were freed by Lincoln as a war measure while their masters were absent, the Negroes would rise in insurrection, or at least desert. However, the majority of slaves, particularly those far from the border states, were content to remain on the plantations; these loyal Negroes were often the only males for miles around. Many of those who took advantage of the Preliminary Emancipation Proclamation were dissatisfied with the conditions of their new lives. When the former slave discovered that he must work for his own support even as he had done before he became free, when he found out that under the new regime he was little better off than he had been as a slave, and when he faced the problem of unemployment, the poor fellow in some cases thought nostalgically of the old-time slave days. Southern composers made the Negro who had searched for happiness away from the old plantation and who had found only misfortune, failure, and calamity a subject of their songs.

The Negroes often became homesick because the mule and forty acres promised by the "liberators" never materialized; the freed slave was not accustomed to shifting for himself. In a song by Hermann L. Schreiner, a Negro implores *Take Me Home* to the place where I first saw the light,

To the sweet sunny South, take me home.

The Unhappy Contraband (words and music by Will S. Hays) felt that, in retrospect, his former life with his master looked mighty good, "kase he allers was so good and kind":

Oh, I wish dat I was back in Louisiana,
    An' a-hoein' ob de cotton an' de cane,
Oh, I knows dat I would be a happy nigger,
    But I'll neber see de sunny Souf again.

CHORUS:
Oh, oh, dey's dun played de debbil wid de land,
I'se gwine back to Louisiana
Kase I'se an unhappy Contraband.

I'se a-libin' in de Norf among de strangers,
    An' dey ain't a-gwine to gib me work to do,
Kase dar is so many white folks in de country
    Dat's got to work an' make a libin' too.

De niggers got no frens 'mong de white folks;
    De white folks got de niggers free;
An' I pities all de balance ob de niggers
    Ef dey ain't any better off dan me!

A contraband had a dream, told in *The Freedman's Song* (words by A. R. Watson, music by F. W. Smith), a Southern composition:

I dreamt last night ole massa came and took us home with he
To de log cabin dat we left when fust dey sot us free;
And dar I built de lightwood fire and Dinah cook de yam.
Dey say dat dreams are sometimes true! I wonder if dis am?

The Happy Contraband (words and music by J. Emerson) felt that the Negroes were better off on the old plantation:

The Negro and the Contraband

I'm a happy contraband, lately come from Ole Virginny,
    For master there I used to dig and hoe.
But as "Secesh" he was rated and his things was confiscated,
    An' I don't know where the debbil for to go;
I haven't got no clothes, my feet are almost froze,
    Cold winter, you know, is coming on.
But I never died yet, so I'll just get up and "git,"
    I'll sing and dance to keep myself warm,
For I tell you I'm a Happy Contraband.

CHORUS:
When this cruel war is over, Oh, won't we live in clover!
    To think of it makes my heart feel bigger!
Then 'way with 'mancipation, give me back the old plantation,
    'Tis the best place in the world for the nigger.

With the darkies gone from the cabins in search of this life which was not for them, with banjo and fiddle gone, it was certainly true that *The Old Home Ain't What It Used to Be* (words and music by C. A. White):

Oh, the old home ain't what it used to be,
    The banjo and the fiddle have gone;
And no more you hear the darkies singing
    Among the sugar-cane and corn;
Great changes have come to the colored man,
    But this change makes him sad and forlorn,
For no more we hear the darkies singing
    Among the sugar-cane and corn.

Now the old man would rather lived and died
    In the home where his children were born;
But when freedom came to the colored man
    He left the cottonfield and corn.
This old man has lived out his three score and ten
    And he'll soon have to lay down and die;
Yet he hopes to go unto a better land,
    So now, old cabin home, goodbye.

Most slaveowners were kind and sympathetic to their wards. The "missus" at home was occupied in keeping the slaves clothed and well fed.

293

At the war's end, many freed Negroes chose to remain on the plantations which they loved, to work as sharecroppers and to aid in the restoration of Southern economy. It was, however, never to be the same; a way of life had disappeared. For many, the "day of Jubilo" was a bitter disappointment.

✳✳✳✳✳✳✳✳

CHAPTER 8

✳✳✳✳✳✳✳✳

The Long, Weary Years

THE CONFEDERATE VICTORY in the First Battle of Bull Run, on July 21, 1861, stunned the North. The populace was thoroughly awakened; men responded more readily than before to the call for troops; and a spirit of determination seized the inhabitants of those states remaining in the Union.

General Irvin McDowell, commander of the defeated Army of the Potomac, was the subject of derision and widespread complaints, and his removal was demanded by everyone. General George B. McClellan, "the Napoleon of the West," who had been aiding the western counties of Virginia, after their refusal to join the Confederacy, in forming the Union state of West Virginia, was the logical successor.[18] All Northerners were urged to stand behind him in *Rally for the Union* (words by C. M. Tremaine, music by Septimus Winner):

Now Uncle Sam has got the dimes, that's so, that's so;
General McClellan is the man for the times, that's so, too.
So with all our money and plenty of men for freedom, for freedom,
I tell you, boys, we're bound to win. Cotton is not king.

[18] McClellan was always one of the most popular Union generals and was the subject of many songs, among them *The Noble George McClellan* (words by Rev. Edwin H. Nevin, adapted to a favorite melody), *McClellan and the Union, a Grand Rallying Song* (words from the Boston Courier, music by Albert Fleming), and *Brave McClellan Is Our Leader Now* (words by Mrs. M. A. Kidder, music by Augustus Cull). After he had been relieved of the command of the Army of the Potomac in November, 1862, Septimus Winner wrote *Give Us Back Our Old Commander.*

News of the victory at Manassas swept the South with a thrill of triumph. The people were understandably proud of their generals' proven competence and results of the first meeting with forces of the opposition. *Chivalrous C. S. A.,* to the lively tune of *Vive la Compagnie,* celebrated the victory:

> I'll sing you a song of the South's sunny clime, Chivalrous C. S. A.!
> Which went to housekeeping once on a time, Chivalrous C. S. A.!
>
> CHORUS:
> Chivalrous, chivalrous people are they!
> Chivalrous, chivalrous people are they!
> In C. S. A.! In C. S. A.!
> Aye, in chivalrous C. S. A.!

Succeeding stanzas showed the triumphant spirit which pervaded the Confederate States of America at this time:

> They have a bold leader, Jeff Davis is his name, Chivalrous C. S. A.!
> Good generals and soldiers, all anxious for fame, Chivalrous C. S. A.!
>
> At Manassas they met the North in its pride, Chivalrous C. S. A.!
> But they easily put McDowell aside, Chivalrous C. S. A.!

These early days of Southern exultation found expression in many songs with the similar theme of urging Southrons to awaken; some of these were cited in Chapter II. *The Southron's Watchword* (words by M. F. Bigney, music by Stephen Glover) was "the grave of a hero or victory," and *God Defendeth the Right* (words by Mrs. Dubose, music by Hermann L. Schreiner) was the theme of a song by a Richmond lady:

> Sons of the South arise!
>   Rise in your matchless might,
> Your war cry echo to the skies:
>   "God will defend the right!"

The fact that the North was so bitterly disappointed over the outcome only served to increase Southern jubilation, and the embarrassed and chagrined Unionists were due for many jibes. *Another Yankee Doodle,* to the tune of *Yankee Doodle,* began:

Yankee Doodle had a mind
To whip the Southern traitors,
Because they didn't choose to live
On codfish and potatoes.
Yankee Doodle, doodle-doo,
Yankee Doodle dandy,
And so to keep his courage up
He took a drink of brandy.

Yankee Doodle drew his sword
And practiced all the passes.
Come, boys, we'll take another drink
When we get to Manassas.
Yankee Doodle, doodle-doo,
Yankee Doodle dandy,
They never reached Manassas' plain,
And never drank the brandy.

The North soon discovered, as the last verse declared, that the South knew
how to use a rifle, so beware:

Yankee Doodle, all for shame,
    You're always intermeddling.
Leave guns alone, they're dangerous things,
    You'd better stick to peddling.
Yankee Doodle, fa so la,
    Yankee Doodle dandy,
When you get to Bully Run,
    You'll throw away your brandy.

And, to the tune of *Pop Goes the Weasel*, the Confederates sang:

King Abraham is very sick,
Old Scott[19] has got the measles,
Manassas we have now at last,
Pop goes the weasel!

A victory which would encourage the North and avenge the disgrace
of Bull Run was the goal toward which McClellan was to work. The

[19] General Winfield Scott, who was in his seventies.

capture of Richmond, for which his countrymen were still calling, became the objective of the Army of the Potomac. With renewed hope, the North anticipated a rapid march toward Richmond and a decisive thrust at the very heart of Secessionism which would terminate the war immediately. Some Unionists even said, *We'll Go Down Ourselves* (words and music by Henry C. Work) :

> What shall we do? What shall we do?
> Why, lay them on the shelves,
> And we'll go down ourselves,
> And teach the rebels something new!

The mismanagement, defeat, timidity, disgust, and dejection which followed all Union efforts to accomplish this end formed a long and unhappy tale. A succession of Union generals had their chances and failed. The minstrel-show tune *Jordan Am a Hard Road to Trabble,* by Dan Emmett of *Dixie* fame, was the setting for the chronological story of these failures :

> Would you like to hear my song, I'm afraid it's rather long,
> Of the half a dozen trips and half a dozen slips,
> And the very latest bursting of the bubble?
> 'Tis pretty hard to sing and like a round, round ring,
> 'Tis a dreadful knotty puzzle to unravel;
> Though all the papers swore, when we touched Virginia's shore,
> That Richmond was a hard road to travel.

> CHORUS:
> Then pull off your coat and roll up your sleeve,
> For Richmond is a hard road to travel;
> Then pull off your coat and roll up your sleeve,
> For Richmond is a hard road to travel, I believe!

> [*The six trips enumerated in succeeding verses were those of Mc-Dowell, Frémont, and Banks, the Union naval forces on the James River, McClellan, Pope, and Burnside, from July, 1861, to January, 1863.*]

> First McDowell, bold and gay, set forth the shortest way
> By Manassas, in the pleasant summer weather,

But unfortunately ran on a Stonewall—foolish man—
And had a "rocky journey" altogether;
And he found it rather hard to ride o'er Beauregard,
And Johnston proved a deuce of a bother;
And 'twas clear, beyond a doubt, that he didn't like the route,
And the second time would have to try another.

CHORUS:
Then pull off your coat and roll up your sleeve,
For Manassas is a hard road to travel;
Manassas gave us fits and Bull Run made us grieve,
For Richmond is a hard road to travel, I believe.

[*Manassas is a hard road. The defeat at Bull Run, unexpected as it was, made the North recognize that the war would be long and that the Union had better "roll up its sleeves" and settle down to a long struggle. Hence the increased calls for volunteers. Johnston and Beauregard were the Confederate generals.*]

Next came the Wooly-Horse with an overwhelming force,
To march down to Richmond by the Valley;
But he couldn't find the road and his "onward movement" showed
His campaign was merely shilly-shally.
Then Commissary Banks with his motley, foreign ranks
Kicking up a great noise, fuss and flurry,
Lost the whole of his supplies and with tears in his eyes,
From the Stonewall ran away in a hurry.

CHORUS:
Then pull off your coat and roll up your sleeve,
For the valley is a hard road to travel;
The Valley wouldn't do and we had all to leave,
For Richmond is a hard road to travel, I believe.

[*The Shenandoah Valley is a hard road. In the Peninsular Campaign of 1862, McClellan aimed to bring his forces by water as far as Fortress Monroe and then reach Richmond by crossing the narrow peninsula between the York and James rivers. McDowell's troops, held in Washington, were to provide reinforcements if needed. But the siege of Yorktown delayed the campaign a month, hence the valley route was tried. Jackson defeated Banks at Winchester in May and Frémont, the "wooly-horse," at Cross Keys in June.*]

Then the great Galena came with her port-holes all aflame,
And the Monitor, that famous naval wonder.
But the guns at Drewry's Bluff gave them speedily enough
The loudest sort of reg'lar Rebel thunder.
The Galena was astonished and the Monitor admonished;
Our patent shock and shell were mocked at,
While the dreadful Naugatuck, by the hardest kind of luck
Was knocked into an ugly cocked hat.

CHORUS:
Then pull off your coat and roll up your sleeve,
For James River is a hard road to travel;
The gunboats gave it up in terror and despair,
For Richmond is a hard road to travel, I declare!

[*The James River route is a hard road. In March, 1862, the Confederate ironclad Merrimac met the Union Monitor and was defeated. In May the Union fleet made an unsuccessful attack on Drewry's Bluff, eight miles below Richmond.*]

Then McClellan followed soon, with spade and balloon,
To try the Peninsula approaches.
But one and all agreed that his best rate of speed
Was no faster than the slowest of "slow coaches."
Instead of easy ground, at Williamsburg he found
A Longstreet indeed, and nothing shorter;
And it put him in the dumps, that spades wasn't trumps,
And the Hills he couldn't level "as he orter."

CHORUS:
Then pull off your coat and roll up your sleeve,
For Longstreet is a hard road to travel;
Lay down the shovel and throw away the spade,
For Richmond is a hard road to travel, I'm afraid.

[*Longstreet is a hard road on the Peninsular approach. Lee, with Jackson's men and with the aid of "Jeb" Stuart's cavalry units, was able to take the offensive and defeat McClellan in the Seven Days' Battle ending at Malvern Hill on July 1, 1862. Longstreet and Hill were the Confederate generals responsible for the defeat at Williamsburg.*]

Then said Lincoln unto Pope, "You can make the trip, I hope.

300

I will save the universal Yankee ration;
To make sure of no defeat, I'll leave no lines of retreat,
And issue a famous proclamation."
But that same dreaded Jackson, this fellow laid his whacks on,
And made him by compulsion a seceder.
And Pope took rapid flight from Manassas' second fight,
'Twas his very last appearance as a leader.

CHORUS:
Then pull off your coat and roll up your sleeve,
For Stonewall is a hard road to travel;
Pope did his very best but was evidently sold,
For Richmond is a hard road to travel, I'm told.

[*"Stonewall" Jackson is a hard road. Halleck replaced General Mc-
Clellan as commander in chief and Pope became head of the Army
of Virginia (with the corps of McDowell, Banks, and Frémont under
his command). Banks was defeated by Jackson at Cedar Mountain;
hence the word "seceder." Lee attacked and defeated Pope disastrously
at the second Battle of Bull Run on August 28–30. Meanwhile Lee
made several thrusts into Maryland, finally being stopped at Antietam.*]

Last of all, the brave Burnside, with his pontoon bridge, tried
A road no one had thought of before him.
With two hundred thousand men for the Rebel slaughter-pen
And the blessed Union flag waving o'er him;
But he met a fire-like hell of cannister and shell
That mowed his men down with great slaughter.
'Twas a shocking sight to view, that second Waterloo,
And the river ran with more blood than water.

CHORUS:
Then pull off your coat and roll up your sleeve,
Rappahannock is a hard road to travel;
Burnside got in a trap which caused him for to grieve,
For Richmond is a hard road to travel, I believe.

[*The Rappahannock is a hard road. Ill-starred Burnside, now remembered for the type of facial adornment he popularized, was known
as the general whose forces (the Army of the Potomac) were stuck
in the mud. The Confederate victory at Fredericksburg on the Rappahannock (December 13, 1862) was probably the worst slaughter of the*

301

entire war. The Southerners characterized the unlucky commander with a parody on a Mother Goose rhyme:

> *Burnside, Burnside, whither doth thou wander?*
> *Up stream, down stream, like a crazy gander?*]

We are very much perplexed to know who is next
To command the new Richmond expedition,
For the Capital *must* blaze and that in ninety days,
And Jeff and his men be sent to perdition.
We'll take the cursed town and then we'll burn it down,
And plunder and hang each cursed rebel;
Yet the contraband was right when he told us they would fight,
"Oh, yes, massa, they fight like the devil."

Then pull off your coat and roll up your sleeve,
For Richmond is a hard road to travel;
Then pull off your coat and roll up your sleeve,
For Richmond is a hard road to travel, I believe!

This type of "topical" song, outlining contemporary campaigns and battles, always enjoyed momentary popularity, particularly in minstrel shows. Stephen Foster composed a song which was typical of hundreds celebrating single victories. Northern theaters, where Dan Bryant's minstrels were performing, resounded to *That's What's the Matter:*

We live in sad and stirring times,
Too sad for mirth, too rough for rhymes;
For songs of peace have lost their chimes,
    And that's what's the matter!
The men we held as brothers true
    Have turned into a rebel crew,
So now we have to put them thro',
    And that's what's the matter.

CHORUS:
That's what's the matter,
The rebels have to scatter;
    We'll make them flee
    By land and sea,
And that's what's the matter.

302

Predicting as it did an immediate finish to the war, the theme proved altogether too optimistic. Foster undoubtedly changed his mind on that score, for he expressed the idea that too many people were attempting to conduct the war through the words of a Revolutionary War soldier, in *I'm Nothing but a Plain Old Soldier:*

> Again the battle song is resounding,
>   And who'll put the trouble to an end?
> The Union will pout and Secession ever shout,
>   But none can tell us now which will yield or bend.
> You've had many generals from over the land,
>   You've tried one by one and you're still at a stand,
> But when *I* took the field we had *one* in command,
>   Yet I'm nothing but a plain old soldier.

The gloom over the failure to travel successfully the long road to the Confederate capital caused Foster to enumerate the more encouraging exploits of the Union forces (the song was probably composed early in 1862) and to express the optimistic opinion that *Better Times Are Coming:*

> Now McClellan is a leader and we'll let him take the sway,
> For a man in his position, he should surely have his way.
> Our nation's honored Scott, he has trusted to his might,
> Your faith in McClellan put, for we are sure he's right.

Though too long and detailed (the complete song had nine verses) to gain widespread success, its rendition in a minstrel show was the signal for a storm of patriotic applause. The hope of "better times" was fruitless, as successive failures of a procession of leaders were to prove.

After Burnside's failure (verse seven of *Richmond Is a Hard Road to Travel),* "Fightin' Joe" Hooker was placed in command of the Army of the Potomac, but he was removed at Chancellorsville (May 2–3, 1863) where "Stonewall" Jackson was killed. Hooker was followed by General George G. Meade, a much more efficient man than any of his predecessors, who remained in command from the date of his appointment until the end of the war. Lee decided to invade the North again, disregarding the warning in *The Battles of July '63* (words by J. Worrall, with music by John Parry):

Now all ye secessioners, mind what I say;
Don't never advance into Pennsylvania.
For sure as you're born, it can easy be shown
Seceshers by Yankees are soon overthrown.

At Gettysburg, on July 1–3 (see Chapter VI), the tide turned against the Confederacy, though Meade failed to follow up his victory. In this battle, Southern soldiers had been reduced to using stones, nails, and railroad iron for missiles. Lee's wagon train was seventeen miles long, yet Meade delivered no thrust at the retreating columns. Thus, even in the midst of victory, this possible chance for ending the war was lost.

Union soldiers sang a parody to the tune of *When Johnny Comes Marching Home,* which memorialized the activities of this long line of generals:

We are the boys of Potomac's ranks, hurrah, hurrah!
We are the boys of Potomac's ranks, hurrah, hurrah!
We are the boys of Potomac's ranks,
We ran with McDowell, retreated with Banks,
And we'll all drink stone blind—Johnny, fill up the bowl.

We fought with McClellan, the Rebs, shakes and fever,
But Mac joined the navy on reaching James River.

They gave us John Pope, our patience to tax,
Who said that out West he'd seen nought but gray-backs.

He said his headquarters were in the saddle,
But Stonewall Jackson made him skedaddle.

Then Mac was recalled, but after Antietam
Abe gave him a rest, he was too slow to beat 'em.

Oh, Burnside, then he tried his luck,
But in the mud so fast got stuck!

Then Hooker was taken to fill the bill,
But he got a black eye at Chancellorsville.

Next came General Meade, a slow old plug,
For he let them get away at Gettysburg.

The soldiers had lost battle after battle because of successive blunders by a series of commanders. The increase in casualties was appalling. The end of the war seemed far off.

The soldiers' discovery of graft in handling Union supplies was destructive to morale and a retarding factor in enlistment. Much of the blanket and clothing material was so shoddy that a finger could be poked through it; the life of a contractor's pair of shoes was between twenty and thirty days, and many pairs would fall to pieces after soldiers tramped through the mud a few times. Several Union songs railed against the corruption which was rampant. *I Wish I Had a Fat Contract,* to the tune of *Barbara Allen,* promised:

Oh, if I had a fat contract
    To make the Army shoeses,
I wouldn't do as some folks do
    Who the so-gi-ers abuses;
I'd make the shoes so tight and strong,
    I'd make them neat and taper;
I'd make them all of leather
    And I wouldn't use no paper.

Oh, if I had a fat contract
    To find de pans and kittles,
De blankets and de oder tings,
    Likewise de soger's vittles,
I wouldn't give them rotten pork,
    A very nasty trick dat—
With salt beef made of leather,
    And de biscuit like a brickbat.

The dishonest army contractors were becoming wealthy, declared *The Shoddy Ball* (words and music by F. E. Garrett):

Sal Jones sells no more fish,
She goes not near her stall,
A contract made her rich,
She's at the shoddy ball.
Contractor Johnson's daughter
Was there, dressed up so fine,
With a diamond of first water
Dug from a shoddy mine.

Says she, "My own true love,

How came you here tonight?
I did not think you'd move
So far off from the fight.
Poor Uncle Samuel called
He wants you right away
To keep up shoddy balls
With Army contract pay."

A Washington telegraphic dispatch to the commander of the Army of the Potomac asked why the forward movement was delayed. The reply stated the impossibility of making a decided thrust until more wagons were obtained; to march with less than a thousand was out of the question, and these were not to be delivered until July 15, 1863. To the tune of *Wait for the Wagon,* an impatient Northerner, "E. F.," made an effort to explain *The Reason Why:*

Now if the army wagons needs, not for compromise you wait,
Just ask them of the farmers of any Union state;
And if you need ten thousand sound, strong, though second-hand,
You'll find upon the instant a supply for your demand.

CHORUS:
You must wait for the wagons,
The real army wagons,
The fat contract wagons,
Bought in the red-tape way.

No swindling fat contractors shall block the people's way,
Nor rebel compromisers—'tis treason's reckoning day.
Then shout again our war-cry, to Richmond onward move!
We now can crush the traitors, and that we mean to prove!

The speculators enjoyed a field day. Worthless, castoff European muzzle-loading muskets of the type used in the Revolutionary War were purchased at double their value: 1,092,000 muskets worth $13.50 in the open market were contracted for $28.00 each; Colt revolvers ordinarily priced at $15.00 cost the government $35.00; $2.50 pants brought a price of $5.00; 10,000 head of cattle fetched 8¢ a pound and were sub-contracted for 6½¢, thus netting $34,368 without any effort. Of 1,000 cavalry horses which cost the government $58,200, 485 were so worthless that they were subsequently condemned. Yet these profits were not unusual. As in all wars, soldiers in the field resented the profiteers. The situation was no better at home, for inflation set in with drains on the Union's economy. *How Are You, Greenbacks?* (words by E. Bowers, music by Charles Glover), complained of this:

> We're coming, Father Abraham,
>   One hundred thousand more,
> And cash was ne'er so easily evoked
>   From rags before,
> To line the fat contractor's purse
>   Or purchase transport craft
> Whose rotten hulks shall stink
>   Before the winds begin to waft!
> With our promises to pay,
> How are you, Gideon Wells, Esquire?
> Promise to pay.
> Oh, can't you fix the date?

Treasury Rats, according to a minstrel song, seemed to be in power:

> Treasury rats now rule the land,
> Everything moves by their command.
> They cut out the work and handle the pay
> And a charming song they sing today.
> Traitors and Copperheads, penniless knaves,
> You are the stuff to fill soldiers' graves!
> The country's great and only need
> Is that we shall make money
> While you shall bleed.
> This is true loyalty, on with the war!
> And this is what you are fighting it for.
> Go on killing each other gloriously
> 'Till we are as rich as we'd like to be.

In the face of superior forces and supplies, Southern military genius had held out through a series of victories. A united policy coupled with unexcelled leadership combined to offset the numerical superiority of the North. But Gettysburg was the beginning of the slow and painful process of Confederate deterioration, though Southerners were to fight long and hard, and to the death, before finally being overwhelmed.

307

The Confederate government cherished the hope that the European nations would intervene in its behalf. Their supply of cotton was cut off by the war, and the later Federal blockade of Southern ports seriously interfered with European commerce. Early Union military disasters formed excellent and convincing arguments for use by President Davis' agents in attempting to woo England and France to the South's support.

In the fall of 1861, while the victories at Bull Run and Ball's Bluff were still impressive arguments, two Confederate commissioners, James W. Mason and John Slidell, former senators from Virginia and Louisiana respectively, were dispatched with full powers to deal with European governments—Mason with England and Slidell with France. They were to ask that the Confederacy be recognized as a separate nation. But Captain Charles Wilkes of the U. S. Navy, bringing home the *San Jacinto,* a Federal warship which had been stationed near Africa, intercepted them on the British mail steamer *Trent* twenty-five miles out of Havana bound for England. After firing two shots across the vessel's bow, Wilkes boarded her and forcibly seized the two commissioners and took them to Boston as prisoners of war. The incident set off internal repercussions, barely avoiding a British declaration of hostilities. This "Trent Affair" called forth a stanza in *We're Marching Down to Dixie's Land:*

> They sent two Envoys Plenipo
> From Dixie's land, from Dixie's land
> To Johnny Bull and Jean Crapeau,
> Lest treason should go down.
> They rowed about from shore to shore,
> In Dixie's land, in Dixie's land.
>
> 'Til John Bull lent a helping oar,
> Lest treason should go down;
> A gallant plucky commodore
> From Yankee land, from Yankee land
> Just bagged them both, though John Bull swore;
> And treason shall go down.

One of the incidents in this capture was celebrated in song by a Confederate who drank a toast to *The Gallant Girl that Smote the Dastard Tory, Oh!.* When Slidell was removed from the *Trent,* a Union officer, Lieutenant Greer, ordered the commissioner's wife and daughter to leave the cabin. Miss Slidell refused, begging that she be taken prisoner with her father, to whom she clung, her arms around his neck. When the Lieutenant, in order to separate her forcefully from her father, grasped her, she briskly slapped him in the face three times. In his testimony later, Lieutenant Greer claimed that he was certainly not ungallant enough to have slapped the maiden, but that at the moment he had approached her father the boat had been struck by a swell and, losing his balance, he had grasped her to prevent them both from falling. Regardless of the truth, this song, with the alternate title of *The Slap*, recounts the story and proposes a "bumper," a glass filled to the brim, accompanied by a "thumper," a banging of the table with the fist, in honor of *The Gallant Girl that Smote the Dastard Tory, Oh!* (words by Klubs, music by Ducie Diamonds):

> Ho, gallants, brim the beaker bowl
> And click the festal glasses, oh!
> The grape shall shed its sapphire soul
> To eulogize the lasses, oh!
> And when ye pledge the lip and curl
> Of loveliness and glory, oh!
> Here's a bumper to the gallant girl
> That smote the dastard Tory, oh!
>
> CHORUS:
> A bumper, a thumper, to loveliness and glory, oh!
> A bumper to the gallant girl that smote the dastard Tory, oh!
>
> Our boys are fighting East and West,
> Our women do not linger, oh!
> They take their diamonds from the breast,
> Their rubies from the finger, oh!
> They send their darlings to the war
> Of honor and of glory, oh!
> They've all the spirit of a man
> To smite a dastard Tory, oh!

With England enraged over this incident, the time was ripe for close co-operation between Richmond and London. Although England remained neutral, she succeeded in arousing the ire of the North not only in the affair of Mason and Slidell, who were later released upon demand, but more particularly in her flagrant collaboration in the outfitting of war-ships for the use of the Confederacy. The Northerners took full advantage of this incident, as shown in *I Don't See It* (words and music by Frederick Hessler):

> The Secessers thought we were bent
>   On having with John Bull a fight;
> Because we made free with the Trent,
>   They hugged themselves up with delight.
> They all felt so sure we had tried
>   A move that we couldn't repair
> When we let the Commissioners slide.
>   "They don't see it" now they declare!

The *Alabama* was the most famous of these British-supplied gunboats. The cruiser, built as no. 290 in a Liverpool shipyard, over the protests of the United States minister, Charles Francis Adams, captured and destroyed —through burning and sinking—fifty-eight ships valued at almost seven million dollars, in all parts of the globe, during the period of the war, and was justly celebrated as a terror of the sea. *The Alabama* (words by E. King, music by Fitz William Rosier) celebrated the exploits of this raider:

> Our country calls all hands to arms,
> We hear but to obey;
> Nor shall home's most endearing charms
> Steal one weak thought away.
> Our saucy craft shall roam the deep,
> We've sworn, lads, to defend her;
> Trim, taut and tight, we'll brave the fight,
> Our motto "No surrender!"
>
> Boys! if perchance it may befall
> When storm of battle raves,
> By shot or shell our noble hull
> Shall sink beneath the waves;
> Yet while a plank to us is left
> To death we will defend her;
> Facing the foe, down, down we'll go,
> But still cry, "No surrender!"

The Long, Weary Years

The wind blows off yon rock-y shore, Boys, set your sails all free; And

soon our boom-ing can-non's roar Shall ring out mer - ri - ly.

Run up your bunt-ing taut a-peak And swear, lads, to de - fend her 'Gainst

ev - ry foe, where-e'er we go, Our mot - to "No Sur - ren - der!" Then

sing the bowl, drink ev-'ry soul, A toast to the A-la-ba-ma; What-

e'er our lot, through storm and shot, Here's suc-cess to the A-la-ba-ma!

The Alabama

The U. S. steamer *Kearsarge* finally sank the pirate ship off the coast of France on June 19, 1864. This event was celebrated in two songs, one of which was *The Last of the Alabama* (words and music by "Eastburn," probably Septimus or Joseph E. Winner), which described the encounter in nine verses, ending with the moral:

Now Britishers, do you beware
And don't to combat Yankees dare,
Or you perhaps the fate may share
Of Semmes' Alabama!

311

For Uncle Sam will never stand
An insult on the sea or land;
The men and ships at his command
    Can sink all Alabamas.

and the other *The Alabama and the Kearsarge* (words and music by Frank Wilder):

The Alabama's gone, hurrah!
To Davey Jones's locker far.
There's nothing left of her to mar
    Our commerce on the sea.

Her sister ships, the *Florida, Georgia, Shenandoah, Sumter,* and others, reported close to 165 additional prizes. Two verses from the Union *Our Neutral Friend* (words and music by J. P. Webster) dealt with these dangers:

Then the Alabama bold, built by British toil and gold
    Armed with British guns and manned by British fee, sirs,
From the Mersey where she lay with John's blessing sailed away
    And our merchant ships were sunk in every sea, sirs.
True, this man-of-war so brave quickly found a watery grave
    When she took the old Kearsarge's gauge of battle,
While the rebel pirates sought refuge on a British yacht
    When the gallant Winslow shot began to rattle.

Also sailed the Shenandoah when the war was wholly o'er,
    Sweeping whalers from the sea with British thunder.
From her cannons grim and black as the desolated track
    Which she made wher'ere she went with wreck and plunder.
Johnny plied a lively trade and a jolly spec he made,
    What with slipping into ports that were blockaded,
And with taking rebel loans though the latter he disowns,
    When he sees the list in public prints paraded.

The ravages of this fleet served to drive from the seas a large part of the Northern merchant marine.

Knowledge of England's part in equipping these frigates was obtained in each case before the ships left dock, but the British government refused, under one pretext after another, to prevent their sailings. England's depreciation of Northern successes and delight in Southern advantages, her claim that the Union was hopelessly disintegrated, and her characterization of the Northern Army as a mob of loose, shiftless, vulgar men brought forth articles by Union editors in opposition to John Bull. A cartoon in *Harper's Weekly* (April 25, 1863) depicted Uncle Sam as keeping John Bull's account on a blackboard. The years 1776 and 1812 had been marked as settled, but many checks for 1862 and 1863 were still outstanding.

One Philadelphia poet termed England *Dixie's Nurse* (words by Eastburn, the pseudonym for Joseph E. Winner, music by M. E.), characterizing the South as a child spoiled and pampered by England:

> Britannia was quite jealous of
>   Her neighbor, Uncle Sam,
> So, full of wicked thoughts did she
>   The head of Dixie cram.
> She nursed him well until she thought
>   He large enough had grown,
> To try the hard experiment
>   Of standing all alone.
>
> She built him many pretty ships
>   With which to sail the sea,
> And taught him how to rob, and play
>   The game of Piracy.
> Of swords and rifles, shot and shell,
>   She gave him quite a store,
> And took his worthless cotton bonds
>   For twice as many more.

The queerest of queer things in the war, related another song, was *English Neutrality* (words and music by William M. Doughty):

> Some queer things occur in this vale of mortality,
> Some that are common and others more rare,
> But the queerest of queer things is English neutrality,
> Shown by her conduct in this present war.
>
> A very queer thing is this English neutrality,
> Crying, "Fair play," but yet helping one side;
> It would be all O. K. if 'twere only reality,
> And it could have been so had she but tried.

Individual verses of many songs during wartime reflected the tenseness of Northern relations with England. The fourth verse of the famed and popular *Abraham's Daughter* contained a word of caution:

> We'll have a spree with Johnny Bull
> > Perhaps some day or other,
> And won't he have his fingers full,
> > If not a deal of bother?
> For Yankee boys are just the lads
> > Upon the land or water,
> And won't we have a "bully" fight,
> > And don't you think we oughter,
> If he is caught at any time
> > Insulting Abraham's daughter?

George Root's last war song, *Good-bye, Old Glory,* written at the close of the war, after having bade farewell to pens and prison holes, disaster, famine, and ruin, gave warning to John Bull:

> Good-bye to muster and parade,
> > Good-bye the grand review,
> The dusty line, the dashing aide,
> > Goodbye the general, too;
> Good-bye to war. But halt! I say,
> > John Bull, a word with you.
> Pay up old scores or we again
> > May don the army blue.

And a verse from *Rebellion's Weak Back* (words and music by F. Wilmarth) was militant in its resentment of England's interference:

> And there's old Johnny Bull, he's confoundedly dull
> Or he'll mind his own business just now, sirs;
> For we Yankees can lick old England right quick
> And the rest of Creation, I vow, sirs!

The same idea was expressed in a verse from *Hoist Up the Flag* (words by Billy Holmes, music by Septimus Winner):

> Old England is trying to kick up a fuss;
> We think they had better not interfere with us!

If they come to fight, they'll find it no fun;
They'll get what they got from General Washington.

Another Union song, *Jonathan to John* (words by Hosea Bigelow, music by F. Boot), included a verse as a challenge to England:

Shall it be love or hate, John?
    Its you that's to decide!
Aint *your* bonds held by fate, John,
    Like all the world's beside?

Great Britain proved not to be dependent upon Confederate cotton, and additional war profits from the blockade, together with the impressive victories of Gettysburg and Vicksburg, made it seem wiser to put confidence in the Union. France was too weak to oppose the Union government alone, although Napoleon III was decidedly unfriendly, even sponsoring the ill-fated monarchy of Emperor Maximilian in Mexico. Both countries, according to a verse in *The Nerves,* were afraid of the North:

Both France and England now look on
    And speak with great reserve,
For Yankee Doodle is the boy
    That will keep up his nerve!

Both eventually came to the conclusion that nothing was to be gained by intervening in what was a purely domestic struggle.

The war inevitably produced military idols in profusion, and victories were always followed by paeans of praise for the successful leaders. When a popular or picturesque figure failed to continue his successes, however, his popularity abruptly ceased, and he was superseded in the public's acclaim by another. A few leaders enjoyed continuous and well-merited celebrity and popular adoration; Robert E. Lee, for example, held the love of the Confederacy and the respect of his enemies to the end and even thereafter. Poems in praise of individuals were set to music in great numbers, far too many to be treated here. Typical tributes to Union heroes Grant and Sherman are included in later sections in connection with their outstanding accomplishments—the former at the siege of Vicksburg, the latter in the march to the sea. Lincoln was a frequent song subject.

315

The affection which Confederates lavished on their leaders was one of the remarkable phenomena of the war. Leaders of the American Civil War were notably beloved and idolized. Today, the expressions of devoted sentiment seem extravagant and excessive. One attribute, however, cannot be denied—the praise of the South for her great men is always thoroughly sincere. During the war, the Southerners were, as never before, a band of brothers. There was, therefore, in relations with their great men, a personal contact and appeal which in the North was not so keenly felt.

Because they are picturesque, yet completely different, personalities of vivid and swift action, two Confederate leaders—"Stonewall" Jackson and "Jack" Morgan—are typical examples of heroes whose exploits inspired musical and poetic outbursts.

Next to General Lee, the most beloved Southern soldier was General Thomas J. Jackson, a man who had kept in training after the Mexican War as professor of mathematics and artillery tactics in the Virginia Military Institute at Lexington. He lacked the social graces to make him a society favorite. Tall, rawboned, with big hands and a peculiar stride, he was impressive as a leader who possessed human qualities and who was always approachable.

The origin of his nickname, "Stonewall," is told in two stories, both possibly fictitious. It is recounted that, during the First Battle of Bull Run, Confederate General Barnard Bee rode over to Jackson and said, "General, they are beating us back." "No, sir," was the reply, "We will give them the bayonet." Bee rode back and spoke to his brigade: "Look at Jackson there standing like a stone wall! Rally behind the Virginians!" The other story, appearing in *Harper's Weekly* on March 14, 1863, claimed that he received his nickname as a result of his promise to General Beauregard that his brigade of new troops should stand like a stone wall before the enemy. His men stood, but they became the opposite of a stone wall; they were exceptionally mobile and soon were called "Jackson's foot cavalry." Even his fellow general and brother-in-law, Daniel H. Hill, said these tales were "sheer fabrication," and "the name was least suited to Jackson, ever in motion, sweeping like an eagle on his prey, but the name spread like wildfire."

Jackson attained his first fame in the Shenandoah Valley in May, 1862. In 48 days he marched 676 miles; fought 5 hard battles, accomplishing in each his purpose; baffled 3 Union armies under McDowell, Frémont, and Banks—his 17,000 men matched against 50,000; brought off his prisoners and much booty; ruined McClellan's campaign; and struck the North with terror. For swift troop movement this campaign was outstanding in the history of warfare. "Mystify, mislead and surprise" was his motto, and then "hurl overwhelming numbers at the point where the enemy least expects attack."

Though he was later blamed for the failure of the Seven Days' Battle of the Peninsular Campaign in June, because of unexpected slowness in his operations, he more than retrieved himself at the Second Battle of Bull Run (August 27–September 2, 1862) and in the Maryland campaign captured Harpers Ferry, marching through Frederick where the aged Barbara Fritchie of later poetic legend was said to have unfurled the Union banner to defy him. On this "invasion" of Maryland, Jackson's troops were the first to cross the Potomac River. They sang *Maryland, My Maryland* as they waded the river in columns of four, each man with his trousers and shoes hung around his neck.

Jackson himself was a very religious man who prayed long and earnestly before every engagement. All of the songs which center about this heroic figure—and there are many—contain references to his prayers. His petitions were the prayers of any devout commander under similar circumstances—prayers for success at arms. A telegram to Richmond announcing a triumph read, "God has blessed our arms with another glorious victory." While his men were out on skirmishes, he would often remain in his tent to pray. In *Riding a Raid,* to the air of *Bonnie Dundee,* we read:

> Now gallop, now gallop, to swim or to ford,
> Old Stonewall, still watching, prays low to the Lord.
> Goodbye, dear old rebel, the river's not wide,
> And Maryland's lights in the windows do shine.

His faithful Negro servant would often meet officers early in the morning and say, "Gentlemen, there's gwine to be hard fightin' today. Marse Tom was on his knees prayin' all night long."

He is pictured as a devoted husband and father in *Stonewall Jackson's Prayer* (words by L. Rieves or Henry P. Jackson, music by B. A. Whaples):

> The tattoo beats, the lights are gone,
>   The camp around in slumber lies.
> The night with solemn face moves on
>   And sad, uneasy thoughts arise.

I think of thee, oh, dearest one,
  Whose love my early life hath blest,
Oh thee, and our dear infant son
  Who slumbers on thy gentle breast.

This well-known love was expressed in a popular poem, *My Wife and Child,* set to music by Fitz William Rosier, the authorship of which was erroneously attributed to him since it was written by John R. Jackson, a field officer in a Southern regiment during the Mexican War.

A Northern newspaper correspondent, John W. Palmer, wrote the poem *Stonewall Jackson's Way* during the roar of the guns at Antietam. The original copy dropped from his pocket in the heart of the Union encampment and was found on the body of a Confederate sergeant of the Second Stonewall Brigade who was killed at Winchester. Published in the *Baltimore Republican,* it was set to music in two versions, the more popular by Frederick Benteen. The Confederate sympathizers in Baltimore became so enthusiastic about the song that the Provost Marshal of the occupying force seized and destroyed all existing copies. But it had already gone through the lines and soon became extremely popular in the South. The spirit of Jackson's men is well shown in this song:

We see him now; the queer slouched hat
  Cocked o'er his eye askew;
The shrewd, dry smile; the speech so pat,
  So calm, so blunt, so true!
The 'cute old Elder knows him well:
Says he, "That's Banks—he's fond of shell;
Lord save his soul! We'll give him ——"
Well! That's Stonewall Jackson's way.

Silence! ground arms! kneel all! caps off!
  Old Blue Light's going to pray;
Strangle the fool that dares to scoff—
  Attention! It's his way!
Appealing from his native sod
In *forma pauperis* to God,
"Lay bare Thine arm! Stretch forth Thy rod!
Amen!"—that's Stonewall's way.

It was a strange stroke of fate that brought this noble man to death

The Long, Weary Years

Come, stack arms, men! pile on the rails, Stir up the camp fire

bright; No mat-ter if the can-teen fails, We'll make a roar-ing night; Here

Shen-an-do-ah crawls a-long, Here bur-ly Blue Ridge ech-oes strong, To

swell the bri-gade's rous-ing song Of Stone - wall Jack - son's way.

Stonewall Jackson's Way

at the hands of his own soldiers. With victory practically in the Union's grasp, Hooker had been outwitted at Chancellorsville, Virginia, on May 3, 1863, by one of Jackson's famous flank movements. While directing these maneuvers, Jackson was accidentally shot in the arm by one of his own pickets. Amputation failed to save the popular idol's life. The next day, General Lee sent a note: "Could I have directed events, I should have chosen, for the good of the country, to have been disabled in your stead. I congratulate you upon the victory which is due to your skill and energy." "General Lee is very kind," said Jackson when this message was delivered to him, "but he should give the praise to God." "You have lost only your left arm, while I have lost my right," Lee said to him on a visit later in the week. Jackson continued to give military orders throughout his delirium, and his last words, though they sound like a religious sentiment, were the culmination of a protracted series of commands—"Let us pass over the river and rest in the shade of the trees." They formed the subject of a song entitled *Stonewall Jackson's Last Words* (words by J. H. S., music by Edward Best).

The entire Confederacy mourned his death, commemorated in at least two songs—one *The Death of Stonewall Jackson* (words and music by C. Blamphin), the other *Stonewall's Requiem* (words and music by M. Deeves), typical of a popular type of tribute to fallen heroes:

The muffled drum is beating,
    There's a sad and solemn tread,
Our banner's draped in mourning
    As it shrouds th' illustrious dead.
Proud forms are bent in sorrow,
    And all Southern hearts are sore;
The hero now is sleeping,
    Noble Stonewall is no more.

His death was the worst single blow the Confederacy sustained during the entire war.

The other popular Confederate hero chosen for special mention here is the cavalry raider, John Hunt Morgan, a man quite the opposite of Jackson and representative of the daring leader whose exploits captured the imaginations of the stay-at-homes. He was a large man, over six feet tall, and was not at all religious. When the impossibility of remaining neutral became evident to the people of his home state, Kentucky, and they tended to favor affiliation with the Union, he stole some United States rifles and horses and, with 200 Confederate sympathizers, set out to join the Southern forces. He and his band, which ranged in number from 860 to over 5,000 men, gained their reputation as guerrilla cavalry when they successfully raided Nashville, Tennessee, in March, 1862, followed by their "terror" forays into Kentucky in July, destroying three Union supply depots. In the December "Christmas Raids," Kentucky was invaded five times by the band, which tore up railroads and burned depots.

But his greatest expedition, in the summer of 1863, was intended to cover General Braxton Bragg's retreat from Tullahoma by causing disturbances in Kentucky to engage the attention of Union forces sufficiently for the retreat to be unobserved. Morgan asked permission to cross the Ohio River into Ohio and Indiana, feeling that he could create such terror that all troops in that section would be sent after him. He was strictly forbidden to carry out this plan, which was based on his desire to make the North feel what actual warfare was like. However, he disobeyed orders and advanced with 2,600 men into Indiana and Ohio. The coming of his soldiers was a signal for terror; inhabitants of villages in the path of his travel fled their homes. His force was actually outnumbered, but skillful maneuvering gave the impression of a very large Southern force. Passing near Cincinnati, the column attempted to re-cross the Ohio but found itself pursued and the way blocked. One of the band who was taken prisoner and sent to Chicago explained in the chorus to *Camp Douglas by the Lake:*

John Morgan crossed the river,
    And I went across with him;
I was captured in Ohio
    Because I could not swim.

Fleeing farther north with the remnants of his forces, Morgan and the 364 remaining men were captured on July 26 near the Pennsylvania border, the northernmost point reached by any armed Confederate force during the war. The story of this raid, showing the terror of Ohioans when the cavalry guerrillas approached, is told in *How Are You, Telegraph?; or, The John Morgan Song* (words by W. Collins, music by G. W. Work). Morgan always captured local telegraph offices on his route, and as he advanced his men tapped out messages containing misleading information or dispatches designed to create panic. On this particular raid he was in territory where "the wires don't run":

John came in excellent style, to be sure,
    With banner and brand came he;
His clattering hoofs made a terrible roar,
    And his cannon numbering three.
The Hoosiers were scared, so entered the race,
    What a rowdyish set were they;
And the Buckeyes mounted to join in the chase,
    As Johnny galloped their way.

CHORUS:

Ho! gather your flocks and sound the alarm
For the Partisan rangers have come;
Bold knights of the road, they scour each farm
And scamper at tap of the drum.
How are you, Telegraph?

These exploits were occasioned by Morgan's bitter resentment of Ken-

How Are You, Telegraph?; or, The John Morgan Song

tucky's allegiance to the Union. He was not a man to be contented with showing his feelings through circuitous actions, and for this reason the Kentuckians were the particular targets of his forays. His men were devil-may-care adventurers who loyally gave *Three Cheers for Our Jack Morgan* (words by Eugene Raymond, pseudonym of John H. Hewitt, music by Dan Emmett):

> The snow is in the cloud,
>   And night is gathering o'er us,
> The winds are piping loud,
>   And fan the blaze before us;
> Then join the jovial band,
>   And tune the vocal organ,
> And with a will we'll all join in,
>   Three cheers for our Jack Morgan!
>
> Jack Morgan is his name,
>   The fearless and the lucky,
> No dastard foe can tame
>   The son of old Kentucky.
> His heart is with his state,
>   He fights for Southern freedom,
> His men their General's word await,
>   They'll go where he will lead 'em.

He escaped from the penitentiary at Columbus, Ohio, on November 27, 1863, by tunneling through stone floors, across the prison yard, and under the outside walls. A popular piano solo, with elaborate musical representations of shots and clatter of horses' hoofs, was *John Morgan's Escape,* by A. E. A. Muse.

His troopers were not mere plundering, roving bands of men out to enjoy themselves; they fully intended to injure the Union Army directly. Morgan had a feeling for the geography of the country which he coupled with keen strategy to outwit his adversaries. His men were fed by foraging parties, and fresh horses were supplied by willing (and unwilling) residents of the country through which he happened to be passing and from captured Union wagon trains. An edition of the nonsense song *Here's Your Mule,* published in Nashville, had an extra verse to be pasted in the margin of copies:

Come on, come on, come on, old man,
    And don't be made a fool;
I'll tell you the truth as best I can,
    "Johnny Morgan's got your mule!"

Kentucky being the scene of his major terrorist activities, a lament
to the state was set to the tune of *Maryland, My Maryland,* titled *Kentucky:*

For feeding John you're paying dear,
    Kentucky! O, Kentucky!
His very name now makes you fear,
    Kentucky! O, Kentucky!
In every valley far and near,
You'll rue his raids for many a year,
    Kentucky! O, Kentucky!

An aroused citizenry finally proved his undoing. His troopers and
horses were continually being captured during the summer raids into
Kentucky in 1864. Finally, surrounded by only a remnant of his men, he
was shot through the heart in September as he left his tent during a surprise attack on his band in Tennessee.

As a daring Confederate raider, he represented the aggressive spirit
of the South and was widely known as "Our Morgan" and "the thunder-
bolt of the Confederacy." In the North, less flattering superlatives were
attached to his name—"the great guerrilla," "the great freebooter," and
"the king of horse thieves." Certainly he was one of the most picturesque
soldiers in either North or South.

In spite of the rigorous blockade, the Confederacy was able to obtain
supplies from Europe by way of Mexico and Texas. As the second largest
port of the United States and the center of Mississippi River traffic, as
well as the key to its use, New Orleans was of strategic importance. Placing
of military emphasis elsewhere caused Confederate failure to fortify the
city properly. In the spring of 1862, a Union naval squadron under Ad-
miral David Farragut attacked the city, which fell on May 1 and was
occupied by troops under General Benjamin Butler. The defender, General Mansfield Lovell, was burlesqued in *A New Ballad of Lord Lovell:*

Lord Lovell, the city he vowed to defend,
    Awaiting, his sword on high;

He swore the last ounce of powder he'd spend
  And in the last ditch he'd die, die, die.

He swore by black and he swore by blue;
  He swore by the stars and the bars;
He never would fly from a Yankee crew
  While he was a son of Mars.

Oh, a wonder it was to see them run!
  A wonderful thing to see!
And the Yankee sailed in without firing a gun
  And captured their great city.

Lord Lovell marched out of New Orleans;
  He went at the double quick
And gallant Old Ben marched in with his men
  Which made the poor rebels feel sick.

The Mississippi River was thus cut off as an avenue of supply. Union forces, however, were never able to prevent completely the running of the Atlantic blockade. New methods of evasion were devised by the Confederates as fast as old ones proved ineffective; the final one was the development of a special type of ship built in England—long, narrow, and swift. Painted gray and practically invisible beyond a distance of several hundred yards, these privateers made nocturnal dashes through the blockading squadrons. Early in 1864, about two out of three runners escaped. During the entire blockade, 1,504 runners of all sizes were captured or destroyed by Union naval forces.

Vicksburg was the only major city along the Mississippi River (the backbone of the Confederacy) which was free of Union forces in the summer of 1862; not a Federal ship was on the river. The town, heavily fortified behind a steep bluff, suddenly assumed tremendous importance. It became Grant's primary objective to take this "Gibraltar of the South." The Northern armies were having setbacks under Burnside and Hooker early in 1863, when an expedition against Vicksburg failed miserably. Grant determined to storm this most important Southern citadel in May, even constructing canals to divert the river from the large bend where it was situated, but the spring floods failed to materialize, as recounted in a verse of *U. S. G., A National Walkaround* (words and music by Daniel D. Emmett):

Grant marched his men, worn out and jaded
To Vicksburg where he was blockaded;
He dug a canal (none dare dispute him);
The river would not rise to suit him.

A fleet under Commander David Porter was dispatched to try to pound the town into submission, as set forth in *Ho, Boys, de Time Am Come* (words and music by C. R. Packard):

Uncle Sam send he Porter as just he orter
To open de doors all 'round dar;
But dey wouldn't let him in and so he begin
Wiv his gum boats to knock 'um all down dar.

Failing in all these devices, his armies bogged down in the surrounding swamplands, in May Grant determined upon a siege which was to be one of the most desperate episodes of the war.

During the siege, Confederate defenders were subjected to the heaviest fire of the war. Minnie balls and Parrot shells literally whistled through the air. The Union river fleet, under General Porter, constantly bombarded the town. The never-ending cannonading was so severe that heads ached splittingly from continuous concussions. Artillery and sharpshooters sent soldiers and civilians alike into cellars and caves burrowed into the hillsides. Next to hunger and starvation, this clamor and pandemonium was a factor in the eventual surrender. Lines of communication having been effectively cut off, available commissary supplies were rapidly exhausted. Before the siege began, Logan, the Confederate commissary officer, drove some herds of Texas beef within the safety of the breastworks. As the weeks passed and the supply of fodder dwindled, these unfortunate beasts grew leaner and leaner, as well as tougher and tougher. The rage of the defending forces was vented on Logan; two members of the Third Louisiana Regiment, A. Dalsheimer and Captain J. W. A. Wright, to the tune of *A Life on the Ocean Wave* (composed by Henry Russell in 1838), sang of *A Life on the Vicksburg Bluff*

A life on the Vicksburg bluff, a home in the trenches deep,
Where we dodge Yank shells enough, and our old pea bread
        won't keep.
On old Logan's beef I pine for there's fat on his bones no more;
Oh! Give me some pork and brine, and truck from a sutler's store.

326

Old Grant is starving us out, our grub is fast wasting away;
Pemb' don't know what he's about, and he hasn't for many a day.
So we'll bury old Logan tonight, from tough beef we'll be set free;
We'll put him far out of sight, no more of his meat for me!

Texas steers are no longer in view, mule steaks are now done up brown,
While pea-bread, mule roast and mule stew are our fare in
      Vicksburg town;
And the song of our hearts shall be, while the Yanks and their
      gunboats rave,
A life in a bomb-proof for me, and a tear on "old Logan's" grave.

Mule meat was actually issued and eaten in Vicksburg four days before the capitulation, when dwindling food supplies made such action necessary. The defenders were exhausted by constant pounding of gun and shell and acutely near actual starvation. Commanding General John C. Pemberton surrendered the town July 4, 1863, as described in *Ulysses Leads the Van* (words and music by E. W. Locke):

This plan had failed and so had that
    And worthless were the ditches.
He saw he'd got to run their fire
    And take them by the breeches.
So, tiger-like, he made a spring
And seized them in the tender;
"Hold on," said Pem, "I've got enough,
    I might as well surrender."

The fall of Vicksburg was a signal for exultation throughout the North. It was a fitting holiday celebration, according to verses in *Vicksburg Is Taken, Boys* (words and music by E. W. Hicks):

The great C. S. A. is now severed in twain,
    And both of them shortly must die;
But he will not forget 'till the end of his reign,
    That wonderful Fourth of July!

Bring out the spare powder and fire the big guns,
    The rebs are surprised at the way
Columbia's loyal and true-hearted sons
    Have honored their country's birthday.

This brilliant culmination of a three-month siege helped greatly to restore confidence throughout the Northern states. From that point on, the tide turned, and Grant, the hero of the hour, was hailed as the hope of the Union. The North's gratitude poured itself out in songs such as *All Hail to Ulysses* (words by Charles Haynes, music by James E. Haynes), which acclaimed him as:

> . . . the patriot's friend, the hero of battles renowned.
> He has won the bright laurel, its garland he wears,
> And his fame throughout the world we will sound.

Coming as it did, simultaneously with the defeat at Gettysburg, this surrender filled the South with apprehension about the future. Already in possession of too few troops, the loss of 30,000 prisoners and arms for 60,000 men was a severe blow. Many Northerners saw a possible immediate end of the war and urged the troops to *Strike While the Iron's Hot!* (words and music by R. Hastings):

> Vicksburg and Gettysburg,
>   Bright and glorious days!
> To the heroes of each fight
>   Grant the Meade of praise!
> On 'till the struggle's o'er;
>   Traitors know their doom.
> Strike, strike in freedom's name!
>   End the matter soon!

This play on words—using names of commanders of the simultaneous victories—was used in several songs, of which *The Union Prayer for Victory* (words and music by Mrs. E. L. Webster) is typical:

> Thy strength impart in time of need
> While hearts and hands are raised to Thee.
> And like an ever-growing Meade
> Grant us a lasting victory!

Sentiment to end the war was expressed in a New Orleans song, *Sheath the Sword, America* (words by Mrs. C. Edmonstone, music by A. Cardone), which called upon the sons of America "to demand rest and to let war and its dread horrors cease." Others, as in *One Flag or No Flag* (words by Ed. Willet, music by R. P. Robbins), felt that the struggle should continue until unity was restored:

> Then bloody and long though the contest may be,
> Our freemen must fight for the cause of the free!
> Though rivers of blood may yet deluge the land
> Our hearts must not fail us nor slacken our hand.
> No counting the cost for the Union is worth
> All the lives of the South and the lives of the North.
> For what is the value to you or to me
> If the stars shall be torn from the flag of the free?

And, according to *Follow the Drum* (words by W. Dexter Smith, Jr., music by Matthias Keller), peace must be won:

> Freemen, this fair land no tyrant can sever,
> Home of the millions of freemen to come.
> Shall they be slaves to a despot forever?
> Strike for the future and follow the drum!
> Never in gladness but ever through sorrow
> Must the bright triumphs of great nations come.
> War is but dross of the peace of tomorrow,
> Peace must be fought for, so follow the drum!

The Union must continue the fight and not lag, affirmed *Uncle Sam, What Ails You?* (words by Charles C. Sawyer, music by John M. Loretz):

> Uncle Sam, we know you're strong
>   Both on land and water.
> Why then, with these rebels play?
>   Meet them as you oughter!
> Meet them with the sword and gun
>   Nor for a moment falter!
> Meet them man to man at least,
>   Meet them with the halter!

The surrender of Port Hudson, the last Confederate stronghold on the Mississippi, a few days after the fall of Vicksburg, on July 9, 1863, cleared the river for the Union, cut the Confederacy in two, and completed the longest effective blockade in history. The 3,500 miles of coast from the Chesapeake River to the Mexican border were already so closely blockaded that the South had difficulty in exporting its cotton and importing desperately needed supplies from foreign countries which were willing and eager to do business. Lincoln summarized this triumph by the remark that "The Father of Waters again goes unvexed to the sea."

Throughout the last months of 1863 and early 1864, the Federal government was attempting to arrange for the purchase of Confederate cotton, of which there was an immense public and private surplus, badly needed by Northern mills, in return for gold, sterling, or supplies. General Nathaniel P. Banks strongly disapproved but wanted to confiscate the cotton, offer it for sale, and give most of the proceeds to the Union treasury, the remainder to collaborating Southerners. But Confederate generals E. Kirby Smith, commander of the Trans-Mississippi Department, and Richard Taylor thwarted the plan by ordering the burning of cotton when necessary to avoid its capture. A Southern parody on *When Johnny Comes Marching Home,* then currently popular, tells how the Unionists went down to New Orleans *For Bales* (words by A. E. Blackmar, music by Louis Lambert):

> We all went down to New Orleans, for bales, for bales;
> We all went down to New Orleans for bales, says I;
> We all went down to New Orleans
> To get a peep behind the scenes.
>
> CHORUS:
> And we'll all drink stone blind,
> Johnny, fill up the bowl.
>
> We thought when we got in the "Ring"
> Greenbacks would be a dead sure thing.
>
> But Taylor and Smith, with ragged ranks
> Burned up the cotton and whipped old Banks.
>
> Our "Ring" came back and cursed and swore,
> For we got no cotton at Grand Encore.
>
> Now let us all give praise and thanks
> For the victory [?] gained by General Banks!

The story of the South's resistance against the Union expedition up the Red River is a tale of Confederate success and Northern miscalculations and military ineptness. While en route to Shreveport, possession of which would have meant complete control of Louisiana and Arkansas, the 30,000 Union soldiers, instead of being massed, were strung out, the roads cluttered with supplies and wagons. Co-ordination of infantry, artillery, and cavalry was impossible when they were surprised by the Confederate forces. At Sabine Crossroads on April 8, 1864, the Northerners were completely routed, retreating in a disorganized panic.

The fallen heroes of the western campaigns are remembered in the Southern *By the Banks of Red River* (words by E. E. Kidd, music by Theodore von La Hache), a type of melancholy song such as followed every major engagement of the war:

> Oh, gone is the soul from his wondrous dark eye,
> And gone is her life's dearest glory.
> The tales of fond lovers unheeded pass by,
> Her heart hears a single sad story;
> How her gallant young hero fell asleep and will never
> Awake from his dream by the banks of Red River.
>
> CHORUS:
> How her gallant young hero fell asleep, and will never
> Awake from his dream by the banks of Red River.

The years 1861, 1862, 1863, and 1864 were indeed long and weary—years in which the balance of victory passed successively from North to South and from South to North, with success in a battle but failure in a campaign or vice versa. Yet nothing seemed decisive, and the months passed almost monotonously with always a ray of hope that the end might be nearer than events seemed to indicate. The tide seemed to have turned late in 1863, and thereafter the Union's vast superiority in supplies, manpower, and resources began to assert itself. The struggle settled down to a finish fight, with continuous hammering and bursts of strength against an almost exhausted but still doggedly courageous and resolute foe.

CHAPTER 9

The Curtain Falls

AFTER THE FALL of Vicksburg, Grant assumed command of the Army of the Cumberland. In a battle around Chattanooga (November 23–25, 1863), he drove the main Confederate Army in the West from Tennessee. General Sherman forced a continued and continuous retreat south toward Atlanta through the spring and summer of 1864, culminating in that city's fall on September 2.

Grant was appointed commander in chief of all Union forces in March and began a showdown with Lee in the East. The battles of the Wilderness, Spotsylvania (which brought forth his famous dispatch: "I propose to fight it out on this line, if it takes all summer"), and Cold Harbor in May and June were bloody but inconclusive. Grant's remark at Spotsylvania gave rise to *We'll Fight It Out Here on the Old Union Line* (words by Chaplain Lozier, music by George F. Root):

> Then rally again, then rally again
> With the soldier and sailor and bummer,
> And we'll fight it out here on the old Union line
> No odds, if it takes all summer.

However, Confederate forces were beginning to dwindle, whereas Northern losses, when heavy, were immediately replaced. Grant and Sherman, as states *Abraham the Great and General Grant His Mate* (words and music by T. Brigham Bishop), were to prove the right combination to end the war:

Then let us work away and care not what we say,
For freedom in the South is plainly dawning;
With Abraham the Great and General Grant his mate
They'll bring us out all right in the morning!

As picturesquely worded by Robert S. Henry, "Grant, with unshakeable grip, was at the throat of the Confederacy, while Sherman's army, whose Atlanta campaign had broken its back, flowed through its body."

Not all Northerners had been eager to continue the war, and support of Lincoln, as the war progressed, was far from unanimous. Though Abolitionist feeling was predominant, some Unionists felt that the injection of the slavery question into politics was hardly merited. To the tune of *Wait for the Wagon,* a ballad titled *Fight for the Nigger* expressed this sentiment:

Fight for the nigger, the sweet-scented nigger,
The wooly-headed nigger and the Abolition crew.

Moreover, if you're drafted, do not refuse to go,
You are equal to the nigger, and can make as good a show;
And when you are in battle, to the Union be true,
But don't forget the darkey is as good a man as you!

The Abolitionist label was encouraged by Southerners, said *Call 'Em Names, Jeff* (words by R. Tompkins, music by Wurzel [George F. Root]):

They really thought that calling names
    Had strengthened their position,
When all their sneaking curs up north
    Ran yelping abolition.
But soon we made the traitors know
    'Twas something else the matter;
The more they abolition howled,
    The more we did not scatter.

The South seemed to have *Nigger on the Brain (N. O. B.)* (words by R. A. C., music by J. C. M.), but there was a cure-all:

But, thank the Lord, an antidote
    Is found to cure its ills,

'Tis labelled on the outer side
    "Grant's anti-nigger pills."
He gives them as preventatives
    On every battle plain
And he's the doctor that will cure
    This "nigger on the brain."

On the other hand, the Copperheads, those opposed to the administration and in favor of peace without military victory, were strong. *What's
the Matter?* (words and music by Charles Boynton) explained the trouble
caused by this disloyal group:

Firing on our Army's rear,
    Trying to scatter
Disaffection far and near,
    That's what's the matter!

Unfortunately the Copperheads, according to *What's the Cause of This
Commotion?* (words by Charles Learned), were supported by certain
Northern editors:

Jeff Davis owns some Northern traitors;
    Traitors, traitors for dirty work,
There's now and then a traitorous sheet
    That for its treason can't be beat!

By the time the major political parties of the North were ready to
select their candidates for the Presidency, Lincoln had become a target of
bitter criticism. A segment of his own party, the Republicans, was increasingly hostile to him and his war policies. These faultfinders, meeting at
Cleveland in May, 1864, nominated John C. Frémont as their candidate,
but he asked to have his name removed from the ballot in September.

Early in June the Republicans met in Baltimore and, amid unprecedented enthusiasm, renominated Lincoln to run with Andrew Johnson.

The Copperheads had from the beginning sought to embarrass the
government by discouraging enlistments and opposing the draft calls.
They criticized the administration's war measures, constantly calling attention to what they considered the inefficiency of Lincoln and his advisers.
They violently opposed the Emancipation Proclamation.

They had become influential in the Democratic party, which held its convention in Chicago late in August. Controlled by Copperheads, they adopted a peace plank in their platform in which they declared the four years' war to be a failure. General George B. McClellan, "Little Mac," became their candidate.

Seldom has an American political campaign reached such heights of excitement and venom. The popular war tunes of the day were freely used by the many campaign songsters of both parties. These parodies are of interest as examples of songs with words of momentary topical appeal, easily sung because of the popularity of the tunes, and even more interesting because both sides would use the same tune to express sentiments appropriate to their aims.

Lincoln's supporters used the chorus of *John Brown's Body* to shout:

Hurrah for the Union, hurrah for the flag,
Down with the traitors and the cursed rebel rag;
With Lincoln and with Johnson we'll gain the victory,
As we go marching on.

And the always rousing tune of *Yankee Doodle* stirred up support:

How are you, Mister Little Mac?
You are a pretty dandy,
But you have got upon a plank
That will throw you very handy.

We're sorry for you, Little Mac,
You've joined a fated party;
So make your mind up to defeat.
How are you now, my hearty?

The *Nomination Song* (words by Charles Haynes, music by J. E. Haynes) said that Lincoln "was driving a wedge in the tyrant's great rail" and deserved to be elected:

Come up to the polls then, from mountain and glen
Stand firm, boys, and work for the right!
We must show the bold traitors we'll triumph again
When we face them once more in the fight.

335

One Pip Van Winkle asserted himself:

> We will *Vote for Uncle Abe,* for he's loyal, true and brave;
> Soon the day will be here but I think we needn't fear;
> We will vote for Uncle Abe, 'tis clear,
> Come along, come along!

A Campaign Song for Abraham Lincoln (words by Charles Haynes, music by J. E. Haynes) expressed the belief that Lincoln could end the war:

> CHORUS:
> Come, all ye truehearted, Let this be your cry,
> Our chieftain must conquer, The traitor shall die!
> 'Neath freedom's proud banner We'll march to the field,
> Now press them with vigor, The traitors shall yield.

The Lincoln supporters emphasized the fact that McClellan had already had his chance to "save the Union" and had failed; hence it seemed not a little paradoxical that he should suddenly come forth with the campaign slogan "The Union must be preserved at all hazards!" on a win-the-war platform. *Liberty's Call; or, Hurrah for Abe and Andy* (words by W. S. Blanchard, music by L. B. Starkweather) asserted that all would be well once the election was assured.

The great accomplishments of the new team of Lincoln and Johnson were foretold in the chorus of *Three Cheers for Abe and Andy* (words and music by Charles P. Brigham):

> Three cheers for Abe and Andy, our gallant boys in blue,
> For General Grant and Sherman who will put the rebels through;
> And with their bristling bayonets will end this cruel war
> And teach men that this Union must never lose a star.

The anti-Lincolnites took delight in hurling abuse, personal and political, upon the President. To the tune of *Dixie,* the campaigners sang *Away Down South There Is Rebellion:*

> Away down South there is rebellion,
> Fighting 'gainst our glorious Union.

Cheer away! cheer away!
Cheer away! cheer away!
Send McClellan to defend it,
That's the only way to end it.
Cheer away, etc.

CHORUS:

Then away down South he'll fix 'em, Oh, oh! Oh, oh!
On Dixie's soil he'll end the broil,
For Union he will ever toil.
Cheer away! cheer away! Then away down South he'll fix 'em!
Cheer away! cheer away! Then away down South he'll fix 'em!

"Peace with Union" is our mission,
The height of Little Mac's ambition.
Cheer away! cheer away!
Cheer away! cheer away!
We'll put him in the first position
To end this war without submission.
Cheer away, etc.

Anticipating Lincoln's leaving the White House, the Democrats sang *Who Will Care for Abra'am Now?* to the tune of *Who Will Care for Mother Now?*:

Why are we so strong and sanguine,
    See our banners waving high!
All around the sky is brightening,
    Mac will give us victory!
He will guide our noble vessel,
    Soon this "cruel war" will cease;
Now we've got our old Commander,
    We'll soon have a glorious peace.

CHORUS:

Soon our country'll be united,
    To McClellan we will bow;
We have promised him our ballots,
    Who will care for Abra'am now?

Using the tune of *When Johnny Comes Marching Home,* then highly popular among war-weary Republicans and Democrats alike, they sang *When Abe Comes Marching Home:*

> When Abe comes marching home again, Huzza, huzza!
> The people all will cry "Amen!", Huzza, huzza!
> The boys will cheer, the ladies shout,
> To see Old Abra'am going out.
>
> CHORUS:
> And we'll all be free
> When Abe comes marching home.

The chorus of *Weeping, Sad and Lonely* was a perfect setting for:

> *Shouting "Mac" and Freedom,*
> Votes and cheers prepare;
> Yet praying, when Abra'am's time is over,
> Mac will take the chair.

McClellan Is the Man, asserted a song with words by Charley Leighton and music by Henry Cromwell, while the belief that *Mac Will Win the Union Back* was expressed in words by A. Oakley Hall and music by Daniel D. Emmett, the composer of *Dixie:*

> They cry hurrah, hurrah for Little Mac,
> For he's the boy to win the Union back
> And sail the ship of state on safer tack.
> Hurrah, hurrah, hurrah for Little Mac!

McClellan's experience would prove useful in ending the war swiftly, according to *Old Abe They Said Was an Honest Man* (words by J. W. Jarboe, music by F. Lafayette):

> He also is the soldier's true friend
> Who fought for the Union under his command.
> He loved his men and they all feel
> That he is quite brave upon the field.
> Now, Little Mac, he is the man,
> He'll make things howl in Washington.
> Old Abe he'll fix as he deserves
> By giving him command, the home reserves.

The war's conclusion could reasonably be expected when *The Presidential Combat* (words and music by E. L. Kurtz) was over:

> The people want McClellan
>   Our Union to restore,
> And when the war we've ended
>   At home we'll war no more.
>
> The soldiers well remember
>   The master of their drill;
> Once loved by all together,
>   We know they love him still.
> McClellan as President
>   Is now the people's will.

Referring to the tavern of Benny Haven, near West Point, which was known to cadets as a place where all was peaceful and serene, *Benny Haven's O, a Campaign Song* (words by Noble Butler) anticipated the time when the academy would have both Northern and Southern trainees:

> Hurrah for George McClellan!
>   To Washington he'll go;
> And to the plots of wicked men,
>   Will give a fatal blow;
> The Constitution o'er the land
>   Its ample shield shall throw,
> And North and South shall meet again,
>   At Benny Haven's O.

Though Stephen Foster had died during the previous January, his music served for one of the campaign songs, *Little Mac! Little Mac!*. Authorship of the words is undetermined, though they were probably the work of his sister, Henrietta, a stanch Democrat:

> Little Mac, Little Mac! you're the very man,
> Go down to Washington as soon as you can.
> Lincoln's got to get away and make room for you,
> We must beat Lincoln and Johnson, too.
>
> CHORUS:
> Hurrah, hurrah, hurrah!

Sound the rally thro' the whole United States,
Little Mac and Pendleton are our candidates.

With the triumphs of Grant and Sherman aiding him, Lincoln's election was assured. McClellan had difficulty in dodging an explanation for his yearlong inactivity as commander of the Army of the Potomac. Twenty-five states took part in the election, and Little Mac carried only three. Out of 233 electoral votes, Lincoln received 212.

Whether or not Lincoln had managed the war badly until now mattered little in view of the Union victories being reported almost daily. Grant was now in full command, and Northerners talked of *The Grant Pill; or, Unconditional Surrender* (words by Harriet L. Castle, music by J. C. Beckel):

> Hurrah! then for our Union,
>   Peace and liberty attend her;
> And henceforth be this our war cry,
>   "Unconditional surrender!"

A song by Henry Tucker asserted:

> *It's All Up in Dixie,* the jig is up in Dixie's land;
> Yes, let Union stand forever!

Uncle Sam is Bound to Win (words by W. Dexter Smith, Jr., music by Ernest Leslie):

> Oh, General Lee, it is no use
>   So now you'd better go;
> You never can whip our gallant boys,
>   We might have told you so.
> So toddle right back to Uncle Jeff
>   And tell him right away
> That old Uncle Sam is bound to fight
>   Until he wins the day.

Secesh was almost played out, said *Cheer Up, Brave Boys* (words and music by G. Lampard):

Secession has almost played out,
    They're whipped and well they know
They're in a trap and can't get out
    And stocks are running low.
We'll show them soon to Yankee boys
    Their honor they'll have to tender,
And Jeff with all his rebel crew
    Will have to soon surrender.

General William Tecumseh Sherman was beginning to take his place as an important Union hero. Striking deep in the Southland, he captured Atlanta on September 2 and sent word that *Atlanta's Ours and Fairly Won* (words and music by Alman K. Virgil):

Though Sherman here to many a soul those glorious words of thine,
"Atlanta's ours and fairly won" come like a draught of wine.
The doubting spirit gains new faith and echoes back
    "Right nobly done!"

Sherman's message to his army before Atlanta, "Hold the fort, I am coming," was the subject of a song entitled *Hold the Fort* (words and music by P. P. Bliss). Septimus Winner celebrated the conquest in

Our Flag O'er Georgia Floats Again,
    By native breezes tossed;
Its starry folds must now remain,
    No matter what it cost!
Though blood may flow 'mid scenes of woe,
    It shall not be in vain.
Let nations know, both friend and foe,
    We can our rights maintain!

During November and December, 1864, the South received the blow from which it was never to recover. Leaving Atlanta, Sherman's army, 60,000 strong, moved in several lines, cutting a swath sixty miles wide across Georgia. Behind it remained a wide wake of ruin, in spite of Sherman's orders against pillaging. The state had been considered the storehouse of the Confederacy; hence, what the army could not eat or carry away, it burned, spoiled, or ruined. So efficient were the soldiers in foraging

341

that they were termed "bummers." Citizens along the path of the historic march were left destitute, their food supplies gone, their livestock stolen or killed, and their homes and barns destroyed. With fork and spade the Yanks dug up treasures which had been buried in the ground; they killed what livestock they could not take along, and numberless curling columns of smoke told the story of burning barns.

The history of warfare has few records as appalling as the destruction spread by Sherman's troops. Carl Sandburg has vividly drawn the picture:[20]

> An army for thirty-two days to the outside world "lost sight of," as Sherman phrased it, now had behind it three hundred miles of naked smokestacks, burned culverts, shattered trestleworks, wailing humanity. Of the railroads, every rail was twisted beyond use, every tie, bridge, tank, woodshed, and depot building burned. Thirty miles ran the devastation on either side of the line from Atlanta to Savannah ... Over many square miles of this area now was left not a chicken, not a pig, nor horse nor cow nor sheep, not a smokehouse ham nor side of bacon, not a standing corncrib with a forgotten bushel, not a mule to plow land with, not a piece of railroad track, nor cars nor locomotives nor a bunker of coal. "The destruction could hardly have been worse," wrote one commentator, "if Atlanta had been a volcano in eruption, and the molten lava had flowed in a stream sixty miles wide and five times as long." War as a reality, a pervasive stench of conquest, had come to Georgia.

Marching Through Georgia, Henry C. Work's stirring song, was to become not only one of the most widely sung of all the war songs, but its fame was destined to outlive the immediate reason for its composition. It is still sung today and is a part of America's singing heritage. The song describes various aspects of the march. Verse one indicates that the Union troops seem to have considered the march in the light of a holiday frolic, although it reduced the army to 50,000 men, whereas there had formerly been over 62,000:

> Bring the good old bugle, boys, we'll sing another song,
> Sing it with a spirit that will start the world along;
> Sing it as we used to sing it, fifty-thousand strong,
> While we were marching through Georgia!

[20] Carl Sandburg, *Storm Over the Land* (Harcourt, 1942), 335–36. Used by permission.

CHORUS:
Hurrah! Hurrah! We bring the jubilee!
Hurrah! Hurrah! The flag that makes you free!
So we sing the chorus from Atlanta to the sea,
While we were marching through Georgia.

The joyful "darkies" in the second stanza were the 7,000 Negroes who joined the rear guard of the army before it reached Savannah. This stanza treats the commissary department with considerably less respect than it deserved, for sweet potatoes and turkeys were only two items in a long list of requisitions. Sherman set out from Atlanta with 5,000 head of cattle, but arrived in Savannah on December 20 with 10,000:

How the darkies shouted when they heard the joyful sound!
How the turkeys gobbled which our commissary found!
How the sweet potatoes even started from the ground
While we were marching through Georgia!

Verse three refers to the Union prisoners who were freed on the route:

Yes, and there were Union men who wept with joyful tears,
When they saw the honored flag they had not seen for years;
Hardly could they be restrained from breaking forth in cheers
While we were marching through Georgia.

And the Union triumph is hailed in the final stanzas:

"Sherman's dashing Yankee boys will never reach the coast!"
So the saucy rebels said, and 'twas a handsome boast,
Had they not forgot, alas, to reckon with the host
While we were marching through Georgia.

So we made a thoroughfare for Freedom and her train;
Sixty miles in latitude, three hundred to the main;
Treason fled before us, for resistance was in vain
While we were marching through Georgia.

One of the phases of the march which attracted the attention of Union song writers was the liberation of Negroes and their eagerness to follow

343

in the wake of the liberators. Sherman's arrival was heralded in *Sherman's on the Track* (words and music by David A. Warden):

> Oh, look away out yonder, for de dust am risin' high,
> General Sherman's comin' 'long and massa's goin' to die;
> He's got some nigger soldiers that make de rebels run;
> Just hold your breff a little while and see the glorious fun!
>
> CHORUS:
> Shout, darkies, shout,
>   Old Sherman's on de track;
> He's knocked de breff from poor ole Jeff
>   And laid him on his back.

The slave in *Who Comes Dar?* (words by Kate Crayon, music by Will Hill and John M. Hubbard) puts on a pretense of fright:

> O, darkeys, hear dat mighty tramp, Who comes dar?
> I guess ole Sherman move his camp, Darkeys, he come dar!
>
> We darkeys play we's mighty scared, Crying "Who comes dar?"
> We got de ole shotguns prepared, Kase Sherman, he comes dar.
>
> But all de time we play be 'fraid, Cryin' "Who comes dar?"
> We knew 'twas Sherman on his raid, A-goin' we knew whar!

That the Union soldiers were often friendly is indicated in *Glory, Glory; or, The Little Octoroon* (words and music by George F. Root):

> Fly, my precious darling, to the Union camp;
>   I will keep the hounds and hunters here.
> Go right through the forest though 'tis dark and damp,
>   God will keep you, dear one, never fear.
>
> When the blazing campfires gleamed amid the wood,
>   And the boys were halting for the night,
> In her wond'rous beauty little Rose stood
>   Trembling and alone before their sight.
>
> Then the brave gunner took her in his arms,
>   Thinking of his own dear ones at home,
> And through all the marches and their rude alarms
>   Safely brought the little octoroon.

344

Even amid the complete devastation, sympathy was sometimes felt for the Southerners, according to a verse of *De Lord He Makes Us Free* (words by Charles Gates, music by Eman C. Pation):

De massa's come back from his tramp, 'pears he is broken quite;
He takes de basket to de camp for rations ebery night.
Dey fought him when he loud and strong, dey feed him when he low,
Dey say dey will forgive de wrong and bid him 'pent and go.

The song *Sherman's March to the Sea* gave the campaign the name by which it came to be popularly known. The author of the words, Lieutenant Samuel Hawkins M. Byers, was at the time a prisoner at Columbia, South Carolina, and he learned of the advance from a newspaper which had been secreted in a loaf of bread brought to him by a faithful Negro. A fellow prisoner, Lieutenant J. C. Rockwell, wrote the music:

Our campfire shone bright on the mountains
    That frowned on the river below,
While we stood by our guns in the morning
    And eagerly watched for the foe;
When a rider came out from the darkness
    That hung over mountain and tree,
And shouted, "Boys, up and be ready,
    For Sherman will march to the sea."

Still onward we pressed 'till our banner
    Swept out from Atlanta's grim walls,
And the blood of the patriot dampened
    The soil where the traitor flag falls;
But we paused not to weep for the fallen
    Who slept by each river and tree,
Yet we twined them a wreath of the laurel
    As Sherman marched down to the sea.

The ballad was memorized by countless Union schoolboys, and the publisher of the song, who gave Lieutenant Byers five dollars for it, sold over one million copies. Sherman later indicated his preference for this song over the even more famous *Marching Through Georgia*.[21]

[21] Another musical setting was composed by Henry Werner, and the poem was published under the titles *When Sherman Marched Down to the Sea* (music by

The concurrent advance of a large Union force under Grant farther north spread throughout the Union the certainty that, with concentrated energy, the war would soon be over. The day of retreating was over; *We Will Not Retreat Any More* (words by E. W. Locke, music by G. Ascher), said the Unionists:

> Our comrades fill many a grave, boys,
>> Our brothers are crippled and maimed,
> Of those who now fall as they fell, boys,
>> Their country need not be ashamed;
> We sigh for the blessings of peace, boys,
>> We tire of the war bugle's blast,
> We'll conquer before we go home, boys,
>> We'll fight for our flag to the last!
>
> CHORUS:
> Oh, we will not retreat any more, boys,
> We will not retreat any more.
> We've numbers to match the traitors we'll catch,
> We will not retreat any more.

The *Rebel Kingdom Falling* (words and music by E. P. Noyes), after reviewing the Union victories of the war in four verses, suggested that the South heed the handwriting on the wall and give up the fight:

> And now, ye rebels of the South,
>> You'd better save your breath
> Before the freemen of the North
>> Have whipped you all to death.
> Your kingdom now is falling fast,
>> Jeff totters on his throne,
> And if you ever wish for peace,
>> Let Uncle Sam alone!

Those slaves not yet free looked forward to the approaching end in *The War Will Soon Be Over* (words and music by Walter Kittredge):

E. Mack) and *The Marching Song of Sherman's Army* (music by W. C. Peters). Other songs were *We Marched with Sherman's Army to the Sea* (words and music by Thomas P. Westendorf) and *Sherman the Brave* (words by Charles Haynes, music by J. E. Haynes). A composition which traced Sherman's course from Shiloh, Vicksburg, Dalton, and Atlanta was *General Sherman and His Boys in Blue* (words and music by G. Ascher, another setting by H. M. Higgins).

If you look a little lower
   The horizon will soon be clear,
And the war will soon be over,
   For the time is drawing near.
And we know that God has promised
   To set the slave, the bondsman, free;
Then we'll raise the starry banner
   And we'll have a jubilee.

The more bitter Unionists naturally gloated over the South's predicament. In the song *Good-bye, Jeff* (words and music by P. P. Bliss), a Northerner depicts a conversation between President Davis and a friend in which both are discouraged about the outcome of the war:

Oh, you told me that you'd meet me at the White House, Jeff,
When I left you on the Chattahoochee shore,
But you're farther from it now than even then, friend Jeff,
And your face it isn't looking tow'rds the door.
You remember what I told you down in Georgia, don't you, Jeff,
When you came to talk secession stuff to me,
That I thought you'd never live to see the White House, Jeff?
You believe it now, and so you're going to flee.

The finish seemed ever closer and closer, and anticipation of the joyful return of their soldier boys led people to grow hopeful for the great day *When Johnny Comes Marching Home:*

When Johnny comes marching home again, Hurrah! Hurrah!
We'll give him a hearty welcome then, Hurrah! Hurrah!
The men will cheer, the boys will shout,
The ladies they will all turn out,

CHORUS:
And we'll all feel gay when
Johnny comes marching home.

The old church bell will peal with joy, Hurrah! Hurrah!
To welcome home our darling boy, Hurrah! Hurrah!
The village lads and lassies say
With roses they will strew the way,

347

Get ready for the Jubilee, Hurrah! Hurrah!
We'll give the hero three times three, Hurrah! Hurrah!
The laurel wreath is ready now
To place upon his loyal brow,

Let love and friendship on that day, Hurrah! Hurrah!
Their choicest treasures then display, Hurrah! Hurrah!
And let each one perform some part
To fill with joy the warrior's heart,

Even today copies of this song erroneously bear the name of "Louis Lambert" as composer. "Lambert" was the pseudonym of Patrick S. ("Pat") Gilmore, the greatest bandleader of the 1860's. He composed the words and adapted the tune from an old Irish air titled *Johnny, I Hardly Knew Ye* and *Johnny, Fill Up the Bowl* while on duty in 1864 at New Orleans as bandmaster in General Nathaniel Banks's command. The tune has survived as one of the brightest ever sung, and Johnny has come marching gaily home from the wars since to its rhythm.

As Union power increased, Southerners began to feel the cumulative impact of four years of suffering and hardship. Their available manpower had been all but exhausted, and as the months dragged on, their hopes of success were correspondingly reduced. When the southernmost states of the Confederacy were invaded and became the scenes of bloody battles, the limit of endurance seemed to have been reached.

The South had never been an industrial area, and the blockade reduced the region to pioneer living conditions. Long unused spinning wheels and looms were brought out, and the women spun, dyed, and wove thread into cloth. Yarn for the warp was purchased from mills, but the woof was homespun thread. Southern belles proudly sang the tune of *Bonnie Blue Flag,* describing *The Homespun Dress; or, The Southern Girl* (words by Carrie Bell Sinclair):

Oh, yes, I am a Southern girl
    And glory in the name,
And boast it with far greater pride
    Than glittering wealth or fame.
We envy not the Northern girl
    Her robes of beauty rare,
Though diamonds grace her snowy neck
    And pearls bedeck her hair.

The homespun dress is plain, I know,
    My hat's palmetto, too;
But then it shows what Southern girls
    For Southern rights will do.
We send the bravest of our land
    To battle with the foe,
And we will lend a helping hand;
    We love the South, you know!

The Southern land's a glorious land
    And has a glorious cause;
Then cheer three cheers for Southern rights
    And for the Southern boys!
We scorn to wear a bit of silk,
    A bit of Northern lace,
But make our homespun dresses up
    And wear them with a grace.

Memoirs of life during the later war years describe the Confederate world of women, old men, and Negroes. Southern women resorted to many makeshirts in providing food for their families—sorghum was used instead of sugar; okra and persimmon seeds replaced coffee. Salt was so expensive that people even reclaimed the precious grains from the dirt floors of smokehouses. Prices were high, for Confederate money was practically worthless. The Confederate dollar bill (with gold as a standard) depreciated from 80¢ in 1861 to 20¢ in 1863 and 1½¢ by April, 1865. A pound of coffee sold for $7.00, sugar for $25.00, butter for $5.00; flour was $1,000 a barrel, shoes $100 a pair, and the rate for wagon transportation was $100 a mile. Under such conditions the prevailing Southern attitude of resignation and total weariness as the end of the war approached is understandable.

The sacrifices made by Southerners were never-ending and extended into almost every phase of life. For example, during the first year of the war, General Beauregard ordered that all bells of Louisiana churches and plantations should be melted into cannons. The response was generous, and the change from peaceful to warlike use of the bells was noted in two songs, one of which was *Those Sabbath Chimes* (words and music by J. R. Stevenson):

A fiercer warning now they tell—
Let the oppressor heed it well!
Now dare the stern, relentless might,
Upholding truth, defending right.

and the other *Melt the Bells* (words by J. Y. Rockett, music by Mrs. Dr. Byrne):

Melt the bells! Melt the bells!
 Still the tinkling on the plain,
And transmute the evening chimes
Into war's resounding rhymes,
 That th' invader may be slain!

Melt the bells! Melt the bells!
 That for years have called for prayer.
And instead the cannon's roar
Shall resound the valleys o'er
 That the foe may catch despair!

But even this gesture was fruitless, for the chimes were seized by General Butler in New Orleans and sent to Boston. It is entirely possible that the cannons made from them were used in the Southland.

The Confederacy was facing extinction. Like a juggernaut, the march to the sea continued on its destructive route, marked, as always, by songs of immediate interest. Many stately homes were entered and ransacked during the advance, making the words of *Deserted Rebel Mansion* (words and music by I. W. Gougler) descriptive of a commonplace occurrence:

Advance, let us enter that dwelling
 Not fearing assaults from the foe.
Its secrets, though dark and forbidding,
 We must with some certainty know.
Hark! Hark! Mystic sounds seem to greet us
 As lightly the threshold we tread;
The silence and gloom widely reigning
 Seem like the dark home of the dead.

Here riches and pleasure and beauty
 Have vied, the best trophies to gain;

These halls now so silent and lonely
    Oft rang with some warbler's sweet strain.
Oh, where are the loves and the friendships
    Which none to this home deigned to spare?
Alas, has the lord of the mansion
    The doom of the traitor to share?

The North was now united in encouraging the advance; *On to Savannah* (author and composer unknown) urged Sherman forward:

On to Savannah! Press to Mobile!
On o'er the southern hills;
Army of heroes, the hope of the world,
Onward! Press onward still!
Ne'er may you rest 'till on the crest
Of all mountains the old flag proudly floats on high;
'Till all who are in bondage and chains in the land
Proudly as free men stand.

Savannah was reached on December 21. In February, Sherman started north on a campaign through the Carolinas to join Grant. Columbia fell, and then the cry was *On to Charleston* (words by O. Wheelock, music by M. H. Frank):

Let those in their rebel homes
    See the conquering heroes come,
Armed with saber, lance and gun,
    On to Charleston! Onward, on!

With the fall of Charleston, the sea was reached, and *Charleston Is Ours!* (words and music by George A. Meitzke) celebrated the event:

Hearts throb with gladness and pulses beat fast,
Patriots are firm and base traitors aghast.
Deep in the dust lies the hope of the foe,
Lifeless and cold as the midwinter snow.

Meanwhile Grant was assaulting Petersburg on the northern road to the Confederate capital, urged on by songs such as *We Are Marching On to Richmond* (words and music by E. W. Locke):

351

Then tramp away while the bugles play,
   We're marching on to Richmond!
Our flag shall gleam in the morning beam
   From many a spire in Richmond!

Capture of Richmond, on April 3, 1865, sealed the doom of the South and left no question as to the eventual success of Union forces. *Richmond Falls!* (author and composer unknown) was the cry on every tongue:

Richmond falls! the war is o'er!
Welcome home to part no more,
Ye who fought with dauntless soul,
Ye who marched to glory's goal.
Lee surrenders! welcome back!
Heroes of the Potomac,
Heroes of the gory James,
Sheridan and Ord and Ames!

Union rejoicing over previous victories—Gettysburg, Vicksburg, and Atlanta—had been tame compared to the outbursts of enthusiasm which followed news of the occupation of the Confederate capital. Bells were rung, cannons fired, flags waved, speeches made, ballads sung, and business practically ceased throughout the North. The end was in sight.

Two songs were titled *Richmond Is Ours!* The version with words and music by William Clifton declared:

Richmond is ours, Richmond is ours!
   Glory to God on high!
Ten thousand thanks to our brave boys
   That made the rebels fly,

while the other (words by A. J. H. Duganne, music by Mrs. E. A. Parkhurst) asserted:

Babylon falls, and her temples and towers
Crumble to ashes before us.

The fall represented the restoration of the Union, said *Triumph of the Dear Old Flag* (words and music by Eastburn, pseud. of J. E. Winner):[22]

Our flag o'er Richmond's fated walls
   In triumph waves again,
No star erased, no stripe effaced,
   But free from blot or stain;
As floating on the gentle breeze
   With field of blue unfurled
Its beaming stars with silvery light
   Show victory to the world!

as well as the restoration of Virginia,[23] which many felt had been unfairly drawn into the Confederate forces, according to *Virginia, Our Home* (words and music by J. Dorley Radford):

Virginia, the birthplace of freedom
   With rebels she went though in vain,
But now that her traitors are routed
   With the Union she joins hands again.
Opposed was she strong to secession
   But traitors from other states came
And sat in Virginia's convention
   To preach up rebellion's great fame.

CHORUS:
Now Richmond, dear boys, we'll together
   Join hands and fly to our land,
Our birthplace be free of all traitors,
   Four years they have made it their stand.

Treason had been crushed, and rebellion was dead, rejoiced *At Eight in the Morning* (words and music by J. E. Haynes):

Now Richmond has fallen, rebellion is done,
Let all men rejoice for the victory is won!

[22] Other songs were *Richmond Falls, the War Is O'er* (words and music by O. Wheelock) and two compositions entitled *Richmond Has Fallen*—one with words and music by J. W. Turner, the other with words by F. S. Chandler, music by A. E. Wimmerstedt.

[23] Maryland was also welcomed back into the Union in two songs set to the tune of *My Maryland*—*The Starry Flag Waves O'er Thy Shore, Maryland, My Maryland* (words by Joseph Merrefield) and *Maryland, Our Maryland; or, Maryland Redeemed* (words by Frank H. Norton)—as well as in *Maryland Free* (words by George L. Taylor, music by Charles H. Greene).

The city where slavery once dwelt in her pride
Is now in our hands and rebellion has died.
Now Richmond is taken, they'll harm us no more,
For treason is crushed and rebellion is o'er.
Our armies have triumphed, the traitors have fled,
We've captured their city, secession is dead.

The Liberty Bird (words by J. P. Johnson, music by George F. Root), the Union, a proud eagle, had triumphed over the reptile, the South:

A moment he poised on his aerial height,
Then downward he swooped like the gleaming of light.
The treacherous snake in his talons he clutched
While his proud plumage fluttered aloft all untouched.
Its vitals, its heart from its bosom he tore,
Then spurned the base carcass and heavenward did soar,
And the wild notes of freedom in triumph were heard
Bursting forth from the throat of the liberty bird!

In a serenade in front of the White House in Washington, the President addressed a jubilant crowd, heralding the return of Southern states to the Union. He ended with a touch of mingled humor and pathos, calling on the band to play a piece of Confederate music. It was one "we captured yesterday, and the Attorney General gave me his legal opinion that it is now our property. So I ask the band to play *Dixie*." Thus this famous song was returned to the Union.

Only a few days later, on April ninth, the end came at Appomattox Court House when Lee surrendered the main Confederate forces to Grant. The love and respect which General Lee held in the hearts of his men and their unwillingness to give up the fight until ordered by him to do so were expressed in *General Lee's Surrender* (words and music by Mrs. J. P. H. of Virginia):

I can never forget the day Lee
    And his soldiers had to part,
There was many a tear to wipe away,
    And many a sad and weary heart.

'Twas vain! for an unnumbered host
    Closed round our small heroic band,

The General saw that hope was lost
  And sadly gave up his command.

But the soldiers would not listen to his story
  'Till their glorious old leader bid them yield;
They would follow him to sorrow or to glory,
  So all silently they left the battlefield.

The surrender of other Southern forces followed rapidly after Appomattox. On April fourteenth, four years to the day after the first inciting incident of the war, the Stars and Stripes was again raised over Fort Sumter as a symbol of the restoration of the Union. *Victory at Last!* (words by Mrs. M. A. Kidder, music by William B. Bradbury) was sung during that ceremony:

For many years we've waited
  To hail the day of peace,
When our land shall be united
  And war and strife shall cease!

while *Hurrah for the Old Flag* (words by W. Dexter Smith, Jr., music by Matthias Keller), dedicated "to all who aided in restoring our flag," proclaimed:

Our old flag is waving o'er Sumter again,
Its bright stars are gleaming o'er fortress and main;
Its broad stripes are floating from rampart to crag.
Our Union forever, hurrah for the flag!

The Fall of Sumter (words and music by J. W. Turner) cited the fort as a symbol of re-established unity:

Sumter is ours! our flag once more
  Upon the ramparts waves,
And 'neath her ruined, shattered wall
  Are many a traitor's grave.
Wave on, old flag, as in the past,
  Thy glittering folds we see,
Wave forth in all thy glories bright,
  Sweet emblem of the free!

355

while *The American Jubilee; or, Freedom Triumphant* (words by Henry O'Rielly, music by John M. Loretz, Jr.), an anthem for the Sumter celebration, expressed the same idea:

> Freedom's flag now floats aloft,
>   Our eagles proudly soar;
> Secession and vile slavery
>   Shall curse the land no more.
> Confederate treason vanished
>   Like foul and fitful dream;
> The great Republic triumphs
>   And freedom reigns supreme!

A wave of relief swept the country, though represented in songs only by Union adherents.[24] Northern jubilation was summarized in *'Tis Finished; or, Sing Hallelujah!* (words and music by Henry C. Work):

> 'Tis finished! 'Tis ended!
>   The dread and awful task is done;
> Tho' wounded and bleeding
>   'Tis ours to sing the vic'try won.
> Our nation is ransom'd,
>   Our enemies are overthrown,
> And now, now commences
>   The brightest era ever known.

CHORUS:

> Then sing Hallelujah! Sing Hallelujah!
> Glory be to God on high!
> For the old flag with the white flag
> Is hanging in the azure sky.

Following the formal truce, the end came quickly. General J. E. Johnston surrendered his troops to Sherman in North Carolina on April 26. President Davis had fled to the safety of the deep South with several of his cabinet members but was captured at Irwinsville, Georgia, on May 10. The

---

[24] Two Union songs were *All Hail to Our Triumph* (words and music by Harry Buckline) and *The Cruel War Is Over* (words by W. Dexter Smith, Jr., music by August Kreissman).

The Curtain Falls

'Tis fin-ished! 'Tis end-ed! The dread and aw-ful task is done; Tho'
wound-ed and bleed-ing 'Tis ours to sing the vic-t'ry won. Our
na-tion is ran-som'd, Our en-e-mies are o-ver-thrown, And
now, now com-menc-es The bright-est e-ra ev-er known. Then
sing Hal-le-lu-jah! Sing Hal-le-lu-jah! Glo-ry be to God on high! For the
old flag with the white flag Is hang-ing in the az-ure sky.

'Tis Finished; or, Sing Hallelujah!

story of his assuming woman's dress as a disguise was the signal for an
outpouring of vituperation and mockery, and Union song writers capitalized on the situation. His disappearance elicited a verse in *O, Jefferson
Davis, How Do You Do?* (words by F. B. Scott, music by Charles G.
Degenhard):

Oh, Jefferson Davis, how do you do?
Rebellion's all ended, the rebels put through.
The country's all saved, and the Union, too;
But give us an answer, dear Jeff, where are you?

and his taking some of the Confederacy's gold, the amount of which was grossly exaggerated, was noted in *Jeff in Petticoats* (words by George Cooper, music by Henry Tucker):

> Now when he saw the game was up,
>   He started for the woods,
> His bandbox hung upon his arm
>   Quite full of fancy goods.
> Said Jeff, "They'll never take me now;
>   I'm sure I'll not be seen;
> They'll never think to look for me
>   Beneath my crinoline."
>
> Jeff took with him, the people say,
>   A mine of golden coin
> Which he from banks and other places
>   Managed to purloin;
> But though he ran like every thief,
>   He had to drop the spoons
> And maybe that's the reason why
>   He dropped his pantaloons!

His actual capture by Union scouts was dealt with in detail in several songs, including *Jeff Davis in Crinoline* (words by Charles Haynes, music by James E. Haynes):

> In crinoline old Jeff was caught
>   By us the other day;
> We'll still take him straight to Washington,
>   He'll never get away!
>
> "Oh, put on your duds," the corporal cried,
>   "Don't make too much delay,
> For we're going to march to Washington;
>   We must be off, I say."
>
> Old Jeff soon came unto the door
>   Led by his wife and son,
> And the way he tried to run from us,
>   I tell you, it was fun.
>
> "I pray you, let my mother pass,
>   Sure she'll do no harm,

For she wants to get some water
    In this bucket on her arm."

"Hello there, boy," the soldier cried,
    "This lady lacks her furs,
And I tell you she looks funny here
    Wearing boots and spurs."

"And whiskers, too," the sergeant said,
    "She wears upon her face!
Now we'll take Old Jeff to Washington
    To suffer his disgrace."

But a verse in *A Confederate Transposed to a Petticoat* (words and music by E. L. Kurtz) was undoubtedly exaggerated:

Poor Jeff was likely dreaming yet
    In the forest camp at dawn,
Then hailed by seizers out of bed,
    For the scene's to change that morn.
Approaching with his face be-veiled
    More to gratify his cause,
A fallen chieftain like he railed,
    Sneering 'bout the Union laws.

The humiliation of the capture was the subject of raillery in *The Sour Apple Tree; or, Jeff Davis' Last Ditch* (words and music by J. W. Turner):

O, when our soldiers found him,
    I'll bet he did look rich
With petticoats around him
    As he stood in the last ditch!
Old Jeff, he wasn't wise
    With boots on, don't you see?
It was a splendid sight, I'm sure,
    Such Southern chivalry!

while his wife's intercession was noted in *Oh, Jeff, Oh, Jeff, How Are You Now?* (words and music by Henry Schroeder):

But on they came, close to his heel, Our boys with cries, "We've got
    you tight!"

What kind are you? Your boots reveal a hundred-thousand
      dollar light.
His wife now like a woman true, said, "Don't provoke the President
Or else he may hurt some of you. He's got a dagger in his hand!"

Invective reached a new high as Davis was blamed for all the slaughter
and division which secession had brought to the country (*Jefferson D,*
words and music by William B. Justice), and there were immediate cries
that he be hanged:

What shall be found upon history's page
When the student explores the Republican age?
He will find, as is meet, that at Judas's feet
    You sit in your shame with the impotent plea
That you hated the land
    And the law of the free!

What do you see in your visions at night?
Does the spectacle furnish you any delight?
Do you feel in disgrace, the black cap o'er your face
    While the tremor creeps down from your heart to your knees
And freedom, insulted, approves the decree?

The "sour apple tree," which had been the goal for Davis in many minds
throughout the war, was again called upon for his execution in *Hang Him
on the Sour Apple Tree* (words and music by James W. Porter):

Now all my friends, both great and small,
    A warning take from me;
Remember when for plunder you start,
    There's a sour apple tree!

The President was imprisoned at Fortress Monroe, and the only Union
song of support was *Jefferson Davis in Prison* (words by Rev. J. Barker,
music by Alfred Schmidt). It maintained that he was bearing the brunt
of all condemnation:

The orb of thy fame to its zenith uprisen
Thy firm spirit yet stands unhurt in the flame;
And vain are the capture, the shackles, the prison,
For freedmen look upwards, still shouting thy name.

Depicted on the cover of this 1865 song is the capture of Confederate President Jefferson Davis by members of the Fifth Michigan Cavalry as he attempted to escape from Richmond in female clothing.

The dark war cloud that poured its ruin around us
Hath rolled its red flood from the hills to the sea,
And the perilous storm that nearly hath drowned us
Reserved all its lightnings, proud eagle, for thee!

Others, however, were not as lenient and demands for vengeance, as in *Requiem for Jeff Davis* (words and music by Bohemia), were numerous:[25]

Oh, plunge the proud secession swell
In darkest pit of deepest hell
To gnash his teeth and roar and yell.

In burning brimstone may he be
While little devils dance in glee
And lock the door and lose the key.

Good devils, see you chain him well
In torture worse than tongue can tell,
In hottest fire of blazing hell.

And 'mid his roars and frantic cries,
Oh, make eternal ashes rise
And blow forever in his eyes.

Condemn each cursed rebel's slave
On no account Jeff Davis save
That hell-deserving scoundrel, knave!

The Confederacy, because of limited communications, fought on in various places. On May fourth the Confederate forces in Alabama were surrendered by General Taylor. The last encounter of the war took place May thirteenth on the Río Grande. The *Shenandoah,* a Confederate cruiser, was in the North Pacific, and its commander did not hear of Lee's surrender until June 23. He did not consider that capitulation meant the war's end and continued the voyage until August 2, when he heard definitely that the Confederacy had ceased to exist. At that time the ship proceeded to Liverpool, flying the Confederate flag, and surrendered to Britain on November 7, 1865. The ravaged Confederacy was too stunned and exhausted to feel anything but a sense of prostrated sorrow.

[25] Two other songs condemning Davis were *Jeff's Race for the Last Ditch* (words by W. Dexter Smith, Jr., music by Fritz Eustace) and *How Do You Like It, Jefferson D?* (words and music by Amos Patton).

Lincoln lived to enjoy the victory only five days; the entire world received the news of his tragic assassination on April fourteenth with unprecedented feelings of horror and sympathy. Scores of songs, all following a common pattern, attempted to express the nation's sorrow. The most famous song, *Farewell, Father, Friend and Guardian,* was composed by George Root (words by L. M. Dawn):

> All our land is draped in mourning,
>> Hearts are bowed and strong men weep,
> For our loved, our noble leader
>> Sleeps his last, his dreamless sleep.
> Gone forever, gone forever,
>> Fallen by a traitor's hand,
> Though preserved, his dearest treasure,
>> Our redeemed beloved land.
>
> CHORUS:
> Farewell, Father, Friend and guardian,
>> Thou hast joined the martyr's band;
> But thy glorious work remaineth,
>> Our redeemed, beloved land.

A Nation Mourns Her Martyr'd Son (words and music by Alice Hawthorne, pseudonym of Septimus Winner) expressed this sentiment:

> A nation mourns her martyr'd son
>> From many hearts there comes a sigh
> For him whose days on earth are done,
>> Whose name and deeds can never die.
>
> Oh, weep for him whose patient heart
>> Gave pardon to a fallen foe,
> Who acted well a manly part
>> Towards those who planned the fatal blow.

We Mourn Our Fallen Chieftain (words and music by M. B. Ladd) attempted to voice the shocked grief:

> A nation's heart is throbbing
>> With grief sincere and strong.

Toll, toll the bell with dirge-like knell,
  The sad refrain prolong.
Mourn, freemen of America;
  Weep, weep through all the land.
The shrine he sanctified in blood,
  A monument shall stand.

Although the national feelings were difficult to express, the presses poured out the people's sorrow. John R. Thomas, to words by George Cooper, said:

Our Noble Chief Has Passed Away,
  His form is lying still and cold,
And hearts that knew the bloom of May,
  Dark sorrow's wings in gloom enfold

while the gratitude of liberated slaves was expressed in *Lincoln (In Memoriam)* (words by William P. Fox, music by Francis Woolcott):

Breathe a sad requiem, ye millions now free,
Saviour of Freedom is waiting for thee.

A Nation Mourns Her Chief (words and music by H. S. Thompson):

Twine our flag with death's dark emblem,
  Mingle crepe and laurel leaf;
Weep, true heart, and pay thy homage,
  For a nation mourns her Chief.

and one C. Archer, said:

Rest, Noble Chieftain, mighty and brave;
Peaceful thy sleep and hallowed thy grave.
No sound shall disturb thy quiet repose,
While o'er thee shall grow the myrtle and rose,

the same idea being expressed in *Toll the Bell Mournfully* (words and music by C. Everest):

Toll the bell mournfully,
  Toll the bell slow;

> Toll the bell solemnly,
>   Toll the bell low;
> The chief of the land
>   Is taken away,
> A nation in grief
>   Is mourning today.

Mere words were powerless to express the nation's grief, said *Rest, Martyr, Rest* (words by James E. Glass, music by George P. Graff):

> Though tongues inspired would tell our woe,
>   And tears in oceans roll,
> Vain would they prove to paint the grief
>   That wrings the nation's soul.

The picture of Mrs. Lincoln standing vigil over the dying President was painted in *Live But One Moment* (words and music by J. W. Turner).[26]

As was to be expected, there were calls for vengeance upon the South centering in one song, *A Gloom Is Cast O'er All the Land* (words and music by Henry Schroeder):

> Oh, nation rouse and let this crime,
> A warning be for future time;
> Avenge the blow! Avenge the blow!
> To traitors now no mercy show!

In the Northern states, feeling was high against John Wilkes Booth, the killer, and *The Assassin's Vision* (words and music by J. W. Turner)

[26] Among other songs mourning Lincoln's death were *Lincoln's Requiem* (words by Irene Boynton, music by J. A. Butterfield), *The Martyr of Liberty* (words and music by James G. Clark), *The Death Knell Is Tolling* (words by H. H. Cody, music by J. F. Fargo), *Our Nation's Captain* (words by Charles Haynes, music by Edward Haynes), *Requiem* (words and music by Matthias Keller), *In Memoriam, Abraham Lincoln* (words by W. Dexter Smith, Jr., music by Matthias Keller), *In Memoriam, A. Lincoln* (words and music by Gertrude I. Ladd), *Dirge—Our Deeply Lamented Martyred President* (words by O. Wheelock, music by E. Mack), *In Memoriam, Quartette on the Death of Abraham Lincoln* (words by Mrs. E. J. Bugbee, music by H. T. Merrill), *The President's Grave* (words by Edwin S. Babbitt, music by L. B. Miller), *A Nation in Tears* (words by R. C., music by Konrad Treuer), *A Nation Weeps* (words and music by J. W. Turner), *The Nation's Honoured Dead* (words by Miss M. J. Bishop, music by J. W. Turner), and *The Flag Is at Half Mast; to the Memory of Lincoln* (words and music by William Willing).

pictured his wild flight through the forest on his horse, startled by the apparition of his victim appearing in the trees and around him:

> Heaven had witnessed, he could not escape,
> The assassin's fate was sealed.
> "Vengeance is mine," said God in his might
> As the vision that night revealed.
> The assassin rode on with his trembling and fear
> And mournfully murmured the breeze;
> Before him, around him, all vivid and drear;
> The vision appeared in the trees.

As the symbol of Unionism, Lincoln had been almost unanimously hated in the Confederacy, and his death was certainly not deplored by Southerners. A. E. Blackmar, under his pseudonym "Armand," wrote *Our Brutus;* as the Brutus of old had freed his people from the tyrant Caesar, it said, so had Booth freed his countrymen from the oppressor, Lincoln. There had been an outcry that Booth should be buried in the ocean so no trace of his resting place could be found by those seeking vengeance; hence, the following sentiment:

> Oh, give him a sepulchre broad as the sweep
> Of the tidal wave's measureless motion,
> Lay our hero to sleep in the arms of the deep
> Since his life was as free as the ocean.
> It was liberty slain that maddened his brain,
> To avenge the dead idol he cherished.
> So 'tis meet that the main never curbed by a chain
> Should entomb the last freeman now perished.

The final grand review of the Union Army, 150,000 strong, was held on Pennsylvania Avenue in the nation's capital before President Andrew Johnson on May 23 and 24. That one last exhibit of military might momentarily recalled the four years of glory and sadness, years etched deeply in the hearts of all who had been affected.

It was inevitable that the subject of homeward bound soldiers should occupy the attention of scores of poets and composers.[27] As victors, the

[27] "Homeward bound" songs not analyzed in this volume are *Coming Home*

Union poets now poured out countless songs of welcome to the returning soldiers. Throughout the North, the beating of the drums, the shouts of "Huzzah!" and the tramp of marching feet indicated that *The Boys Are Marching Home* (words and music by J. G. Huntting):

> Now the fight is over peace will come again,
>> Union boys have conquered on the bloody plain;
> Welcome to the fireside, never more to roam,
>> With victory and Union, the boys are marching home!

They Have Broken Up Their Camps (words by Major John B. Jewell, music by George F. Root) and are greeting the homefolks once again:

> They are coming from the wars
> With their wounds and with their scars,
> But they're bringing back the dear old flag in glory;
> They have battled long and well,
> And let after ages tell
> How they won the proudest name in song or story.

from the Old Camp Ground (words and music by John Baker), *O, 'Twill Be a Happy Time When the Boys Come Home* (words and music by T. O. Conant), *Oh, the Boys Are Marching Home* (words and music by Henry Crofts), *Rejoice, Our Boys Are Coming Home* (words and music by George C. Deming), *We'll Soon Be Marching Home* (words by G. R. Herbert, music by James Harrison), *Welcome to the Returned Volunteers* (words by Charles Haynes, music by J. E. Haynes), *Our Boys Have All Come Home* (words and music by Will S. Hays), *We'll Soon Be Marching Home* (words and music by G. R. Herbert), *Once More at Home* (words and music by John H. Hewitt), *The Boys in Blue Are Marching Home* (words and music by J. G. Huntting), *The Soldier's Welcome Home* (words by Marion McMynn, music by J. P. Jones), *Welcome to Our Gallant Boys* (words by B. Fenton Smith, music by Matthias Keller), *The Boys Are Coming Home; or, The Bells Are Ringing Sweet And Clear* (words by Lilly Lovette, music by Herman T. Knake), *The Soldier's Return* (words by William H. Morris, music by Herman T. Knake), *The Union Restored and Soldier's Welcome* (words and music by E. Ludewig Kurtz), *Our Boys Are Marching Home* (words by Ednor Rossiter, music by E. Mack), *Cheer! Cheer! Cheer! The Prisoner at Home After the War* (words by George F. Worthington, music by James E. Magruder), *The Boys Are Coming Home* (words by Mary L. Masters, music by J. W. Turner), *Our Soldier's Welcome Home* (words by E. B. Dewing, music by J. P. Webster), *After the War; or, Won't We All Be Happy Then?* (words by J. Augustus Signaigo, music by B. A. Whaples), *Home the Boys Are Marching; or, Ring the Merry Bells* (words by C. St. John, music by F. Wilmarth), and *The Boys in Blue Are Coming Home* (words by Samuel H. M. Byers, music by A. E. Wimmerstedt).

The elation and happiness extends to all, according to *Our Boys Are Coming Home* (words and music by Thomas M. Towne; other versions under the same title by R. E. Henninges, Robert Lowry, August Kreissman, and J. E. Hartel):

> The vacant fireside places
>   Have waited for them long;
> The love-light lacks their faces,
>   The chorus waits their song;
> A shadowy fear has haunted
>   The long deserted room;
> But now our prayers are granted,
>   Our boys are coming home!
>
> O mother, calmly waiting,
>   For that beloved son!
> O, sister, proudly dating
>   The victories he has won!
> O maiden, softly humming
>   The love song while you roam—
> Joy, joy, the boys are coming—
>   Our boys are coming home!

They Are Coming from the Wars (words by Eugene H. Munday, music by J. H. Ross) amidst general exultation and excitement:

> They have broken up their camps,
> They are laughing o'er their tramps;
> They are joking with the girls
>   Who flock around them.
> They have left the scanty fare,
> They have left the fetid air
> They have dashed to earth the
>   Prison walls that bound them.

Coming Home; or, The Cruel War Is Over (words and music by Charles Carroll Sawyer) declared:

> Hearts that seemed as breaking throb with joy today;
> Eyes are bright that long were dimmed with tears.

Hopes that seemed as vanished now are light and gay,
Doubting ones have banished all their fears.

All acknowledge the debt they owe to their defenders *When They Come Marching Home* (words and music by Walter Kittredge):

Their country was in danger
    And they started at the call,
And said the starry banner
    Should yet wave over all.
And in many a hard-fought battle
    They stood their ground alone.
God bless the brave defenders
    As they come marching home!

The same thanks is expressed in *Wearing of the Blue* (words by H. E. Church, music of Henry Macarthy's setting of the *Irish Jaunting Car*):

Now that the war is over,
    What better can we do
Than sing a song of grateful praise
    To the boys who wore the blue?
Who nobly faced the traitors,
    Tore down secession's rag?
Here's a welcome for the laddies
    Who rallied round the flag.

The waiting and watching are over, and prayers have been answered now that *Our Boys Are Home to Stay* (words by Mrs. E. S. Kellog, music by T. Martin Towne):

The weary, weary night is passed,
    All hail the joyful day!
Our boys are home, safe home at last,
    Our boys are home to stay.

Each member of the soldier's family, as well as his sweetheart, has a reason for joy and thanksgiving, asserts *Peace Has Come* (words by W. Dexter Smith, Jr., music by August Kreissman):

369

How many mothers of our land
    Who hear the beat of drum
Look for the absent soldier boy
    So dearly loved to come?
She loves him dearer, dearer far
    Than e'er she did before,
And murmurs with a thankful heart,
    "I'm glad the war is o'er."

The father hears a well-known step,
    A well-remembered voice,
And happiness he cannot speak
    Bids him again rejoice.
The wanderer now has come again,
    To leave him nevermore,
And he can say with tears of joy
    "I'm glad the war is o'er."

The sister waits, how anxiously,
    To welcome a brother home,
The maiden knows that home again
    Her lover soon will come.
We see on every side such joy
    As we never saw before.
Thank God that everyone can say,
    "I'm glad the war is o'er."

The family welcomes its soldier boy in *Heard Ye the News?* (words and music by William B. Adamson) and *Our Soldier's Return* (words by Tom Russell, music by George H. Barton), while the soldiers themselves express their joy in *Home from the War* (words and music by J. W. Turner):

Home from the war, among our friends
    And those we love most dear;
With happy hearts we'll try to glad
    The hours that have been drear.

And *We're Coming Again to the Dear Ones at Home* (words and music by G. M. Wickliffe):

Hurrah, then, for peace, my brave comrades and brothers!
Raise, raise your glad shouts to the heaven's blue dome;

The Curtain Falls

Three cheers for our sisters, our wives and our mothers,
We're coming again to the dear ones at home!

A soldier returns unharmed to his mother in *My Own Loved Home
Again* (words and music by H. S. Thompson), while a freed prisoner in
The Prisoner's Return (words and music by Frank M. Davis) greets his
mother:

> I am coming, dearest Mother,
>   To my peaceful home again
> From the Southern rebel prison
>   Where the thousand have been slain.

Jimmy's mother, in a companion piece to *Grafted into the Army*, reports
that *He's Got His Discharge from the Army* (words and music by William
A. Field):

> My Jimmy's got home, I am ever so glad,
>   He's got his discharge from the Army.
> He behaved himself well and he was a brave lad
>   So they gave him his discharge from the Army.
> The boys, they all loved him, his Captain did say;
> In battle around him dead rebels did lay;
> He fought for his country and not for the pay
>   So he got his discharge from the Army.

> CHORUS:
> Oh, Jimmy, my dear, your mammy's so glad
> That you're safely at home from the Army.
> He's a dear, darling boy, and a brave little lad,
> And he's got his discharge from the Army.

A soldier greets his father in *The Soldier Coming Home* (words and
music by H. M. Slade):

> I'm coming, dear father, the battle is o'er,
> Wait my footsteps at mealtime, spread another plate more;
> Set a chair by the doorside, for I'm weary and sore.
> I'm coming, dear father, the battle is o'er.

The New England wife who sent her John to the war in *Take Your Gun and Go, John* welcomes him home in its sequel, *The Happy Day Has Come, Kate* (words and music by H. T. Merrill).

The sweethearts get attention in *He Is Coming Home Today* (words by Lilly Lovette, music by Henri Cromwell), *The War Is Over, Darling Kate* (words and music by M. B. Ladd), and *We Are Coming Home Tomorrow* (words from the Waverley Magazine, music by Frank Wilder). One girl tells her friend that Tom, her sweetheart, has carried out his promise now that *The Cruel War Is Over, Jenny* (words and music by George P. Graff):

> The cruel war is over, Jenny,
> And Tom came home last night.
> He quickly came to keep his promise
> And make me his own bride.
> He led me to the altar, Jenny,
> Yes, solemn vows we made;
> And I am now his bride, dear Jenny,
> His own beloved Kate

while Geraldine's soldier lover, in *Once More at Home* (words and music by John H. Hewitt), wants to make her his bride:

> Once more at home and by thy side
> My hand close-pressed in thine;
> Say, wilt thou be the soldier's bride,
> My meek-eyed Geraldine?
> I've done my duty on the field
> And 'mid the battle cry;
> Thy fairy form has been my shield
> When whistling balls flew by.

Most sweethearts will be reunited forever *When We All March Home from the War* (words and music by S. W. Paine):

> There'll be weddings today and weddings tomorrow,
> And honeymoons gay to take the place of our sorrow;
> Our care's all aside and no trouble we'll borrow
> When we all march home from the war.

The boys will receive *A Hearty Welcome Home* (words and music by Eastburn, pseud. of J. E. Winner, sometimes attributed to his brother, Septimus):

With wreaths of laurel crown them, they have glory won;
Give them a hearty welcome home!
Right nobly have they battled, now their task is done;
Give them a hearty welcome home!

even though, according to *The Boys Will Soon Be Home* (words by Major John Hay, music by Tullius C. O'Kane):

Their bayonets may be rusty and their uniforms be dusty,
But all shall see the traces of battle's royal graces
In their brown, bearded faces when the boys come home.

For the soldier it is *Good-bye, Old Glory* (words by L. J. Bates, music by George F. Root), good-bye to drums and bugles, pens and prison holes, muster and parade, general and dashing aide, glory and death:

Four weary years of toil and blood,
    With loyal hearts and true,
By field and fortress, plain and flood,
    We've fought the rebel crew;
But victory is ours at last,
    The mighty work is through,
Sound drums and bugles loud and fast,
    This is your last tattoo.

CHORUS:
Farewell, farewell to march and fight!
Hardtack, a fond adieu!
Good-bye, Old Glory, for tonight
We doff the army blue.

After the long separation, the soldiers are *Coming Home from the Old Camp Ground* (words and music by William T. Rogers):

We are coming home again from the old camp ground
And the scenes of war and strife.
We are coming home again to the things we love
And the joys of a peaceful life.

373

Even the slackers could now return, and a drafted boy who became a bounty jumper asks his mother (words and music by J. W. Turner):

Can I Come Home from Canada?
   To live with you again?
Oh, I am longing for the day,
   My heart is filled with pain.
You know I always told you
   That for native land I'd fight,
But when the time came, Mother dear,
   I took an awful fright.

So down I went to Canada
   Among the Johnny B's,
But they call me a deserter
   From the land of the Yankees.
Dear Mother, I am tired now
   Of living on this way.
Can I come home from Canada?
   Is the battle over, say?

The sweetheart in *My Beau that Went to Canada* (words by Eben E. Rexford, music by Wurzel [George F. Root]) does not want her Jim back now that he has proved himself a coward:

Oh, Jim, my dear, you need not fear
   That we shall grieve about you.
The war is done, the boys have come,
   And we can do without you!

Even the Negro in *The Southern Contraband* (words and music by M. B. Leavitt) had reason to be happy:

Oh, now the war is over, I'm gwine to hab some fun,
Hang up the knapsack and lay down de gun.

In striking contrast, the boys in gray, paroled by Grant after the surrender, made their separate ways south to homes which often were destroyed, to waiting loved ones who had suffered immeasurably, and to a society which had been uprooted, an economy blighted. For them there were no cheers and banners, but only the numb exhaustion of defeat. In

374

The Curtain Falls

The boys are com-ing home a-gain This war will soon be o'er. The

South-ern land a-gain will stand As hap-py as of yore. Yes,

hand in hand and arm in arm To-geth-er we will roam, Oh,

won't we have a hap-py time When all the boys come home? We'll

hoist the star-ry cross a-gain On free-dom's lof-ty dome; And

live in peace and hap-pi-ness When all the boys come home.

When the Boys Come Home!

the closing months of the conflict, Blackmar had published a song of Union origin which was highly optimistic in its hopes for postwar happiness—*When the Boys Come Home!* (words and music by Charles Carroll Sawyer):

> The boys are coming home again,
> This war will soon be o'er.
> The Southern land again will stand
> As happy as of yore.
> Yes, hand in hand and arm in arm
> Together we will roam,

Oh, won't we have a happy time
    When all the boys come home?

CHORUS:
We'll hoist the starry cross again
On freedom's lofty dome;
And live in peace and happiness
When all the boys come home.

The happy time envisioned in this song was far from being reality for most of the Southerners. Life would never be the same for many, says *My Southern Sunny Home* (words and music by Will S. Hays):

Oh, mother dear, I have come home,
    The home I loved so true,
But I'm unhappy, all is changed,
    Yet there's no change in you.
Each flower lifts its blushing face,
    The birds are glad I've come
But nature seems to weep around
    My Southern sunny home.

Quite apart from the personal side, there was deep-felt relief that the war was over, calling for a *Peace Jubilee* (words by Mrs. M. A. Kidder, music by Mrs. E. A. Parkhurst):

Send a shout o'er the foam-crested ocean
To the farthermost isles of the sea,
For a people by four years' devotion
Have earned this, their peace jubilee.

A poem by George P. Morris, set to music by T. Martin Towne, said:

Take Your Harps from the Silent Willows,
Shout the chorus of the free;
States are all distinct as billows,
Union one, as is the sea.

The hope of many was that the dream of a united North, South, East and West might at last come true. The North naturally had faith that the end of the war would mean a harmonious nation with past differences forgotten; hence, all songs expressing this ideal were by Union poets and composers. George Root, always one to express a current idea, hailed this new day in *Columbia's Call*:

> Come, then, O North and South united,
>> Come, then, O East and West as one;
> Rejoice in the light which has chased away the night
>> And heralds now the rising sun!

Another Union poet exclaimed, *All Hail to the Reign of Peace* (words by George C. Street, music by George C. Pearson):

> Joy, joy, the war is over,
>> Joy, joy, the contest's done;
> Foemen embrace as brothers,
>> North and South henceforth are one.
> Praise to Him who rules the nations,
>> He doth first our thanks demand,
> Then we'll crown with glad ovations
>> All the heroes of our land.

Still another composer-author, William H. Stevens, conceived the notion of Yankee Doodle and *Dixie Doodle* as brothers together:

> Now Dixie Doodle wears the cap
>> Of Liberty and Union,
> And thinks the change becomes him well,
>> The gray one for the blue one;
> Hand in hand the brothers bear
>> The banner of our freedom,
> Ever ready for their work
>> When Uncle Sam shall need them.
>
> CHORUS:
> Dixie Doodle Doodle Doo,
>> And Yankee Doodle Dandy,
> Together live in Washington
>> With Uncle Sam and Andy.

But amidst the jubilation, as the aftermath of the war, in addition to political, social, and economic readjustments, were the grief and sorrow which were to be a blight for years to come.

CHAPTER 10

The Aftermath of the War

JOY AND RELIEF at the war's end were overshadowed by grief on both sides for those who had made the final sacrifice.[28] Those left behind could only *Weep for the Brave* (words and music by S. L.):

Mourn for the fallen,
    Weep for the brave
Who to a holy cause
    His young life gave.
Sadly, yet proudly,
    Read we thy name,
Fondly entwining
    Fresh wreaths of fame

[28] Typical dirges were the Union *Dirge Sung at the Consecration of the Soldiers' Cemetery at Gettysburg, November 19, 1863* (words and music by Alfred Delaney), *Sleep, Comrades, Sleep* (words and music by J. H. Dwyer), *Bring Him Back to the Home of His Childhood* (words by M. C. S., music by L. O. Emerson), *Sleep, Boys in Blue* (words by James A. Martling, music by Charles H. Greene), *Weep Not for the Slain, O Columbia* (words and music by Mrs. O. N. Haskins), *Ode to the Brave* (words and music by Ferdinand Mayer), *Hushed Be Each Sorrowing Murmur* (words and music by Guy F. North), *Tread Softly! A Soldier's Sleeping There* (words and music by D. S. Shallenberger), *Weep for the Heroes As They Fall* (words by Charles W. Butler, music by J. W. Turner), and *Oh, Fallen Hero* (words by Bayard Taylor, music by J. P. Webster), and the Confederate *We Sleep, But We Are Not Dead* (words by James R. Randall) and *Kneel Where Our Loves Are Sleeping* (words by G. W. R., music by L. Nella Sweet): "They lost, but still were good and true, Our father, brothers fell still fighting; We weep, 'tis all that we can do."

and at the time *When the War Is Over* (words by M. W. Packard, music by J. B. Packard):

> Every heart shall beat with gladness,
> But our tears will fall in sadness
> For the brave who fell in battle,
> Far from home and children's prattle,
> 'Mid the cannon's dreadful rattle,
>   When the war is o'er.

All sections of the country had reasons for sorrow. *Our Dear New England Boys* (words by Mattie, music by Mrs. E. A. Parkhurst) were mourned:

> Let them rest, the work is finished;
>   Nothing now their sleep annoys;
> Angels guard th' unbroken slumbers
>   Of our dear New England boys.

These mournful songs often expressed the thought that memories of loved ones are kept vivid and will never die. *Old Stonewall* (words by C. D. Dasher, music by F. Younker), a Southern melody, recalled the glories of Jackson's military victories and the cause. The battlefields are covered with green grass as life begins anew:

> The harvest waves over the battlefield, boys,
> And where bullets once pattered like rain
> The peach blooms are drifting like snow in the air
> And the hillocks are springing in grain.
> Oh! green in our hearts may the memories be
> Of those heroes, in blue or in gray,
> As new-growing grain, for never again
> Can they meet in dread battle array.

The *Nation's Orphans* (music by P. G. Anton) would "bear witness of their sires":

> Thus around our fallen heroes,
>   Stricken in their pride of place,

379

On the gory field of battle,
   Cluster scions of their race.
From each lowly grave uprising,
   From each lone dismantled hearth,
Spring these peerless perfect pledges
   Of the nation's newest birth.

Many of the slain were returned to their homes, where due honor was
paid to them, as in *From the Red Battlefield* (words by J. W. Parker, music
by Nathan Barker):

Silently, tenderly, mournfully, home
Not as they marched away, volunteers come;
Not with the sword and gun, not with the stirring drum,
Come our dead heroes home.
Now all his work is done. Thoughtfully, prayerfully, bear ye the dead,
Pillow it softly, the volunteer's head.

The Hero's Grave was at home (words and music by T. H. Howe):

Dig his grave where the soft green sod
By traitors' feet has never been trod,
Where sweet flowers are the smile of God
   For the patriot pure and true.
There let a graceful fadeless tree,
Emblem of hope and liberty,
Rise, while his epitaph there shall be
   Sweet flowers red, white and blue.

The pride of the homefolks, mingled as it was with grief, came to the fore
in *Bear Them Home Tenderly* (words and music by T. H. Howe):

Tenderly, tenderly bear them home,
Life and its trials are over.
Tenderly, tenderly, bear them all home
Calm in their silent slumber.
Cherish in memory the noble and brave
Dying for country its honor to save;
Sacred in all your hearts 'grave each dear name
Shining in heaven's bright record of fame.

Let this thought check this sigh
Not in the grave they lie;
Angels are bearing them homeward so tenderly.

The Blue and the Gray were both grieved (words and music by J. H. McNaughton):

Now calmly they rest from the march and the fray,
They sleep side by side, both the blue and the gray.
For them let us weep, both for them and our own—
Ah, both have a mother now weeping and lone.

Far south is a cottage whence cometh a wail,
Far north is a home and a face sad and pale.
Each mourns o'er her brave and for both we will pray,
The birds sing the same o'er the blue and the gray.

Many Northern boys failed to return home (words by W. W. Montgomery, music by Charles H. Lovering):

They Sleep in the South on a hundred fields
    As they sank to rest where war's thunders pealed.
On the shore they rest where pineapples grow,
    By the foaming surf where the Gulf winds blow.
They sleep in the dust 'neath palmetto shade,
    Their bones lie bleaching on the Everglades;
And Virginia's coast by Atlantic's wave
    Is a resting place for our heroes brave.

They Sleep in a Lonely Southern Grave (words by Thomas Manahan, music by N. B. Hollister) far from their mourning loved ones:

He is sleeping, lonely sleeping,
    Where all who sleep are free;
Where southern winds are breathing
    Soft music tenderly.
Would I were sleeping with him,
    He was so dear to me!
But he's sleeping, sweetly sleeping,
In a lonely southern grave.

Two other songs on this theme were *They Sleep in the Far Sunny South-land* (words and music by Mrs. O. N. Haskins) and *New England Soldiers* (words and music by C. A. White).

In the midst of jubilation came the vivid realization that many of the boys in blue and gray would not be returning, as in a verse from *Our Boys Are Coming Home* (see Chapter IX):

> And yet, oh, keenest sorrow!
> They're coming, but not all;
> Full many a dark tomorrow
> Shall wear its sable pall.
> For thousands who are sleeping
> Beneath the empurpled loam;
> Woe, woe, for those we're weeping
> Who never will come home!

As in all wars, there were *The Unknown Dead* (words and music by John H. Hewitt)—those (Confederate) soldiers who had been "plucked from Fame's diadem" and "whose records are not found on white marble stones but in the sad hearts of those for whom they fought and died":

> Then let them sleep on 'neath the sod of the valley,
> Where night dews will lave the long grass o'er their beds;
> Above, on the great day of muster they'll rally
> And glory will twine a bright wreath round their heads.
> No white marble stone shall rise o'er the Unknown,
> But in our sad hearts a fresh record shall be;
> Tho' named nevermore, they will live in the core,
> The bravest who fought and who died to be free.
>
> CHORUS:
> Let the requiem be sung, let the sad prayer be said
> For the heroes forgotten—the Unknown Dead.

Many of the bereaved kin were never to know the location of their loved ones' graves; the dead were *Sleeping in the Battle Field* (music by Karl Reden):

> At last the war is over,
> At last comes golden peace,

At last the cruel strife and bloodshed cease;
But where's our darling Willie,
Who was our pride and joy?
Oh, where's our noble soldier boy?

CHORUS:
Sleeping in the battle field
Lies our soldier boy;
Far from home and loved ones
Rests our soldier boy.
Sweetest of roses bedeck his lonely grave,
But sweeter blooms his memory brave.

The battlefields were the final resting place for many brave soldiers, since it had often been necessary to *Bury the Brave Where They Fall* (words and music by Lieutenant Henry L. Frisbie):

Oh, bury the brave on the field where they fall,
    Let them sleep beneath the sod
That drank up their blood in the deadly affray
    When their spirits went home to God;
Let their resting place be where their brave deeds were done,
    The banner, the banner for their shroud;
And its stars shall keep watch as they peacefully sleep
    Far away from the gathering crowd.

Though the volunteer's grave was unmarked, it was not forgotten (*Tread Lightly, Ye Comrades,* words by Annie, music by Mrs. F. L. Bowen):

And, oh, tho' no marble may point to the spot
Where bravely they've fallen, they'll not be forgot,
For o'er them our banner forever shall wave,
Encircling with glory the volunteer's grave.

Many were the graves unidentified[29] (*The Unknown Soldier,* words by General W. H. Hayward, music by Major Wilson G. Horner):

[29] Two songs on this subject were *Tenderly Bury the Fair Young Dead; or, Somebody's Darling Is Sleeping Here* (words and music by William Cumming) and *The Nameless Graves Where Our Heroes Lie* (words by John H. Lozier, music by C. M. Currier).

The flowers will bloom as brightly
    O'er the unknown soldier's grave,
With his heart's loved idols near him
    And the flag he died to save.
No stone will mark the spot
    Of the stranger 'neath the sod
Where so peacefully he slumbers
    Unknown, save to his God.

Even before Memorial Day was officially established, the custom of decorating graves had begun. *The Rebel's Grave* (words and music by E. A. Ambold) became a shrine to all visiting it:

There is a spot the herd will pass
Nor taste its long luxuriant grass;
There is a mound that flower or sun
Can never tempt the child upon;
But on that mound have old men lain
Bedewing it with tears like rain;
And young men filled with purpose brave
Come there to bless the rebel's grave.

In *Memorial Flowers* (words by Mrs. Fanny Downing, music by Mendelssohn Coote):

Each nameless nook and scattered spot
Where sleeps a Southern soldier true,
I mark with the forget-me-not,
    In Heaven's own blue.

The decoration of graves became an annual ceremony, as in the Confederate *Our Young Soldier's Grave* (words and music by F. W. Smith):

Scatter flowers, bright spring flowers,
Let their fragrance fill the air,
Sprinkle softly April showers,
For our boy is lying there.

Bring the blossoms from the wildwood,
Lay them gently o'er his breast,

384

Touch the sod with shrinking footsteps
Where our soldier takes his rest.

The author of *I Love the Sunny South* (words by Colonel L. T. Dogal,
music by Henry Schoeller) celebrated the visits of those left behind to the
graves of their loved ones:

I love the land where willow waves
    And fragrant valleys weep,
With sorrowing tears upon the graves
    Where patriot heroes sleep.

I love the land where woman goes
    At sunset's stilly hour,
To scatter where the dead repose
    The teardrops and the flower.

A Northern mother said, *Oh, Send Me One Flower from His Grave* (words
by Mrs. M. A. Kidder, music by Mrs. E. A. Parkhurst):

One blossom, though withered, how precious 'twill be,
That has bloomed near that fair sunny head;
But one dear little flowerlet, though trampled and crushed,
That has grown o'er my darling's lone bed.

These floral tributes were given to both *The Blue and The Gray* (words
by M. F. Finch, music by Felix Schelling), a postwar G. A. R. song:

From the silence of sorrowful hearts
    The desolate mourners go;
They are lovingly laden with flowers
    Alike for the friend and the foe.

CHORUS:
Under the sod and the dew, waiting the judgment day,
Under the one the blue, under the other the gray.
Love and tears for the blue, tears and love for the gray.

Fortunate were those who knew of their soldier boys' deaths. Throughout the war many deaths had been unreported, and, as a result, anxious
and agonized hours of waiting would forever go unrewarded. Stephen

Foster pictured the victim of such a fate, a mother who repeated over and over again, *My Boy Is Coming from the War* (words by George Cooper):

My boy is coming from the war,
    He's coming home to me;
Oh, how I long to see his face,
    And hear his voice of glee!

My boy is coming from the war,
    The mother fondly said,
While on the gory battle plain
    Her boy was lying dead!

His comrades came with lightsome steps
    And sound of martial drum,
But now that mother sadly waits
    For one who'll never come.

Another Union mother asked, *I Wonder Why He Comes Not?* (words by J. B. Murphy, music by E. Chamberlin), while still another moaned that *They All Came Home But Mine* (words and music by J. H. Mc-Naughton):

They all came home but mine again,
Why lingers he so long away?
I gaze in every face in vain
And watch through all the weary day.

CHORUS:
No more my darling, my boy, no more will come.
He sleeps by Rappahannock's wave;
Sweet birds, oh, sing him songs of home,
Kind angels, guard his lonely grave.

Wives, children, and parents, as long as they were to live, would watch at the door for the familiar step, ever hoping and *Waiting for the Loved One* (music by Henry Tucker):

They have waited for thy coming,
    They have watched beside the door,
'Till the bees have ceased their humming

And have gathered in their store,
And the coming years will find them
  Walking paths that sorrow's crossed,
Grieving o'er the faded flowers,
  Mourning still the loved and lost.

CHORUS:
Still they're waiting for the coming of a loved one
Who may never, who may never come again,
And the weary days will tell them
Of the sorrow that befell them
When their watching and their waiting was in vain.

To many *That Missing Voice* (words by Mrs. E. S. Kellogg, music by Thomas M. Towne) would always be with them, though others might rejoice in the victory:

That missing voice, that missing voice,
No more I hear its thrilling tone.
What though all earth and heav'n rejoice,
I turn aside and weep alone.

Many who did return would bear forever the marks of their years of service, a vivid reminder of their sacrifice. The homefolks would revere them *When the Boys Come Home* (words by Robert Morris, music by J. A. Butterfield):

What though our boys are wounded, and many a ghastly scar!
These are their marks of glory, the trophies of the War.
We'll be their hands and feet; yes, and voices of the dumb,
The crutch shall be an honor, when the boys come home.

Amputations had been numerous (see Chapter V), and the sight of armless and legless veterans was a common one (*The Wounded Soldier*, words by Rev. Edward C. Jones, music by David D. Wood):

They walk amid the crowded throng
  With eye of kindling rage,
Though cannon balls that whizzed along
  Have borne their limbs away.

The friendly crutch the place supplies
    Of mutilated limb,
To tell the spirit's masteries
    When pain no hope could dim.

For next to those who passed in gore
    Up to the patriot's heaven
Are those whose limbs a martyr's store
    So joyously were given.

The Union veteran in *Dear Wife, I'm with You Once Again* (words and music by Frank B. Ray) returned to her as an amputee:

Now I am with you once again,
    Look not upon this maimed form;
Let not the thoughts of it give pain
    While life remains and love is warm.
To my country I have given a limb,
    To my wife I bring an unchanged heart.

Another soldier says to his sweetheart, *Will You Wed Me Now I'm Lame, Love?* (words by Avanelle L. Holmes, music by George F. Root); he recalls her promise to wed him on his return:

And so I will not blame you, love, should you recall your vow
And think because I'm lame, love, you cannot wed me now.
What! Your eyes are full of tears, love, and your lips are trembling, too;
You turn your blushing cheek, love, from my long and earnest view.
When I hope—Ah, no! The thought is vain, love, but the hand,
Why comes it near? And those murmured words! Oh, joy, love,
      they have banished fear.
Oh, yes! Your heart's the same, love, in all that we passed through;
You'll wed me though I'm lame, love, my beautiful! My true!

A very popular war poem, set to music by Henry Badger, was *The Empty Sleeve:*

Until this hour I could never believe
What a tell-tale thing is an empty sleeve!

Blindness was also frequent, (*The Blind Soldier's Lament,* words by Mrs. A. B. Lathrop, music by Edgar Spinning):

> Our health and limbs and life, friends, for right we cast away,
> 'Twas mine the fearful destiny to lose the light of day;
> On Liberty's high altar lies many a stalwart limb
> But, oh! Accept these sightless eyes, the sacrifice I bring!

But the blind have their memories, as well (*I'm Blind,* words and music by William Leigh), and these may take the place of sight:

> I hear the drum at morn and eve,
>   I hear the trumpet sound,
> I hear the war horse's clattering hoof,
>   The sentry pace his rounds.
> My fancy sees the tinted field,
>   The flag I left behind;
> I see no more its starry folds:
>   I'm blind, I'm blind!

Those mutilated in one manner or another were a visible reminder of the human toll taken by the Civil War.

It was easy for the North, as the victor, to extend a hand of forgiveness to the South, considering the latter as a recalcitrant prodigal now returned to the fold and ready to rejoin the Union. This idea was expressed in *Wayward Brothers* (words and music by J. H. McNaughton):

> Wayward brothers, don't despair
>   You'll come in and take a chair,
> And we'll all be friends and happy as of yore.
> But before you enter now,
> You must make an earnest vow
>   To adore the starry banner evermore

and in *Shake Hands with Uncle Sam* (words and music by Charles Carroll Sawyer):

> Let brothers live as brothers,
>   All angry passion cease;

Bury deep the hatchet
    And we'll smoke the pipe of peace.
We'll have one flag, one country
    If we will man to man
Be friendly to the Union
    And shake hands with Uncle Sam.

Forgiveness seemed so rapid that the causes of the war and its scars were often oversimplified, as indicated in *North and South* (words by Beulah Wynne, music by George F. Root):

United now, once more we stand
As sisters should, a loving band;
The North and South with East and West
In one great Union, sweetly blessed;
Each fancied wrong, each hasty word,
Each unkind thought within us stirred
Shall now and aye forgotten be
Throughout our land, so great and free!

Some authors adopted an almost condescending tone in offering to patch up the differences; after verses of *Be Merciful to the South* (words by Miles O'Reilly, music by William Ketchum) urging the North to be merciful, generous, tender, and just towards the erstwhile enemy, the acceptance of the erring brother is hailed:

Let us join hands once more,
Renewing the vows that our fathers swore;
Forgetting all strife save the lessons it taught
And meeting as reconciled brothers ought,
A reconciled North and South.

Again like two parted friends
With our quarrel fought out, the hatred ends
And none more welcome this happy day
Than the boys in blue and the boys in gray
Who fought for the North and the South.

Although all Confederates were pardoned and the Union was ready to "forgive and forget" and welcome the seceded states back, many Southerners were unwilling to accept the North's condescending tone. No song of resistance was actually issued, but an "unregenerate" Confederate was presented in *Oh, I'm a Good Old Rebel* (words by either Adelbert Volck or Innes Randolph, music to the tune of *Joe Bowers,* by R. Bishop Buckley) as saying:

Oh, I'm a good old rebel, that's just what I am;
For this "Fair Land of Freedom" I don't care a damn!
I'm glad I fit against it, I only wish we'd won,
And I don't want no pardon for anything I've done.

I hates the Constitution, this great Republic too,
I hates the Freedman's Buro in uniforms of blue;
I hates the nasty eagle with all his brag and fuss,
The lyin', thievin' Yankees, I hates them wuss and wuss!

I hates the Yankee nation and everything they do,
I hates the Declaration of Independence, too;
I hates the glorious Union—'tis dripping with our blood,
I hates the striped banner, I fit it all I could.

Three hundred thousand Yankees lie stiff in Southern dust;
We got three hundred thousand before they conquered us!
They died of Southern fever and Southern steel and shot,
I wish they was three million instead of what we got!

I can't take up my musket and fight 'em now no more,
But I ain't a-going to love 'em, now that is sartain sure;
And I don't want no pardon for what I was and am,
I won't be reconstructed, and I don't care a damn!

This melody is assumed to have been published by Blackmar, in New Orleans, in 1866.

A Kentucky lady, Mrs. C. A. Warfield, had already, in 1864, told the Northerners:

You Can Never Win Us Back, never! never!
Tho' we perish in the track of your endeavor!
Tho' our corpses strew the earth that smiled upon our birth
And blood pollutes each hearthstone forever.

You have no such noble blood for the shedding;
In the veins of cavaliers was its heading;

391

You have no such stately men in your abolition den
To wade through fire and fen, nothing dreading.

As in all wars, hatred of the conqueror was at white heat. The wanton destruction by Sherman's army was a blow difficult to excuse, even as a part of the strategy of war, and for many, impossible ever to forgive. Some Southerners, however, were willing to accept defeat, although taking pride in their effort. The feeling that in victory the North was not being completely fair and free from recrimination was expressed in *We Know that We Were Rebels; or, Why Can We Not Be Brothers?* (words by Clarence J. Prentice, music by Charlie L. Ward):

> Why can we not be brothers? The battle now is o'er;
> We've laid our bruis'd arms on the field to take them up no more.
> We've fought you hard and long, now overpowered stand
> As poor, defenseless prisoners in our native land.
>
> We know that we were rebels, and we don't deny the name,
> We speak of that which we have done with grief but not with shame!
> And we never will acknowledge that the blood the South has spilt
> Was shed defending what we deemed a cause of wrong and guilt!

Many Southerners merely wanted their leaders freed and themselves left unhampered to take up the work of reconstruction.

It should not be assumed, however, that all Northerners were filled with forgiveness; hatred of the vanquished was long to endure, as in *Up with the Blue and Down with the Gray* (words by James L. Dalzell, music by A. C. Rose), in a highly vindictive and uncharitable mood:

> You may sing of the blue and the gray
>   And mingle their hues in your rhyme,
> But the blue that we wore in the fray
>   Is covered with glory sublime.
> So no more let us hear of the gray,
>   Symbol of treason and shame!
> We pierced it with bullets. Away!
>   Or we'll pierce it with bullets again.
> Then up with the blue and down with the gray
> And hurrah for the blue that won us the day!

The Aftermath of the War

Victors find it easy to live and forget the animosities which inflamed them during a struggle, but the vanquished find it difficult to erase the stigma of defeat from their minds. The latter situation was particularly true of the South after the Civil War. With so much of their land laid waste, with the cream of their manhood sacrificed, with thousands of homeless families relying on charity for support, and with the burden of an army of freed slaves—often ignorant, lazy, and superstitious—the Southerners were reminded at every turn that they were vanquished. Disappointment, frustration, and failure are evident in *The Wearing of the Gray* (words by H. L. Schreiner to the Irish tune *Wearin' of the Green*), describing the sorrow with which the Confederate flag was laid away:

Oh, have you heard the cruel news?
   Alas, it is too true!
Upon the Appomattox down
   Went our cross of blue.
Our armies have surrendered,
   We bow to Northern sway,
And forevermore forbidden is
   The wearing of the gray.
No more on fields of battle waves
   The banner of our pride,
In vain beneath its crimson folds
   Stuart and Stonewall died.
Like a meteor of the evening
   That flag has passed away,
And low lie they who guarded it,
   The wearers of the Gray.

The Sword of Robert E. Lee (words by Father Abram J. Ryan, "the poet-priest of the Confederacy," who often wrote under the pseudonym "Moina"; several musical settings, the most famous by A. E. Blackmar ["Armand"], others by E. Louis Ide, Henry Weber, and C. C. Nordendorf) is set in a heroic vein and exhibits the dignity and strength of the General, who, even in defeat, held the respect of the enemy, whose name still called forth the glory of the South's struggle, and who seemed to be the incarnation of the Confederacy itself:

393

Forth from its scab-bard, pure and bright, Forth flash'd the sword of Lee!

Forth from its scab-bard, pure and bright, Forth flash'd the sword of Lee!

Far in the front of the dead-ly fight, High o'er the brave, in the cause of right,

Its stain-less sheen, like a bea-con light, Led us to vic-to-ry.   Sword!

sword of brave Rob-ert Lee! Sword! sword of brave Rob-ert Lee!

The Sword of Robert E. Lee

Forth from its scabbard, pure and bright,
    Forth flashed the sword of Lee!
Far in the front of the deadly fight,
High o'er the brave, in the cause of right,
Its stainless sheen, like a beacon light,
    Led us to victory.

Out of its scabbard, never hand
    Waved sword from stain as free,
Nor purer sword led braver band,
Nor braver bled for a brighter land,
Nor brighter land had a cause as grand,
    Nor cause a chief like Lee!

Forth from its scabbard! All in vain!
    Forth flashed the sword of Lee!
'Tis shrouded now in its sheath again,

It sleeps the sleep of our noble slain,
Defeated, yet without a stain
   Proudly and peacefully.

Carolina (tune by A. E. Blackmar) is particularly martial for a "defeat" lyric, despite the fact that the sufferings of her dead sons seemed to have been in vain. The first stanza voices the true Southern pride which meant salvation of the region in its struggle during reconstruction years:

'Mid her ruins proudly stands, Our Carolina!
Fetters are upon her hands, Dear Carolina!
Yet she feels no sense of shame,
For upon the scroll of Fame
She hath writ a deathless name,
   Brave Carolina!

Southern pride in the uniform was still strong, as expressed in one of Blackmar's last songs, *Wearing of the Gray,* published under his pseudonym, "Armand," to the tune of *Wearin' of the Green:*

The fearful struggle's ended now
   And Peace smiles on our land,
And though we've yielded we have proved
   Ourselves a faithful band;
We fought them long, we fought them well,
   We fought them night and day
And bravely struggled for our rights
   While wearing of the Gray;
And now that we have ceased to fight
   And pledged our sacred word
That we against the Union's might
   No more will draw the sword,
We feel despite the sneers of those
   Who never smelt the fray,
That we've a manly, honest right
   To wearing of the Gray.

No, we are men, though overpowered
   By numbers in the fight,
We'll not deny that we have fought
   For what we deemed the Right;

Tho' we our fondest, dearest hopes
    Aside forever lay,
We cherish still with honest pride
    The wearing of the Gray.
When in the battle's fiercest hour
    We faced the deadly hail,
Our simple suits of gray composed
    Our only coats of mail.
And still we'll wear that glorious suit
    (Let those deride who may)
In memory of the brave who fell
    While wearing of the Gray.

Though the cause was lost, the pride of the Southerners in their heroic but fruitless struggle never ended, and the putting away of *The Conquered Flag* (words from the Louisville Courier, music by Charlie L. Ward) was the symbol of all the grief and hopelessness of the struggle:

Fold tenderly that banner, and gently lay it by
As we do the tear-wet garments of our loved ones when they die.
Is it treason now to mourn it? If so, we're traitors all
For we cannot keep the tears back that fast around it fall.

We fought bravely to uphold it, but valor was in vain;
It is now the sad memento of our gallant brothers slain.
'Tis a relic sad and holy of a past forever fled,
And we see in it a symbol, coffin of a Cause that's dead.

Finally, Father Ryan's *The Conquered Banner,* set to music by Theodore von La Hache and published by Blackmar, epitomized the weariness, the sacrifice of young blood, and the unconquerable pride of the South:

Furl that banner, for 'tis weary,
Round its staff 'tis drooping dreary,
    Furl it, fold it, it is best;
For there's not a man to wave it,
And there's not a sword to save it,
And there's not one left to lave it
In the blood which heroes gave it,
And its foes now scorn and brave it,
    Furl it, hide it, let it rest.

CHORUS:

Furl that banner, softly, slowly,
Treat it gently—it is holy,
   For it droops above the dead;
Touch it not, unfold it never,
Let it droop there, furled forever,
   For its peoples' hopes are dead.

Furl that banner, furl it sadly,
Once ten thousand hailed it gladly,
And ten thousand wildly, madly,
   Swore it should forever wave;
Swore that foeman's sword should never
Hearts like theirs entwined dissever,
Till that flag would float forever
   O'er their freedom or their grave.

Furl that banner! True, 'tis gory
Yet 'tis wreathed around with glory,
And 'twill live in song and story
   Though its folds are in the dust;
For its fame on brightest pages,
Penned by poets and by sages,
Shall go sounding down the ages,
   Furl its folds though now we must.

It is fitting that *The Conquered Banner* should terminate this survey of the war songs, for it expresses perfectly the spirit which dominated the Confederacy. Though staggering under a burden of human loss and material destruction, the Southerners immediately sought to re-establish a place in the life of the nation. Ordinances of Secession were repealed or declared null and void, slavery was abolished in the respective states, and ratification of the Thirteenth Amendment to the Constitution was effected by the state legislatures. By August, 1866, the "state of insurrection" was officially declared at an end, and the South was then ready to enter upon a period of growth and prosperity hand in hand with her reunited brothers in the North.

That "brother," however, showed a deplorable desire for vengeance and failed to support the program for peace which Lincoln had blueprinted and which President Johnson attempted to carry out. The story of the Congressional plan of reconstruction, led by Thaddeus Stevens in the

House of Representatives and Charles Sumner in the Senate, of treating the Southern states as conquered provinces, with military rule, unreasonably high taxation, Negro suffrage, and officeholding by Northern adventurers or "carpetbaggers," still remains a disgraceful blot on the generally proud record of American history. This period has rightly been termed "the tragic era." However, home rule, free from Federal interference, was fully restored by 1877, and political, economic, and social reconstruction was thereafter slowly but surely attained. As the years passed, memories of hatred and resentment were in great measure obliterated.

By the late 1940's the ranks of the Grand Army of the Republic and the United Confederate Veterans had so thinned that final reunions were held. The Union organization, which at its peak in 1890 numbered 409,000 members, held its eighty-third and last encampment in Indianapolis, Indiana (the scene of its first meeting in 1866), on August 28–September 1, 1949. Only sixteen G. A. R. veterans were living at that time, and of the six in attendance, the average age was 103. At the time of this last reunion, the United States Post Office issued a red commemorative three-cent stamp. As recently as June 30, 1956, the government was still paying pensions to over 5,000 widows and children of Civil War veterans. The sole surviving Union soldier died in August, 1956.

The United Confederate Veterans held its sixty-first and final encampment in Norfolk, Virginia, on May 31, 1951. The reunion was attended by three survivors, each 105 years old. The United States Post Office issued a gray commemorative three-cent stamp in celebration. The Sons of Confederate Veterans, meeting in Jackson, Mississippi, in June, 1952, at their fifty-second annual convention, voted to dissolve the Confederate Veterans of America as an organization. The last Southern soldier died on December 19, 1959, at the age of 117. Widows of Confederate veterans were granted government pensions in 1958.

The physical, moral, and mental wounds of the house divided have long since healed. Many of the songs have been forgotten; most were stowed away with the cannon and the flags or died with the contemporaries who had sung them. They are now recalled as the sad story of a fratricidal conflict and as expressions of the sincerity and heroism of our forefathers. Through these songs, the Civil War is relived in all of its sorrow, humor, and grandeur. These stirring melodies of the 1860's are national songs, and their strains serve to keep alive a spirit of patriotism which has welded millions of Americans into one mighty republic, undivided and indivisible.

Bibliography

I. SONG BOOKS (WORDS AND MUSIC)

MOST AVAILABLE BOOKS containing music of the Civil War period include extensive duplications of the most popular songs. The majority of compositions in this volume are to be found only in the original sheet music form, often in limited editions, available only in the largest libraries in the United States.

Adler, Kurt (ed.). *Songs of Many Wars, from the 16th to the 20th Century.* New York: Howell, Soskin, 1943. Civil War, pp. 95–111. Music, with short notes, to six popular songs of the war.

The Bugle Call, a Collection of the Most Celebrated War Songs, for the Use of G. A. R. Posts, Soldiers' Reunions, etc., and Intended Also as a Souvenir of the Musical Features of the Great Rebellion. Cincinnati: John Church, 1886. Words and music of eighty-two Union songs, some with four-part arrangements.

Dolph, Edward A. *"Sound Off!" Soldier Songs from the Revolution to World War II.* New York: Farrar & Rinehart, 1942. Civil War section, pp. 226–367. Words and music of fifty songs.

Downes, Olin, and Elie Siegmeister. *A Treasury of American Song.* 2nd edn. New York: Knopf, 1943. Section IV, "Year of Jubilo," pp. 188–97. In addition to several Abolitionist and Negro songs, words and music, with descriptive introductions, are included for nine Civil War tunes.

Harwell, Richard B. (ed.). *Songs of the Confederacy.* New York: Broadcast Music, 1951. Facsimiles of thirty-eight significant "songs that stirred the South," with historical notes.

Jordan, Philip D., and Lillian Kessler. *Songs of Yesterday.* New York: Doubleday Doran, 1941. Section 17, "Songs of the Stars and Stripes," pp. 347–60; Section 18, "Songs of the Stars and Bars, pp. 361–72. Complete music in photostat form for eight songs.

Luther, Frank. *Americans and Their Songs.* New York: Harper, 1942. In various chapters are the words of twenty-six Civil War songs and the music of eight.

Our National War Songs: A Complete Collection of Our Grand Old War Songs, National Hymns, Memorial Hymns, Decoration Songs, Quartettes, etc. Cleveland and Chicago: S. Brainard's Sons, 1884. Words and music of fifty-seven of the most popular Union songs.

Our War Songs, North and South. Cleveland: S. Brainard, 1887. The most complete book of songs; it includes 157 Union and 32 Confederate songs in a special edition originally available only to subscribers, but now found in some libraries.

The Patriotic Glee Book. Chicago: H. M. Higgins, 1863. Words and music, in four parts, of thirty-six Union songs.

Smith, Wilson G. (ed.). *Grand Army War Songs, a Collection of War Songs, Battle Songs, Camp Songs, National Songs, Marching Songs, etc., As Sung by Our Boys in Blue in Camp and Field.* (Compiled expressly for the Grand Army of the Republic.) New York: S. Brainard's Sons, 1886. Words and music of forty-seven war, battle, and camp songs and sixteen G. A. R. memorial songs.

Songs of the Confederacy and Plantation Melodies. (Issued under the auspices of the Richard Hawes Chapter of Paris, Ky.; selected and arranged by Mrs. A. L. Mitchell.) Cincinnati: George B. Jennings Co., 1901. Words and music of twenty-one Confederate songs.

War Songs, for Anniversaries and Gatherings of Soldiers, to Which Is Added a Selection of Songs and Hymns for Memorial Day. Boston: Oliver Ditson Co., 1891. Words and music of thirty-two war songs and seventeen G. A. R. memorial songs.

II. POEMS AND SONGS (WORDS ONLY)

THE VOLUMES listed below contain full texts of many poems which were set to music, none of which have been included in this volume unless the music was examined by the authors.

Browne, Francis F. (ed.). *Bugle-echoes; a Collection of the Poetry of the Civil War, Northern and Southern.* New York: White, Stokes & Allen, 1886.

Capps, Claudius M. (ed.). *The Blue and the Gray.* Boston: Humphries, 1943.

Daniel, Mrs. Lizzie (compiler). *Confederate Scrap-Book.* (Published in 1893 for the benefit of the Memorial Bazaar, held in Richmond, April 11, 1893.)

Eggleston, George Cary (ed.). *American War Ballads and Lyrics.* 2 vols. New York: Putnam, 1889. Civil War, vol. I, pp. 165–226; vol. II, pp. 1–278.

Fagan, William L. (ed.). *Southern War Songs, Campfire, Patriotic & Sentimental.* New York: M. T. Richardson & Co., 1890.

Miller, Francis T. (ed.). *Photographic History of the Civil War.* 10 vols. New York: Review of Reviews Co., 1911. "Songs of the War Days," ed. by Jeanne R. Foster, vol. IX, pp. 342–53. Same in reprinted edition (New York: Yoseloff, 1957).

Moore, Frank (ed.). *The Civil War in Song and Story, 1860–1865.* New York: P. F. Collier, 1889.

———. *Lyrics of Loyalty.* New York: Putnam, 1864.

———. *Personal and Political Ballads.* New York: Putnam, 1864.

———. *Rebel Rhymes and Rhapsodies.* New York: Putnam, 1864.

———. *Songs of the Soldiers.* New York: Putnam, 1864.

National Society of Colonial Dames of America. *American War Songs.* Philadelphia, 1925. Civil War, pp. 71–140.

Parks, Edd Winfield (ed.). *Southern Poets.* New York: American Book Co., 1936. Civil War ballads, songs, and poems, pp. 136–61.

Simms, William Gilmore (ed.). *War Poetry of the South.* New York: Richardson & Co., 1866.

Staton, Kate E. (ed.). *Old Southern Songs of the Period of the Confederacy.* New York: Samuel French, 1926.

War Lyrics and Songs of the South. London: Spottiswoode & Co., 1866.

Wharton, H. M. (ed.). *War Songs and Poems of the Southern Confederacy, 1861–65.* (By an ex-Confederate.) Philadelphia: Privately printed, 1904.

Williams, Henry L. (ed.). *War Songs of the Blue and the Gray, As Sung by the Brave Soldiers of the Union and Confederate Armies in Camp, on the March and in Garrison.* New York: Hurst & Co., 1905.

Index

This book was set into type on the Linotype machine in Granjon, a type which has achieved great popularity as a book face. The text paper was especially selected to present the illustrations and musical examples at their best. Color and ornament were used liberally in order to echo the stir and excitement of the "Singing Sixties."

University of Oklahoma Press: Norman

on l
gran
No.

T·

DATE DUE

#47-0108 Peel Off Pressure Sensitive